MCSD: Visual Basic 6 Companion CD-ROM

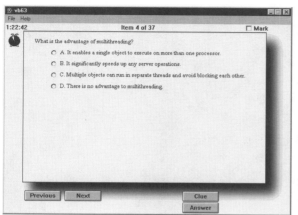

To start the CD-ROM included with this book, just pop it in your CD-ROM drive, use Explorer to locate the root directory for your CD-ROM, and double-click Clickme.exe. You'll see Sybex's easy-to-use interface.

The following products are on the CD:

MCSD Test Engine. Created for Sybex by EdgeTest. All the questions and answers in this book are included on the test engine, an easy-to-use program for test preparation.

VB6 Code. Try your hand at tweaking the examples and demos created by the author for this Study Guide.

VB5 Code and Chapters. Bonus database coverage from the last edition of this book.

MCSD Offline Update. The latest Microsoft information on the MCSD certification program. NOTE: Internet Explorer 4 or above is required to run this HTML-based document.

Internet Explorer 4.01. This powerful browser includes everything you need for accessing the Net.

MCSD on the Web. Popular MCSD Web site listed in order of importance to MCSD students.

Using the Test Engine

The MCSD test engine is created for Sybex by EdgeTest. To prepare for the exam:

1. Close all active and minimized applications.

2. Access the test engine through the Sybex CD interface.

3. Follow the installation prompts to install and launch the engine.

4. If you choose not to run the program after it installs, you can start it later by clicking Start ➢ Programs ➢ The Edge Tests.

5. When the main screen appears, type your name and press Enter. Select an exam, select Start Practice Exam, and click Go.

To access other elements of the CD, use the Sybex interface.

MCSD: Visual Basic 6
Desktop Applications
Study Guide

MCSD: Visual Basic® 6 Desktop Applications Study Guide

Michael McKelvy

San Francisco • Paris • Düsseldorf • Soest

SYBEX®

Associate Publisher: Gary Masters
Contracts and Licensing Manager: Kristine O'Callaghan
Acquisitions & Developmental Editor: Brenda Frink
Editor: Sharon Wilkey
Project Editor: Malka Geffen
Technical Editor: Tracy Liveoak
Book Designers: Patrick Dintino, Bill Gibson
Electronic Publishing Specialist: Franz Baumhackl
Production Coordinator: Blythe Woolston
Indexer: Ted Laux
Companion CD: Ginger Warner
Cover Designer: Design Site
Cover Illustrator/Photographer: Design Site

Screen reproductions produced with Collage Complete.
Collage Complete is a trademark of Inner Media Inc.

Library of Congress Card Number: 98-88946
ISBN: 0-7821-2438-0

Manufactured in the United States of America

10 9 8 7 6 5 4 3 2

Microsoft
CERTIFIED PROFESSIONAL
Approved Study Guide

November 1, 1997

Dear SYBEX Customer:

Microsoft is pleased to inform you that SYBEX is a participant in the Microsoft® Independent Courseware Vendor (ICV) program. Microsoft ICVs design, develop, and market self-paced courseware, books, and other products that support Microsoft software and the Microsoft Certified Professional (MCP) program.

To be accepted into the Microsoft ICV program, an ICV must meet set criteria. In addition, Microsoft reviews and approves each ICV training product before permission is granted to use the Microsoft Certified Professional Approved Study Guide logo on that product. This logo assures the consumer that the product has passed the following Microsoft standards:

- The course contains accurate product information.
- The course includes labs and activities during which the student can apply knowledge and skills learned from the course.
- The course teaches skills that help prepare the student to take corresponding MCP exams.

Microsoft ICVs continually develop and release new MCP Approved Study Guides. To prepare for a particular Microsoft certification exam, a student may choose one or more single, self-paced training courses or a series of training courses.

You will be pleased with the quality and effectiveness of the MCP Approved Study Guides available from SYBEX.

Sincerely,

Holly Heath
ICV Account Manager
Microsoft Training & Certification

MICROSOFT INDEPENDENT COURSEWARE VENDOR PROGRAM

To my wife, Wanda, and my children, Laura and Eric, for their love and support, and for their patience during the long hours of the project.

Acknowledgments

A book like this is not the effort of a single individual; it takes a talented team of people to create a book that is useful to the reader and is a quality publication. I would like to thank all the members of the team that helped me put this book together. First, the team at Sybex—Brenda Frink, Malka Geffen, Blythe Woolston, and Bill Gibson; second, our editor—Sharon Wilkey. Finally, I would like to thank my friend and colleague, Tracy Liveoak, who worked as the technical editor to make sure that all explanations were right.

Contents at a Glance

Table of Contents

Appendices

Table of Exercises

Introduction

These days, almost every job requires some level of computer literacy. You will even find computers being used in most restaurants to handle order processing, a task that was previously done by hand. For all the tasks that are being performed by computer, someone needed to write the software to handle the task. This is the role of the software developer. Finding qualified software developers is a major issue for many companies today.

But how is a company supposed to determine who is qualified and who is just a computer user with a few elementary programming skills? Determining the qualifications of people is difficult when there are so many who claim to be computer experts, even if their expertise is limited to setting up their own Web page. To help with the task of determining who is qualified and who is not, Microsoft developed its Microsoft certification program to certify those people who have the skills to work with Microsoft products and networks.

For developers, this certification is in the form of the Microsoft Certified Solution Developer. This certification establishes that a person is familiar with the inner workings of Windows and has skills in working with multiple programming languages or development environments. Visual Basic is one of the languages in which you can be certified on your way to becoming an MCSD. Even if MCSD certification is not your goal, being Microsoft certified in Visual Basic can make it easier for you to get a programming job or to command a higher salary for the job.

The purpose of this book is to make it easier for you to pass the Visual Basic certification exam. After working through the book, you will understand the objectives covered by the test and will know the types of questions to expect on the test.

Your Key to Passing Exam 70-176

This book provides the key to passing Exam 70-176, Designing and Implementing Desktop Applications with Microsoft Visual Basic 6.0. You'll find all the information relevant to this exam, including hundreds of practice questions, all designed to make sure that when you take the real exam, you are ready for even the picky questions on less frequently used options.

Understand the Exam Objectives

To help you prepare for certification exams, Microsoft provides a list of exam objectives for each test. This book is structured according to the objectives for Exam 70-176, designed to measure your ability to create applications in Visual Basic.

Exam objectives are subject to change at any time without prior notice and at Microsoft's sole discretion. Please visit Microsoft's Web site (www.microsoft.com\train_cert) for the most current listing of exam objectives.

Is This Book for You?

The target audience for this book is the programmer who has some experience with Visual Basic but needs to understand the topics covered in the exam objectives. Although the explanations and exercises are written to be easily understandable, a certain level of Visual Basic programming background is assumed. If you are not familiar with the basics of programming in Visual Basic, you would probably do well to take an introductory class or read an introductory book before continuing toward certification.

Understanding Microsoft Certification

Microsoft offers several levels of certification for anyone who has or is pursuing a career as a professional developer working with Microsoft products:

- Microsoft Certified Professional (MCP)
- Microsoft Certified Professional + Internet
- Microsoft Certified Solution Developer (MCSD)
- Microsoft Certified Systems Engineer (MCSE)
- Microsoft Certified Systems Engineer + Internet
- Microsoft Certified Database Administrator (MCDBA)
- Microsoft Certified Trainer (MCT)

The one you choose depends on your area of expertise and your career goals.

Microsoft Certified Professional (MCP)

This certification is for individuals with expertise in one specific area. MCP certification is often a stepping stone to MCSE or MCSD certification and allows you some benefits of Microsoft certification after just one exam.

By passing one core exam (meaning an operating system exam), you become an MCP.

Microsoft Certified Solution Developer (MCSD)

The MCSD certification identifies developers with experience working with Microsoft operating systems, development tools, and technologies. To achieve the MCSD certification, you must pass four exams:

1. Analyzing Requirements and Defining Solution Architectures

2. A desktop application development exam selected from the following:

   - Designing and Implementing Desktop Applications with Visual Basic 6.0

   - Designing and Implementing Desktop Applications with Microsoft Visual C++ 6.0

3. A distributed application development exam selected from the following:

   - Designing and Implementing Distributed Applications with Microsoft Visual Basic 6.0

   - Designing and Implementing Distributed Applications with Microsoft Visual C++ 6.0

4. One Elective Exam

Some of the electives include:

   - Implementing a Database Design on Microsoft SQL Server 6.5

   - Designing and Implementing a Database with Microsoft SQL Server 7.0

   - Designing and Implementing Data Warehouses with Microsoft SQL Server 7.0

   - Developing Applications with Microsoft Visual C++ Using the Microsoft Foundation Class Library

- Designing and Implementing Web Sites with Microsoft Front Page 98

- Designing and Implementing Commerce Solutions with Microsoft Site Server 3.0, Commerce Edition

- Designing and Implementing Web Solutions with Microsoft Visual InterDev 6.0

Desktop and distributed application exams for Microsoft Visual J++ 6.0 and Microsoft Visual FoxPro 6.0 are in development and will be available in 1999.

Microsoft Certified Systems Engineer (MCSE)

For network professionals, the MCSE certification requires commitment. You need to complete all the steps required for certification. Passing the exams shows that you meet the high standards that Microsoft has set for MCSEs.

The following list applies to the NT 4.0 track. Microsoft still supports a track for 3.51, but 4.0 certification is more desirable because it is the current operating system.

To become an MCSE, you must pass a series of six exams:

1. Networking Essentials (waived for Novell CNEs)

2. Implementing and Supporting Microsoft Windows NT Workstation 4.0 (or Windows 95)

3. Implementing and Supporting Microsoft Windows NT Server 4.0

4. Implementing and Supporting Microsoft Windows NT Server 4.0 in the Enterprise

5. Elective

6. Elective

Some of the electives include:

- Internetworking with Microsoft TCP/IP on Microsoft Windows NT 4.0

- Implementing and Supporting Microsoft Internet Information Server 4.0

- Implementing and Supporting Microsoft Exchange Server 5.5
- Implementing and Supporting Microsoft SNA Server 4.0
- Implementing and Supporting Microsoft Systems Management Server 1.2
- Implementing a Database Design on Microsoft SQL Server 6.5
- System Administration for Microsoft SQL Server 6.5

Microsoft Certified Database Administrator

The MCDBA certification is the premier certification for database support and development professionals. This certification requires four core exams in the subjects of Microsoft SQL Server 7.0 and Windows NT platform support. The core exams include:

1. Implementing and Supporting Microsoft Windows NT 4.0
2. Implementing and Supporting Microsoft Windows NT 4.0 in the Enterprise
3. System Administration of Microsoft SQL Server 7.0
4. Designing and Implementing a Database with Microsoft SQL Server 7.0

In addition, you must pass one elective exam. Some of the more popular include:

- Designing and Implementing Distributed Applications with Microsoft Visual Basic 6.0
- Designing and Implementing Distributed Applications with Microsoft Visual C++ 6.0
- Designing and Implementing Data Warehouses with Microsoft SQL Server 7.0
- Implementing and Supporting Microsoft Internet Information Server 4.0
- Internetworking with Microsoft TCP/IP on Microsoft Windows NT 4.0

Microsoft Certified Trainer (MCT)

As an MCT, you can deliver Microsoft certified courseware through official Microsoft channels.

The MCT certification is more costly because, in addition to passing the exams, it requires that you sit through the official Microsoft courses. You also need to submit an application that must be approved by Microsoft. The number of exams you are required to pass depends on the number of courses you want to teach.

> For the most up-to-date certification information, visit Microsoft's Web site at www.microsoft.com/train_cert.

Preparing for the MCSD Exams

To prepare for the MCSD certification exams, you should try to work with the product as much as possible. In addition, there are a variety of resources from which you can learn about the products and exams:

- You can take instructor-led courses.

- You can take online training. This is a useful option for people who cannot find any courses in their area or who do not have the time to attend classes.

- If you prefer to use a book to help you prepare for the MCSD tests, you can choose from a wide variety of publications, including test-preparedness books similar to this one.

> For more MCSD information, point your browser to the Sybex Web site, where you'll find information about the MCP program, job links, and descriptions of other quality titles in the Network Press line of MCSD-related books. Go to http://www.sybex.com and click the MCSD logo.

Scheduling and Taking an Exam

When you think you are ready to take an exam, call Prometric Testing Centers at (800) 755-EXAM (755-3926). They'll tell you where to find the closest testing center. Before you call, get out your credit card because each exam costs $100. (If you've used this book to prepare yourself thoroughly, chances are you'll only have to shell out that $100 once!)

You can schedule the exam for a time that is convenient for you. The exams are downloaded from Prometric to the testing center, and you show up at your scheduled time and take the exam on a computer.

After you complete the exam, you will know right away whether you have passed. At the end of the exam, you will receive a score report. It will list the six areas that you were tested on and how you performed. If you pass the exam, you don't need to do anything else. Prometric uploads the test results to Microsoft. If you don't pass, it's another $100 to schedule the exam again. But at least you will know from the score report where you did poorly, so you can study that particular information more carefully.

Test-Taking Hints

If you know what to expect, your chances of passing the exam will be much greater. The following are some tips that can help you achieve success:

Get there early and be prepared   This is your last chance to review. Bring your Study Guide and review any areas you feel unsure of. If you need a quick drink of water or a visit to the restroom, take the time before the exam. After your exam starts, it will not be paused for these needs.

When you arrive for your exam, you will be asked to present two forms of ID. You will also be asked to sign a paper verifying that you understand the testing rules (for example, the rule that says that you will not cheat on the exam).

Before you start the exam, you will have an opportunity to take a practice exam. It is not related to Windows NT and is simply offered so that you will have a feel for the exam-taking process.

What you can and can't take in with you   These are closed-book exams. The only thing that you can take in is scratch paper provided by the testing center. Use this paper as much as possible to diagram the questions. Many times diagramming questions will help make the answer clear. You will have to give this paper back to the test administrator at the end of the exam.

Many testing centers are very strict about what you can take into the testing room. Some centers will not even allow you to bring in items like a zipped-up purse. If you feel tempted to take in any outside material, be aware that many testing centers use monitoring devices such as video and audio equipment (so don't swear, even if you are alone in the room!).

Prometric Testing Centers take the test-taking process and the test validation very seriously.

Test approach   As you take the test, if you know the answer to a question, fill it in and move on. If you're not sure of the answer, mark your best guess, then mark the question.

At the end of the exam, you can review the questions. Depending on the amount of time remaining, you can then view all the questions again, or you can view only the questions that you were unsure of. I always like to double-check all my answers, just in case I misread any of the questions on the first pass. (Sometimes half of the battle is in trying to figure out exactly what the question is asking you.) Also, sometimes I find that a related question provides a clue for a question that I was unsure of.

Be sure to answer all questions. Unanswered questions are scored as incorrect and will count against you. Also, make sure that you keep an eye on the remaining time so that you can pace yourself accordingly.

If you do not pass the exam, note everything that you can remember while the exam is still fresh on your mind. This will help you prepare for your next try. Although the next exam will not be exactly the same, the questions will be similar, and you don't want to make the same mistakes.

After You Become Certified

Once you become an MCSD, Microsoft kicks in some goodies, including:

- A one-year subscription to the Microsoft Beta Evaluation program, which is a great way to get your hands on new software. Be the first kid on the block to play with new and upcoming software.

- Access to a secured area of the Microsoft Web site that provides technical support and product information. This certification benefit is also available for MCP certification.

- Permission to use the Microsoft Certified Professional logos (each certification has its own logo), which look great on letterhead and business cards.

- An MCSD certificate (you will get a certificate for each level of certification you reach), suitable for framing or for sending copies to Mom.

- A one-year subscription to *Microsoft Certified Professional Magazine*, which provides information on professional and career development.

How to Use This Book

This book is designed to help you prepare for the MCSD exam. The book reviews each of the exam objectives and explains how to accomplish the objectives. The explanations include exercises that help you understand how to implement the programming concepts.

Each chapter of the book contains review questions to help you make sure you understand the material in the chapter and to prepare you for the exam itself.

For each chapter:

1. Review the exam objectives as you work through the chapter. (You may want to check the www.microsoft.com/train_cert Web site to make sure the objectives haven't changed.)

2. Study the chapter carefully, making sure you fully understand the information.

3. Complete all hands-on exercises in the chapter, referring to the text so that you understand every step you take.

4. Answer the practice questions at the end of the chapter. (You will find the answers to these questions in Appendix A.)

5. Note which questions you did not understand, and study those sections of the book again.

At this point, you are well on your way to becoming certified! Good Luck!

PART

I

Getting Started with Visual Basic

CHAPTER

1

Getting Started
with Visual Basic

Microsoft Exam Objectives Covered in This Chapter:

- Install and configure Visual Basic for developing desktop applications.

- Establish the environment for source code version control.

- Implement navigational design.
  - Add controls to forms.
  - Set properties for controls.
  - Assign code to a control to respond to an event.

- Assess the potential impact of the logical design on performance, maintainability, extensibility, and availability.

- Write code that processes data entered on a form.
  - Given a scenario, add code to the appropriate form event. Events include Initialize, Terminate, Load, Unload, QueryUnload, Activate, and Deactivate.

When you are ready to start programming with Visual Basic, you need to do two things. First, you obviously need to install the program and its components on your development machine. Second, you need to gain an understanding of the basics of creating a form and writing program code. These two items are the subject of this chapter.

You will take a look at how to install Visual Basic on your machine and to set up Visual SourceSafe to handle version control of your projects. Although this is not a difficult task, it is a somewhat lengthy and involved process.

In the second part of the chapter, you will cover the creation of forms for your program. Typically, you think of designing forms and creating the visual interface of your program by adding controls to the forms of your program while you are in design mode. The exam is not concerned with your ability to arrange the controls of your form in an aesthetic manner; however, it is concerned with your ability to control the functions of the forms and controls of your program through properties, methods, and events.

Installing Visual Basic

On the surface, the installation of Visual Basic is very similar to the installation of many other programs. However, because of the complexity of the product and the requirement for several auxiliary programs, you must step carefully through the Installation Wizard and make several choices during the installation.

The steps discussed here are based on the installation of the Enterprise Edition of Visual Basic. Some steps will be different for other versions of the program.

Microsoft
Exam
Objective

Install and configure Visual Basic for developing desktop applications.

To install Visual Basic on your development machine, you need to perform the following steps outlined in Exercise 1.1.

EXERCISE 1.1

Installing Visual Basic

1. Place the CD-ROM in your drive. The installation program should start automatically and display the opening screen of the Installation Wizard. (If your CD-ROM does not have the AutoPlay feature installed, you can run the installation program by running the *Setup.exe* program from the root directory of the CD-ROM.)

2. You are shown the License Agreement. You need to accept this agreement before you can proceed.

EXERCISE 1.1 (CONTINUED)

3. Next, the installation program checks your machine for the correct version of Internet Explorer. Visual Basic requires that Internet Explorer 4.01 or higher be available on your machine. If Internet Explorer is not present, it will be installed for you. If Internet Explorer is installed by the VB Installation Wizard, you have to reboot your machine to finish setting up Internet Explorer and continue the installation.

4. If you are using the Enterprise Edition, you are asked if you want to install Distributed Component Object Model (DCOM) 98. This technology is necessary for creating distributed applications and is recommended for the Enterprise Edition of Visual Basic.

5. If you have Visual Basic version 5 on your machine, you are asked if you want to remove it. Visual Basic 6 can coexist with VB5, so if you are supporting programs with both versions, you should keep VB5 on your machine.

Microsoft ✓ *Exam* *Objective*

Establish the environment for source code version control.

6. You finally come to the Visual Studio 6.0 Enterprise-Custom dialog box (see the following illustration) that lets you specify which options to include with your installation of Visual Basic. These options include data access options, enterprise tools (for the Enterprise Edition), ActiveX controls, and Visual SourceSafe. Visual SourceSafe is the version control tool that is designed to work with Visual Basic to manage changes between versions of your programs. For programs that are stored in Visual SourceSafe, a copy of each component of the program is stored in the repository. As the program is modified, Visual SourceSafe tracks what changes were made and who made the changes. This is particularly useful in a multi-programmer environment. To make version control available for your programs, you need to have the Visual Source-Safe option checked in the installation dialog. If you install Visual SourceSafe, you need to decide whether to use the old repository format, which supports VB5 and VB6, or the new format, which supports VB6 only.

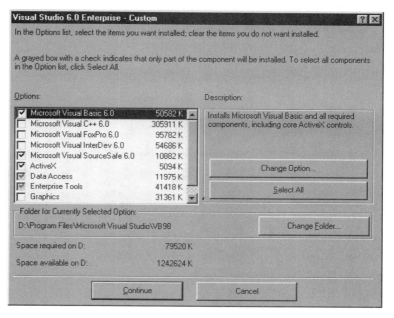

7. Next, the Microsoft Developer's Network Library is installed. MSDN provides all the documentation and sample code for Visual Basic. The documentation and help is in HTML format and uses a browser interface as shown in the following illustration.

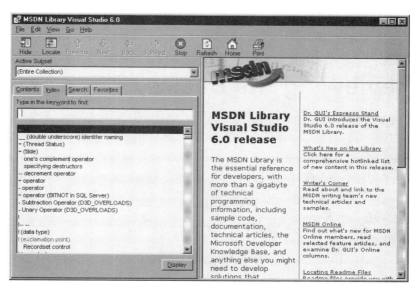

EXERCISE 1.1 (CONTINUED)

8. Finally, you need to choose whether to install any additional tools such as InstallShield. These tools are displayed in the Installation Wizard dialog box shown in the following illustration. After the installation of any additional tools, your Visual Basic development environment is completely set up and ready for you to use.

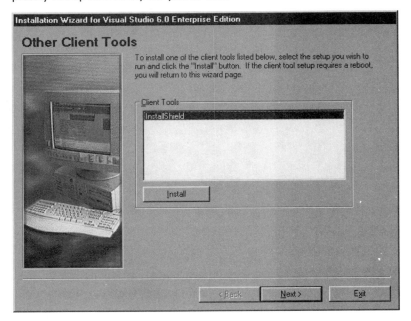

Reviewing the Basics of Forms and Controls

Microsoft ✓ **Exam** **Objective**

Implement navigational design.

- Add controls to forms.

Most programs that you create in Visual Basic contain at least one form, which in turn contains a number of controls. About the only programs that do not contain a form are ActiveX servers, which are discussed in Chapter 10, "Creating COM Components." The forms and controls of your programs are the only parts that your user sees. Therefore, much effort is expended by programmers to ensure that the interface created by the forms and controls is intuitive to use, visually pleasing, and makes it easy for the user to accomplish the desired task. This is true whether you are writing a custom database program to handle membership tracking (such as the program shown in Figure 1.1) or a simple game (as shown in Figure 1.2).

FIGURE 1.1

The interface of a data entry program may be complex...

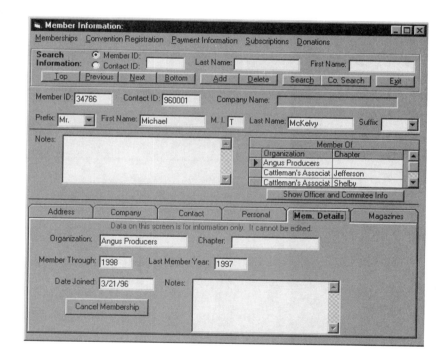

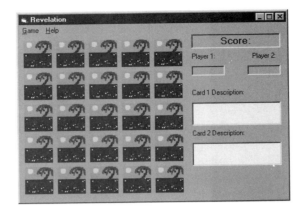

Working with Properties

Microsoft Exam Objective

Implement navigational design.

- Set properties for controls.

As you add controls to the forms of your program, you control the behavior
and appearance of these controls, and of the forms themselves, through the
properties of each control. Properties such as Left, Top, Height, and Width
determine the size and position of each control. These four properties, along
with the Name property, are common to every control you use. The other
properties available depend on the specific control you are using. Three categories of properties are available for each control:

- Properties that are available only at design time

- Properties that are available only at run time

- Properties that can be set at any time

While you are in design mode, you change the properties available at design
time through the Properties window of the Visual Basic design environment.
This window, shown in Figure 1.3, enables you to easily set the properties by
providing descriptions of the properties, drop-down lists for properties that

have only a specified set of values, and even dialog boxes for some properties such as Font or ForeColor and BackColor. All these elements are designed to make it as easy as possible for you to create your programs.

FIGURE 1.3

Visual Basic's Proper-
ties window provides
easy access to control
properties.

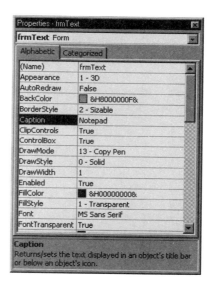

To further facilitate the design process, many controls (especially third-party controls) have a Custom button in the Properties window that brings up a set of property pages for the control. These property pages help you set up all the necessary properties of a control. The property pages are particularly useful for complex controls such as ImageList or TreeView. The TreeView Property Page shown in Figure 1.4.

Although you will work with the properties of the form and controls mostly while in design mode, there are times when you will want to change the appearance and behavior of controls while your program is running. A typical case is changing the Enabled property of controls as program conditions change. The Enabled property determines whether the user can interact with the control. (A disabled control is indicated by showing it as "grayed out.") To change a property in program code, you simply use an assignment statement to set the new value of the property. This statement, like the one shown below, specifies the name of the control, the name of the property, and the new value to be set.

```
cboFieldName.Enabled = True
```

FIGURE 1.4

The property page for
the TreeView control

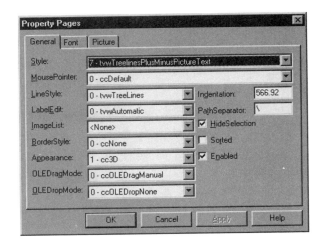

Some properties, such as the Name property, can be set only at design time,
but most properties can be set with program code. This manipulation of properties will make up a large portion of the Visual Basic code that you write.

Writing Code for Events

Microsoft ✓ *Exam Objective*

Implement navigational design.

- Assign code to a control to respond to an event.

The properties of the forms and controls determine their appearance and
behavior, but it is code that you write for the events of the forms and controls
that makes your program perform tasks. You can have the most well-planned,
perfectly designed user interface; but without program code, your application
won't accomplish anything, no matter how good the interface looks.

Events are Visual Basic's way of notifying you that the form has received
a Windows message from the operating system. These messages can indicate
that the user has pressed a key, clicked a mouse button, or taken some other
action. The events can also be triggered in response to system events or control events, such as having a specified amount of time elapse. Although many

events are available for each control and for forms (take a look at the form event list in the Code window), your program responds only to events for which you have written program code. All other events are ignored.

Program code can be divided into two major categories:

Assignment statements   Used to set the value of a control's property or of a variable. You saw such a statement earlier in this chapter.

Control statements   As their name implies, control the flow of a program. These statements include For...Next loops, If...Then...Else...End If structures and others. You will learn more about controlling program flow in Chapter 2, "Working with ActiveX Controls."

You should be familiar with writing event procedures; Exercise 1.2 provides a brief refresher for those who aren't. The code takes the input from two text boxes, performs a calculation, and displays the results in another text box. The code is executed when a user clicks the command button on a form.

EXERCISE 1.2

Writing an Event Procedure

1. Start a new project in Visual Basic.

2. Place three text boxes on the form and name them **txtInput1**, **txtInput2**, and **txtOutput**.

3. Add a command button to the form and name it **cmdCalculate**.

4. Open the Code window by clicking the Code button on the Project window.

5. In the object list, select the command button (named cmdCalculate). The Click event is the default event and the header and footer for the procedure are automatically created for you.

6. You can go directly to this event procedure from your form by double-clicking the command button.

7. Enter the following code in the Code window:

```
Dim iNumber1 As Integer, iNumber2 As Integer
iNumber1 = txtInput1.Text
iNumber2 = txtInput2.Text
txtOutput.Text = iNumber1 * iNumber2
```

You can omit the Text property from your code. Most controls have what is called a Value property, which is the default property for the control. If you do not specify a property name, the default or Value property is assumed. Text is the default property of the TextBox control.

The program works only if you input numbers in the text boxes. If you enter letters, the program generates an error. You can learn about handling errors in Chapter 14, "Handling and Logging Errors in Visual Basic Programs."

Planning the Design

Microsoft Exam Objective	Assess the potential impact of the logical design on performance, maintainability, extensibility, and availability.

You know that creating a user interface for a program can be as simple as placing controls on a form. Add program code for specific events, and you have a working program. We all know that creating a good program is more involved than this, however, and many design issues can make a program either a good one that users will use or a bad one that users will avoid. Although this section doesn't cover a large number of design issues (whole books have been devoted to the subject), you should be aware of a few key areas.

Because the MCSD exam uses multiple-choice questions, you will not find questions specifically related to design. The exam is designed, however, to measure your ability to apply programming theory and to test your experience. These design considerations are an integral part of the practical application of programming theory.

Tab Order

One of the first concepts that you need to understand is tab order, the order in which controls on your form are accessed as the user presses the Tab key. The tab order of controls is determined by the TabIndex property of each control. As you add controls, the TabIndex of each control is set to the next lowest number not already taken by the other controls on the form. If you design a form perfectly, tab order is not a problem. However, many programmers add all the labels to a form first, then the text boxes, then other controls. Although this makes it easy to initially set up the controls, it plays havoc with the tab order.

The most desirable tab order starts at the top left of the form and moves from left to right and from top to bottom on the form. Because this is the way most users read, it is a logical order in a form. To set the tab order, start with the control you want your users to hit first and set its TabIndex to zero. Then proceed in the order you want for the tab order, setting the TabIndex property of each control to the next available number.

The other property that affects the tab order of your program is the Tab-Stop property. This property is available for any control that can receive focus, such as a text box or combo box. The default setting of the TabStop property is True, indicating that the user can tab to the control. If the Tab-Stop property of a control is set to False, the control is skipped as the user presses the Tab key to move from control to control.

Keyboard Navigation

Another key design issue is keyboard navigation for your forms. Setting the tab order enables a user to move through the form in a logical manner; however, users may often need to go directly to a specific control. They can do this by clicking on the control with the mouse, but a good design enables them to move directly to a control without moving their hands from the keyboard. You can provide hot key functionality to other input controls. Exercise 1.3 shows how to enable a text box for keyboard navigation.

EXERCISE 1.3

Allowing a User to Move Directly to a Text Box

1. Place a text box on the form.

2. Place a label control near the text box. Set the TabIndex property of the label to zero. This automatically increments the TabIndex of the text box to one.

3. Set a hot key in the Caption property of the label using an ampersand (&), for example, &Name.

4. Add some other controls to the form.

When the user presses the hot key combination for the label, Visual Basic tries to set the focus to the label. However, because a label cannot receive focus, the control next in the tab order (the text box) receives the focus. The *KeyBoard.vbp* project on the CD-ROM shows how this is implemented.

Creating Applications with Multiple Forms

You can create some useful programs with a single form, but most of the programs you create will involve multiple forms. Many large projects can have 50 forms or more. You must have a way to create and display other forms from within your program code, because Visual Basic loads only a single form on start-up.

Displaying Forms in a Program

You create all the forms of your program in the design environment. The key to using these forms is to display them in your program at the proper time, typically in response to user actions. Visual Basic provides a form method and a command to enable you to display additional forms in your program. The simplest way to handle displaying a form is to use the Show method, which loads the form into memory and displays it on-screen. Exercise 1.4 provides a simple example of this method.

EXERCISE 1.4

Displaying a Second Form in a Program

1. Start a new project in Visual Basic.

2. Add a second form to the project by choosing the New Form item from the Project menu or by clicking the New Form button on the toolbar.

3. Place some controls on the second form.

4. Return to the first form.

5. Place a command button on the form.

6. In the Click event procedure, place the following statement:

   Form2.Show

7. Run the program.

The Show method handles all the work of displaying the second form. An optional parameter can also be specified with the Show method, which enables you to make the form modal; that is, the user cannot move to another form in the program until this form is hidden or unloaded. Modal forms are often used for dialog boxes that you want to have the user complete before moving on. To display a form as modal, use the following variation of the Show method:

```
Form2.Show vbModal
```

If you can display a form, you also want to be able to hide it. The Hide method removes the form from the display, but does not remove it from memory. The Hide method is used as shown in the following line:

```
Form2.Hide
```

In addition to the Show and Hide methods, two commands are used in manipulating forms: Load and Unload.

Load   The Load command places the form in memory but does not display it on the screen.

Unload   The Unload command is used to remove the form from memory, freeing up most of the memory used by the form definition.

Because a form is automatically loaded when the Show method is invoked, why would you want to use the Load command? Often, a large form takes a long time to load. If you have one or two large forms in your program, you can use the Load command to load them into memory during program start-up when users are more tolerant of delays. Then, issuing the Show method quickly displays the form. You can also use the Load command if several options need to be set by your program code before the form is displayed.

The Load and Unload commands are shown in the following lines of code:

```
Load Form2
Unload Form2
Unload Me
```

The last code line shows the use of the Me keyword to refer to a form. This keyword tells a command to operate on the form that contains the code line. Using the Me keyword to internally refer to a form helps avoid any problems that can arise from renaming a form after it is created. You will also find that the Me keyword is essential in properly using object variables to manipulate forms and in creating MDI applications, which are discussed in the next sections.

Using Variables to Manipulate Forms

Using the Show and Hide methods and Load and Unload commands with the name of a form enables you to work with a single instance of each form that you create in your program. Because forms are Visual Basic objects, however, you can use object variables to work with forms. Using object variables enables you to create multiple instances of any form you have designed.

To use a variable to handle form operations, you need to declare a variable for the form to be used. You can then use the variable in place of the form name in any form operation. By using the New keyword in either the variable declaration or in the Set command that assigns a form to the variable, you can create multiple instances of the form. Exercise 1.5 illustrates how to create two instances of a form using object variables. An example of this technique is contained in the *FormObj.vbp* project on the CD-ROM.

EXERCISE 1.5

Creating Multiple Form Instances

1. Create the primary form for your project. This form should contain a command button for creating and displaying the instances of the second form.

2. Create a second form to be used as a template for your form objects. For the example, name the form **frmPerson**.

3. Open the Code window for your main form (the first one you created).

4. Place the variable declarations in the Declarations section of the form. The variables are declared using the following code:

```
Dim frmVar1 As frmPerson, frmVar2 As frmPerson
```

5. In the Click event of the command button, place the code to create and display the form instances. The Set command with the New keyword creates a new instance of the frmPerson form. The Show method applied to each form variable displays the form.

```
Set frmVar1 = New frmPerson
Set frmVar2 = New frmPerson
frmVar1.Show
frmVar2.Show
frmVar2.Move 500, 500
```

EXERCISE 1.5 (CONTINUED)

6. Run the program. When you click the command button on the main form, two instances of the frmPerson form are created. Each of these instances is independent of the other.

WARNING

When you are creating multiple instances of a form, you should always refer to them by the variable that you used to create the instance of the form. Attempting to refer to either form using the form name (that is, frm-Person.Show) does not affect either of the instances assigned to variables, but does create an additional instance of the form.

Creating MDI Applications

The most common method of using variables to create multiple instances of a form is in the creation of a multiple-document interface (MDI) application. You have used MDI applications when you worked with multiple documents in a word processor. Also, the interface for Visual Basic 5 is an MDI application, placing each form and each Code window in a separate child window of the main form.

In an MDI application, a single parent form contains a menu and optionally contains toolbars that enable you to create, arrange, and work with the child forms. The MDI parent form does not contain standard controls such as labels and text boxes. It can, however, hold a Panel, StatusBar, or Image-List control, or any other control that has an Align property. Each child form provides an interface with which you can work on a document, a spreadsheet, a data entry form, or any other type of program interface. Each child form is contained within the borders of the parent form, but each child form is capable of independent operation.

A typical example of an MDI application is a notepad or simple word processor. Without going into all the details, Exercise 1.6 illustrates the basics of creating an MDI application.

EXERCISE 1.6

Creating an MDI Application

1. Start a new project in Visual Basic.

2. Add an MDI form to the project using the Add MDI Form item of the Project menu.

EXERCISE 1.6 (CONTINUED)

3. Make the MDI form the start-up form for the program. To do this, select the Properties item from the Project menu, then select the MDI form in the Startup form drop-down list.

4. Using the original Form1 that was created when the project was created, change the name to **frmText** and set the MDIChild property to True.

5. Add a text box to this form to allow the user to input text.

6. On the MDI form, add a menu item called File and a submenu called New. (Menu creation is discussed in detail in Chapter 4, "Advanced Design Features.")

7. In the Click event for the New menu item, place the following code:

```
Dim frmVar As frmText
Set frmVar = New frmText
frmVar.Show
```

8. Run the program. Each time you select the New item from the File menu, a new instance of the child form is created within the MDI parent.

Coding for Events in a Form

Microsoft ✓ **Exam Objective**

Write code that processes data entered on a form.

- Given a scenario, add code to the appropriate form event. Events include Initialize, Terminate, Load, Unload, QueryUnload, Activate, and Deactivate.

Properties control the appearance and behavior of a form, and a method enables the form to perform tasks, but it is the events of the form that tell it when to take action. If you look at the event drop-down list in a form's Code window (see Figure 1.5), you will see that there are several events that a form recognizes and to which it can respond. All these events can cause action to be taken, but only the events for which you write code perform any functions in your program. If you have no code in the procedure for an event, the event is ignored.

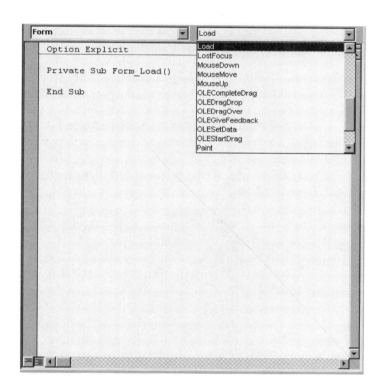

FIGURE 1.5

Forms are capable of responding to a multitude of events

This section does not examine each event to which a form can respond. Rather, it looks specifically at some of the events that occur when a form is loaded and when it is closed. You will also see the sequence in which some of these events occur. Knowing the sequence of events is important in knowing where to place your code to get the desired results.

Events Occurring When a Form Loads

Several key events occur when a form is loaded for the first time. These events are summarized below. Table 1.1 lists these start-up events and indicates when they are triggered.

T A B L E 1.1	Event	When Triggered
Event and Trigger	Initialize	When the form is first referenced in any manner by your program
	Load	When the form is first placed in memory using the Load statement or Show method
	Activate	When the form receives focus as it is shown or the user moves back to the form from another form or application
	Resize	Whenever the user or the program changes the Height, Width, or WindowState properties of the form
	Paint	Whenever any part of the form needs to be refreshed

Figure 1.6 shows how some of these events are used in a program.

F I G U R E   1.6

Multiple events may be accessed when a form loads.

```
Form                        ▼   Load                        ▼
     Private Sub Form_Activate()
     Dim I As Integer
     If FrstCapture Then
         LocnSet.Index = "PrimaryKey"
         'Set captions for table 1
         SetCaptions
     End If
     End Sub
     Private Sub Form_Load()
     Dim I As Integer
     On Error GoTo CaptureErr4
     cmdLocate.Caption = TextLoad(654) & ProdTitle
     'Set path for data controls.
     For I = 0 To 2
         Me.datCapture(I).DatabaseName = LabData
     Next I
     DatSelSQL = "SELECT DISTINCTROW Archives.*, Location.Roo
     'Set Window size and position
     Me.Top = 0
     Me.Left = 0
     Me.Height = 6705
     Me.Width = 9390
     End Sub
     Private Sub Form_Resize()
     If Me.WindowState <> 1 And AllowResize Then
         dbgTable1.Width = Me.ScaleWidth - 240
         dbgTable1.Height = Me.ScaleHeight - dbgTable1.Top -
         fraMain.Height = Me.ScaleHeight - 45
         fraMain.Width = Me.ScaleWidth - 15
```

Initialize Event

The Initialize event is triggered only once during the lifetime of a form. The Initialize event is triggered by one of the following actions:

- When a property or method of the form is referenced by another part of the program.

- When an object variable is used to create a new instance of the form. (This was covered in the section "Using Variables to Manipulate Forms.")

- Automatically when the form is loaded by the Load command or the Show method.

You can use the Initialize event to set initial values of custom properties that you create for a form. Giving a custom property an initial value ensures that a valid value will always be available for the property.

Load Event

Like the Initialize event, the Load event is triggered only once during the lifetime of a form. The Load event is triggered by one of the following actions:

- When the Load command is issued to load the form into memory

- Automatically when the Show method is used to display a form that was not previously loaded

The Load event is often used to set the initial properties of the form itself and of the controls contained by the form. Most control properties can be set from the Load event.

Resize Event

The Resize event occurs when the form is initially loaded or whenever the form changes size. If you have controls, such as a grid, that need to be sized to match the dimensions of the form, the Resize event is the location for that code.

Paint Event

The Paint event is another event that occurs when a form is initially displayed. It also occurs whenever a part of the form needs to be refreshed, such as when the form is initially loaded or after it has been covered up by another form.

The Paint event is where you place code that prints on the form or draws graphics on the form. For example, if you are printing labels instead of using the label controls, you place the code in the Paint event to assure that the labels get reprinted whenever part of the form has been covered.

Activate Event

The Activate event occurs whenever the form receives focus from another form or another program. It is also triggered when the form is initially shown using the Show method. This event may be used to initialize the state of a form each time it is shown. For example, you may place code in the event to set the focus to a particular control, so the user always knows where to start. Also, some initial settings, such as the RecordSource property of a data control, cannot be set during the Load event and must be initially set in the Activate event.

Sequence of Events

It is important to know which events are good for specific tasks, but it is also necessary to understand the sequence in which these events occur, because the code in one event may be dependent on code in other events. For example, the code in Figure 1.6 sets a variable in the Load event that determines whether controls on the form will be moved or sized in response to the Resize event. The Load event is the proper location for this assignment because it occurs before the Resize event.

For the first four events listed earlier, the proper sequence is

1. Initialize

2. Load

3. Resize

4. Paint

If you want to experiment with the sequence of other events, simply place a message box in the event procedure for each event of interest. Then, as you perform operations on the form, you can see the order in which events occur. A sample program is contained in the *FormEvent.vbp* project on the CD-ROM.

The Activate event also occurs between the Load and the Paint events, but it is not triggered if your program has code for the Resize event.

Events Occurring when a Form is Unloaded

In a manner similar to loading the form, a series of events occur when the form is unloaded. The three key events are

1. QueryUnload

2. Unload

3. Terminate

The characteristics of these three events, as well as the Deactivate event, are summarized below.

QueryUnload Event

The QueryUnload event occurs when the form is closed using the Control menu, the Close button, or the Unload command. The QueryUnload event enables you to determine the method by which the form was closed. The QueryUnload event occurs before the Unload event; it can be used to determine how the form was closed and to cancel the Unload if desired. The UnloadMode argument of the QueryUnload event procedure tells you how the form was unloaded. The argument can have one of five values, as listed in Table 1.2.

T A B L E 1.2 UnloadMode Values	**UnloadMode Value**	**Cause of Unload action**
	vbFormControlMenu	The Close option of the Control menu (upper-left corner of the form) was chosen or the Close button (upper-right corner) was clicked.
	vbFormCode	Your program code issued the Unload statement for the form.
	vbAppWindows	The user is shutting down Windows.
	vbAppTaskManager	The application was closed by the Task Manager.
	vbFormMDIForm	The child form is being closed because the MDI parent form was closed.

Unload Event

The Unload event occurs when the form is unloaded by any of the means specified in Table 1.2. This event is used to close objects, such as recordsets, that were opened within the form. It can also be used to return a program to the same state it was in before the form was loaded. The Unload event always occurs after the QueryUnload event.

Terminate Event

The Terminate event is unique in the closing events of a form. The Terminate event always occurs after the Unload event, but it occurs only when all references to the form are destroyed either by being set to Nothing or by an object variable going out of scope. The Terminate event typically is used for clean-up code to handle tasks such as releasing memory used by form variables, resetting a program state, or other similar tasks.

Deactivate Event

The Deactivate event occurs when the focus is transferred to another form or program. You can use this event to ensure that certain operations are completed before the user leaves the form.

To illustrate how these events might be used in a program, Exercise 1.7 demonstrates how to prevent a user from closing a form using the Control menu or the Close button.

EXERCISE 1.7

Preventing the User from Using the Control Menu or the Close Button

1. Start a new project.

2. Place a command button on the form and set the caption to Exit.

3. Open the Code window for the form.

4. Place the statement Unload Me in the Click event of the command button.

5. Select the QueryUnload event of the Form object.

6. Use the following code to check for the method by which the form was closed and to cancel the unload if the Close button was clicked.

   ```
   If UnloadMode = vbFormControlMenu Then Cancel = 1
   ```

7. You can test the program by running it, then trying to exit the program using the Control menu or the Close button. You can exit the program by clicking the Exit button.

Coding Events for Control

Microsoft ✓ ***Exam Objective***

Implement navigational design.

- Assign code to a control to respond to an event.

Like forms, controls are also capable of responding to events. And, like the events of a form, control events occur in a specific order. Control events are too numerous to list here, but a few worth special mention are outlined in this section because questions about them may appear on the certification exam.

Almost all controls respond to the user pressing a key. For these controls, there are three events of importance:

KeyDown   Occurs as the user presses the key

KeyUp   Occurs as the user releases the key

KeyPress   Occurs between the KeyDown and KeyUp events

These events not only detect keystrokes, but also can tell you which key was pressed and enable you to modify the keystroke if you want. The KeyPress event tells you only the ASCII code of the key that was pressed, making it useful for limiting input—for example, making sure that the user enters only numbers. The KeyDown and KeyUp events are also capable of telling you whether any Shift or Control keys were being held down while the key was being pressed.

The other action that almost all controls respond to is the mouse click. As with a keystroke, three events occur whenever the user clicks the mouse on a control (in order of firing):

- MouseDown
- MouseUp
- Click

If the user double-clicks the mouse, these three events are fired, followed by the DblClick event and a second MouseUp event. Because of this sequence, you can see why you need to be careful regarding what code is placed in an event. The double-click not only fires the DblClick event, but also fires the Click event and the MouseUp event twice. The Click event only detects that the left mouse button was clicked. The MouseUp and MouseDown events tell you which mouse button was clicked, whether a Shift key was pressed, and the position of the mouse cursor. Therefore, these two events are useful for handling functions such as context-sensitive pop-up menus.

Extending Forms through Custom Properties and Methods

You are familiar with the built-in properties and methods of forms. The properties of a form control its appearance and behavior, and the methods of the form handle performing tasks in your programs. However, you are not limited to using only the internal properties and methods of forms; you can create your own, enabling you to pass data back and forth between forms and extend the functionality of forms.

Creating a Property in a Form

The properties that you create for a form are variables of the form that have a public interface; that is, they can be accessed from other parts of your program. The capability of accessing custom form properties enables you to do more with forms than is possible with the built-in properties alone. For example, a program could use the same form to enable a user to input information about customers or employees. Because both functions require the input of a name, address, and phone number, using a single form makes sense. However, suppose you want the form's caption and some of the command buttons to have a different appearance depending on whether a customer or employee is input. The solution to this problem is to create a property in the form that can be set before the form is loaded. Then, code in the Form_Load event sets up the form based on the value of the property. The code for this is shown below:

```
Private Sub Form_Load()
' This will be loaded from 2 forms; Security &
' Customer.  The form title will vary based
' upon the calling form.
On Error GoTo AddUserErr1
'Use TextLoad function to load language appropriate
captions, etc.
'   Captions for this form will be in the range of 151 to 175
If AddType = 1 Then
    'Called from Security screen
```

```
        frmAddUser.Caption = TextLoad(151)
        lblAddUser.Caption = TextLoad(153)
        'Add button is default, called if user presses Enter
        cmdAddUser(0).Caption = TextLoad(156)
        txtNewUser.MaxLength = 20
    Else
        'Called from Customer screen
        frmAddUser.Caption = TextLoad(152)
        lblAddUser.Caption = TextLoad(158)
        'Add button is default, called if user presses Enter
        cmdAddUser(0).Caption = TextLoad(159)
        txtNewUser.MaxLength = 50
    End If
    'Cancel button is default, called if user presses Esc
    cmdAddUser(1).Caption = TextLoad(157)
    Exit Sub
AddUserErr1:
    LogError "AddUser", "Load", Err.Number, Err.Description
    Resume Next
    End Sub
```

There are two methods of creating a property in a form:

- Declaring a Public variable in the Declarations section of the form

- Using Property procedures

You will look at both of these methods, but using Property procedures is recommended for reasons that will be covered later.

Going Public with a Variable

The first and simplest way of creating a property in a form is to declare a Public variable in the Declarations section of the form using a statement such as the one below:

```
Public iFormType As Integer
```

Using this statement, you create a variable that can be accessed from anywhere in your program by specifying the name of the form and the name of the property (variable) using the same dot notation as you would for built-in properties. In fact, if you are using the Auto List Members feature of Visual Basic, you will see your Public variable listed right along with the built-in properties of the form in the member list.

Using a Public variable is the easiest way to create a property, but it has two major drawbacks. First, it is not possible to validate the values that are set by other parts of the program or by your users (if you are basing the value of the property on user input). With a Public variable, the user can set any value regardless of what values may be appropriate for the form. Second, you cannot use the variable for information only. That is, other parts of your program always have the capability to modify the value of the variable.

Creating a Property through Procedures

The second and preferred method of creating a property in a form is through the use of Property procedures. These procedures enable your program to perform validation on the values passed to the property to assure that the values are appropriate for the function. Also, you can restrict the property to be read-only, which enables you to use the value within the form and provide access to the value of the property to determine the state of the form. You can create three types of Property procedures:

Property Let   Used to set the value of a property that is stored as a standard variable type (an integer, floating point number, string, and so on).

Property Get   Used to retrieve the current value of the property.

Property Set   Variation of the Property Let procedure. Property Set is used to set the value of properties that are objects. For example, you can use a Property Set to pass a recordset to a form.

Typically, you create a Property Let and Property Get procedure together to allow read/write capabilities for the property. However, you can create a read-only property by omitting the Property Let procedure. Likewise, you can create a write-only property by omitting the Property Get procedure. Exercise 1.8 demonstrates how to create a read/write property using both the Property Let and Property Get procedures.

EXERCISE 1.8

Creating a Property

1. Open the Code window of the form in which you wish to create a property by clicking the code icon in the Project window or double-clicking the form itself.

2. In the Declarations section of the form's code, create a Private variable of the same type as the property you are creating. This variable will be used internally by the form code to reference the value of the property.

3. Select the Add Procedure item from the Tools menu in Visual Basic to bring up the Add Procedure dialog box shown here.

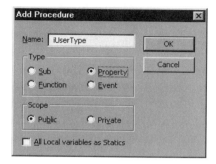

4. Specify a name for the procedure, choose the Property button in the Type group, choose the Public button in the Scope group, and then click the OK button in the dialog box. The skeleton code for a Property Let and a Property Get procedure is created in the Code window, as shown here.

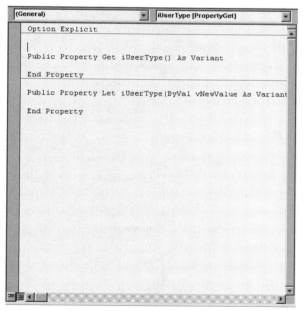

5. Change the type specification of the variable in the Property Let procedure to match that of the internal variable you created in step 2.

6. Change the type specification of the Property Get procedure to match the variable in step 2.

EXERCISE 1.8 (CONTINUED)

7. In the Property Let procedure, set the value of the internal variable to the value passed to the procedure. The Property Let procedure is where you place the validation code for the property. For example, the following code verifies the input and sets the value of the internal variable.

```
If iInptType < 0 Then
    iFormType = 0
ElseIf iInptType > 10 Then
    iFormType = 10
Else
    iFormType = iInptType
End If
```

8. In the Property Get procedure, set the value of the Property to the internal variable to enable other parts of your program to determine the current value of the property. For example,

```
PersonType = iFormType
```

9. The complete code for the PersonType property is shown here.

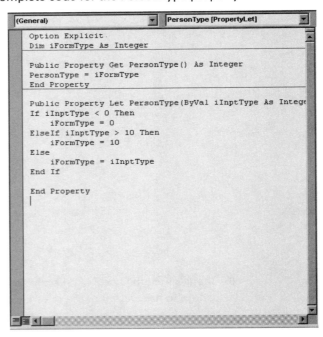

As with the property created using a Public variable, properties created with these procedures behave like the built-in properties of a form. The following code line shows how the type of form is set from another part of the program.

```
frmPersonInfo.PersonType = 1
Load frmPersonInfo
```

Creating a Method in a Form

Custom properties help you pass data to a form, but custom methods help you extend the functionality of a form. Methods can be used to handle simple tasks such as centering a form, or more complex tasks such as populating a grid with database information. A properly written method makes it easier to maintain your code and to create reusable forms that can be used in multiple projects.

A custom method of a form is simply a Sub or Function procedure that has a public interface. You will learn more about procedures and functions and their scope in Chapter 2. Exercise 1.9 shows you how to create a method that centers the form.

EXERCISE 1.9

Creating a Method to Center the Form

1. As with creating a Property procedure, open the Code window for the form.

2. Select the Add Procedure item from the Tools menu in Visual Basic.

3. Specify the name of the procedure (CenterMe), choose the Sub button in the Type group, choose the Public button in the Scope group, and then click the OK button in the dialog box to create the skeleton of the procedure in the Code window.

4. Add the following code to the procedure to perform the operation:

```
If Me.WindowState <> 0 Then Exit Sub
Me.Top = (Screen.Height - Me.Height) / 2
Me.Left = (Screen.Width - Me.Width) / 2
```

The CenterMe method can now be called like any of the built-in methods of the form. You can call the method from within the form's code to center the form, such as after a Resize event. You can also call the method from other parts of the program. In addition, the method will show up in the member list just as if it were a built-in method. This is illustrated in Figure 1.7 where the method is called to center a form after it is initially shown.

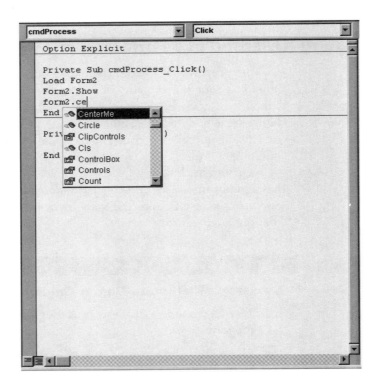

Summary

In this chapter you have reviewed several aspects of programming the forms and controls that make up your programs. The chapter has provided you with some of the basic information that you will need to create most of your Visual Basic programs, including how:

- Event sequences can have an impact on your programs.

- Choosing the right event enables your program to perform the tasks that you want it to perform.

- Multiple instances of a form can be created by using object variables.

- The functionality of forms can be extended by creating your own properties and methods.

An understanding of these topics will help you meet these Microsoft certification exam objectives:

- Install and configure Visual Basic for developing desktop applications.

- Establish the environment for source code version control.

- Implement navigational design.

   - Add controls to forms.

   - Set properties for controls.

   - Assign code to a control to respond to an event.

- Assess the potential impact of the logical design on performance, maintainability, extensibility, and availability.

- Write code that processes data enterd on a form.

   - Given a scenario, add code to the appropriate form event. Events include Initialize, Terminate, Load, Unload, QueryUnload, Activate, and Deactivate.

Also, and perhaps more importantly, understanding these topics will prepare you for the real-world test of creating professional programs to meet real needs. Now it is time to put your knowledge to the test. The following questions are typical of those you might find on the Visual Basic certification exam.

Review Questions

1. What is the sequence in which the following events are triggered when a form is loaded?

   A. Initialize, Resize, Paint, and Load

   B. Load, Initialize, Resize, and Paint

   C. Initialize, Load, Paint, and Resize

   D. Initialize, Load, Resize, and Paint

2. What is the sequence of events when a form is unloaded?

   A. Unload, QueryUnload, and Terminate

   B. QueryUnload, Unload, and Terminate

   C. Unload only

   D. QueryUnload and Unload

3. How can you keep the user from exiting a form by using the Close item on the Control menu or by clicking the Close button?

   A. Place code in the Unload event.

   B. Place code in the QueryUnload event.

   C. This can only be done using a Windows API call.

   D. This cannot be done in Visual Basic.

4. How do you create a read-only property in a form?

   A. Create only a Property Let procedure.

   B. Create only a Property Get procedure.

   C. Create both a Property Get and Property Let procedure.

   D. Declare a Public variable in the Declarations section of the form.

5. Given the following code segment, how many instances of the form are created and displayed?

```
Dim frmVar1 As frmPerson, frmVar2 As frmPerson
Set frmVar1 = New frmPerson
Set frmVar2 = frmVar1
Load frmVar1
frmVar2.Show
```

   A. None

   B. Three

   C. One

   D. Two

6. Given the following code, what happens when the frmPerson.Show method is called?

```
Dim frmVar1 As frmPerson, frmVar2 As frmPerson
Set frmVar1 = New frmPerson
Set frmVar2 = frmVar1
Load frmVar1
frmPerson.Show
```

A. The current instance of the form is displayed.

B. A second instance of the form is created and displayed.

C. An error occurs.

D. Nothing.

7. Which event(s) enable you to determine which key was pressed by the user? Check all that apply.

A. Click

B. KeyPress

C. KeyDown

D. KeyUp

8. Which event(s) allow you to determine if a control or Shift key was pressed by the user? Check all that apply.

A. Click

B. KeyPress

C. KeyDown

D. KeyUp

9. When is the Terminate event of a form triggered?

A. When the user moves to another form or program

B. When the form is unloaded

C. Never

D. When all references to the form are deleted

10. Which event is triggered when the user moves to another form?

   A. Unload

   B. Deactivate

   C. Terminate

   D. Load

CHAPTER

2

Working with ActiveX Controls

Microsoft Exam Objectives Covered in This Chapter:

- Add an ActiveX control to the toolbox.

- Create data input forms and dialog boxes.
  - Display and manipulate data by using custom controls. Controls include TreeView, ListView, ImageList, Toolbar, and StatusBar.

Developers, particularly Microsoft, seem to always be adding new interface features to their programs. For example, a menu used to be the main interface mechanism for handling tasks. Now, programs have not one, but multiple toolbars for providing easier access to tasks. Another added feature is the status bar, the area at the bottom of the program window that keeps the user informed as to the state of the program. There have been interface shifts. For example, the TreeView and ListView elements that make up the Windows Explorer interface represent a change from some older ways of presenting data. And most recently, the interface is shifting toward the browser interface, where many applications either are or look like an extension of a Web browser.

Fortunately for Visual Basic developers, the development tool has kept pace with many of these new design features. For the most part, if you see a feature in Microsoft's programs, you will probably see a way to implement it in the next version of Visual Basic. And if you can't wait for the next version, third-party vendors will come out with tools that let you implement the features. The controls that you use, whether from Microsoft or other vendors, are ActiveX controls.

One such set of controls is the Microsoft Windows Common Controls. This control set was first added in Visual Basic 4 and has been enhanced in each succeeding version. In version 6, the collection includes eight controls for adding design features to your applications. These controls are:

TreeView   Displays information in a hierarchical tree, like the left pane of Windows Explorer

ListView   Displays information in a multi-column list, like the right pane of Windows Explorer

Toolbar   Enables you to create the push button toolbars that you see in most programs

StatusBar   Enables you to present information to the user in a concise manner

ProgressBar   Enables you to keep the user informed of the progress of a long operation

ImageList   Provides an easy way to manage the images that are used by several of the other controls

TabStrip   Enables you to create multiple pages on a single form, with each page accessible by pressing a tab

ImageCombo   Enables you to display a list of items, each with its own icon and with multiple indentation levels

All these controls are contained in a single OCX file that comes with Visual Basic. To use any of these controls, you have to add them to the Visual Basic toolbox. You can do this through the Components dialog box, which is accessible by choosing the Components item on the Project menu. To add the controls, check the box next to Microsoft Windows Common Controls 6.0 in the dialog box. The dialog box and the toolbox with the controls added are shown in Figure 2.1.

F I G U R E   2.1

Microsoft Windows Common Controls let you add advanced interface elements to your programs.

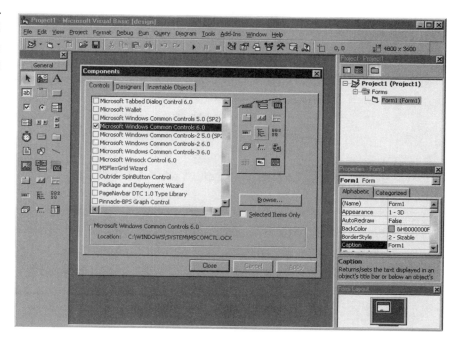

In this chapter you will learn how to use the TreeView, ListView, Image-List, Toolbar, and StatusBar controls. This chapter focuses on these specific controls out of all the Windows Common Controls because these five are called out in the Microsoft exam objectives.

Keeping the User Informed

Most users want to have constant information about the status of the program they are using. For example, your word processor keeps up with the page number you are currently working on, the total number of pages in the document, your position on the page, the status of several options, and whether any spelling errors are in the document. The purpose of status information is twofold:

- First, the user should be able, at a glance, to determine which options are in effect and where the user is in a program, for example, on which record of a database application, on which cell of a spreadsheet, or on which page in a word processor.

- Second, status information indicates the progress of a long operation. Keeping up with the status lets the user know that the program is still working, and is not hung for some reason.

Visual Basic provides two controls for handling the different jobs of status information. The StatusBar control provides easy access to information about the current state of the program. The ProgressBar control supplies information about the progress of a long operation. You will look at both of these controls in this section.

Creating a StatusBar for Your Program

Microsoft ✓ *Exam Objective*

Create data input forms and dialog boxes.

- Display and manipulate data by using custom controls. Controls include TreeView, ListView, ImageList, Toolbar, and StatusBar.

For most applications, the status bar is a thin bar at the bottom of the screen that contains information about the program. This bar typically contains a variety of panels that are used to display bits of information—for example, the state of toggle keys such as Caps Lock and Num Lock, the date and time, short messages about current operations, and location information as described above. Figure 2.2 shows a typical status bar.

F I G U R E 2.2

A status bar keeps the user informed.

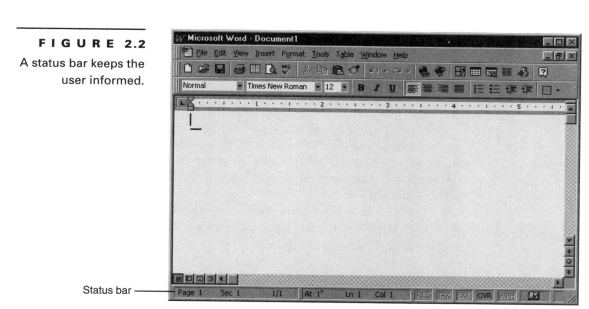

Status bar

For most applications, you design the basic StatusBar setup in the design environment, then update the information by using code. However, you can handle the complete StatusBar setup with code if you desire. This chapter covers both of these techniques.

Creating the Panels of the StatusBar

The first step in creating a StatusBar is, of course, placing the control on your form. When you first place the control on the form, it defaults to a position at the bottom of the form and expands to cover the full width of the form. This is the default behavior and is the one that you will use for most programs. If you wish to use a status bar position other than the default, you can choose from one of five options. These options are assigned to Visual Basic constants as described in Table 2.1.

TABLE 2.1	Constant	Location of the Control's Position
Visual Basic Assigned Constants	vbAlignNone	Enables the control to be placed anywhere on the form
	vbAlignTop	Positions the control at the top of the form
	vbAlignBottom	(Default) Positions the control at the bottom of the form
	vbAlignLeft	Positions the control along the left side of the form
	vbAlignRight	Positions the control along the right side of the form

After you place the control on the form, you are ready to start adding panels to the StatusBar. The panels are objects that contain the information displayed in the StatusBar. To create the panels in the design environment, you simply access the property pages of the control. You can do this by selecting the Custom property in the Properties window and clicking the ellipsis button, or by right-clicking the control and choosing the Properties item from the pop-up menu. Either way, you are shown the Property Pages dialog box, as illustrated in Figure 2.3.

FIGURE 2.3

The property pages of the StatusBar control

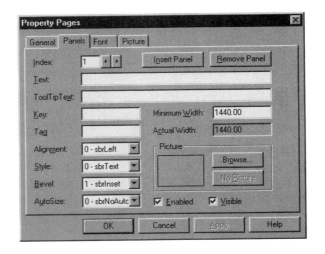

To start creating the panels, click the Panels tab of the dialog box. You will see that the first panel object is created for you; you only have to set the properties. To create more panels, you simply click the Insert Panel button on the dialog box. As you create each panel, you need to set its properties to control what information is displayed and how it is displayed. Now, take a closer look at these properties.

One key property for each panel is the Style property. This property determines whether the panel shows text that you assign to the panel or automatically displays status information about key states or dates and times. The Style property has eight possible settings:

sbrText   Enables you to insert the text to be displayed. The panel displays the information contained in the Text property of the panel object or displays the bitmap contained in the Picture property. This is the only setting that enables you to modify the information in the panel.

sbrCaps   Displays the text CAPS in the panel. When Caps Lock is on, the text is shown in normal text. When Caps Lock is off, the text is displayed dimmed.

sbrNum   Similar to the sbrCaps option, except that this panel style displays NUM to indicate the status of the Num Lock key.

sbrIns   Similar to the sbrCaps option, except that this panel style displays INS to indicate the status of the Insert key.

sbrScrl   Similar to the sbrCaps option, except that this panel style displays SCRL to indicate the status of the Scroll Lock key.

sbrDate   Displays the current date.

sbrTime   Displays the current time.

sbrKana   Similar to the sbrCaps option, except that this panel style displays KANA to indicate the status of a special setting used for handling katakana characters in Japanese language programs.

If you are creating a sbrText Style panel, two properties determine what appears in the panel—the Text property, which contains any text to be displayed, and the Picture property, which determines if a bitmap will be displayed, and which bitmap. Each panel is capable of handling the text and a bitmap simultaneously.

The relative position of the text and the picture depends on the Alignment property. If Alignment is set to Left (the default), any picture appears at the left side of the panel, followed immediately by the text. With Alignment set to Right, the picture appears at the right edge of the panel immediately preceded by the text; and if Alignment is set to Center, the picture appears on the left side of the panel, with the text centered in the remaining space of the panel.

You can also use several other properties to control the appearance of the panels of the StatusBar:

ToolTipText   Specifies the text to be shown if the user rests the mouse cursor on the panel.

Key   A text string that uniquely identifies the panel in the collection.

Bevel   Determines whether the panel has a raised, indented (default), or flat appearance.

MinWidth   Specifies the minimum width of the panel.

AutoSize   Controls how the panel is sized, while observing the minimum width constraint. This property has one of three settings:

  sbrNoAutoSize   Causes the panel size to be set to the size specified in the MinWidth property.

  sbrSpring   Causes the panel to occupy the remaining space in the status bar after all other panels have been sized. If more than one panel uses the sbrSpring setting, the remaining space is shared equally among these panels.

  sbrContents   Causes the panel size to be adjusted to fit the contents of the panel, whether text or picture or both.

Exercise 2.1 shows how to set up a simple StatusBar that keeps up with key states and the current date and time, and provides a space for other information.

Microsoft ✓ *Exam* *Objective*   **Add an ActiveX control to the toolbox.**

EXERCISE 2.1

Creating a Status Bar

1. Start a new project.

2. Add the Microsoft Windows Common Controls to your toolbox.

3. Add a StatusBar control to the form. Name the control **stbSample**.

4. Access the property pages of the control and select the Panels tab of the pages.

5. For the first panel, set the following properties:

Property	Value
Text	Sample Text
Styles	sbrText
AutoSize	sbrSpring
Key	CurStatus

6. Click the Insert button to create another panel in the StatusBar. For the second panel, set the Style property to sbrCaps, and set the MinWidth property to **700**.

7. Repeat the process in step 6 to add four more panels. Set the Style properties of these panels to sbrNum, sbrIns, sbrDate, and sbrTime, respectively. For the Date and Time panels, set the AutoSize property to sbrContents.

8. Accept all the panels by clicking the OK button in the property pages. Then, run the program. Your status bar should look similar to the one in Figure 2.4.

Modifying the Status Bar with Code

As you can see, you can set up the entire status bar from the property pages. However, you still need to use code to handle changes in the status of the program. Because the sbrText Style panel is the only one that enables you to modify the contents, you will look at how to access this panel in code. The other types of panels have their information updated automatically, based on the conditions of the computer and the system date and time.

FIGURE 2.4

The status bar created
in Exercise 2.1

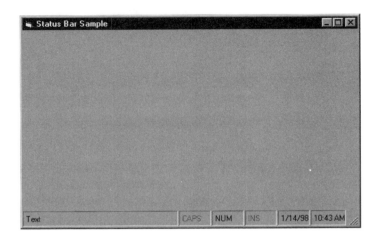

To modify the contents of the panel, you need to access the Text property of the Panel object. This is handled through the Panels collection of the StatusBar. You can work with a specific panel by listing its index number in the collection or by using its Key property. For the text panel created in Exercise 2.1, you can change the Text property using either of the following lines of code:

```
stbSample.Panels(1).Text = "Text"
stbSample.Panels("CurStatus").Text = "New Text"
```

The index numbers of the Panels collection start with one instead of zero as is customary for other collections. If you try to access a Panel object with an index of zero, an error occurs.

In addition to being able to modify the contents of the Text property, you can set up the entire StatusBar control from code. The following code shows how to create the same status bar that you created in Exercise 2.1. The code uses the Add method of the Panels collection to add new panels to the control.

```
Dim pnlNew As Panel
With stbSample.Panels(1)
    .Text = "Text"
```

```
                  .Key = "CurStatus"
                  .AutoSize = sbrSpring
                  .Style = sbrText
              End With
              Set pnlNew = stbSample.Panels.Add
              pnlNew.Style = sbrCaps
              pnlNew.MinWidth = 700
              pnlNew.AutoSize = sbrContents
              Set pnlNew = stbSample.Panels.Add
              pnlNew.Style = sbrNum
              pnlNew.MinWidth = 700
              pnlNew.AutoSize = sbrContents
              Set pnlNew = stbSample.Panels.Add
              pnlNew.Style = sbrIns
              pnlNew.MinWidth = 700
              pnlNew.AutoSize = sbrContents
              Set pnlNew = stbSample.Panels.Add
              pnlNew.Style = sbrDate
              pnlNew.MinWidth = 700
              pnlNew.AutoSize = sbrContents
              Set pnlNew = stbSample.Panels.Add
              pnlNew.Style = sbrTime
              pnlNew.MinWidth = 700
              pnlNew.AutoSize = sbrContents
```

You can learn more about working with collections in Chapter 6, "Working with Collections."

Working with the ProgressBar

The StatusBar control provides one method of giving information to the user. The ProgressBar control is designed to enable you to display the percentage of progress of a long operation, such as a database search or a file copy. You have probably seen a progress bar when you have copied large files or when you have connected to the Internet or retrieved e-mail. The progress bar indicates that the program is still working and is not hung up. It also provides the user with some indication of how much time is remaining until the completion of the operation.

The ProgressBar is easy to set up. The only properties you need to set to make it work are the Min, Max, and Value properties. The Min and Max properties specify the numbers that make up the range of the ProgressBar. The Value property is a number between the Min and Max properties that indicates the relative progress of the operation. The ProgressBar represents the Value as a percentage fill based on the range of the Min and Max properties. For example, if you set the Min property to 0 and the Max property to 500, you could set the Value property to 100 to indicate that an operation is one-fifth complete. This shows up in the progress bar as one-fifth of the space being filled, as shown in Figure 2.5.

FIGURE 2.5

A progress bar in operation

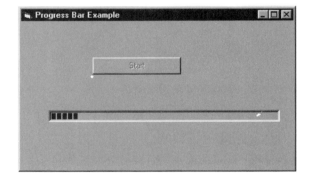

Exercise 2.2 shows you how to create a progress bar. The exercise uses the Timer control to provide an event for updating the ProgressBar's Value property.

EXERCISE 2.2

Creating a Progress Bar

1. Start a new project and add the Windows Common Controls to the toolbox.

2. Add a ProgressBar to your form and set its Name property to **prgSample**. Set the Min and Max properties to **0** and **100**, respectively.

3. Add a Timer control to the form and set its Name property to
tmrProgress.

4. Place the following code in the Timer event of the timer. This code
updates the Value property of the ProgressBar and stops the timer
when the Value property reaches 100.

```
prgSample.Value = prgSample.Value + 10
If prgSample.Value >= 100 Then
    tmrProgress.Interval = 0
    cmdStart.Enabled = True
End If
```

5. Add a command button named **cmdStart** to the form. Set the button's
Caption property to Start. This button will be used to start the timer
and set the initial value of the ProgressBar.

6. Place the following code in the Click event of the command button.

```
prgSample.Value = 0
tmrProgress.Interval = 1000
cmdStart.Enabled = False
```

7. Run the program.

Two new features of the ProgressBar have been added in version 6—
orientation and scrolling. The ProgressBar can now be created with either
a horizontal or a vertical orientation. In previous versions, only the horizontal orientation was possible. You control the orientation of the bar
using the Orientation property. The other new feature enables you to
specify the scrolling of the bar. In previous versions, the bar would always
appear segmented. Although this is still the default behavior, you can also
choose to have the bar appear smooth (unsegmented) as it moves across
the control. This behavior is controlled by the Scrolling property.

Setting Up the ImageList Control

Microsoft ✓ *Exam Objective*

Create data input forms and dialog boxes.

▪ Display and manipulate data by using custom controls. Controls include TreeView, ListView, ImageList, Toolbar, and StatusBar.

Among the Windows Common Controls, the ImageList is unique. The ImageList control cannot be accessed directly by the user. Instead, the control provides a repository for images that are used by several other controls—the Toolbar, TreeView, and ListView controls. The ImageList control adds images to the control through the design environment or through code, then references the index of the image to use it in another control.

In this section, you will look at both methods of setting up the ImageList control. How the control is used with the other controls will be covered in later sections.

Working in the Design Environment

For most of your applications, you will want to set up the ImageList control from the design environment. The reason for this is that after the control is created in the design environment, all the images associated with the control are included as part of your application. You do not need to distribute the bitmap files in addition to your application. Setting up the ImageList from the design environment is simply a matter of choosing pictures and specifying one or two optional properties.

The ImageList control maintains the images in a collection of ListImage objects. (The collection name is ListImages.) Each ListImage object has three key properties:

Picture   Contains the image that is stored for the ListImage object.

Key   A text string that uniquely identifies the image. You can use the Key property to refer to the image instead of using the Index of the collection.

Tag   Enables you to associate other data with the image. The property is not used by Visual Basic itself, so you can set the value to anything that would be useful to you in your program.

Exercise 2.3 shows you how to set up an ImageList control from the design environment.

EXERCISE 2.3

Setting Up the ImageList Control

1. Start a new project and add the Microsoft Windows Common Controls to the toolbox.

2. Add an ImageList control to the form and set the Name property to **iml-Toolbar**. (You will use this ImageList in the Toolbar creation exercise later.)

3. Open the property pages of the ImageList control and select the Images tab. The Images page is shown here.

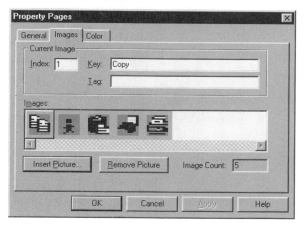

4. To add the first image to the control, click the Insert Picture button at the bottom of the dialog box to bring up the Select Picture dialog box shown here.

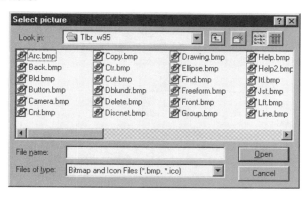

EXERCISE 2.3 (CONTINUED)

5. For the first image, select the `Copy.bmp` file from the `Tlbr_w95` folder. This folder is located in the `Graphics\Bitmaps` folder of VB.

6. After the image is selected, it is added to the Images window of the property pages. At this point, you can set a value for the Key property to make it easy to access the ListImage object from code.

7. You can add additional images in the same way. Click the Insert Picture button, choose the image from the dialog box, and set a value for the Key property. Using this procedure, add the following bitmaps for use in Exercise 2.4: `Cut.bmp`, `Paste.bmp`, `New.bmp`, `Open.bmp`, `Save.bmp`, `Print.bmp`, `Bld.bmp`, `Itl.bmp`, and `Undrln.bmp`. After you add these images, the property page for the image control looks like the graphic below.

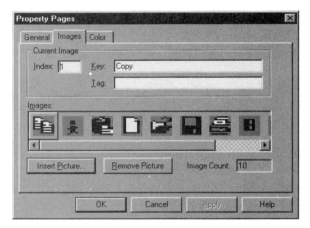

In addition to being able to add images to the ImageList control with the property pages, you can also delete pictures from the control. To do this, simply select the picture by clicking on it, then click the Remove Picture button.

 You cannot modify an ImageList using the property pages after the control has been bound to another control. You can however, add pictures using code.

Adding and Deleting Images with Code

As with most other controls, the ImageList control can be modified by code. The main task that you may want to handle in code is the addition or removal of pictures in the ImageList by using the ListImages collection. Like most collections, the ListImages collection has three key methods:

Add   Adds a new ListImage object to the collection

Remove   Deletes a ListImage object from the collection

Clear   Removes all ListImage objects from the collection

To add pictures to the ImageList control, you use the Add method and specify:

- The index of the picture (optional parameter)

- The Key property, which specifies a unique identifier for the picture (also an optional parameter)

- The picture to be included

The picture source can be the Picture property of another control, such as an Image or PictureBox, or you can load a picture from a bitmap file using the LoadPicture command. The following code shows how to load some of the pictures that were used in Exercise 2.3 into an ImageList control.

```
Dim imgCode As ListImage, sPicturePath As String
Dim sPicture As String
sPicturePath = _"C:\Graphics\
Files\DevStudio\Vb\Graphics\Bitmaps\Tlbr_w95\"
sPicture = sPicturePath & "Copy.bmp"
Set imgCode = imlCode.ListImages.Add(, "Copy", _
LoadPicture(sPicture))
sPicture = sPicturePath & "Cut.bmp"
Set imgCode = imlCode.ListImages.Add(, "Cut", _
LoadPicture(sPicture))
sPicture = sPicturePath & "Paste.bmp"
Set imgCode = imlCode.ListImages.Add(, "Paste", _
LoadPicture(sPicture))
```

To remove one of the images, use the Remove method of the collection and specify the index of the image to be removed.

NOTE A collection is an object that is used extensively in Visual Basic for managing groups of related objects. For controls such as the ImageList where you are working with a group of items (ListImages), using a collection makes it easy to add, remove, or reference individual images. You can learn more about working with collections in Chapter 6.

Accessing Functions with Toolbars

Microsoft ✓ *Exam Objective*

Create data input forms and dialog boxes.

- Display and manipulate data by using custom controls. Controls include TreeView, ListView, ImageList, Toolbar, and StatusBar.

Toolbars provide a program with a great complement to menus. The toolbars of most programs provide quick access to the most commonly used functions of the program. For a word processor, these functions could be formatting options or the creation of tables. For most programs, the toolbar includes functions to enable the user to create new files, open existing files, save files, and print files. Many toolbars also include the standard editing functions of Cut, Copy, and Paste. There are several advantages to using toolbars to supplement your menus in a program:

- Toolbars provide one-click access to functions instead of requiring the user to navigate several menu levels.

- You can create multiple toolbars that the user can choose to display, which enable users to customize their work area to their liking. As an example, look at the four toolbars in Visual Basic—Standard, Form Editor, Format, and Debug. The user can choose to have any, all, or none of these open at any given time. This customization is something that is not easily done with menu items.

- You can allow users to customize the toolbars themselves, to add or remove buttons. Again, this is not easily achieved with menus.

Creating a toolbar in Visual Basic requires the use of two controls. The first is the ImageList control, which contains the images used for the toolbar buttons. The second control is the toolbar itself. The previous section showed you how to create an ImageList control. This section uses that control to help you create a toolbar.

The first step in creating a toolbar is to place the control on your form. When you do this, the toolbar is initially placed at the top of the form and spans the width of the form—the default behavior of the toolbar. You can, of course, change the default by setting the Align property of the toolbar. The settings of the property enable you to align the toolbar with any edge of the form or to have no alignment (which allows the creation of a "floating" toolbar).

If you add multiple toolbars to a form, the second one is placed, by default, directly below the first toolbar, the third below the second, and so on.

The other key properties of the toolbar specify the ImageList controls used with the toolbar. The toolbar supports three ImageList properties. These properties are:

ImageList   Specifies the images used for the normal state of the toolbar buttons

DisabledImageList   Specifies the images used for the disabled buttons on the toolbar

HotImageList   Specifies the images shown when the mouse is above a toolbar button

If used, each of these properties must be set to the name of an ImageList control on the same form as the toolbar. The ImageList is the only way to provide the images that are placed on the buttons of the toolbar. As is the case with setting up many of the Windows Common Controls, the easiest way to set up the toolbar is by using the property pages. The three ImageList properties are on the General page of the property pages, as shown in Figure 2.6.

As you can see in Figure 2.6, several other general properties control the appearance and behavior of the toolbar:

BorderStyle   Causes the toolbar to be displayed with a single line border or no border (default)

Appearance   Causes the toolbar to have a 3-D (default) or flat look

FIGURE 2.6

The property pages of the Toolbar control

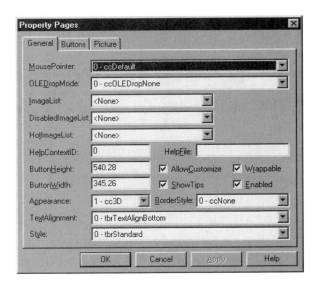

TextAlignment   Determines whether text on the toolbar button is placed below or to the right of the picture on the button

Style   Determines whether the toolbar appears as a standard or flat toolbar

ButtonHeight and ButtonWidth   Specify the size of the buttons in the toolbar

ShowTips   Specifies whether the tool tip information entered in the ToolTips property of the Button object is displayed

Wrappable   Specifies whether the toolbar creates a second row of buttons if there is insufficient space for all the buttons on a single row

AllowCustomize   Specifies whether the user is allowed to customize the toolbar

Creating Buttons for the Toolbar

After you have created an instance of the Toolbar control and set the general properties, you are ready to start creating the individual buttons that will be on the toolbar. Creating the buttons is most easily accomplished by moving to the Buttons page of the property pages, as shown in Figure 2.7.

FIGURE 2.7

Creating buttons from
the property pages

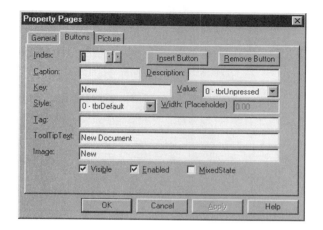

Key Properties of a Toolbar Button

To create a button in the property pages, click the Insert Button button in the dialog box, and then set the properties of the button. The main properties that you need to set include:

Key The name by which the button is referenced in code

Style The appearance and behavior of the button

Image The picture to be shown on the button

The Toolbar control supports six styles of Button objects. Table 2.2 summarizes these styles.

TABLE 2.2 Button Types Available on a Toolbar	**Style**	**Description**
	tbrDefault	Standard button that can be clicked to launch a task.
	tbrCheck	A two-state button, such as the Bold button, that turns an option on or off and indicates the status of the option by the button's appearance.
	tbrButton-Group	One button of a group that enables a single option to be selected from the group. An example is the alignment buttons group that enables the user to choose right-justified, left-justified, or centered.

T A B L E 2.2 *(cont.)*	**Style**	**Description**
Button Types Available on a Toolbar	tbrSeparator	A button that has a width of eight pixels and provides a space between other groups of buttons.
	tbrPlaceHolder	Provides a space on the toolbar for other controls such as a combo box that can be used for providing multiple options.
	tbrDropdown	Creates a drop-down menu that is shown when the button is pressed. The items of the menu are created with the ButtonMenu portion of the Toolbar dialog box.

Optional Toolbar Properties

In addition to the Image, Key, and Style properties, several other properties define the behavior of the Button object.

Caption   Specifies the text that appears on the face of the button. If only a Caption is specified (no Image property), the text appears in the center of the button. If an Image and Caption are both specified, the text appears below the picture in the button.

Description   Provides a description of the button for the user if customization of the toolbar is allowed.

Value   Sets or returns the current state of the button. The value is zero if the button is not pressed, one if the button is pressed.

Width   Specifies the width of the button for the PlaceHolder style only. For all other button types, the width is ignored.

Tag   Assigns other data to the button for use in your program.

ToolTipText   Specifies the text that is displayed when the user pauses the mouse over the button. This text is displayed only if the ShowTips property of the toolbar is set to True.

As you create each button, it is added to the toolbar on your form. This way, you can see the results of setting the properties as they happen. Exercise 2.4 shows you how to create a toolbar that you would typically find in a word processing program.

EXERCISE 2.4

Creating a Toolbar

1. Open the project that you created in Exercise 2.3. This project contains the ImageList control that you will use to provide images for the toolbar.

2. Add a Toolbar control to the form. Name the toolbar **tlbSample**. Then, open the property pages of the toolbar.

3. In the General section of the property pages, set the ImageList property to the name of the ImageList control created in Exercise 2.3 (imlToolbar).

4. Click the Buttons tab of the property pages, then click the Insert Button button on the page.

5. Set the following properties for the first button:

Property	Value
Key	New
Style	tbrDefault
ToolTipText	New Document
Image	New

Notice that you used the Key value of the ListImage object instead of its index number for setting the Image property of the button. Assigning key values makes it easier to remember which picture is contained in the ListImage object. If you assigned different Key values when you created the ImageList control, use those Key values instead of the ones presented here.

6. Create two more buttons using the tbrDefault Style setting. These buttons should be **Open** and **Save**. Be sure to use the appropriate image from the ImageList control, and be sure to assign appropriate Key values to the buttons. Both are necessary to write program code to activate the buttons.

7. Create a new button and set the Style property to tbrSeparator to provide a space between the first group of buttons and the second.

8. Create three additional buttons for **Bold**, **Italic**, and **Underline**. The Style property of these buttons should be set to tbrCheck.

9. Close the property pages and run the program to see how the toolbar looks and behaves. Notice that the ImageList control is not visible while the program is running. The completed sample toolbar is shown in Figure 2.8.

FIGURE 2.8

The toolbar created in Exercise 2.4

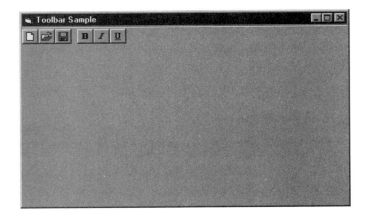

Creating Toolbar Buttons from Code

Of course, this discussion would not be complete if it did not include how to create toolbar buttons from code. As you might expect from the discussion of the ImageList control, you can manipulate the toolbar using the methods of the Buttons collection. With the collection methods, you can add buttons to the toolbar, remove buttons, or clear the entire toolbar.

The following code shows you two techniques for adding buttons to the toolbar. The first technique uses the Add method alone and specifies all the necessary information for the button. The second technique uses the Add method to create a Button object, then sets the properties of the object. Both techniques work equally well.

```
Dim btnNew As Button
'Adding a button with the Add method alone.
```

```
tlbSample.Buttons.Add , "Paste", , tbrDefault, "Paste"
'Adding a button by creating a button object and setting
properties
Set btnNew = tlbSample.Buttons.Add
btnNew.Key = "Print"
btnNew.Style = tbrDefault
btnNew.Image = "Print"
```

Running Functions with the Toolbar

After you have created the toolbar, you need to add code to make the buttons of the toolbar perform tasks. When the toolbar button is clicked, the Button-Click event of the toolbar is fired, passing the object reference for the button that was pressed. The object reference enables you to determine which button was pressed and to take appropriate action.

The simplest way to determine which button was pressed is to check the Key property of the button. (This is why I recommend that you always include a value for the Key property.) Because the toolbar is often closely tied to the menu of a program, you can use the same event code for both the toolbar and the menu. The following code shows how you would use a Select Case structure to identify the button, then fire the Click event of the appropriate menu item to perform the task.

```
Select Case Button.Key
    Case "New"
        filNew_Click
    Case "Print"
        filPrint_Click
    Case "Bold"
        fmtBold_Click
End Select
```

You can use the Index property of the Button object to determine which button was pressed, but this requires you to remember the index number of the button. Also, the Index property can change if you later modify the toolbar through the property pages or with code. Therefore, it is strongly recommended that you include a value for the Key property for each button and use that value in your code.

Customizing the Toolbar

These days, most applications that use toolbars (which includes almost all applications) enable the user to customize the toolbar to their own liking. The Toolbar control of Visual Basic makes it easy for you to incorporate this functionality in the toolbars you create. All you have to do is set the Allow-Customize property to True. The Toolbar control takes care of the rest for you. When the user double-clicks the toolbar, the Customize Toolbar dialog box, shown in Figure 2.9, pops up. The user can then move buttons around on the toolbar or add or remove buttons. When the user clicks the Close button of the dialog box, the changes are displayed in the toolbar.

FIGURE 2.9

The Customize Toolbar dialog box lets the user modify the toolbar.

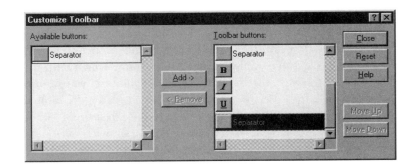

Displaying Data with the TreeView Control

The TreeView control provides you with a versatile way to look at related data. The TreeView presents data in the form of a hierarchical tree. The data starts with a root node that is directly related to a number of branch nodes. Each of the branch nodes is known as a child of the root node. Each of the children can have their own children, and so on. As you look at the various nodes of data, the overall appearance is that of an inverted tree, hence the name. The most widely known example of a TreeView control is the tree used in the left-hand pane of Windows Explorer, as shown in Figure 2.10.

FIGURE 2.10

Windows Explorer as an example of a Tree-View control

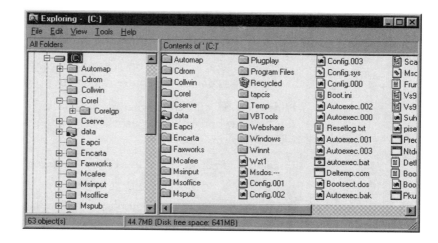

The main attraction of the TreeView control is the capability to show direct relations between various levels of data. For example, you could use the TreeView control to display all the orders shipped to a particular customer. The root node of such an application would be the customer name. The next level of nodes would be the individual orders shipped to the customer. The next level would be the specific details of each order.

The TreeView control enables the user to view all this information at once, or to collapse or expand specific branches to change the view of the data. In addition, the TreeView control gives you the capability to modify individual nodes by assigning values to the properties of the nodes. Also, the TreeView control gives you the capability to display pictures with the nodes—including pictures that indicate which node is selected. For the order-processing example, you could indicate shipped orders with one icon and mark pending orders with another icon. The TreeView control also enables you to associate a check box with each node of the tree. This feature can be useful in allowing the user to mark particular nodes for a task.

Setting Up the TreeView Control

There are two major functions required to create a TreeView control in your application: setting up the control itself by setting general properties, and creating the nodes of the tree. You can set the general control properties in the design environment by using the property pages or the Properties window. You can also set most of the properties of the control with code. Creating the nodes is something that can be done only in code. You will look at creating nodes in the next section.

After you have drawn an instance of the TreeView control on your form, you can set several general properties to determine the appearance and behavior of the control. The more important properties include:

HideSelection Specifies whether the selected node is highlighted when the TreeView control loses focus. The default value is to not show the selection in this case.

ImageList Specifies the name of the ImageList control that contains the pictures used for the nodes of the tree.

Indentation Specifies the number of twips that each level of the tree hierarchy is indented from its parent node.

LabelEdit Specifies how the user can edit the label of the tree node. If the property is set to Automatic, the user can click on the node label and begin editing. In this case, the BeforeLabelEdit event is fired when the user clicks on the node. If the property is set to Manual, the user can edit the label only after the StartLabelEdit method has been invoked. In this case, the BeforeLabelEdit event is fired after the method is run.

LineStyle Determines whether lines are drawn between root nodes. The default is to not draw the lines. In either case, the control draws lines between parent and child nodes.

Sorted Determines whether the root nodes of the tree are sorted alphabetically. There is also a Sorted property for each node of the tree, which determines whether the child nodes of a given node are sorted.

CheckBoxes Determines whether a check box is placed next to each node of the tree.

Style Determines which combination of elements (images, text, lines, +/– signs) is displayed by the TreeView control to indicate the expansion of branches. There are eight possible settings of the Style property, as summarized in Table 2.3.

TABLE 2.3 Settings of the Style Property	Setting	Description
	0	Only text is shown.
	1	Both text and images can be shown.
	2	Text and the +/– signs can be shown.
	3	Text, images, and the +/– signs can be shown.
	4	Only text is shown, but with lines between parent and child nodes.
	5	Text and images are shown, with parent/child lines.
	6	Text and +/– signs are shown, with parent/child lines.
	7	Text, images, and the +/– signs can be shown, with parent/child lines. This is the default value.

Creating the Nodes of the Tree

After you create the control and set the general properties, it is time to start creating the nodes of the tree. As stated previously, you must create the nodes of the tree using program code. You create TreeView nodes by using the Add method of the Nodes collection of the TreeView control. The general syntax of the Add method is as follows:

```
TreeView.Nodes.Add relative, relationship, key, text, image, _
selectedimage
```

Of these parameters, only the Text parameter is required. However, if other parameters prior to Text are omitted, their places must be held by commas. Each of these parameters specifies information about the node, as summarized here:

Relative   Specifies the Key value of the node to which the added node is related.

Relationship   Specifies the type of relationship that exists between the new node and the node specified in the Relative parameter. The following list indicates the possible relationships:

Setting	Description
tvwFirst	The new node is placed ahead of all other nodes at the same level of the node named in the Relative parameter.
tvwLast	The new node is placed after all other nodes at the same level of the node named in Relative.
tvwNext	The new node is placed immediately after the node named in Relative.
tvwPrevious	The new node is placed immediately before the node named in Relative.
tvwChild	The new node is created as a child node of the node named in Relative.

Key   Specifies a unique identifier for the new node.

Text   Specifies the text to be displayed in the node.

Image   Specifies the index of an image in the ImageList control that is associated with the TreeView control. This image is shown whenever the node is visible unless the node is the selected node and the SelectedImage has been specified.

SelectedImage   Specifies the index of an image in the ImageList control that should be displayed when the node is selected.

The Add method of the Nodes collection can be used directly to create a node, or the method can be used to create a reference to a Node object so that other properties of the node can be set. Both methods are shown in the following code.

```
'Create node directly
TreeView1.Nodes.Add , , "Employee", "Employees"
'Create node object and set additional properties
Set nodX = TreeView1.Nodes.Add(, , "Customer", "Customers")
nodX.Expanded = True
```

In addition to the parameters used in the Add method to create a node, there are several other properties of the Node object that you use in writing a TreeView application:

Checked   Returns whether the check box next to the node is filled.

Children   Returns the number of child nodes for the current node.

Child, FirstSibling, Next, Previous, LastSibling   Returns a node that is a child of the current node. You can check the help file for a complete description of the differences between the properties.

Parent   Returns a reference to the node that is the parent of the current node.

Root   Returns a reference to the node that is the root node for the current node.

Expanded   Specifies whether the child nodes of the current node are shown or the node is shown in its collapsed form.

ExpandedImage   Specifies the index of the image in an ImageList control that should be shown when the current node is expanded.

To illustrate how to create a TreeView control, Exercise 2.5 walks you through all the necessary steps to create a control that displays the players of Little League teams.

EXERCISE 2.5

Creating a TreeView Control

1. Start a new project and add the reference to the Windows Common Controls.

2. Add an ImageList control to the form and add three images of your choosing to the control. You can refer to Exercise 2.3 to refresh your memory on creating an ImageList control.

3. Add a TreeView control to the form.

4. Set the ImageList property of the TreeView control to the name of the ImageList control created in step 2.

5. Add the root node to the tree using the following code. All the code in this example can be placed in the Load event of the form.

```
Dim nodBB As Node
'Create league
```

```
Set nodBB = tvwBaseball.Nodes.Add(, , "Shelby", _
"North Shelby")
nodBB.Expanded = True
nodBB.Sorted = True
```

6. Next, add a team to the tree as a child of the root node. Use the following code to add the first team:

```
'Create Teams
tvwBaseball.Nodes.Add "Shelby", tvwChild, "Cubs", "Cubs", _
"Diamond", "Check"
```

7. Add several more teams of your choosing to the tree. Use the same syntax as was used in step 6. Remember to specify a Key value for each team.

8. Add a player to the first team using the following code. The player node is a child of the team node.

```
'Add Players
tvwBaseball.Nodes.Add "Cubs", tvwChild, "Eric", "Eric", _
"Player"
```

9. Add players to the other teams using the same syntax as in step 8.

10. Run the program. Your application should look something like the one in Figure 2.11. Try clicking and double-clicking on the various nodes to see the effects. The code for this project is contained on the CD-ROM in *BaseBall.vbp*.

The control itself is useful for displaying data, but you will probably also want to be able to take action when the user clicks on one of the nodes. You can accomplish this with the NodeClick event. This event is triggered each time a node is clicked. The event passes an object reference to the selected node. You can use this object to determine which node was selected and take the appropriate action.

The CD-ROM includes a project named *TreeList.vbp*. This project uses a TreeView and a ListView control to display order information for all the customers listed in the *Nwind.mdb* database. The TreeView control contains the names of the customers and information about each order. As an order node is selected, the ListView control is updated to display the details of the order. The code in the NodeClick event is used to determine which order was selected and to retrieve the appropriate details. Figure 2.12 shows how this program looks.

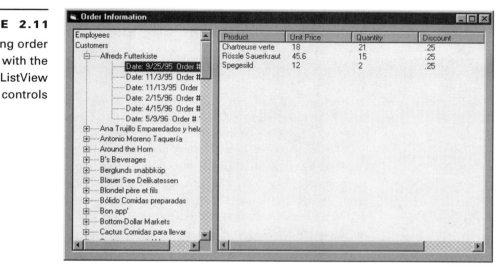

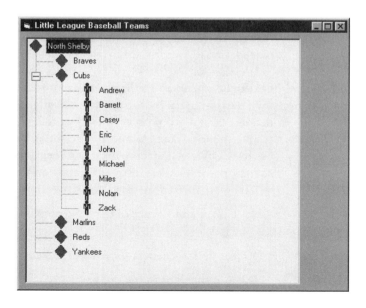

Displaying Data in a List

Microsoft ✓ *Exam Objective*

Create data input forms and dialog boxes.

- Display and manipulate data by using custom controls. Controls include TreeView, ListView, ImageList, Toolbar, and StatusBar.

The sample project, *TreeList.vbp*, showed you how data can be displayed in a ListView control. This section shows you how the control is set up.

A ListView control is best exemplified either by the right side of the Windows Explorer application or by the directory listings shown in the MyComputer application of Windows 95. Both applications enable you to view the files and folders on your computer as small icons, large icons, a simple list, or a report with detailed information. You can create each of these four views with the ListView control.

Because the report view of the ListView control is the most complex view, you will examine how to create this view. The other three views show a subset of the information displayed in the report view.

The report view provides you with a souped-up version of a ListBox control. Whereas the ListBox is limited to a single text string for each list item, the report view of the ListView control can have any number of columns displayed, making it ideal for displaying detailed information about anything. In addition, the ListView control enables you to display an icon or check box next to each item and to apply different formatting to the individual cells in the ListView. The *TreeList.vbp* used the ListView control to display the details about a given order, including the product, unit price, quantity, discount, and total cost. As another example, a membership application might use the ListView control to display information about family members, such as their name, gender, birth date, and social security number.

To create the report view, you need to perform three tasks:

1. Create an instance of the control and set the general properties of the ListView.

2. Set up the headers for each of the columns of the report.

3. Add the data to the report.

Setting Up the Control

The simplest way to set up the general properties of a ListView control is, of course, through the use of the property pages. As shown in Figure 2.13, the property pages for the ListView control consist of seven tabs of information. Of these, the first three contain information that is unique to the ListView control. The fourth page is column header information, which you will get to in a moment. The other pages cover information about fonts and colors, information that is familiar from working with other controls. Take a look at the properties on the first three pages and what they do (this section doesn't cover every property).

FIGURE 2.13

The property pages for the ListView control

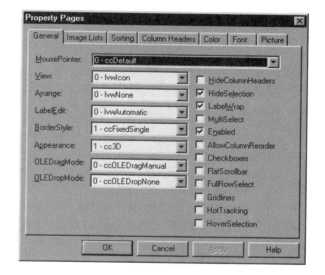

The first page has the general information for the ListView control—which style to use, how to edit labels, whether to show column headers, and so on. In particular, these properties are as follows:

Arrange　Specifies whether items are aligned along the left edge of the control, the top edge of the control, or are not aligned.

HideColumnHeaders　Specifies whether column headers are shown. This property affects only the report view of the ListView control.

HideSelection　Specifies whether the selected item is highlighted when the ListView control loses focus. The default value is to not show the selection in this case.

LabelEdit   Similar to the LabelEdit property of the TreeView control described earlier.

LabelWrap   Determines whether the label of an item is wrapped to additional lines if the length of the line is greater than the icon spacing defined by the operating system. This option affects only the icon views of the ListView control.

MultiSelect   Specifies whether the user can select multiple ListItems in the ListView control, similar to the MultiSelect property of the ListBox control.

View   Specifies how the ListItems are shown in the control. The four options are to display items as standard icons with text, as small icons with text, as a single column list, or as a report with detailed information presented for each item.

Checkboxes   Specifies whether check boxes appear next to the items of the list.

After setting the general information for the ListView control, you need to specify the names of the ImageList controls that are used to provide the icons for the ListView control. Because the ListView is capable of showing items as either standard or small icons, the control requires two ImageList controls. The names of the ImageList controls are stored in the Icons and SmallIcons properties of the ListView. You can set these names either through the ImageLists page of the property pages or through code, using a standard assignment statement. There is also an ImageList for the column headers that enables you to specify icons that will appear in the header of each column of the list.

The final general characteristic of the ListView control is the sort order for the list. You probably know that you can sort a ListBox control by setting the Sorted property, which sorts the list in ascending alphabetical order. The ListView control has the same capability, but with enhancements. The ListView control is capable of sorting the list based on the contents of any of the columns defined for the list and can sort in either ascending or descending order. You have seen this capability if you have changed the sort order of files in the Windows Explorer. The sorting of items in the ListView control is dependent upon three properties. Each of these properties needs to be set before the sort will work:

Sorted   Specifies whether items are sorted in accordance with the information in the SortKey and SortOrder properties.

SortKey   Specifies which column of information is used to sort the list. If SortKey is zero, the Text property of the ListItem object is used for the sort. If SortKey is one or greater, the sub-item (detail column) whose index is equal to the SortKey value is used as the sorted field. For example, if you have sub-item information specifying the type of a file, size of a file, and date of modification (in that order), specifying a SortKey value of two causes the information to be sorted on the file size.

SortOrder   Specifies whether the information is sorted in ascending (Sort-Order=0) or descending (SortOrder=1) order.

When you have a report view showing in the ListView control, you can allow the user to change the sort order of the items by clicking the column header. This is accomplished by placing the following line of code in the ColumnClick event of the control.

```
LvwGrades.SortKey = ColumnHeader.Index 1
```

Now, put all this information to use by creating a sample program. The program uses the ListView control to display class grades in a report view. This enables the user to sort information based on any of several test results. Exercise 2.6 starts the project. Exercises 2.7 and 2.8 show you how to complete the program.

EXERCISE 2.6

Creating a ListView Control

1. Start a new project and add the reference to the Windows Common Controls.

2. Add two ImageList controls to the form and set up images in the controls as described in Exercise 2.3.

3. Add a ListView control to the form and activate the property pages of the control.

4. On the General page of the property pages, set the View property to Report View.

5. On the ImageLists page of the property pages, set the Icons and Small-Icons property to the names of the ImageList controls created in step 2.

6. On the Sorted page of the property pages, set the Sorted property to True. You will use code to handle changing the sort order and field.

7. Add the following code to the ColumnClick event of the ListView control. The code checks the SortKey property. If this does not match the index of the column that was clicked, the order is set to the new field and defaults to ascending order. If the SortKey property matches the index, the sort order is reversed, enabling the user to not only change the field that is the basis of the sort, but to also change the order of the sort.

```
If lvwGrades.SortKey = ColumnHeader.Index - 1 Then
    If lvwGrades.SortOrder = lvwAscending Then
        lvwGrades.SortOrder = lvwDescending
    Else
        lvwGrades.SortOrder = lvwAscending
    End If
Else
    lvwGrades.SortKey = ColumnHeader.Index - 1
    lvwGrades.SortOrder = lvwAscending
End If
```

8. Save the project as Grades.vbp. This project is also included on the CD-ROM.

Setting Up the Headings for Columns

The next task in setting up the report view of the ListView control is to create the column headers for the list, either from the design mode or from code. In the design mode, you simply go to the Column Headers page of the property pages (shown in Figure 2.14) and click the Insert Column button for each column you want to create. As you create the column, you need to set the following properties:

Text   Specifies the information that is shown in the column header

Alignment   Specifies whether the text is left or right justified, or centered in the column header

Width Specifies the width of the column

Key Specifies a string that uniquely identifies the column

Icon Index Specifies the icon from the ImageList control that should be displayed in the column header

FIGURE 2.14
Column Headers
Property Page

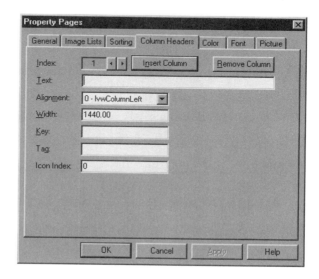

The first column header that you create (index value of one) is the one that corresponds to the text of the ListItem object and is the main information that you will want to display for each item. The value of the text property is also the only information shown when you are using a view other than the report view. Exercise 2.7 walks you through creating the column headers for the Grades list.

EXERCISE 2.7

Adding the Column Headers

1. Starting from the previous project (Exercise 2.6), open the property pages of the ListView control and select the Column Headers page.

2. Click the Insert Column button to create the first header.

3. Set the Text property of the first header to Name and set the Key property to Name as well.

4. Repeating steps 2 and 3, create additional headers as described in the following list:

Text	Key
First Test	Test1
Second Test	Test2
Final Exam	Final
Average Score	Average

5. Save the project.

Adding Column Headers with Code

In addition to using the property pages, you can also create column headers with code. The column headers are objects that are handled by the Column-Headers collection. To add a column header from code, use the Add method of the ColumnHeaders collection. The following code shows how to create the headers for the Grades list.

```
Dim clmHead As ColumnHeader
lvwGrades.ColumnHeaders.Add , "Name", "Name", _
lvwGrades.Width / 5
Set clmHead = lvwGrades.ColumnHeaders.Add(,"Test1", _
"First Test")
ClmHead.Width = lvwGrades.Width / 5
Set clmHead = lvwGrades.ColumnHeaders.Add(,"Test2", _
"First Test")
Set clmHead = lvwGrades.ColumnHeaders.Add(,"Test3", _
"Second Test")
Set clmHead = lvwGrades.ColumnHeaders.Add(,"Final", _
"Final Exam")
Set clmHead = lvwGrades.ColumnHeaders.Add(,"Average", _
"Average Score")
```

Adding Data to the ListView Control

The final step in creating the ListView control is to add the data to the list. The data is added in two steps. First, you add the ListItem object to the ListItems collection. Then you set the values of the SubItem properties of the ListItem. SubItems is an array of values that correspond to the columns of information that are displayed in the report view. The following code shows how the List-Item object is created, then how the SubItem values are set. Exercise 2.8 takes you through the process.

```
Dim liStudent As ListItem
Set liStudent = lvwGrades.ListItems.Add( , , "Jackson")
With liStudent
    .SubItems(1) = 75
    .SubItems(2) = 90
    .SubItems(3) = 95
    .SubItems(4) = (Val(.SubItems(1) + Val(.SubItems(2)) _
+Val(.SubItems(3)))/3
End With
```

EXERCISE 2.8

Adding the Student Information

1. Continuing with the project from Exercise 2.7, open the Code window for the Load event of the form.

2. Place the code shown above in the Load event to create the data for the first student.

3. Repeat the last seven lines of the previous code to add more students. You can repeat this process for as many students as you like.

4. Run the program. You can now click on the column headers to see how the sort order changes due to the code created in Exercise 2.6. A sample grade list is shown in Figure 2.15.

FIGURE 2.15

The completed grade
list project

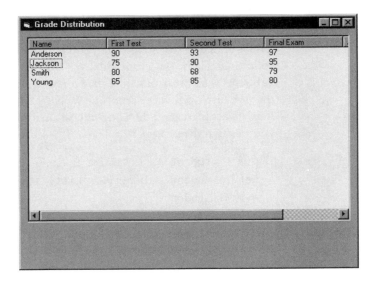

Summary

This chapter has covered a lot of material. You have seen how to use most of the controls in the Microsoft Windows Common Controls group. The chapter has shown you how to create toolbars to allow quick access to functions, and how to use the StatusBar and ProgressBar controls to provide information to the user. You have also seen how to display information using the TreeView and ListView controls.

Yet you have only scratched the surface of the capabilities of several of the controls. The TreeView and ListView controls in particular are powerful and take a significant amount of time to master. Also, for these controls, the real power lies in being able to display data from sources such as databases or directory information, not merely the simple examples shown in the exercises. The *TreeList.vbp* project on the CD-ROM shows you a little of this capability. As with many other activities, the best way to learn is to acquire a good understanding of the basics (from the information in this chapter) and then experiment.

This chapter covered the material that you need to know to achieve the following exam objectives:

- Add an ActiveX control to the toolbox.

▪ Create data input forms and dialog boxes.

– Display and manipulate data by using custom controls. Controls include TreeView, ListView, ImageList, Toolbar, and StatusBar.

The inner workings of several of these controls, particularly the TreeView and ListView controls, can be very complex. Make sure that you have a complete understanding of the steps in all the exercises before you take the exam.

Review Questions

1. Which control lets you display information in a hierarchical structure?

A. TreeView

B. ListView

C. ListBox

D. StatusBar

2. Which style of StatusBar panel can be modified by your program? Check all that apply.

A. sbrText

B. sbrCaps

C. sbrNum

D. sbrIns

3. How do you update the status of a sbrCaps style panel?

A. It is handled for you automatically by the control.

B. You need to place code in the KeyPress event of the form.

C. You must place code in the KeyPress event of the StatusBar.

D. You use a Windows API call to find out when the key is pressed.

4. Name the two techniques for identifying a Panel object in the Panels collection.

   A. Refer to it by the Index property.

   B. Refer to it by the Text property.

   C. Refer to it by the Style property.

   D. Refer to it by the Key property.

5. What property of the ProgressBar determines how much of the bar is filled?

   A. Min

   B. Max

   C. Value

   D. All of the above

6. What is the purpose of the ImageList control?

   A. To display bitmaps for the user to view

   B. To provide a repository for images used by other controls

   C. To allow easy editing of icons

   D. Both A and B

7. What are valid methods of adding a picture to the ImageList control? Check all that apply.

   A. Select a picture using a dialog box in the property pages.

   B. Set the Picture property of the ImageList control to the name of a PictureBox control.

   C. Set the Picture property of the ListImage object to the Picture property of another control.

   D. Set the Picture property of the ListImage object using the Load-Picture command.

8. What does a button of a button group on a toolbar do?

   A. Shows you the current status of an option

   B. Enables you to select one option from several

   C. Simply starts a function of the application

   D. Provides a space in the toolbar

9. All of the following statements are true about toolbars except:

   A. You can have only one toolbar on a form.

   B. Toolbars can be positioned anywhere on the form.

   C. Toolbars can be customized by the user.

   D. Toolbar buttons can display both text and images.

10. What do you have to do to allow the user to customize the toolbar?

   A. Write code to add buttons or remove buttons based on the user selection.

   B. Set the AllowCustomize property to True and the control takes care of the rest.

   C. You cannot do this with Visual Basic toolbars.

   D. You don't have to do anything. Toolbar custom action is automatic with any toolbar you create.

11. How many root nodes can a TreeView control have?

   A. One

   B. Up to five

   C. Maximum of two

   D. No limit

12. What must you specify to make a new node the child of another node? Check all that apply.

   A. The Key value of the node to which it is related

   B. The text of the related node

   C. The Relationship must be specified as tvwChild

   D. The image to be associated with the new node

13. What property determines whether lines are drawn between parent and child nodes? Check all that apply.

   A. Appearance

   B. Style

   C. Indentation

   D. LineStyle

14. What advantages does the ListView control have over the standard ListBox? Check all that apply.

   A. ListView can display multiple columns of data.

   B. ListBox is limited in the number of items that are allowed.

   C. Only the ListView can be sorted.

   D. ListView enables you to sort on different fields and to specify the sort order.

   E. ListView can display headers over columns of information.

15. Which of the following views displays the Text property of the List-Item objects? Check all that apply.

   A. Icon view

   B. Small icon view

   C. List view

   D. Report view

16. Which views display the detailed information of a ListItem that is contained in the SubItem array? Check all that apply.

A. Icon view

B. Small icon view

C. List view

D. Report view

17. Which property of the ListView control determines which field a sort is based on?

A. Sorted

B. SortOrder

C. SortField

D. SortKey

CHAPTER

3

Creating Menus for Your Programs

Microsoft Exam Objectives Covered in This Chapter:

- Implement navigational design.
  - Add a pop-up menu to an application.
  - Dynamically modify the appearance of a menu.
  - Create an application that adds and deletes menus at run time.

Forms and the controls in the Visual Basic toolbox will make up the bulk of the visual interface of your programs. However, two other key elements are used in most of the programs that you will create—menus and dialog boxes. If you look at almost any commercial program today, you will find that the functions of the program are conveniently organized in a menu system. This system consists of the menu bar at the top of the screen and a series of drop-down choices that provide single-click access to the program's functions. You will find menus in programs from simple games to the most sophisticated word processing or database software. Visual Basic, of course, provides you with the tools to create your own menus. Using menus gives your programs a professional appearance and helps the user work with your program.

Creating a Menu System

There are several types of menus you can create for your programs. Most people are familiar with the main menu that is shown at the top of a program's main screen. However, most programs also include a variety of pop-up menus that present context-driven options. For example, if you right-click the mouse on a paragraph in a word processor, you are typically presented with a Format menu that enables you to modify the characteristics of the paragraph, as shown in Figure 3.1. These pop-up menus are displayed right next to the mouse cursor.

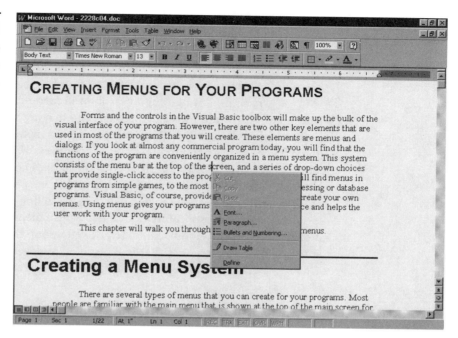

F I G U R E 3.1

Pop-up menus provide context-sensitive options.

Visual Basic provides you with the tools to create an application's main menu as well as pop-up menus. In fact, you are not limited to a single menu in your programs. Although it is customary to have a menu on the main form of a program, Visual Basic enables you to place a menu on any form in your program, so you can have multiple menus based on the tasks that need to be performed.

Designing the Menu

Although designing a menu is not specifically covered in the exam, you do need to know how to plan and lay out your menu before you begin creating it. Also, understanding Microsoft's expectations about menu design will help you if you want to have programs certified as "Windows 95 compatible."

The first step in creating a good menu is to design the layout of the menu—not how wide the drop-down menu will be, or where it will be located on the screen, but what functions will need to appear on the menu and how the functions will be grouped. Grouping of menu items is important for several reasons. For instance, unless you have only a few items, it is impractical to place them all on the main menu bar. Therefore, you will have to create submenus. The main consideration for grouping items is determining where a user could logically expect to find each item. For example, most users would not look for the Cut and Paste functions on a Tools menu; they would look for them on an Edit menu because the functions relate to editing.

This expectation brings out a key point in menu design. Interface guidelines that were established by Microsoft and that are in common use should determine certain aspects of your menu. If your menu design conforms to these guidelines and common practices, your users will have a head start on being able to use your program. If your menu does not conform, your users may become confused and frustrated, and they may not use your program.

Therefore, the best way to design a menu is to first determine which functions of your program fit into one of the typical menu groups, such as File, Edit, View, Tools, Window, and Help. Then, group the rest of the functions into a few other categories that will be your top-level menus. When you finally are ready to create your menu, you need to remember some other design guidelines:

- Group menu list items by their functions.

- Keep the function groups limited to five items or less.

- Separate function groups in a menu list with separator bars.

- Limit the number of submenu levels to two, if possible. Too many levels make your menu hard to navigate.

As you are designing your menu groupings, you may want to lay them out on paper to make sure the menu meets your needs. Then, with this listing in hand, it will be easy to create the menu in the Menu Editor.

Creating the Menu with the Menu Editor

The Menu Editor is the only means in Visual Basic to create or modify a menu in the design mode. And, although you can make some changes to the menu at run time, you create the vast majority of the menu in the Menu Editor. To begin creating a menu for your program, you must have a Form Design window active in Visual Basic, as shown in Figure 3.2. You can then access the Menu Editor by clicking the Menu Editor button on the toolbar, choosing the Menu Editor item from the Tools menu, or pressing Ctrl+E.

FIGURE 3.2

A form must be active in order to create a menu on it.

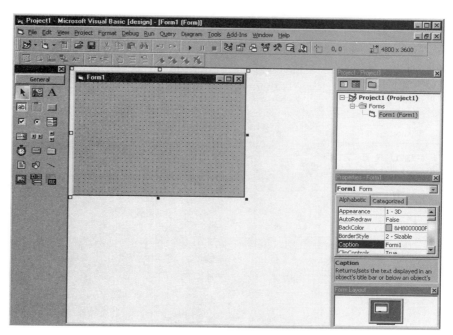

Microsoft ✓ **Exam Objective**

Implement navigational design.

After you have opened the Menu Editor, you can begin creating the items of your menu. For each item on the menu, you must specify two key properties—the Name property and the Caption property. The caption identifies the menu item to the user and the name identifies the menu to your program. The first item you create is a main menu bar item. After you accept the values for the Name and Caption properties, by pressing Enter or clicking the Next button, the menu item appears in the selection area at the bottom of the dialog box, as shown in Figure 3.3. The Name property must be unique for each menu item on a given form. However, because Visual Basic supports menus on any form, you can use the same name on multiple forms.

The only property that you are required to specify for a menu item is the Name property. However, even if you plan to specify the menu captions using code, it is a good idea to set the Caption property of each item to help you with your program design.

FIGURE 3.3

Creating menus in the Menu Editor

Notice that the item is positioned against the left edge of the dialog box, indicating that it is a top-level menu item. As you create other items, you should make them submenus of one of the top-level items. You can do this by clicking the Right Arrow button or pressing Alt+R before you accept the properties of the menu item. Figure 3.3 also displays several levels of indentation. Each indentation indicates another menu level, similar to the organization of an outline.

Of course, the best way to learn to create a menu is to do it. Exercise 3.1 shows you how to create a basic File and Edit menu system.

EXERCISE 3.1

Creating a Menu with the Menu Editor

1. Start a project and make sure that the main form is active in the design environment.

2. Start the Menu Editor by clicking the Menu Editor button.

3. Type in the values for the Caption and Name properties for the first item. Use **File** and **mnuFile** respectively.

4. Press Enter to accept the properties and clear the input area for another item.

5. Press Alt+R to indent the next item in the menu. Type **New** for the Caption property and **filNew** for the Name property. Press Enter. Notice that the next item is automatically indented to the same level as the item you just created.

6. Add two more items with the following Caption and Name properties: **Open** and **filOpen** for the first item, **Save** and **filSave** for the second item.

7. Next create a separator bar by typing a hyphen (-) for the Caption property and **filSep1** for the Name property. Even though this item cannot be accessed by the user, you must still specify a name for the item.

8. Create the Exit item by entering **Exit** in the Caption property and **filExit** in the Name property. Then press Enter to accept the values.

9. Press Alt+L to move the next item back to a top-level menu.

10. Type **Edit** in the Caption property and **mnuEdit** in the Name property. Then press Enter.

11. Press Alt+R to indent the Edit menu items.

12. Add the following items to the Edit menu, using the Caption and Name properties listed here: **Cut**, **edtCut**; **Copy**, **edtCopy**; **Paste**, **edtPaste**.

13. Accept the entire menu by clicking the OK button. Figure 3.4 shows the completed menu in the Menu Editor, and Figure 3.5 shows the menu as it appears on the form.

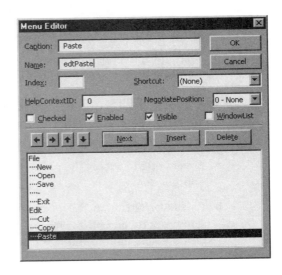

FIGURE 3.4

A completed menu in
the Menu Editor

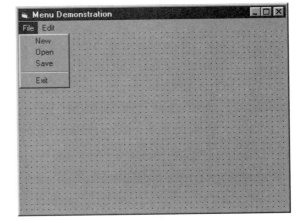

FIGURE 3.5

The menu as seen by
the user

If you forget to enter a Name property for any menu item, the Menu Editor
notifies you of the problem and does not let you exit.

After you have completed creating the menu in the Menu Editor, you need
to add code to make the menu items perform a task. You write code for the

Click event of each menu item, similar to writing code for the Click event of a command button. The easiest way to access the Code window for a menu item is to select the item on the form. This action places you in the Click event procedure of the menu item. You can then write any code you want to take an action.

The Click event is the only event supported by the menu items.

As an example, you can write code to terminate the application in the Exit menu item by following two simple steps:

1. Click the Exit item to access the Code window.

2. Insert the code **Unload Me** in the event procedure.

Adding Shortcut and Access Keys to Menu Items

Menus are designed primarily for navigation with the mouse; however, most users have come to expect menu access from the keyboard as well. The ability to select items without using the mouse is particularly important to data entry users. These users do not want to move their hands from the keyboard to the mouse and back. Visual Basic provides two ways to enable keyboard access to menu items:

- Access keys
- Shortcut keys

Accessing menu items from the access keys or shortcut keys has the same effect as clicking a menu item with the mouse: the Click event for the item is triggered and the corresponding code is run.

Creating Access Keys

An access key enables the user to press Alt plus a key to cause the drop-down list of a top-level menu to appear. The user can then press a single key to access an item on the list. In Visual Basic, you can see this type of access in the menu. For example, you can press Alt+F to access the File menu, then press the N key to start a new project. With access keys, you should have a unique key combination for each top-level menu, then a unique key for each item within a top-level menu. It is permissible to assign the same key to different items in different menus. For example, the Paste item in the Edit menu and the Print item in the File menu both use the same access key, P.

Multiple top-level items can have the same access key. The user can repeatedly press Alt plus the key to loop through all the menus assigned the same access key. However, the user then has to use the cursor keys to have the menu drop down, instead of this happening automatically as is the case if an access key is assigned to only one item.

To create an access key for a menu item, you simply place an ampersand (&) in front of the character to be used as an access key in the Caption property of the menu item. For example, to make F the access key for the File menu, you would place an ampersand in front of the F in the caption. This makes the Caption property &File. Your users do not see the & in the menu. Instead, they see the access key underlined. When you assign access keys, you typically make the key the first letter of the caption. This is the most intuitive letter for the user to hit. You should, however follow some simple conventions:

- The File menu should always use F as the access key. Within the File menu, you should use the following keys: N for New, O for Open, C for Close, P for Print, S for Save, A for Save As, and x for Exit.

- The Edit menu should always use E as the access key. Within the Edit menu, you should use the following keys: t for Cut, C for Copy, P for Paste, F for Find, D for Delete, and e for Replace.

- Other top-level menus should use the following keys: V for View, T for Tools, W for Window, and H for Help.

From time to time, you will want to display an ampersand (&) in a menu caption, such as "Save & Exit." To do this, place two ampersands side by side (&&) in the Caption property of the menu item.

You should use these conventions because the user is probably familiar with them from other programs and will be confused by your interface if you deviate from them. Exercise 3.2 shows you how to add access keys to the menu created in Exercise 3.1. Figure 3.6 shows how the menu appears after the access keys are added.

EXERCISE 3.2

Adding Access Keys to Your Menu

1. Open the project containing the menu sample program.

2. Open the Menu Editor for the main form.

3. Place an ampersand (**&**) in front of the following letters in the specified items:

Item	Access Key
File	F
New	N
Open	O
Save	S
Exit	x
Edit	E
Cut	t
Copy	C
Paste	P

4. Click the OK button to accept the menu changes.

FIGURE 3.6

Menu with access keys added

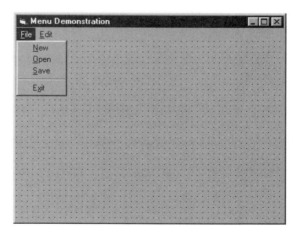

Creating Shortcut Keys

Shortcut keys enable the user to access a menu function using a single key or key combination. Typical examples of shortcut keys are Ctrl+X for Cut, Ctrl+C for Copy, and the Delete key. Visual Basic enables you to create shortcut keys for your menu items. A given shortcut key can be used only for a single item, limiting you to about 75 shortcut keys you can use in your program.

As with access keys, there are a number of shortcut keys with which users are already familiar. Some of the more common shortcut keys are identified in the following list:

Function	Shortcut Key
New	Ctrl+N
Open	Ctrl+O
Print	Ctrl+P
Save	Ctrl+S
Cut	Ctrl+X
Copy	Ctrl+C
Paste	Ctrl+V
Find	Ctrl+F
Replace	Ctrl+H
Undo	Ctrl+Z
Redo	Ctrl+Y
Help	F1

To create shortcut keys in your program, open the Menu Editor, select the item to which you want to assign a shortcut key, and then select the specific key combination from the Shortcut Key list in the Menu Editor. Figure 3.7 illustrates the process of selecting a shortcut key from the drop-down list. As you select a key, the shortcut is automatically shown in the caption of the menu (though it is not part of the Caption property). Exercise 3.3 shows you how to add shortcut keys to the menu created in the previous exercises. Figure 3.8 shows the completed menu.

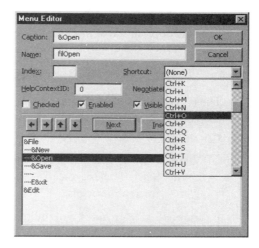

FIGURE 3.7

Selecting shortcut keys for menu items

EXERCISE 3.3

Creating Shortcut Keys

1. Open the Menu Editor.

2. Select the New item, then select the Ctrl+N key combination from the Shortcut drop-down list.

3. Repeat this process for the Open, Save, Cut, Copy, and Paste items, using the key combinations identified in the list above.

4. Click OK to save the menu changes.

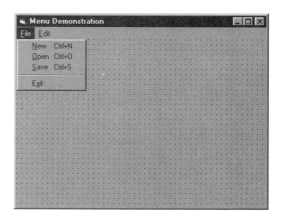

FIGURE 3.8

The menu with shortcut keys added

If you assign the same shortcut key to more than one menu item, the Menu Editor reports an error and does not let you exit.

Using Other Menu Item Properties

The preceding sections discussed how to create a menu. To create a menu, you used the Caption, Name, and Shortcut properties of the menu item object. Several other properties control the appearance or behavior of menu items.

Checked   Indicates whether a check mark appears in front of the item in the menu list. This is typically used to indicate that an option of your program is turned on or off.

Enabled   Determines whether the user can access the functions of the menu. If the Enabled property is set to False, the user can see the menu as a grayed item, but cannot click on it or access any of the sub-level menus.

Visible   Determines whether the menu can be seen by the user. If the Visible property of a menu is set to False, the item and any sub-level menus are not shown in the menu.

WindowList   Determines whether this menu item is used to keep up with MDI child windows in an MDI application. This property is usually set for only a top-level menu item but can be set for other levels as well. Only one item in a menu may have this property set to True.

Index   The index of a menu item within a control array. The items of the menu control array all have the same Name property, but different indexes. The use of indexes enables you to create additional items at run time. Indexes are discussed further in the "Adding Menu Items at Run Time" section later in this chapter.

HelpContextID   Identifies the help topic that is accessed if F1 is pressed while the menu item is selected.

Creating and Accessing Pop-Up Menus

Pop-up menus are becoming more and more commonplace in today's generation of applications. The pop-up menu is designed to provide you with the menu options you need for dealing with a particular object. Therefore, many applications support a variety of pop-up menus. For example, in Visual Basic, if you right-click the mouse on the menu bar, you see a pop-up menu that enables you to show or hide toolbars. Right-click on the form, and you see a menu that provides quick access to the Menu Editor, Code window, and properties of the form. Right-click on a control, and you get a menu that contains editing functions and access to the control's properties. As you can see, help is where you need it, when you need it, and exactly what you need (or at least what the developers think you need).

Microsoft *Exam* *Objective*	**Implement navigational design.** ▪ Add a pop-up menu to an application.

Because users have come to expect to be able to use pop-up menus, you will probably want to include them in your programs. Fortunately, Visual Basic makes this easy to do. Implementing a pop-up menu requires only two steps: creating the menu in the Menu Editor and activating the menu using the PopupMenu method of a form.

Creating the Pop-Up Menu

Creating the menu for a pop-up menu is the same as creating a top-level menu for the main menu bar. You use the Menu Editor to define the Caption and Name properties for each item you want to appear in the pop-up menu. You can even include separator bars and access keys if you want. Exercise 3.4 shows you how to create a Format pop-up menu that you might use to change the properties of text in a text box.

 Although it is typical to use a top-level menu for the pop-up menu, you can use any menu item that contains sub-level items.

EXERCISE 3.4

Creating a Pop-Up Menu

1. Open the Menu Editor on the form where you will want the pop-up menu to appear.

2. Move to a new item at the bottom of the menu list, and make sure that the item is not indented.

3. Create the top-level item for the Format menu using **Format** as the Caption property and **popFormat** as the Name property. This name will be used later to display the pop-up menu.

4. Set the Visible property of the menu item to False, then accept the item by pressing Enter.

5. Create several font items in the menu by using the following Name and Caption properties.

Caption	Name
&Bold	fmtBold
&Italic	fmtItalic
&Underline	fmtUnder

6. Create a separator bar by placing a hyphen in the Caption property and typing **popSep1** in the Name property.

7. Add several items for controlling the color of text using the following Name and Caption properties.

Caption	Name
Blac&k	fmtBlack
B&lue	fmtBlue
&Red	fmtRed
&Green	fmtGreen

8. Close the Menu Editor.

9. Open the Code window of the form to add code to each of the menu items. Because the items are not visible on the form's menu, you have to select each item by name in the Code window's object list to edit the code for the item. Place the code shown in Figure 3.9 in the menu items for the pop-up menu. The ActiveControl object is used to identify the control being operated on by the code, because these menu items could be called from a number of locations.

FIGURE 3.9

Code for handling the
pop-up menu items

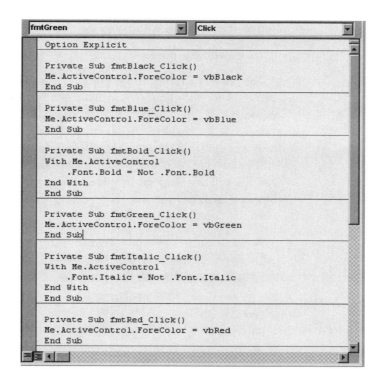

```
fmtGreen                        ▼  Click                              ▼
Option Explicit

Private Sub fmtBlack_Click()
Me.ActiveControl.ForeColor = vbBlack
End Sub

Private Sub fmtBlue_Click()
Me.ActiveControl.ForeColor = vbBlue
End Sub

Private Sub fmtBold_Click()
With Me.ActiveControl
    .Font.Bold = Not .Font.Bold
End With
End Sub

Private Sub fmtGreen_Click()
Me.ActiveControl.ForeColor = vbGreen
End Sub

Private Sub fmtItalic_Click()
With Me.ActiveControl
    .Font.Italic = Not .Font.Italic
End With
End Sub

Private Sub fmtRed_Click()
Me.ActiveControl.ForeColor = vbRed
End Sub
```

The pop-up menu can be derived from one of the items on the main menu
or from a sub-level menu. However, it is atypical to show the pop-up
menu as part of the main menu. Also, a pop-up menu can have sub-level
menus, but this too is atypical.

Exercise 3.4 showed how to create a pop-up menu. To activate the menu,
you need to place code in an event of the form or another control. This is discussed in the following section.

Activating the Pop-Up Menu

After the menu is created, it is a simple matter to activate the pop-up menu.
The PopupMenu method of the form object handles all the work for you.
You simply specify the method and the name of the menu item that is the

top-level item of the pop-up. For example, to activate the pop-up menu created in Exercise 3.4, you would use the following code:

```
Me.PopupMenu popFormat
```

The real key to activating a pop-up menu is choosing the event that will be used to show the menu. Typically, users expect to see the pop-up menu in response to clicking the right mouse button. You can handle this by placing the code for the PopupMenu method in the MouseDown or MouseUp event of the form or a control. These events tell you which button was clicked, whether a Shift key was pressed, and the location of the mouse pointer when the button was pressed. Knowing the location enables you to activate separate menus for different areas of the form. The following code displays the Format menu when the user clicks the right mouse button on any open area of the form:

```
Private Sub Form_MouseDown(Button As Integer, Shift As _
Integer, X As Single, Y As Single)
If Button = vbRightButton Then
    Me.PopupMenu popFormat
End If
End Sub]
```

Figure 3.10 shows you how the menu appears.

FIGURE 3.10

A pop-up menu activated by a right mouse button

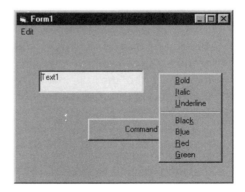

Modifying Menus at Run Time

Creating a menu in the Menu Editor is not the end of the menu management process. You often need to modify the appearance of your menu while your program is running. You might need to make several types of modifications in your program, such as:

- Changing the caption of a menu item

- Changing the Checked property to indicate that an option has been turned on or off

- Showing or hiding a particular menu based on the state of the program

---

Microsoft
Exam
Objective

Implement navigational design.

- Dynamically modify the appearance of a menu.

All these modifications require changing one of the properties of the menu items. The properties that you typically change in modifying a menu are:

- Caption

- Checked

- Enabled

- Visible

Several other properties of the menu items cannot be changed at run time: Name, WindowList, Index, Shortcut, and NegotiatePosition properties.

Although the HelpContextID property can be changed at run time, this is not typically done.

Changing Menu Item Properties

Changing any of the available menu item properties is simply a matter of assigning the property a new value using an assignment statement. The following program line illustrates the use of an assignment statement for the Checked property of a menu item:

```
frmMain.toolOption1.Checked = True
```

Take a look first at the properties that affect the appearance of the menu item: the Caption property and the Checked property.

The Caption property contains the text that is displayed in the menu. This text identifies to the user what the menu item is supposed to do. By changing the Caption property, you can change the text that the user sees. Also, because access keys are defined by placing an ampersand (&) in front of a letter in the Caption property, you can change the access key for a menu item by changing the caption.

Most of the time you should not change the Caption property of a menu item because this will lead to confusion on the part of the user. However, one very beneficial use of this capability is in handling menu setup for programs that may be used by people who speak different languages. In such a case, you may wish to read the Caption properties for the menu items from a resource file and load the caption appropriate to the user's language. The following code shows how to set the captions for the main menu of an international program.

```
mnuDatabase.Caption = TextLoad(209)
datExport.Caption = TextLoad(210)
datImport.Caption = TextLoad(211)
datUtility.Caption = TextLoad(212)
utlRepair.Caption = TextLoad(213)
utlCompact.Caption = TextLoad(214)
mnuSecurity.Caption = TextLoad(215)
secUser.Caption = TextLoad(216)
secConfig.Caption = TextLoad(217)
secChange.Caption = TextLoad(218)
secLogon.Caption = TextLoad(219)
```

 TextLoad is a user-defined function that determines the selected language and pulls the appropriate resource string from the Resource file.

The other visual property of the menu item is the Checked property. This property determines whether a check mark appears next to the menu item. Figure 3.11 shows how the play-level options of a game are indicated using the Checked property. The Click event of each of the option menu items contains code to turn on its own Checked property and turn off the Checked property of all the other options. The following code gives an example of how this would work when a user chooses the Custom level. The code would be placed in the gamCustom Click event:

```
gamStudent.Checked = False
gamScholar.Checked = False
gamPilgrim.Checked = False
gamCustom.Checked = True
```

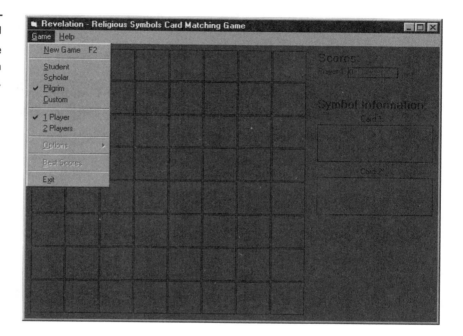

FIGURE 3.11

Game options are indicated with a check mark.

Enabling Menu Items in Response to Program State

The other common modification of a menu at run time is to show and hide, or enable and disable, menu items as the status of the program changes. Consider a word processor. When you first start most word processors, only the File and Help menus are visible, because all the other menus are related to working with a document. If there are no documents open, you do not want the user to have access to the document-handling menu items. As soon as you open a document, however, all the other menus appear. You can set up this type of behavior by setting the Visible property of one or more top-level menus.

Word processors also provide a good example of dynamically changing the Enabled property of menu items. If you examine the Edit menu, you find that the Cut and Copy options are disabled (indicated by their grayed appearance) unless text is selected in the document. Likewise, the Paste option is disabled if there is no text in the Clipboard. The Cut and Copy options are enabled when the user highlights text, that is, changes the status of the program.

Like changing the Caption or Checked properties, a simple assignment statement changes the Enabled and Visible properties. Exercise 3.5 shows you how to create an MDI application that shows and hides the Edit and Window menus depending on whether documents are open. Figures 3.12 and 3.13 show the different views of the menus.

EXERCISE 3.5

Displaying Menu Items in Response to Program Changes

1. Start a new project.

2. Add an MDI form to the project by selecting the Add MDI Form item from the Project menu. Name the form **mdiMain**.

3. Select the Properties item from the Project menu to bring up the Properties dialog box. Change the StartupForm property to **mdiMain**. Then close the dialog box.

4. Open the Menu Editor for the MDI form. Create a File menu with the name **mnuFile** for the top-level item. The menu should contain items for New, Open, Save, and Exit. (Refer to Exercise 3.1 for a refresher on creating a menu.)

5. Create an Edit menu with the name **mnuEdit** for the top-level item. Set the Visible property of the mnuEdit item to False. Add the following sub-level items to the menu: **Cut, Copy, Paste**.

6. Create a Window menu with the name **mnuWindow**. As with the Edit menu, set the Visible property to False. Add the following sub-level items to the menu: **Arrange, Tile**.

7. Create a Help menu with the name **mnuHelp**. Make sure its Visible property is set to True. Add sub-level items for **Topics** and **About**.

8. Switch to the standard form in the project. Change the Name of the form to **frmNotepad** and set the MDIChild property to True.

9. Add a text box to the form. Set the Name property to txtNotepad and set the MultiLine property to True.

10. In the Resize event of the frmNotepad form, add the following code to make the text box fill the form:

```
txtNotepad.Top = 0
txtNotepad.Left = 0
txtNotepad.Height = Me.ScaleHeight
txtNotepad.Width = Me.ScaleWidth
```

11. Switch back to the Code window of the mdiMain form. This is where you start adding the code to display menus. In the filNew menu item (you may have named yours slightly differently), add the following code to the Click event. This code creates a new instance of the frmNotepad form, changes the caption of the form, and displays the Edit and Window menus, ensuring that the menus are displayed whenever a document is open.

```
Dim frmVar As frmNotepad
Static iNumNewForms as Integer
Set frmVar = New frmNotepad
iNumNewForms = iNumNewForms + 1
frmVar.Caption = "Document" & Trim(Str(iNumNewForms))
frmVar.Show
mdiMain.mnuEdit.Visible = True
mdiMain.mnuWindow.Visible = True
```

12. The final step is to add code to hide the menus when the last document is closed. To handle this, place code in the Unload event of frmNotepad. The following code checks the number of open forms using the Count property of the Forms collection. If the count is two, implying that only the MDI form and the current document are open, the code sets the Visible property of the mnuEdit and mnuWindow menu items to False in order to hide them.

```
If Forms.Count = 2 Then
    mdiMain.mnuEdit.Visible = False
    mdiMain.mnuWindow.Visible = False
End If
```

13. You can now run the program and watch how the menus are displayed and hidden as documents are opened or closed. The complete source for this project is included on the CD-ROM as *ModMenu.vbp*.

Only two menus are visible when no documents are open.

More than two menus are shown when the documents are open.

Adding Menu Items at Run Time

Microsoft ✓ *Exam* *Objective*	**Implement navigational design.** ▪ Create an application that adds and deletes menus at run time.

Changing the properties of menu items is not the only way you can modify your menus at run time. You can also dynamically add menu items to the menu. There are two ways to add menu items at run time:

- You can have the program automatically add the names of MDI child forms to the menu to enable the user to quickly switch back and forth between documents.

- You can use a menu item control array to add your own menu items to the menu.

Adding Items for MDI Child Forms

Adding the MDI child forms to a menu is simple. You have to do three things:

1. Create an MDI application.

2. Create a menu on the MDI form.

3. Set the WindowList property of one of your menu items to True.

In Exercise 3.6, you modify the program created in Exercise 3.5 to add the capability of keeping up with the child documents in the form.

EXERCISE 3.6

Keeping a List of MDI Child Forms

1. Open the project you created in Exercise 3.5. You can also use the *ModMenu.vbp* code included on the MCSD VB6 companion CD-ROM.

2. Move to the MDI form and open the Menu Editor.

EXERCISE 3.6 (CONTINUED)

3. Run your program and observe the effect of the WindowList property. Figure 3.14 shows the menu with several child windows added. Notice that the WindowList automatically adds a separator bar and adds the new items at the bottom of the menu.

FIGURE 3.14

MDI child windows listed in a menu

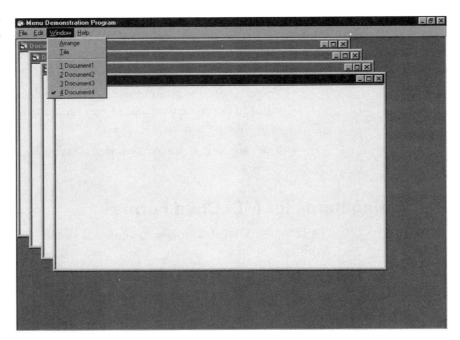

Using Menu Item Arrays

The other method of adding menu items at run time is to use a menu control array. An array is a group of menu items with the same Name property and different values of the Index property. One of the most common uses of a menu control array is to keep a list of the most recently used files for a program. You can see this in programs such as Word or Excel where the File menu contains the names of the last three or four files that you accessed.

Although creating menu items on the fly is not difficult, you must follow several steps:

- You must create at least one element of the array in the Menu Editor. Visual Basic does not enable you to create a control array completely in code. It enables you only to add or remove items from the array.

- You must use the Load command to add items to the array. To use the Load command, you must specify the name of the control array and the index of the element to be added. This index value must be unique. To ensure that the index value is unique, you can use the Ubound property of an array to determine the index of the last element and add one to that value.

- You must use the Unload command to remove elements from the array. To use the Unload command, you must again specify the name of the control array and the index to be removed. If you remove an item within the middle of the control array, the Index properties of the other elements of the array are not affected. For example, if you have a control array of five controls (index values 0, 1, 2, 3, 4) and you Unload the control with Index=2, the result is a control array with the following indexes: 0, 1, 3, 4.

- You can write code only in a single procedure to handle all the elements of the array. The Click event is tied to the Name of the array; however, the index information is passed to the procedure, and you can use a Select statement to handle separate tasks for individual array elements.

To give you an understanding of adding and removing menu array items, Exercise 3.7 adds some files to a most recently used list in the File menu. The menu also has an option to clear the list. This Exercise shows the process of removing array items. The code in the Exercise uses made-up names for the files. To use this in an actual program, you would read the names of the files from the Registry or an .ini file.

EXERCISE 3.7

Adding and Removing Menu Items

1. Open the project created in Exercises 3.5 and 3.6.

2. Open the Menu Editor for the MDI form.

3. Insert a menu item ahead of the Exit item. Set the Caption property of the item to **Clear MRU List**, set the Name property to **filMRUFile**, and set the Index property to **0**, creating the first element of the menu item array. Also, set the Visible property to False. You don't want the Clear List item to be visible if there are no items in the MRU list.

4. Insert a separator bar between the filMRUFile and filExit items. Set its Visible property to False.

5. Close the Menu Editor.

6. In the Load event of the MDI form, place the following code. This code creates the additional items of the MRU list and assigns the Caption property of the menu item. When an item is loaded from code, it is not visible to the user. Therefore, you need to set the Visible property to True. The code also displays the first element of the list and the separator bar.

```
Dim I As Integer, J As Integer

For I = 1 To 4
    J = filMRUFile.UBound + 1
    Load filMRUFile(J)
    filMRUFile(J).Caption = Trim(Str(I)) &
" - File" & Trim(Str(I))
    filMRUFile(J).Visible = True
Next I
filMRUFile(0).Visible = True
filSep2.Visible = True
```

7. In the Click event of the filMRUFile item, place the following code. This code unloads all the menu items except the first one and hides the first element of the array and the separator bar. This code is activated only if the user selects the Clear List item. (The Clear List item has an index value of 0.)

```
Dim I As Integer
If Index = 0 Then
    If filMRUFile.UBound > 0 Then
        For I = filMRUFile.UBound To 1 Step -1
            Unload filMRUFile(I)
        Next I
    End If
End If
filMRUFile(0).Visible = False
filSep2.Visible = False
```

8. Run the program. Figure 3.15 shows the menu after the items are added to the File menu. Figure 3.16 shows the menu after the list is cleared.

FIGURE 3.15

The appearance of the menu after the items have been removed

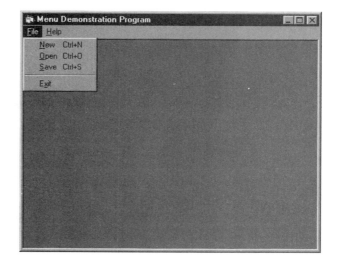

FIGURE 3.16

Items added to a menu item array

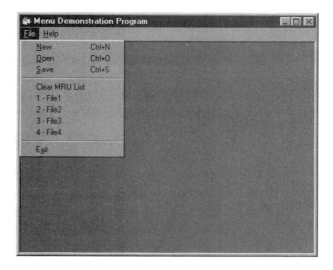

WARNING In step 7 of Exercise 3.7, make sure you do not try to remove the original element of the menu array. Any elements of a control array that are created at design time cannot be removed with the Unload command. Attempting to do so generates an error.

Summary

This chapter has provided you with a refresher in the creation of menus in your Visual Basic programs. You have seen how to create a main program menu and how to create and activate a pop-up menu. You have also seen how to change the appearance of a menu on the fly. Finally, you saw how you can use control arrays and the WindowList property to add and remove menu items while your program is running.

The Microsoft exam tests your ability to create menus, both main menus and pop-up menus. If you complete all the exercises presented in this chapter and understand the concepts behind them, you should have no problem with the following objectives:

- Implement navigational design.

  - Add a pop-up menu to an application.

  - Dynamically modify the appearance of a menu.

  - Create an application that adds and deletes menus at run time.

Review Questions

1. What properties are required to be specified for a menu item? Check all that apply.

   A. Checked

   B. Index

   C. Name

   D. Caption

2. How can you enable the user to access a menu item from the keyboard? Check all that apply.

A. Define an access key by designating a letter in the Caption property.

B. Define a shortcut key by setting the Shortcut property in the Menu Editor.

C. The user can press F10 and use the cursor keys.

D. Define a shortcut key by setting the Shortcut property in code.

3. All of the following statements about access keys are true except:

A. You can have items on different menus with the same access key.

B. The user must hold the Alt key while pressing the access key to open a top-level menu.

C. All top-level menus must have a unique access key.

D. Access keys are indicated to the user by an underlined letter in the caption.

4. Which of the following statements about pop-up menus are true? Check all that apply.

A. A pop-up menu can be used as a main menu.

B. A pop-up menu can be created from a sub-level menu.

C. A pop-up menu can have multiple levels.

D. A pop-up menu can be activated by any event the developer chooses.

5. Which Form event would you use to activate a pop-up menu when the user clicks the right mouse button? Check all that apply.

A. MouseDown

B. Click

C. MouseUp

D. MouseMove

6. What is the proper syntax for activating the pop-up menu fmtFormat?

   A. Popup = fmtFormat

   B. Set PopupMenu = fmtFormat

   C. Me.PopupMenu fmtFormat

   D. Me.PopupMenu = fmtFormat

7. Which menu item properties can you change at run time?

   A. WindowList, Caption, Index, Checked

   B. Name, Caption, Index

   C. Caption, Checked, Enabled, Visible

   D. Caption, Checked, Visible, Shortcut

8. What does the WindowList property do?

   A. Maintains a list of all forms in your program

   B. Enables you to add menu items to any menu at run time

   C. Keeps a list of MDI child windows

   D. Works with any application

9. What is the proper syntax for adding an item to a menu array?

   A. filMRUFile.AddItem 1

   B. filMRUFile.Load 1

   C. Load filMRUFile(1)

   D. Load New filMRUFile

10. Which command is used to remove an item from a menu array?

   A. Delete

   B. RemoveItem

   C. Drop

   D. Unload

11. When removing items from the menu array, which of the following best describes restrictions in doing this?

   A. You can remove all elements of the array.

   B. You must keep at least one element of the array.

   C. You cannot remove any elements that were created at design time.

   D. You cannot remove any elements of the array.

CHAPTER

4

Advanced Design Features

Microsoft Exam Objectives Covered in This Chapter:

- Write code that validates user input.
  - Create an application that verifies data entered at the field level and the form level by a user.
  - Create an application that enables or disables controls based on input in fields.

- Create data input forms and dialog boxes.
  - Create an application that adds and deletes controls at run time.

Chapter 1, "Getting Started with Visual Basic," introduced you to the creation of programs. You saw how to use forms and controls to create the visual interface of the program. You also saw how the methods and events of controls and forms are used to perform tasks in the program and to control the program. Chapter 1, however, covered only the basics of creating programs. You will use advanced techniques in many of your programs. Two of these techniques are so important that they are covered in the objectives of the Visual Basic certification exam. These techniques are:

- Data validation

- Adding and removing controls at run time

Data validation is important to almost every program that you will write. Validation ensures (to as great a degree as possible) that the information that is input by the user of the program is correct. This validation helps maintain the integrity of any databases that you are working with and helps avoid errors in your program. (You can learn more about handling errors in Chapter 14, "Handling and Logging Errors in Visual Basic Programs.")

The second technique, adding and deleting controls, enables you to create more powerful forms that change in response to the conditions of the program or to handle different tasks with the same form. Several examples of this flexibility include:

- Creating an enhanced message box that allows more command button options and user input

- Creating a data entry form that works with any data source

- Adding menu options (remember that menu items are simple controls) such as a list of recently used files

This chapter discusses both of these techniques in detail and, of course, tells you how learning these techniques fits in with the objectives of the Visual Basic certification exam.

Validating User Input

Microsoft *Exam* *Objective*	**Write code that validates user input.**

Data validation is simply checking the input of the program against a set of conditions that are specified in the program's design. Some validation rules are quite obvious for all programs. For example:

- A state code must match one of the fifty U.S. states.

- A person's age cannot be a negative number.

- A percentage number should not be greater than 100%.

In addition, there are many rules that are specific to a company. These might include:

- A person's raise cannot exceed 15% of the base salary.

- A sales tax rate for a customer cannot be zero or negative.

- A social security number must be input for a new employee.

Just as there are many types of validation rules that can exist in a program, there are also many ways to implement the rules. For rules that require a selection from a certain limited set of values, you may choose to use a list box, combo box, check box, or set of option buttons to handle the user input. In this way, the available options are controlled by your program, and it is difficult (if not impossible) for a user to input an invalid value. For other types of validation rules, you need to write code to implement the rules. This type of validation is the subject of this section.

In many cases, you will want to embed business rules in a server component that validates input before data is written to a database. You can learn about creating Automation servers in Chapter 10, "Creating COM Components."

When you are handling the validation for data on a form, you first need to choose whether to validate each field as it is entered or to validate all fields when data is saved or the form is exited. The following sections address both of these methods.

Handling Field-Level Validation

Microsoft **Write code that validates user input.**
Exam
Objective • Create an application that verifies data entered at the field level and the form level by a user.

Field-level validation means that the data in each field is checked by the program after the user enters the data and before the user is allowed to move to another field. In previous versions of Visual Basic, a programmer could enable field-level validation by placing code in the LostFocus event of the control where the data was to be entered. In theory, the code would be executed when the user moved from the current control to another control. In practice, however, this method was less than perfect. This was because several user actions could move the focus from the current control without causing the LostFocus event to fire.

In Visual Basic 6, a new event and a new property were introduced that make handling field-level validation easier and more reliable. Version 6 introduced the Validate event and the CausesValidation property.

The Validate event fires before the focus shifts from the current control to another control. The firing occurs, however, only if the second control has the CausesValidation property set to True. By placing code in the Validate event of a control, you can check the input of the control and force the focus to stay on the current control if the input is incorrect. Exercise 4.1 shows you how to use the Validate event and the CausesValidation property to ensure that a user enters name and address information on a data input form.

EXERCISE 4.1

Validating Data at the Field Level

1. Open a new project in Visual Basic.

2. Create a data entry form with text boxes to handle the input of a person's first name, last name, address, city, state, and zip code. The complete form should look something like the one shown in the following illustration.

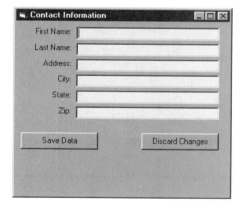

3. Verify that the CausesValidation property of each of the text boxes is set to True. This is the default setting of any control that can receive focus.

4. Set the CausesValidation property of the Save Data command button to True (the default) and set the CausesValidation property of the Discard Changes button to False. These settings are necessary to allow the user to exit a form without saving the data and without having to enter valid data in each field.

5. Place the following code in the Validate event of the First Name and Last Name text boxes of the form.

```
Private Sub txtFirst_Validate(Cancel As Boolean)
Dim sCheckName As String
sCheckName = txtFirst.Text
```

EXERCISE 4.1 (CONTINUED)

```
If Len(Trim(sCheckName)) = 0 Then
    MsgBox "First name cannot be blank.", _
 vbExclamation + vbOKOnly, "Data Entry"
    Cancel = True
End If
End Sub

Private Sub txtLast_Validate(Cancel As Boolean)
Dim sCheckName As String
sCheckName = txtLast.Text
If Len(Trim(sCheckName)) = 0 Then
    MsgBox "Last name cannot be blank.", _
 vbExclamation + vbOKOnly, "Data Entry"
    Cancel = True
End If
End Sub
```

The code in the Validate event causes a message box to be displayed if the field is left blank. Setting the Cancel variable to True indicates that the validation failed and that the focus should stay with the current control.

To ensure that the Validate event works correctly, every control on your form that can receive focus should have the CausesValidation property set to True (the default). The exception is a control such as a Discard button illustrated in Exercise 4.1

Using Form-Level Data Validation

Microsoft ✓ Exam Objective

Write code that validates user input.

- Create an application that verifies data entered at the field level and the form level by a user.

The other way to validate user input is to wait until the user has entered all the information required on a form and then check the data before a Save operation or before the form is unloaded. To handle this type of validation, you typically write a function that returns a True or False value. This function checks each required field. Then if a field is invalid, the function displays a message, sets the focus to the offending control, and cancels the Save or Exit operation. Exercise 4.2 shows you how to implement this type of validation for the same data entry form that you created in Exercise 4.1

EXERCISE 4.2

Implementing Validation at the Form Level

1. Create a data entry form just like the one created in Exercise 4.1.

2. Open the Code window of the form. Then, using the Add Procedure dialog box from the Tools menu, create a new function called **Check-Data**. The Add Procedure dialog is shown in the graphic below.

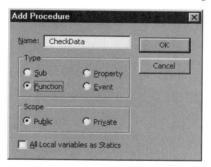

3. Add the **As Boolean** clause to the declaration of the function. This causes the declaration to look like the following code line.

```
Public Function CheckData() As Boolean
```

4. Add the following code to the CheckData function.

```
Dim sCheckName As String
CheckData = True
sCheckName = txtFirst.Text
If Len(Trim(sCheckName)) = 0 Then
    MsgBox "First Name cannot be blank.", _
  vbExclamation + vbOKOnly, "Data Check"
    txtFirst.SetFocus
```

```
        CheckData = False
        Exit Function
    End If
    sCheckName = txtLast.Text
    If Len(Trim(sCheckName)) = 0 Then
        MsgBox "Last Name cannot be blank.", _
     vbExclamation + vbOKOnly, "Data Check"
        txtLast.SetFocus
        CheckData = False
        Exit Function
    End If
```

5. Add the following code line to the Click event of the Save button. This code calls the validation function and takes appropriate action if the validation fails.

```
If Not CheckData Then Exit Sub
'Save the data
```

Enabling Controls

Microsoft Exam Objective

Write code that validates user input.

- Create an application that enables or disables controls based on input in fields.

In another form of data validation, you allow the user to access only controls that are necessary for a certain function. In Chapter 3, "Creating Menus for Your Programs," you saw how you could enable and disable menu items based on the condition of the program or because of a user action. You can do the same with controls on your form.

Each control that you add to a form has an Enabled property (except for certain controls such as the line or shape). By manipulating the Enabled property of one control from the event procedures of another control, you can determine which controls are accessible by the user, based on their input in other controls. Exercise 4.3 shows a simple example of this technique.

Manipulating Controls Based on User Input

1. Open a new project in Visual Basic.

2. Add an array of four option buttons to the form. Set the captions of the buttons to **Radio**, **Television**, **Magazine**, and **Other**. This type of form might be used to determine where customers learned of your product.

3. Add a text box next to the Magazine option button and set the Enabled property of the text box to False. Set the Name property of the box to **txtMagazine**.

4. Add a second text box next to the Other option button and set its Name property to **txtOther**. Also set the Enabled property of this text box to False. The completed form should look like the following graphic.

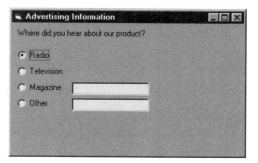

5. Place the following code in the Click event of the option buttons.

```
Private Sub optAd_Click(Index As Integer)
txtMagazine.Enabled = False
txtOther.Enabled = False
Select Case Index
    Case 2
        txtMagazine.Enabled = True
```

```
         Case 3
             txtOther.Enabled = True
    End Select
    End Sub
```

6. Run the program. Notice that you can input the name of a magazine only if the Magazine option is checked.

Changing Forms on the Fly

You know that you can change the appearance of your forms—fonts, colors, backgrounds, and so on—by changing the properties of the forms at run time. You can also change the properties of controls on the forms to respond to differing needs. But how can you make the forms really responsive to the needs of your program? For example, is there a way to create a dialog box that enables multiple inputs as well as a variable number of user-defined command buttons?

The answer is yes. One method of creating this type of dialog box is to add a whole bunch of text boxes and command buttons to the form and then display only the ones you need. This approach, however, has two main drawbacks—it wastes resources, and it imposes an upper limit on the number of controls your form can display (you can display only as many controls as you create during design mode). The better approach to responsive forms is to create and delete controls as necessary.

The easiest way to handle the addition and deletion of controls is to create a control array (or multiple control arrays) and add elements to the control array at run time. You can also, of course, remove elements from the control array. Two great uses of this technique are enhanced message boxes (as shown in Figure 4.1) and generic data entry forms (as shown in Figure 4.2). These types of forms enable you to use a single form to perform multiple tasks throughout your program and are discussed later in the chapter. First, however, the basics of control arrays.

F I G U R E   4.1

F I G U R E   4.1

An enhanced message box lets the program specify the number and captions of the command buttons.

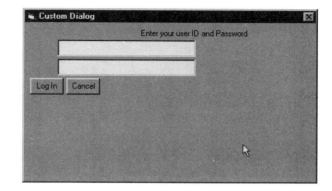

F I G U R E   4.2

A generic data entry form enables the same form to be used for multiple recordsets.

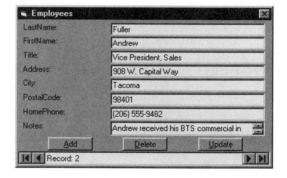

Microsoft
✓ *Exam*
Objective

Create data input forms and dialog boxes.

- Create an application that adds and deletes controls at run time.

Understanding Control Array Basics

At the simplest level, a control array is a group of controls of the same type that all have the same name. For example, you can have a series of text boxes on your form, all having the name txtMember. Because all the controls have the same name you must have another means of identifying the individual control—the Index property of the control. As you add members to the control array, you must specify a unique value for the Index property of the control. No two controls in an array may have the same value of the Index property.

It is possible to specify nonconsecutive numbers for the Index property of controls; however, this can lead to a variety of errors in your programs and is not recommended.

Using control arrays has several important programming benefits:

- You can easily set the property values of all the controls in the array by using a For loop.

- You can write code in a single event to handle a number of controls.

- You can add controls to the array and remove them from the array at run time. (This is the most important benefit for this discussion.)

Creating Control Arrays

The first step in using control arrays is to create the array. Whether you create the entire control array in the design mode or add and remove controls while your program is running, you must create at least one element of the control array at design time. It is not possible to change a single control into an element of a control array while the program is running.

After the initial element of the array is created, you can add more controls to the array by placing them on the form in design mode or by using the Load statement to add the controls at run time. You will look at both methods in this section.

Each control in a control array can have its own set of properties. The only property that the members of an array are required to have in common is the Name property.

Setting up the First Element of an Array   Two methods exist for starting a control array in the design environment. You can create the first element of the array specifically by assigning a value to the Index property of the control, or you can let Visual Basic create the array for you by copying a second instance of the control onto the form.

Both methods of starting a control array begin by drawing a control on your form. After drawing the control, you give it a name and set other various properties of the control. To have Visual Basic start the control array for you, select the control on the form, copy it to the clipboard, and then paste the copy back onto the form. At this point, you are presented with a dialog box (shown in Figure 4.3) that asks if you want to create a control array. If you answer "yes," the second copy of the control is added to the form using the same name as your base control. In addition, the Index properties of the controls are set to zero and one respectively. You now have a control array on your form with two elements.

FIGURE 4.3

Visual Basic asks if you want to create a control array.

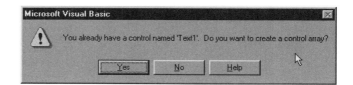

With the second method, you can create only the first element of the control array. After setting up the control, choose the Index property and set its value to zero. You now have a control array with a single element. You typically use this method if you intend to create additional controls at run time.

Control arrays should be zero-based, meaning that the first element of the array should have an Index property value of zero. Additional elements of the array should be numbered consecutively. Although Visual Basic does not enforce this convention, failing to follow it can result in problems in your programs.

Adding Controls to the Array at Design Time   After you have created the initial element(s) of the array, you can add more controls to the array while you are in the design mode. You can do this in either of two methods:

- Copy an existing element of the control array and paste it to a new location on the form.

- Create a new control of the same type as the control array and set the Name property to the name of the control array.

With either of these methods, each new control automatically has the Index property set to the next sequential number in the array. Which method you use is a matter of personal choice.

Adding Controls to the Array at Run Time One of the great benefits of control arrays is that you can add more elements to the array while your program is running. This advantage enables you to modify your forms to handle different situations on the fly. You add controls to the array using the Load statement. This statement specifies the name of the array and the element number that you wish to add. The Load statement is illustrated in the following code:

```
iUpper = txtMember.UBound + 1
Load txtMember(iUpper)
```

The code uses one of the properties of the array to determine the last element number of the array. The four properties of a control array are:

Count Specifies the total number of elements in the array

Item Returns a reference to a specific element of the array

LBound Specifies the lowest index value of the array

UBound Specifies the highest index value of the array

When adding new elements to a control array at run time, you must meet two specific criteria or an error occurs. These criteria are:

- The control array must already exist. You cannot create the initial element of the array at run time.

- The Index value specified in the Load statement must be unique.

After you have created the control using the Load statement, you can set its properties as you would for any other control on your form. One important property to set is the Visible property. Like the Load statement used with a form, the Load statement for a control array creates only the array element in memory. It does not display the control on the form. Therefore, you must set the Visible property to True to have the control seen by the user.

The properties of the newly added control are based on the properties of the first element of the array. Therefore, you also need to adjust the position of the new element, or it will be displayed in the same location as another control.

Removing Controls from the Array   Removing controls from the array is similar to adding the controls. To remove controls, you use the Unload statement. With this statement, you specify the name of the array and the element to be removed. For an element to be removed from a control array without error, it must meet two criteria:

- The Index value must be valid.

- The element must have been added at run time. You cannot remove a control array element that was added in the design environment.

The Unload statement is illustrated in the following code:

```
iUpper = txtMember.UBound
Unload txtMember(iUpper)
```

Writing Code for Control Arrays

Controls that are part of a control array respond to all the same events and use the same methods as individual controls of the same type. In addition, the array itself has properties and methods. To work with the properties and methods of the array, you just specify the array name. If you want to work with an element of the control array, you must specify the Index value of the element.

To invoke the methods or modify the properties of a control array element, you simply place the Index value in parentheses immediately following the name of the control. This format tells your program that you are working with the individual control, not the array itself. The following code shows how to move a control and make it visible:

```
txtMember(iUpper).Visible = True
txtMember(iUpper).Top = txtMember(iUpper - 1).Top + 500
```

WARNING   You cannot set the property values of multiple controls by using just the control name, without the Index value. Each control is a separate entity and its properties must be set individually.

For the events of a control, the event procedure declaration is modified to pass the Index value of the particular control in which the event occurred.

This modification is handled automatically by Visual Basic. The modified declaration is shown in the following code:

```
Private Sub txtMember_Change(Index As Integer)
End Sub
```

Having the Index passed to the event procedure means that you have only one procedure for a particular event for all the elements of a control array. Using this procedure, you can take the same actions for each control in the array, or use a Select statement or If statements to check the Index value and take appropriate actions for specific elements of the array.

Creating an Enhanced Message Box

If you are familiar with Visual Basic's MsgBox and InputBox dialog boxes, you know that although they are very useful, they are limited in what they can do. For example, you cannot specify your own captions for the command buttons, nor can you use command button sets other than the defaults. Also, the InputBox is limited to a single input value. However, you can create your own enhanced message and input dialog box using control arrays. With this custom dialog box, you can determine how many command buttons to use, what the captions of the buttons are, and how many input values you want to handle. Exercise 4.4 shows you how to create the skeleton of an enhanced message dialog box. The complete project is included on the CD-ROM as *Custom.vbp*. Feel free to use and customize this dialog box to suit your needs.

EXERCISE 4.4

Creating a Custom Dialog Box with Control Arrays

1. Start a new project.

2. Add a second form to the project and name the new form **frmCustom**.

3. Set the BorderStyle property of frmCustom to Fixed Dialog.

4. (The next several steps refer to the frmCustom form.) Add a label control to the form and name it **lblMessage**. Set the Alignment property of the label to Center.

5. Add a text box to the form and name it **txtInput**. Set the Index property of the control to zero to create the first element of the text box array used for inputs. Set the Visible property of the control to False.

   6. Add a command button to the form and name it **cmdSelection**. Set the Index property of the command button to zero to create the command button control array.

This completes the initial setup of the visual portion of the custom dialog box. The rest of the work of the dialog box is in the code for adding and displaying additional elements of the control arrays.

   7. Add a Property Let procedure to the form and name it **Buttons**. This procedure will handle creating the command buttons and setting their captions. You can start the Property Let procedure by choosing the Add Procedure item from the Tools menu.

   8. The code for the procedure is too long to include all of it here. The purpose of the procedure is to parse a string of button names and create the buttons for the dialog box. The names are passed to the procedure as a single string, with the individual names separated by a vertical bar (|). The key part of the procedure that loads the additional command buttons is shown below:

```
iMaxWidth = 0
For I = 0 To iBtnCount - 1
    iTextWidth = Me.TextWidth(sCommandText(I))
    If iTextWidth > iMaxWidth Then iMaxWidth = _
iTextWidth
    If I > 0 Then Load cmdSelection(I)
    cmdSelection(I).Caption = sCommandText(I)
Next I
```

   9. Create another Property Let procedure named **Input**. This procedure tells the dialog box the number of input text boxes to be displayed on the form. The code for the procedure loads additional text box controls if needed. The code for the Input procedure is:

```
Dim I As Integer
If iNumInputs > 0 Then
    txtInput(0).Visible = True
    If iNumInputs > 1 Then
        For I = 1 To iNumInputs - 1
            Load txtInput(I)
```

```
        Next I
    End If
End If
```

10. Create one final Property Let procedure to handle passing the message information to the dialog box. This procedure should be named **Message** and contain the following code:

```
lblMessage.Caption = sMessageText
```

11. The final programming for the dialog box consists of code in the Activate event of the form. This code sets the Visible property of all the appropriate controls and sets the positions of the controls on the form. The code for the Activate event is:

```
Dim I As Integer, iBtnWidth As Integer, iBtnCount As _
  Integer
Dim iInputCount As Integer
iBtnCount = cmdSelection.Count
iBtnWidth = cmdSelection(0).Width
Me.Width = iBtnCount * (iBtnWidth + 60) + 240
If Me.Width < 6450 Then Me.Width = 6450
lblMessage.Width = Me.Width - 480
lblMessage.WordWrap = True
lblMessage.AutoSize = True

If txtInput(0).Visible = True Then
    iInputCount = txtInput.UBound
    For I = 0 To iInputCount
        txtInput(I).Top = Message.Top + _
  lblMessage.Height + I * (txtInput(0) _
.Height + 60) + 60
        txtInput(I).Left = lblMessage.Left
        txtInput(I).Visible = True
    Next I
Else
    iInputCount = 0
End If
```

```
For I = 0 To iBtnCount - 1
    cmdSelection(I).Left = I * (iBtnWidth + 60) + 120
    If iInputCount = 0 Then
        cmdSelection(I).Top = lblMessage.Top + _
lblMessage.Height + 60
    Else
        cmdSelection(I).Top = _
txtInput(iInputCount).Top + _
txtInput(iInputCount).Height + 60
    End If
    cmdSelection(I).Visible = True
Next I
```

12. After setting up the dialog box, you need to call the dialog box from another form. Return to the original form of your project and add a command button to the form. In the Click event of the command button, you need to place code to set the properties of the enhanced message dialog box and show the form. An example of this code is shown below. The results of the code can be seen in Figure 4.4.

```
frmCustom.Message = "Enter your user ID and Password"
frmCustom.Inputs = 2
frmCustom.Buttons = "Log In|Cancel"
frmCustom.Show
```

FIGURE 4.4

A sample of the dialog box you can create with the enhanced message dialog box

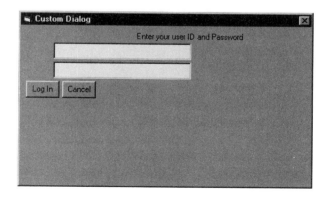

Summary

This chapter has shown you how to implement two advanced design features—data validation, and adding and deleting controls during run time. An understanding of these two features will help you meet several Microsoft certification exam objectives:

- Write code that validates user input.
  - Create an application that verifies data entered at the field level and the form level by a user.
  - Create an application that enables or disables controls based on input in fields.
- Create data input forms and dialog boxes.
  - Create an application that adds and deletes controls at run time.

If you are still not comfortable with the concepts covered in this chapter, review each of the exercises to help solidify those ideas. Then it is time to put your knowledge to the test. The following questions are typical of those you might find on the Visual Basic certification exam.

Review Questions

1. How do you create the first element of a control array?

   A. Set the Index property of a control while in the design mode.

   B. Use the Load statement to load a control with an index value of zero.

   C. Use the CreateObject statement to create an instance of the control.

   D. Change the Index property of a single control at run time.

2. Which of the following restrictions apply to adding a control to a control array at run time? Check all that apply.

   A. The form must be visible when the control is added.

   B. The control array must already exist.

C. The Index value must be the next sequential number after the upper bound of the array.

D. The Index of the new control must be unique.

3. Which of the following are properties of a control array?

A. Count, Type, and Name

B. Count, Item, LBound, and UBound

C. Count, Name, and Index

D. Index, LBound, and UBound

4. Which of the following statements can be used to change the value of a property in an element of a control array?

A. txtMember.Top = 120

B. txtMember(0).Top = 120

C. txtMember.0.Top = 120

D. txtMember0.Top = 120

5. What are the restrictions on removing controls from a control array? Check all that apply.

A. The control must have been created in design mode.

B. The control must have been added at run time.

C. The control element must exist.

D. All data must have been unloaded from the control.

6. Which of the following statements removes a control from an array?

A. Delete txtMember(5)

B. Remove txtMember(5)

C. Unload txtMember(5)

D. Load txtMember(5) vbRemove

CHAPTER

5

Creating Classes in a Program

Microsoft Exam Objectives Covered in This Chapter:

- Design the properties, methods, and events of components.

- Compile a project with class modules into a COM component.
  - Set properties to control the instancing of a class within a COM component.

V isual Basic's capability to create classes is one of the most significant capabilities that has been added to the language. Being able to create classes in Visual Basic lays the groundwork for creating reusable components, creating COM servers, and creating ActiveX controls. A good understanding of classes is essential to most Visual Basic projects.

In this chapter, you will learn the basic concepts of a class and then proceed to the creation of classes. You will see how to create the properties, methods, and events of a class. You will also learn how and when to use the Friend declaration and the purpose of the different settings of the Instancing property. In addition, you will see how using the Class Builder add-in can make creating and managing classes in your Visual Basic project easier. Finally, you will see how to create an instance of a class and use it in your program.

Understanding Classes in Visual Basic

V isual Basic has always been based on the principles of object-oriented programming (OOP). When Visual Basic was originally developed, it enabled programmers to create programs using predefined objects, specifically forms and controls. These objects implemented the OOP principles of encapsulation and polymorphism, but not the principle of inheritance. When classes were introduced to Visual Basic, programmers could create their own objects for use in a program. Like the controls built into Visual Basic, the objects created with a class allow the encapsulation of data and procedures, and allow polymorphism, but do not allow inheritance. Also, the classes created in Visual Basic are code-only objects; they do not have a visual component.

ActiveX controls extend the class model by providing a visual interface to a class so you can use it as a control. ActiveX controls are discussed in detail in Chapter 12, "Creating ActiveX Controls with Visual Basic." However, the techniques you learn here about creating classes also are quite valuable in the creation of ActiveX controls.

Having the capability to create classes makes it easier for a programmer to create reusable objects that can be used within the current project, in other projects by the same programmer, and by other programmers in a multi-programmer work environment. Using classes enables a program segment, whether it is a business rule or an interface to programming tasks, to be created once and then easily reused through the properties and methods of the class.

Understanding Object-Oriented Programming

Three major principles you will hear quite often in the discussion of object-oriented programming are:

Encapsulation   The data about an object and the code used to manipulate the data are contained within the object itself. The data is stored as the properties of the object and the code as the methods of the object. Encapsulation enables the object data and code to stand alone, independent of outside routines.

Polymorphism   Relates to the use of the same method name in various objects, for example, a Print method for the printer, a form, or a picture box. Although the name of the method is the same, the code for the method in each object can be different. However, because the code for the method is encapsulated in the object, each object knows how to perform the correct task when the method is called.

Inheritance   Enables one object to be created based on the properties and methods of another object. With inheritance, you do not have to code the properties and methods that are derived from the parent object. You have to code only new or modified properties and methods.

As stated earlier, Visual Basic does not support inheritance between objects. For each class you create, you have to code all the methods and properties that will be a part of the class. This lack of true inheritance causes a great debate over whether Visual Basic is object-oriented or simply object-based. You are left to form your own opinions about this. However, even without true inheritance, classes in Visual Basic provide a powerful tool for creating applications.

Using Classes

You can use classes in your Visual Basic applications in a number of ways. These uses can typically be categorized as one of three general types—creation of business objects, encapsulation of programming functions, and Visual Basic add-ins. No matter how you use the classes, you create reusable components that make your programs easier to create and easier to maintain.

Creating business objects is probably the most common use of classes in a program. A typical example of a business object is an employee object. When you create an employee object, you create properties that describe the employee, such as name, social security number, department, job level, pay grade, home address, and so on. You also create methods to handle tasks associated with the employee, such as retrieving the employee data from a database, saving changed data to the database, and calculating payroll for the employee. By placing all this information in a class, you make it easier to use the information in your program. More importantly, you can compile the class as an ActiveX EXE or DLL server to allow other programmers to use the same properties and methods. Using classes to create business objects enables you to set up business rules and information in one location, instead of having each program repeat the code. This is the basis of multi-tier, client-server programming.

You will look at creating COM servers in detail in Chapter 10, "Creating COM Components."

Classes can also be used to encapsulate program functions for easy use. For example, you might want to encapsulate the code that opens a recordset in a class module. This class can handle the operations and include all the necessary error-handling functions. You can then use the class each time you need to create a recordset. Using this approach eliminates the need to repeat the code and the error-handling routines in multiple locations throughout your program. Another advantage of this approach is that if you change databases, requiring a change in the access methods, you need to change the code only in a single location, making code maintenance much easier.

Finally, you can use classes to create add-ins, which extend the functionality of Visual Basic itself. Add-ins can be used to build program wizards or to provide functions such as automatic comments at the beginning of a form or module.

Creating a Class

Design the properties, methods, and events of components.

Part of how you create a class depends on its intended use. You may do a few things differently if the class is used only within stand-alone programs as opposed to compiling the class in an ActiveX server. However, there are five basic steps to creating any class in Visual Basic:

1. Create the class module and set its properties.
2. Create the properties of the class.
3. Create the methods of the class.
4. Create any events needed for the class and include the code to raise the events at the appropriate time.
5. Create any constants needed by the class using the Enum structure.

You will look at each of these steps in detail in the following sections.

Setting Up the Class Module

Class modules are files that contain program code. This code sets up the properties, methods, and events that define the class. Each class is created in a special file with the `.cls` extension. This extension tells Visual Basic that the code is a class module, not a standard program module containing general functions and procedures.

To create a class in your program, first you must add a class module to your project. To do this, choose the Add Class Module item from the Projects menu, or press the Add button on the toolbar and select the Class Module item. You are presented with a dialog box that asks you the type of module you want to create. This dialog box is shown in Figure 5.1. Your choices are to create a class module, create a Visual Basic add-in, or open the Class Builder utility. Choose the Class Module option and click the Open button. (You will look at the Class Builder a little later.)

FIGURE 5.1

Add Class Module
dialog box

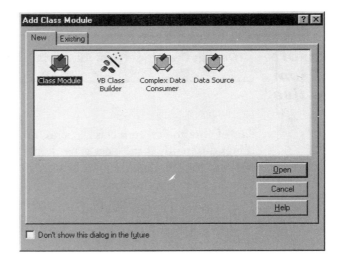

After you select the Class Module option, you are placed in the Code window for the class; notice that a new class has been added to the Project window as shown in Figure 5.2. At this point, you need to set the properties of the class module. For all classes, you need to set the Name property. You want the name of your classes to be descriptive of their function, as well as to identify the object as a class. My personal preference is to start class names with a *c* and to use a descriptive term, such as cUser, for a user information class. Other programmers use other naming conventions. The key is to pick a style that you are comfortable with and to use it consistently.

FIGURE 5.2

The initial appearance of a new class module

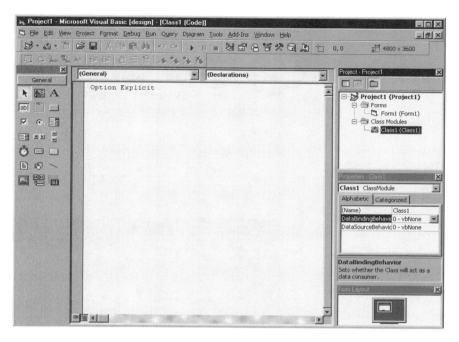

If you are creating a class in a standard program, the Name property is the main property you need to set. If you are creating an ActiveX server, the class also contains the Instancing property, which determines how the class can be used in programs that access the server. You will look at the settings of the Instancing property in the section "Setting the Instancing Property" later in this chapter.

As an exercise in this chapter, you will create a user information class that handles several aspects of logging users into a system and verifying security settings. Exercise 5.1 details the steps needed to start creating this class.

EXERCISE 5.1

Creating the Basic Class Module for the User Information Class

1. Start a new project.

2. Add a class module to the program by choosing the Add Class Module item from the Project menu. Choose the Class Module item from the Add Class dialog box.

3. Name the class **cUserInfo**.

4. Place comments in the Code window that identify the name of the class, the creator of the class, and the purpose of the class. Although this information is optional, it is good practice in order to enhance the reusability of the class. Figure 5.3 shows an example of a class header.

5. Save the project.

FIGURE 5.3

Class headers provide information about the creation of the class.

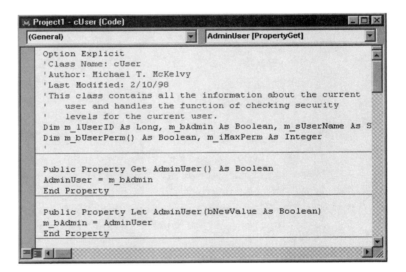

```
Option Explicit
'Class Name: cUser
'Author: Michael T. McKelvy
'Last Modified: 2/10/98
'This class contains all the information about the current
'    user and handles the function of checking security
'    levels for the current user.
Dim m_lUserID As Long, m_bAdmin As Boolean, m_sUserName As S
Dim m_bUserPerm() As Boolean, m_iMaxPerm As Integer
'

Public Property Get AdminUser() As Boolean
AdminUser = m_bAdmin
End Property

Public Property Let AdminUser(bNewValue As Boolean)
m_bAdmin = AdminUser
End Property
```

Creating the Properties of a Class

Microsoft ✓ *Exam Objective*

Design the properties, methods, and events of components.

When you are working with classes, you have to have a way to get data into the class where it can be processed. You pass data between your program and a class (actually an object created from the class) through the properties of the class. These properties provide the public interface of the class, enabling your program to set and retrieve data in the class.

You can create properties in a class module in two ways:

- Create a Public variable

- Create a Property procedure

You can create a Public variable by using the Public keyword in the variable declaration statement in the Declarations section of the class module. The following line shows an example of this:

```
Public lUserID As Long
```

Although this is the simplest way to create a property of a class, it is not the recommended method. Using a Public variable provides open access to the information in the class without providing any means of verifying the data or processing the data for returning a value. This means that invalid information can be passed to a class as easily as good information. Also, using a Public variable does not enable you to create read-only properties that are often needed in a class.

Therefore, the recommended method of creating a property requires three steps:

1. Creating an internal variable to hold the information for use within the class.

2. Creating a Property Let or Property Set procedure to enable the data to be set in the class. These procedures often provide additional processing of the information and validate the data being input.

3. Creating a Property Get procedure to enable the data from the class to be retrieved. Like the Let and Set procedures, a Get procedure often provides additional processing of data prior to returning a value.

Using Internal Variables

The first step in creating a property is to create a variable to hold the information internally in the class. These variables are declared as Private in the Declarations section so that only the class can perform operations on them. After you create the variables, you typically assign default values to them to ensure that valid information is always in the variable, even if no property assignment has been made. Setting the initial values of the internal variables is usually handled in the Initialize event of the class. Exercise 5.2 shows the setup of the internal variables for the user information class.

Creating Internal Variables for a Class

1. Start with the project created in Exercise 5.1.

2. Add Private declaration statements to the Declarations section of the class module to create the internal variables. You need variables to hold the username and the user ID, and to indicate whether the user has administrative rights. For this class, a variable also holds the number of user permissions defined for the application. The code for these declarations is shown below:

```
Private m_lUserID As Long
Private m_bAdmin As Boolean
Private m_sUserName As String
Private m_iMaxPerm As Integer
```

3. In the Code window of the class module, open the Initialize event procedure for the class. You do this by selecting Class from the object list and Initialize from the event list. (Initialize is the default event for the Class object.)

4. Place the following code in the event procedure to set the initial values of the internal variables:

```
m_bAdmin = True
m_lUserID = 0
m_sUserName = "System"
m_iMaxPerm = 0
```

5. Save the project.

The internal variables defined above are preceded by m_. This notation indicates that the variables are module-level variables defined for the class but cannot be used outside the class. You may choose to use a different naming convention in your programming, but be sure you are consistent.

Creating Property Procedures for the Public Interface

As stated above, using Property procedures is the best method for creating the public interface of a class module. There are three types of Property procedures:

Property Let   Enables you to set the value of an internal variable (property) that contains a standard data type, such as integer, single, string, and so on.

Property Set   Enables you to set the value of an internal variable that contains an object reference. For example, you would need to use a Property Set procedure to pass a database to the class.

Property Get   Enables you to retrieve the value of information from the class. You use this procedure whether the information is of a standard data type or an object.

Typically, for each property you create a procedure pair containing either a Let or Set procedure and a Get procedure. If you want to create a read-only property, you create a Get procedure but omit the Let or Set procedure. If you want to create a write-only property, you omit the Get procedure and create only the Let or Set procedure.

You can create Property procedures either by typing code directly into the Code window of the class module or by using the Add Procedure dialog box. Using the dialog box creates a framework for a Property Let and Property Get procedure in your code. To open the Add Procedure dialog box (shown in Figure 5.4), select the Add Procedure item from the Tools menu.

F I G U R E 5.4

Add Procedure
dialog box

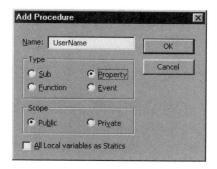

In the dialog box, type the name of the procedure, select the Property option button in the Type selection, and select the Public option in the Scope selection. After setting the options, click the OK button to create the procedure framework, shown in Figure 5.5.

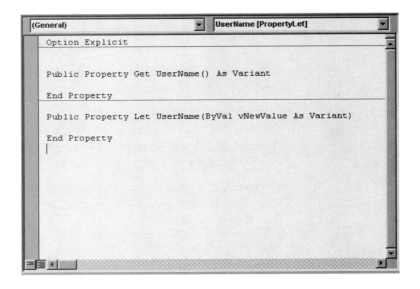

Using a Property Let Procedure   In the Property Let procedure, you need to specify an argument that contains the value being passed to the property. If you use the Procedure dialog box, notice that a variable is created for you with a variant type. Also notice that the argument is passed by value, preventing the Property procedure of your class from changing the value of the variable passed to the procedure.

Unless you have a good reason to do otherwise, pass all arguments to a Property procedure by value (ByVal).

In the declaration of the Property procedure, you need to change the variable type from variant to whatever data type your property will contain. Also, you probably want to change the name of the variable in the argument. If you are creating your procedure by typing in the declaration, you can set up the correct name and type initially. After completing the declaration of the procedure, you need to place code in the procedure that assigns the value passed by the procedure's argument to an internal variable. This is how the data is made available to the class. The following code shows an example of a completed Property Let procedure:

```
Public Property Let FileName(ByVal sInptFile As String)
'Set name of INI file
```

```
'If the input value is null or a zero length string, 'use
current file
If IsNull(sInptFile) Or Len(sInptFile) = 0 Then Exit
Property
m_iniFileName = sInptFile
End Property
```

Using a Property Set Procedure   The Property Set procedure is the only
Property procedure you cannot create automatically with the Procedure
dialog box. You can, of course, type the entire declaration (not a hard task),
or create a Property Let procedure and change the Let keyword to Set. When
you are creating the Set procedure, you need to specify the argument for the
procedure and specify the type of object that is being passed to the procedure. Then, in the code for the procedure, use the Set statement to assign the
argument to the internal object that is used in the class. The following code
shows an example of a Property Set procedure:

```
Public Property Set CurWorkSpace(newWS As Workspace)
'Allow user to set a workspace other than the default.
Set m_WS = newWS
End Property
```

Using a Property Get Procedure   The Property Get procedure is used to
return a value (either a variable or an object) from the class. As such, this
procedure works very much like a function procedure in a standard program
module. In the declaration of the Property Get procedure, you specify the
data type of the procedure. This is the type of information that is being
returned from the class.

WARNING   Make sure that the program statements or variables in the calling program
are of the same or compatible type as the Get procedure.

When you create a Get procedure with the Procedure dialog box, you
must change the data type to the one that you need. After properly setting up
the declaration for the Get procedure, you need to place code in the procedure that sets the value being passed back to the calling program. For standard data types, use a simple assignment statement. If you are passing an

object, you have to use a Set statement. Examples of both types of Property Get procedures are shown in the following code:

```
Public Property Get DBOpen() As Boolean
DBOpen = m_bDBOpen
End Property
Public Property Get CurDataBase() As Database
'If the database is open, return the database object
If m_bDBOpen Then
    Set CurDataBase = m_DB
Else
    Set CurDataBase = Nothing
End If
End Property
```

Creating the Properties of the User Information Class   The user information class that you are creating in the exercises has four main properties. Three of these properties contain the name of the user, the ID of the user, and a flag that indicates whether the user has administrative rights. The fourth property is a read-only property that determines whether the user has access to a specific program function. Exercise 5.3 takes you through the steps of creating the properties of the class.

EXERCISE 5.3

Creating Class Properties

1. Start with the project you created in Exercises 5.1 and 5.2.

2. Add a Property procedure and assign it the name **AdminUser**. This property has both a property Let and Get component. If you create the properties using the Procedure dialog box, you need to change the data type of the argument of the Let procedure and the Get procedure to Boolean.

3. Add code to the Property procedures to set and retrieve the value from the internal variable. The complete code for these Property procedures is:

```
Public Property Get AdminUser() As Boolean
AdminUser = m_bAdmin
```

```
End Property
Public Property Let AdminUser(bNewValue As Boolean)
m_bAdmin = bNewValue
End Property
```

4. Add a second property and name it **UserName**. The data type for this procedure is String. As before, add code to the procedures to handle transferring data to and from the internal variable. The complete code for the Let and Get procedures is:

```
Public Property Get UserName() As String
UserName = m_sUserName
End Property
Public Property Let UserName(sNewValue As String)
m_sUserName = sNewValue
End Property
```

5. Add a third property to the class and name it **UserID**. Set the data type for this property to Long. Add the code to the procedures as shown below:

```
Public Property Get UserID() As Long
UserID = m_lUserID
End Property
Public Property Let UserID(lNewValue As Long)
m_lUserID = lNewValue
End Property
```

6. Finally, add a property named **SecurityOK** to the class. This property is used to determine whether the user has access to a particular function in a program. If you are creating the property by typing in the declarations, you need to create only the Property Get procedure, because this property is read-only. If you are using the Procedure dialog box, you need to erase the Property Let procedure that is created by the dialog box. The Get procedure needs to have an argument passed to it to determine which program function is being checked. This argument is passed ByVal and is an Integer data type. The property itself is a Boolean data type. The complete code for the procedure is:

```
Public Property Get SecurityOK(iPermID As Integer) _
```

```
As Boolean
'Check whether current user has appropriate security
' level
SecurityOK = False
If m_bAdmin Then
    SecurityOK = True
Else
    If iPermID > m_iMaxPerm Or iPermID <= 0 Then _
    Exit Property
    If m_bUserPerm(iPermID) Then SecurityOK = True
End If
End Property
```

7. Save the project.

The m_bUserPerm variable referenced in step 6 of Exercise 5.3 will be created in a later section.

Creating Methods of the Class

After you have created the properties of the class, you need to add procedures to the class to perform tasks with the information. The procedures that
you use are of two varieties:

- Private procedures that are used only within the class

- Public procedures that are the methods of the class exposed to other
  programs

Using Private Procedures for Internal Functions

A variety of small procedures are used in many programs, such as date conversions or particular formatting functions. Typically, you have a library of
such functions that you create over time. These procedures may be stored

in a module to enable you to reuse them in many programs. However, for a class to be truly reusable, it should be completely independent of other modules. Any special functions you need must be included in the class as internal procedures.

To create a private procedure, you can use the Procedure dialog box or declare the procedure by typing in the declaration statement. In either case, you should specify the procedure as Private. Code within the class can use the code, but the procedure is unavailable to any parts of a program outside the class. As an example, the following code might be used to un-encrypt strings that were passed from an encrypted database. This routine is used inside the class but should not be available for the rest of the program.

```
Private Function StringDecrypt(ByVal sInptString As _
String) As String
Dim iChrVal As Integer, I As Integer, sPassStr As String
'Decrypt string
sPassStr = ""
For I = 1 To Len(Trim(sInptString))
    iChrVal = 255 - Asc(Mid(sInptString, I, 1))
    sPassStr = sPassStr & Chr(iChrVal)
Next I
StringDecrypt = UCase(sPassStr)
End Function
```

Using Public Procedures for the External Methods of the Class

Creating methods for a class is the same as creating internal procedures, except that you use the Public keyword in the procedure's declaration statement to enable any program using an object created from the class to access the procedure. These procedures are the same as the Sub and Function procedures that you create for other parts of your program. The procedures can have arguments passed to them and can return a value. Exercise 5.4 shows you how to create the method necessary to set up the permissions array for the user information class.

EXERCISE 5.4

Creating Methods for a Class

1. Start with the project created in previous exercises.

2. Using the Procedure dialog box, add a procedure named **SetPermissions** to class. This is a Sub procedure and must be made Public to make it a method of the class. The appropriate settings of the dialog box are shown in the following graphic.

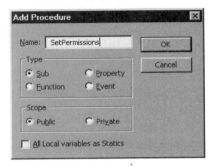

3. Add an argument to the procedure declaration. This argument will be a database object that is passed to the procedure to enable the procedure to retrieve permission information from a security database. The complete declaration of the method is:

    ```
    Public Sub SetPermissions(ByVal m_DB As Database)
    ```

4. Add the code to the procedure to accomplish the task of setting up the permissions array. This code is relatively long and therefore is not shown here. The complete code can be found in the *cUser.cls* file on the CD-ROM.

5. Save the project.

Creating Events for the Class

If you are familiar with forms and controls, you know that these objects have properties, methods, and events that control their behavior. The classes that you create in Visual Basic can also have events. These events enable your class to notify the calling application of occurrences in the class. Creating an event in a class requires two steps:

1. Declaration of the event

2. Writing code to raise the event

When you create the event, you can use the event to pass information to the calling program in the form of parameters. These parameters will show up in the event procedure of an object created from your class. The events that you create behave like the events that are built into Visual Basic's forms and controls. The events are triggered whenever a certain condition occurs, but the calling program responds to the events only if code is written in the event procedure.

One of the key uses of an event in a class is to provide the calling program with information about the status of a long operation. For example, if a class is being used to perform a spell check of a long document, you might want to use an event to indicate when the task has reached certain completion points. Exercise 5.5 shows you how to create such an event in a class.

EXERCISE 5.5

Creating an Event in a Class

1. Start a new project.

2. Add a class module to the project.

3. Using the Procedure dialog box, create a public Sub procedure named **SpellCheck**.

4. Open the Procedure dialog box a second time to create an event procedure. To do this, check the Event button in the Type selection and specify the name of the procedure as **CheckStatus**. Click the OK button to create the procedure in the Code window. The code created by the Procedure Wizard will be placed in the Declarations section of the class module.

5. Add a parameter to the event procedure declaration to enable the event to pass information to the calling program. Name the variable

Status and set it to be passed by value. The final appearance of the declaration is shown in the next graphic.

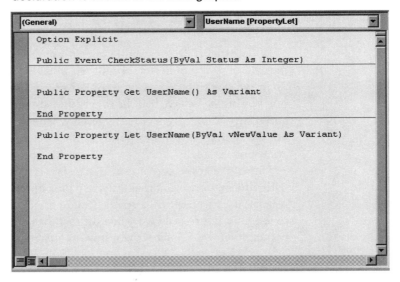

6. Add the following code to the SpellCheck procedure to raise the event.

```
iStatus = Int(100 * iCurrentPage / iTotalPages)
RaiseEvent CheckStatus(iStatus)
```

Using the Friend Declaration

One useful option in the declaration of properties and methods in a class is the Friend declaration. This option is particularly useful in creating ActiveX servers. The Friend declaration enables you to make a property or method available to other modules in the current project (the one in which the class is defined), without making the routine truly public. You can create necessary routines for data conversion or other functions and declare them as Friend. Your ActiveX server can then use these routines internally, but programs that call the classes of the server are not permitted to use the methods or view the properties, increasing the functionality of classes in your programs.

To make a property or method a Friend function, simply replace the Public or Private (typically Private) keyword in the procedure declaration with the Friend keyword. The following code shows an example of the Friend declaration.

```
Friend Function StringDecrypt(ByVal sInptString As String) _
As String
Dim iChrVal As Integer, I As Integer, sPassStr As String
'Decrypt string
sPassStr = ""
For I = 1 To Len(Trim(sInptString))
    iChrVal = 255 - Asc(Mid(sInptString, I, 1))
    sPassStr = sPassStr & Chr(iChrVal)
Next I
StringDecrypt = UCase(sPassStr)
End Function
```

Creating Classes with the Class Builder

Adding class modules to your project is one way to build classes in your programs. Visual Basic provides you with an additional way to create and manage classes in your programs—the Class Builder utility. The Class Builder enables you to implement a sort of inheritance in Visual Basic classes by handling all the work of copying properties and methods from a base class to child classes. In addition, the Class Builder makes it easy for you to create collections of classes.

The Class Builder is one of the add-ins that ships with Visual Basic. To use the Class Builder, you first have to add it to the Add-Ins menu by choosing the Add-In Manager item from the Add-Ins menu. This action displays a dialog box, shown in Figure 5.6, that enables you to choose the add-ins you want loaded for Visual Basic. Choose the Class Builder add-in and click the OK button.

After you have made the Class Builder add-in available, you need to start it in order to start building classes. Start the Class Builder by choosing the Class Builder item from the Add-Ins menu. This brings up the Class Builder form, shown in Figure 5.7.

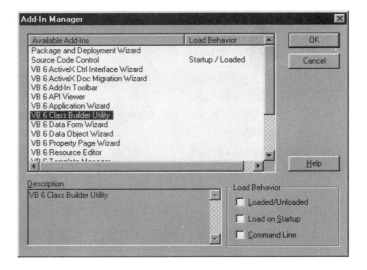

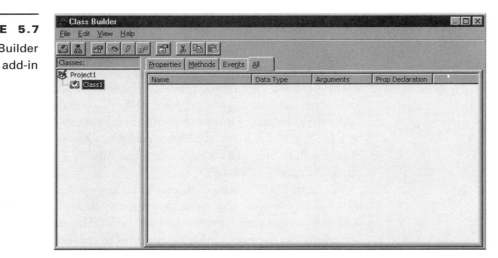

Creating the Base Class

After the Class Builder is open, you are ready to start creating classes. This section covers how to create a class from scratch, assuming that the class is not based on one that already exists.

To start a new class, you can click the New Class button at the upper left of the Class Builder. You can also select the New item from the File menu and then select the Class item. In either case, you are shown the Class Module Builder seen in Figure 5.8. From this dialog box, you can set the name of the class and, if applicable, set the Instancing property on the Properties tab of the dialog box. The Properties tab also includes a drop-down list that enables you to specify the name of a class on which the new class should be based. The names in the list are classes that are defined in the current project. The Attributes tab of the dialog box lets you include a description of the class and provide a help context ID for use in creating online help. After filling out the information in the dialog box, click the OK button to create the class module.

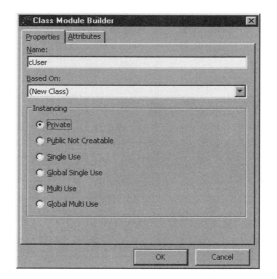

Adding Properties to the Class

After the class is created, you can begin adding properties, methods, and events to the class. Start with properties. To add a new property to the class, click the New Property button on the toolbar, which brings up the Property Builder dialog box shown in Figure 5.9.

You can immediately see one advantage of using the Property Builder over using the Procedure dialog box described earlier: You can specify the property's data type as well as declare the property a Friend function, which cannot be done from the Procedures dialog box. On the Properties tab of the Property

FIGURE 5.9

Creating properties
with Property Builder

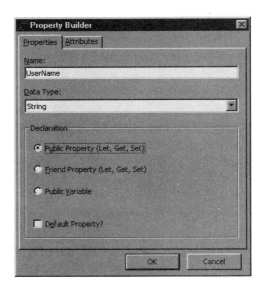

Builder, you specify the name, data type, and declaration type of the property. If you need to use arguments in the Property procedure, you must add these by hand after the Class Builder creates the class in your project. As with the Class Module Builder, the Attributes tab of the Property Builder enables you to create a description of the property and to provide a help context ID. After filling out the information, you can click the OK button. The new property then appears on the Properties tab of the Class Builder.

Adding Methods and Events to the Class

After creating the properties, you can continue creating your class by adding methods and events to the class. To add a method to the class, click the New Method button to bring up the Method Builder dialog box shown in Figure 5.10.

To complete the information in the dialog box, you first need to specify a name for the method. Next, you can specify the type of data to return from the method. Specifying the return data type determines the type of procedure that is created. If you specify a data type, the Method Builder creates a Function procedure. Otherwise, a Sub procedure is created. Next, you need to choose whether the method is declared as a Friend method. If you choose not

F I G U R E 5.10

Method Builder dialog
box for creating
methods in the class

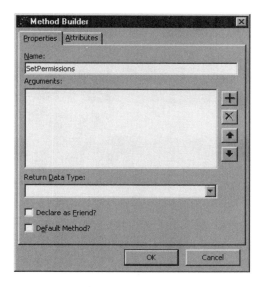

to declare the method as Friend, the method is declared as a Public procedure. Finally, you can choose whether to make this method the default method of the class.

After setting the basic properties of the method, you can specify the arguments that will be used to pass data to the method. Using this process makes it easier to create the declaration of the method than typing in the declaration by hand. You add a new argument by clicking the plus (+) button on the Method Builder. This brings up the Add Argument dialog box shown in Figure 5.11. In this dialog box, you set the name and data type of the argument and indicate whether the argument should be passed by value or by reference. You can also specify whether the argument is optional or required. After adding an argument, it appears in the argument list of the Method Builder.

The Method Builder also lets you remove arguments and change the order in which they are called in the declaration. You manage the arguments through the buttons to the right of the argument list in the Method Builder.

Adding events to the class is similar to adding methods. You click the New Event button to bring up the Event Builder shown in Figure 5.12. You then fill in the name of the event and create any needed arguments for the event.

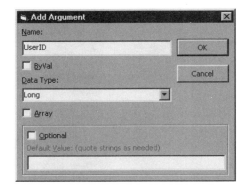

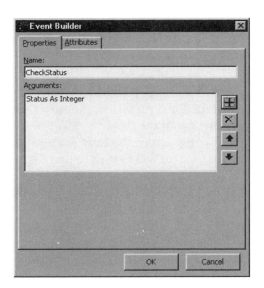

Creating the Child Classes

After you have created at least one class in the Class Builder, you can create additional classes that are based on another class in the project. When you add a new class, you simply select the parent class from the drop-down list in the Class Module Builder. As the class is created, the properties, methods, and events of the parent class are copied to the new child class. This process helps in creating hierarchies of classes, but does not provide true inheritance.

Creating the Classes for the Project

After you have defined all the necessary classes for a project, you can create the classes. Choose the Update Project item from the File menu to create the declarations of all properties, methods, and events for all classes that you defined. At this point, you can enter the code that is required to implement all the functions that you want your classes to perform. For all the properties you defined for a class, the Class Builder creates a local variable to hold the value of the property and sets up the assignment statements to set and retrieve the value of the property. The Builder always creates a Property Let/Get or Property Set/Get pair of procedures. If you want to create a read-only or write-only property, you need to delete the appropriate procedure. The output of the Class Builder for a defined class is shown in Figure 5.13.

F I G U R E 5.13

Procedure built by the Class Builder

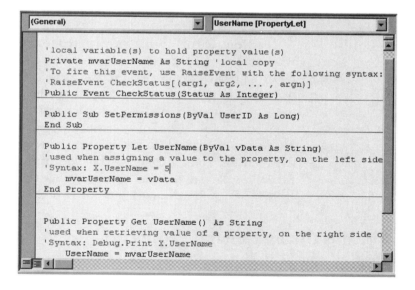

```
(General)                              ▼   UserName [PropertyLet]        ▼

'local variable(s) to hold property value(s)
Private mvarUserName As String 'local copy
'To fire this event, use RaiseEvent with the following syntax:
'RaiseEvent CheckStatus[(arg1, arg2, ... , argn)]
Public Event CheckStatus(Status As Integer)

Public Sub SetPermissions(ByVal UserID As Long)
End Sub

Public Property Let UserName(ByVal vData As String)
'used when assigning a value to the property, on the left side
'Syntax: X.UserName = 5
    mvarUserName = vData
End Property


Public Property Get UserName() As String
'used when retrieving value of a property, on the right side o
'Syntax: Debug.Print X.UserName
    UserName = mvarUserName
```

Defining the Scope of the Class

Like variables and standard procedures, classes have a specifically defined scope. That is, the use of a class can be confined to a certain application or can be made available to numerous applications. The scope of a class is determined by two things: where the class is defined and the setting of the Instancing property.

You can include a class module in almost any project. Making the class available to multiple applications refers to its availability after it is compiled into a program or ActiveX server.

Public and Private Classes

A class can have one of two scopes, Private or Public. By design, any class defined in a standard executable program is a Private class. It can be used from anywhere in the program but cannot be called by other applications running at the same time.

Therefore, the only time that you need to define the scope of a class is when you are creating an ActiveX server. In a server application, you can still create a Private class. A Private class can be used by the program routines within the server, but it is not exposed to other applications as an object available for use. However, an ActiveX server can have Public classes as well as Private classes. These Public classes are used to make business objects and business rules available to multiple programs in a multi-tier client-server environment. You can create several types of Public classes. Whether a class is Public or Private and which type of Public class is created are determined by the setting of the Instancing property of the class.

Setting the Instancing Property

Microsoft
Exam
Objective

Compile a project with class modules into a COM component.

- Set properties to control the instancing of a class within a COM component.

The Instancing property lets you determine how your class will be used by other programs. Again, this property is available only for classes that are created in an ActiveX server (either EXE or DLL) or in an ActiveX control. The Instancing property has six possible settings:

Private   The class cannot be used outside the application in which it is defined. This is the default setting of the property.

PublicNonCreatable   The class can be used by other applications. However, in order for the other applications to use the object, it must first be created by the server. Other applications cannot use the New keyword or the CreateObject function to create instances of the class.

SingleUse   Other applications can create and use objects of the class. However, each time an object is created from the class, a new instance of the class is started.

GlobalSingleUse   Similar to SingleUse, but an application does not have to specifically create the object to use its methods and properties. The methods and properties are treated as global functions.

MultiUse   Similar to SingleUse, but only a single instance of your class is created. All objects from the class are generated from the single instance.

GlobalMultiUse   Similar to MultiUse except that the methods and properties are treated as global functions. Applications do not have to specifically create an instance of the class.

To set the value of the Instancing property, you simply select the desired value from the list of available values in the Properties window. You cannot set the value of the Instancing property at run time.

Using a Class in a Program

Up to this point, you have seen how to create a class and how to add properties, methods, and events to the class. However, a class by itself is not very useful. A defined class is like a Visual Basic control that is in the toolbox. It is available for use, but you are not using it in your program until you create an object from the class. Although controls are created visually in the design mode, in order to create an object from a class, you have to write code.

Creating an Instance of the Class

Before you can use an object that is based on your class, you have to create the object. There are two methods of creating objects in Visual Basic: using the CreateObject function and using the New keyword.

For most objects you create, using the New keyword is the preferred method. Using this method enables you to specify the type of object that the program will be creating, and the compiler can bind the class information to the object variable during compilation. This is known as early binding of an object. Because the binding is handled during compilation, the creation of objects with the New keyword is faster than using the CreateObject function. Another benefit is that the compiler can perform program checking for correct method and function calls. In addition, using the New keyword makes it easier for you to use the objects as you are programming. Because Visual Basic knows the type of object you are creating, it can provide you with a drop-down list of properties and methods, as shown in Figure 5.14.

F I G U R E 5.14

Early-bound objects enable Visual Basic to display lists of properties and methods.

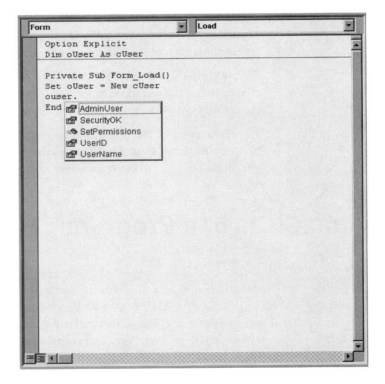

There are two ways to use the New keyword in creating an object from a class. First, you can specify the New keyword in the declaration of the object variable. Then, when you use any of the properties or methods of the object, the object is created. This is illustrated in the following code:

```
Dim oUser As New cUser
oUser.UserName = "Mike"
```

The second way to use the New keyword is in conjunction with the Set command. In this method, you declare an object variable and then use the Set command to explicitly create the object. This is illustrated in the following code:

```
Dim oUser As cUser
Set oUser = New cUser
```

The CreateObject function is typically used when you do not know in advance which type of object will by created for a specific object variable. In this case, the information about the object is not known until the program is run and the object is created. This is known as late binding of the object. CreateObject is also typically used with objects that are created from ActiveX servers. To use the CreateObject function, you declare a variable as an object and then use the function to create the specific instance of the object, as shown in the following code:

```
Dim oUser As Object
Set oUser = CreateObject("excel.sheet")
```

Accessing the Properties and Methods of the Class

After you have created an object from the class, you can access the properties and methods of the object as you can for forms and controls. Using dot notation, you specify the object variable, then the method or property you want to use. Depending on the setup of the Property procedures (Let or Get), you can set or retrieve property values. You can also invoke methods using the dot notation. The following code shows how the properties and methods of the user information class are used in a program.

```
oUser.UserID = LogRset!UserID
oUser.UserName = LogRset!FirstName & " " & LogRset!LastName
oUser.AdminUser = LogRset!AdminUser
```

```
oUser.SetPermissions MainDB
If Not oUser.SecurityOK(5) Then
    MsgBox "You are not authorized to access this
function.", _ vbExclamation
    Exit Sub
End If
```

Destroying the Class Instance

After you have finished using an object, it is good practice to destroy the object, because destroying the object frees up any memory that was used by the object and performs housekeeping operations in your program. Although objects are supposed to be destroyed automatically by Visual Basic when the object variable goes out of scope, it is best to specifically destroy the object.

To destroy an object, you set the object variable to the keyword Nothing. This action clears the object variable and releases memory assigned to it. The following code shows how to destroy the object created from the user information class.

```
Set oUser = Nothing
```

Summary

This chapter has provided you with a detailed look at how to create classes in Visual Basic. You have seen how to create the class module and how to add properties, methods, and events to the class. You have also seen how to use the Class Builder to create and manage a hierarchy of classes in a project. You learned about the Friend declaration and how the Instancing property affects the scope of a class. To successfully pass the sections of the certification exam that deal with classes, you should pay particular attention to the creation of properties and methods. You should also have a good understanding of the scope of a class and the use of the Instancing property. The specific exam objectives covered in this chapter were:

- Design the properties, methods, and events of components.

- Compile a project with class modules into a COM component.
    - Set properties to control the instancing of a class within a COM component.

If you still don't feel comfortable with all the concepts, go over the exercises a second time before you start the review questions.

Review Questions

1. What are the three types of Property procedures that can be created for a class?

    A. Add, Retrieve, Remove

    B. Item, Add, Remove

    C. Let, Set, Get

    D. Let, Get, Object

2. Which Property procedure is used to retrieve the value of a property?

    A. Retrieve

    B. Get

    C. Item

    D. Value

3. How do you create a method for a class?

    A. Use a Method procedure declaration.

    B. Use a Property Set procedure.

    C. Create a Public procedure in the class module.

    D. Create a Private procedure in the class module.

4. What command triggers an event created in a class?

   A. RaiseEvent

   B. SetEvent

   C. Trigger

   D. FireEvent

5. How do you create a Public class in a standard executable?

   A. Set the Public property to True.

   B. Set the Instancing property to SingleUse.

   C. No special requirements.

   D. You cannot create a Public class in a standard executable.

6. What does the Friend declaration do?

   A. Makes a class available for use by any program

   B. Makes the methods of the class usable by other parts of the program in which the class is defined

   C. Limits your program to creating a single object from the class

   D. Keeps you from having to specify the object name to reference the methods of the class

7. What does the Instancing property do?

   A. Sets the number of objects that can be created from the class

   B. Determines whether the class inherited properties from another class

   C. Specifies how the class in an ActiveX server can be used by other programs

   D. Specifies how the class in a standard program can be used by other programs

8. How do you use a class in your program?

    A. Simply call the methods and properties like any other procedure.

    B. Create an object based on the class using the Set statement or New keyword.

    C. Use the Call statement to access the class directly.

    D. Drag a copy of the class from the Project window to the form where you will need it.

9. Which of the following statements can be used to create an object based on a class? Check all that apply.

    A. Set oUser = New cUser

    B. oUser = cUser

    C. Dim oUser As New cUser

    D. CreateObject("cUser")

CHAPTER

6

Working with Collections

Microsoft Exam Objectives Covered in This Chapter:

■ Create data input forms and dialog boxes.

  – Use the Forms collection to manipulate forms at run time.

  – Use the Controls collection to manipulate controls at run time.

Have you ever had a collection of something, like coins, dolls, baseball cards, or even bottle caps? If you have had collections, and probably even if you haven't, you know that a collection is a group of similar objects that are organized in some fashion. If you are a serious collector, you probably change the contents of your collection through buying, selling, and trading items. You also probably have a method of uniquely identifying each item in your collection.

Well, if you have even a basic understanding of the concept of collections, you are well on your way to understanding collections in Visual Basic. Visual Basic uses collections to provide an organizing structure for groups of related objects. In this chapter, you will look first at collections in general, then at a few of the specific collections that are used in Visual Basic. There are two collections that you will pay particular attention to—the Forms collection and the Controls collection. These two collections are of particular interest because they are the subject of two of the certification exam objectives.

Understanding Collections

Collections in Visual Basic are similar to the collections that you find in real life. Visual Basic collections provide a means of organizing a group of related objects. Some examples of collections used in Visual Basic are:

- Forms
- Controls
- Database fields

- TreeView nodes
- ListView items
- Toolbar buttons

In addition to these built-in collections, Visual Basic enables you to create your own collections through the use of the Collection object. A Collection object can be used to create and manage a group of class objects, or a collection can be used as a way to store data instead of using an array.

Although a collection is typically used to handle a group of related items, Visual Basic does not require that all the members of a collection be the same. For example, you can have collection members that are different data types.

All collections in Visual Basic have the following attributes in common:

- You can add items to the collection.
- You can remove items from the collection.
- There is a method to refer to specific members of the collection.
- The Collection object keeps a count of the number of members in the collection.

Although the mechanics of handling these attributes may differ (for example, forms are added to the Forms collection using the Load statement instead of the Add method), all collections in Visual Basic support these attributes.

Using the Methods of a Collection

The Collection object in Visual Basic has three methods that you can use to manage the collection of objects: Add, Item, and Remove. These methods are responsible for adding and removing elements from the collection and retrieving individual items from the collection. If you need additional methods, you can create a wrapper class around the Collection object and create new methods by using Sub procedures. Although this particular task is beyond the scope of this book, you have learned about creating classes and their methods in Chapter 5,

"Creating Classes in a Program." In this section, you will focus on the built-in methods of the Collection object.

Using the Add Method

Most collections in Visual Basic, whether they are built-in collections or ones you create with the Collection object, use the Add method to enable you to add members to the collection. The syntax of the Add method specifies the name of the collection, the method itself, and the item to be added to the collection. In addition, several optional parameters are often included:

Key Defines a unique character string used to identify the item

Before Specifies that the new item should be placed in the collection in front of the item identified in the Before parameter

After Specifies that the new item should be placed in the collection behind the item identified in the After parameter

The use of the Before or After parameters enables you to handle the sorting of items in a collection as they are added, which can be a powerful method of storing information in a sorted order. The Before and After parameters can be specified as either the numeric index of an item or as the Key value of the item. The following code shows how the Add method is used to place a new item in a collection.

```
Dim colUsers As New Collection
Dim oUser As New cUser
oUser.UserID = 101
colUsers.Add oUser, "mmckelvy"
```

Using the Remove Method

Of course, if you can add items to a collection, you need to be able to remove items from the collection as well. With the Collection object, this is handled by the Remove method. To use the Remove method, you simply specify the name of the collection, the method name, and the index of the item to be removed. The index used by the Remove method can be either the numeric index of the item or the Key property of the item in the collection. The following code shows the use of the Remove method.

```
colUsers.Remove 1
```

An error occurs if the item specified in the Remove method does not exist in the collection.

Using the Item Method

The final method of a collection is the Item method. This method is used to access a specific item from the collection. The Item method is used in all collections, including the Forms and Controls collections, making it the only method that is truly common to all collections. The Item method is also the default method of any collection, meaning that if you do not specify the name of a method, the Item method is assumed. The Item method can be used in one of two manners—using the Index value of an item or using the Key value of an item.

Referencing an Object by Its Index   One use of the Item method is to retrieve a specific item of a collection using its Index value. When used in this manner, the index is enclosed in parentheses following the method name, as shown in the following code:

```
Debug.Print colUsers.Item(1).UserID
```

Also, because the Item method is the default method of a collection, the following code can be used to achieve the same results:

```
Debug.Print colUsers(1).UserID
```

Because it is difficult to keep track of the index location of a number of items, the Index value is typically used with the Item method to process all the members of a collection. This can be accomplished through the use of a For loop, as illustrated in the following code:

```
Dim I As Integer
For I = 1 To colUsers.Count
    Debug.Print colUsers.Item(I).UserID
Next I
```

Using the Key Property of an Object   The other way to use the Item method is with the Key value of the items in the collection. The use of the Key value makes it easier to retrieve a specific item in the collection because these string identifiers are not dependent on the location of the item in the collection. When the Key value is used, your program must pass a string (either in the form of a literal string or a string variable) to the Item method. The following code shows the use of both a variable and a literal string:

```
colUsers.Item("mmckelvy").UserID = 101
Dim sItemKey As String
sItemKey = "mmckelvy"
colUsers.Item(sItemKey).UserID = 101
```

Also, as with specifying the Index value, you can leave out the Item method name in referencing an item with the Key value, as shown in the following code:

```
colUsers("mmckelvy").UserID = 101
Dim sItemKey As String
sItemKey = "mmckelvy"
colUsers(sItemKey).UserID = 101
```

Working with the Properties of a Collection

As stated earlier, the Collection object has only a single property, the Count property. The purpose of the Count property is to tell you how many items are in the collection. This property is read-only, meaning that you can retrieve the value of the property, but you cannot set a new value. The value of the Count property changes as items are added or removed from the collection using the Add or Remove methods. The following code shows the use of the Count property to run a loop that populates a list box with the names of all current users in a program.

```
Dim I As Integer
lstUsers.Clear
For I = 1 To colUsers.Count
    lstUsers.AddItem colUsers(I).Name
Next I
```

Working with the Forms

Microsoft ✓ *Exam* *Objective*

Create data input forms and dialog boxes.

- Use the Forms collection to manipulate forms at run time.

The Forms collection is a specialized collection created by Visual Basic. The collection contains a reference to each form in a program that is loaded in memory, including all MDI child forms, an MDI parent form, and any standard forms that may be loaded at a given time. It is important to note that the Forms collection contains only a list of loaded forms, not a list of all forms that you may have defined in your program. For example, Figure 6.1 shows the Project window indicating all the forms defined for a program. However, the Forms collection would list only the loaded forms, like the ones shown in Figure 6.2.

The Forms collection has several primary uses in a program. The most common uses are:

- Changing the common properties (such as Font) of all loaded forms

- Determining if a specific form is loaded

- Ensuring that all forms are explicitly closed prior to exiting a program

Working with the Collection Methods

As stated in the general discussion of collections, a Collection object uses the Add and Remove methods to change the membership of the collection. The Forms collection does not support the Add or Remove methods, but instead uses the Load and Unload statements to control the membership of the Forms collection. To illustrate this, Exercise 6.1 walks you through creating a simple program for checking the names of loaded forms.

FIGURE 6.1

Many forms can be
defined for a program.

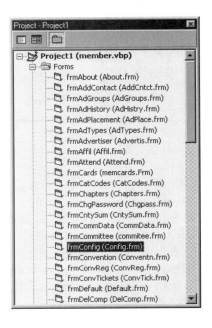

FIGURE 6.2

Only loaded forms are
part of the collection.

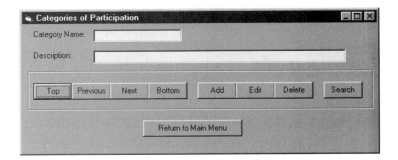

EXERCISE 6.1

Determining Which Forms Are Loaded

1. Start a new project.

2. Add a second form to the project.

3. On the second form, place a single command button that unloads the
   form. Place the command **Unload Me** in the Click event of the command button.

EXERCISE 6.1 (CONTINUED)

4. On the first form of the project, place two command buttons named **cmdForm2** and **cmdListForms**.

5. In the Click event of the cmdForm2 button, place the code **Form2.Show**. This code loads and displays the second form.

6. The cmdListForms button is used to displays the names of the currently loaded forms in the program. In the Click event of the cmdListForms button, place the following code:

```
Dim I As Integer
For I = 0 To Forms.Count - 1
    Debug.Print Forms(I).Name
Next I
```

7. Run the program and check the list of forms as you start the program, after you show Form2, and after you unload Form2. Figure 6.3 shows the output in the Immediate window when both forms are loaded.

FIGURE 6.3

Displaying a list of loaded forms

The Forms collection is zero-based, meaning that the first Index value of the forms collection is zero instead of one, as is the case for many other collections.

When using collections, whether built-in or user-created, be sure to test the operation of the collection for the item with an Index value of zero. Performing this check is the only way to avoid program errors because some collections are zero-based, and others are one-based.

Using the For...Each Loop

As you saw in Exercise 6.1, you can reference the properties of a form by specifying the item in the Forms collection and specifying the property of interest. You can retrieve or set property values for any item in the Forms collection. As shown in the exercise, you can use the Index value to access a specific item, or you can use the Key value as explained in the general discussion of collections. The Key value for a form is simply its Name property.

Exercise 6.1 showed the use of a For loop to display the names of all the forms. This form of the loop used *I* as an index variable and used the Count property of the Forms collection to determine how many times to run through the loop. Although this is one way to write the code, there is another preferred method. A special case of the For loop is used for handling collections—the For...Each loop. This type of loop performs the enclosed code once for every item in a collection. The following code shows how the loop to display the form names would appear if a For...Each loop were used:

```
Dim tstForm As Form
For Each tstForm In Forms
    Debug.Print tstForm.Name
Next tstForm
```

Exercise 6.2 shows you how to use a For...Each loop to change the background color of all loaded forms.

EXERCISE 6.2

Using a For...Each Loop with the Forms Collection

1. Starting with the project created in Exercise 6.1, add another command button to Form1 of the project. Name the command button **cmdColor** and set the Caption to **Change Colors**.

2. Add the following code to the Click event of the cmdColor button.

```
Dim tstForm As Form
For Each tstForm In Forms
tstForm.BackColor = vbGreen
Next tstForm
```

3. Run the code, load the second form, and click the Change Colors button.

You can use this method to set a specific property of all the loaded forms in a program. You can also use the For...Each loop in an exit routine to ensure that all loaded forms are closed before you ultimately exit the program. The following code shows how this is handled:

```
Dim frmLoaded As Form
On Error Resume Next
'Unload forms
For Each frmLoaded In Forms
    If frmLoaded.Name <> "frmMain" Then
        Unload frmLoaded
    End If
Next frmLoaded
Unload frmMain
'Exit the program
End
```

If you want to work with only some of the forms in the Forms collection, do not use the For...Each loop.

Working with the Controls Collection

Microsoft Exam Objective	**Create data input forms and dialog boxes.**
	▪ Use the Controls collection to manipulate controls at run time.

The Controls collection is very similar to the Forms collection. The Controls collection provides you access to each of the controls that are on a particular form. As you might guess, this implies that there is a Controls collection for each form in your program. Like the Forms collection, the Controls collection does not support the Add and Remove methods. Instead, controls are added to or removed from the collection using the Load and Unload statements.

Like all collections, the Controls collection implements the Item method (the default method) to enable you to access a specific control, and the Count property, which tells you the number of controls in the collection and, therefore, on the given form. Some typical uses of the Controls collection are:

- Modifying a specific property of every control, such as Font or ForeColor

- Working with database routines to create a generic data access form or data display routine

- Showing or hiding specific types or groups of controls

Understanding the Differences between Control Arrays and the Controls Collection

Because both control arrays and the Controls collection work with groups of controls and because both use an Index value to reference a specific control, you might think that similarities exist between the Controls collection and a control array. However, these are two different entities with two very different purposes. The following lists of characteristics should help you understand the differences between these two entities.

Control Arrays

A control array has the following characteristics:

- All elements of a control array are the same type of control.

- All elements of a control array have the same name.

- The Index properties of the control are set when the control is created and cannot be changed.

- The elements of a control array share the same set of event procedures.

- In code, an element of the control array is referenced by its name and Index property, as shown in the following example:

```
cmdNavigation(1).Caption = "First Record"
```

Controls Collection

By contrast, the Controls collection has the following characteristics:

- The Controls collection contains all controls (including control arrays) on a form regardless of type.

- The elements of the Controls collection can have different names.

- The Index value of an element in the collection is determined by the order in which the control was added to the form.

- There are no events associated with the Controls collection.

- In code, a member of the Controls collection is referenced by its index within the collection, as shown in the following example:

```
Debug.Print Controls(0).Name
```

You do not have to specify a form name when using the Controls collection. If you do not specify a name, the form containing the code is assumed to be the active form.

Making Global Changes to Controls

Like the Forms collection (and other collections), the elements of the Controls collection can be manipulated with a For loop or a For...Each loop. This process makes it easy to change the controls on a form, for example, to select a font to be used for all the controls. After the user selects the font, a loop can be used to implement the requested change. Exercise 6.3 illustrates this technique.

EXERCISE 6.3

Making Changes to All the Controls on a Form

1. Start a new project.

2. Add a series of labels, text boxes, and command buttons to the form to create a data entry form like the one shown in Figure 6.4.

3. Add another command button to the form and name it **cmdChange-Text**. Set the Caption of the control to **Change Text**.

4. Add the following code to the Click event of the cmdChangeText button:

```
Dim chgControl As Control
For Each chgControl In Controls
    chgControl.Font.Name = "Times New Roman"
```

```
        chgControl.Font.Bold = True
Next chgControl
```

5. Run the program and see what happens when you click the Change Text button. Figure 6.5 shows the new appearance.

F I G U R E   6.4

Initial appearance of the data entry form

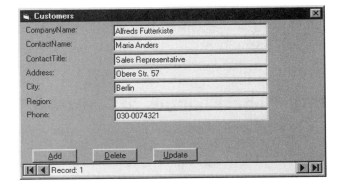

F I G U R E   6.5

The data entry form after the font change

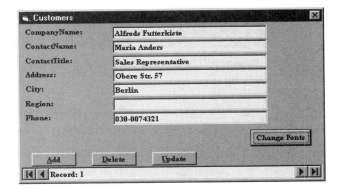

Typically, you should use a Common Dialog control to enable the user to select any font, and then use the selected font as the new value for the Font properties of the controls.

Working with Specific Controls in the Collection

You might have noticed in Exercise 6.3 that you used only labels, text boxes, and command buttons—controls that all have a Font property. You probably know that not all controls have a Font property. If you had such a control on your form, the code in Exercise 6.3 would still try to set a value for the property, but would, of course, cause an error. Obviously, you need a way to determine which type of control is being accessed and process or skip the control accordingly.

Determining the Type of a Control

The first step in handling multiple types of controls within the Controls collection is determining the type of control that is being accessed. You determine the type of control using the TypeOf clause. This statement is used as part of a conditional statement, as illustrated in the following code:

```
If TypeOf chgControl Is CommandButton Then
    chgControl.Font.Name = "Times New Roman"
    chgControl.Font.Bold = True
End If
```

Each control in Visual Basic has a type constant that can be used with the TypeOf keyword to determine if the current control is of a particular type. You can access a list of these constants in the VB library using the Object Browser, as shown in Figure 6.6.

FIGURE 6.6

Control types
displayed in the
Object Browser

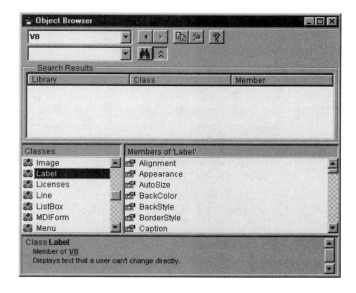

Setting the Properties of Specific Control Groups

Using the TypeOf clause and a series of If statements, you can handle processing for any type of control. The following code modifies the code presented in Exercise 6.3 to change the Font of text boxes and labels, but leaves other controls alone.

```
Dim chgControl As Control
For Each chgControl In Controls
    If TypeOf chgControl Is TextBox Then
        chgControl.Font.Name = "Times New Roman"
        chgControl.Font.Bold = True
    ElseIf TypeOf chgControl Is Label Then
        chgControl.Font.Name = "Times New Roman"
    End If
Next chgControl
```

Using code such as this eliminates possible errors from trying to set properties for controls that do not support them, such as setting a Font property for a Line control.

Although it would seem that a Select Case structure would be preferable to the nested If statements, this is not feasible due to the nature of the TypeOf clause. The TypeOf clause requires the use of the Is keyword, which cannot be used in a Select Case structure.

Summary

This chapter has taught you about how collections work. You have learned about the three methods common to most collections—Add, Item, and Remove methods. You also learned that all collections have a Count property that tells you how many elements are in the collection. In addition to the general information about collections, you learned how to use the Forms collection to manipulate the loaded forms in a program and how to use the Controls collection to work with all the controls on a specific form.

This information will help you meet two of the following Microsoft certification exam objectives:

- Create data input forms and dialog boxes.
  - Use the Forms collection to manipulate forms at run time.
  - Use the Controls collection to manipulate controls at run time.

Review Questions

1. What three methods does the Collection object support?

   A. Load, Unload, Count

   B. Add, Remove, Item

   C. Add, Delete, Index

   D. Add, Remove, Sort

2. What method is common to all collections?

   A. Add

   B. Delete

   C. Remove

   D. Item

3. What is the only property supported by a collection?

   A. Name

   B. Index

   C. Count

   D. Type

4. What does the Forms collection contain?

   A. A list of all forms in a project

   B. A list of all currently loaded forms

    C. A list of all visible forms

    D. All the child forms of an MDI application

5. How are forms added to the Forms collection?

    A. By adding a form to a project

    B. By using the Add method of the Forms collection

    C. By using the Load statement

    D. By activating a form

6. What does the Controls collection contain?

    A. A list of all controls on a form

    B. A list of all the controls used by your program

    C. A list of visible controls

    D. The names of all control arrays on the form

7. What are key differences between a control array and the Controls collection? Check all that apply.

    A. A control array contains controls of a single type; the Controls collection contains controls of many types.

    B. The elements of a control array all have the same name; the elements of the Controls collection can have different names.

    C. The elements of a control array do not share any events; the elements of the Controls collection do.

    D. A control array is simply another name for the Controls collection.

8. How do you determine the type of a control?

    A. Use the IsType function.

    B. Use the TypeOf clause.

    C. Check the Type property of the control.

    D. Use the prefix of the control name.

9. Why is it important to determine the type of a control?

   A. To process only controls that support a given property.

   B. Some control types are not included in the Controls collection.

   C. For programmer information only.

   D. To skip controls that are part of an array.

10. What are the two methods of referencing an element of a collection?

   A. Using the name value or the Index value

   B. Using the Index value and the Key value

   C. Using the name and type

   D. Using name and Key

11. Which of the following code segments can be used to process all the controls on a form? Check all that apply.

   A.

```
For I = 0 To Controls.Count - 1
    Debug.Print Controls(I).Name
Next
```

   B.

```
For All Controls
    Debug.Print Control.Name
Next Control
```

   C.

```
Dim chgControl as Control For Each chgControl In Controls
    Debug.Print chgControl.Name
Next chgControl
```

   D.

```
For I = 0 To Controls.UBound
    Debug.Print Controls.Item(I).Name
Next I
```

PART

II

Working with Databases

CHAPTER 7

Accessing Data with the ADO Data Control

Microsoft Exam Objectives Covered in This Chapter:

- Access and manipulate a data source by using ADO and the ADO Data control.

- Use data binding to display and manipulate data from a data source.

Each new version of Visual Basic provides the developer with new ways to access and work with data in databases. The first major step along this path was the introduction of Data Access Objects (DAO) and the Data control introduced in version 3. DAO was great for desktop databases but was not as good on remote databases such as Microsoft SQL Servers. Next came Remote Data Objects (RDO) and the Remote Data control introduced in version 4. RDO made it easier to link to database servers and remote databases. Now in version 6 of Visual Basic, you have a new way of accessing data—ActiveX Data Objects (ADO) and the ADO Data control (ADODC). ADO provides a way to access almost any database (local or remote) using the same code and the same data control. Although Visual Basic 6 supports DAO and RDO, Microsoft recommends ADO for all new projects because ADO is where Microsoft will focus their attention for future enhancements.

Although there are numerous ways to access data from a Visual Basic program, by far the easiest is through the ADO Data control (ADODC) and bound controls. The ADODC provides an easy-to-use link between your program and the data you are trying to access. This link can be created by placing an ADODC on a form and setting a few properties (as few as two for a default setup). After the link is established, data can be displayed on the form by using bound controls. Bound controls, in most cases, are the standard Visual Basic controls for which you set the data access properties.

Bound controls enable you to specify an ADODC and a field from the recordset accessed by the ADODC. The bound controls then handle the interface between your program and the information in the database.

In this chapter, you will look at how to create a data access program using the ADODC and bound controls. You will see how to use the data access properties of the standard controls and look at some enhanced controls that were created specifically for data access programs. Chapter 8, "Creating Programs with the ActiveX Data Objects," shows you how to create a similar program without the use of the ADODC. In that chapter, you will also learn about the advantages and drawbacks of each method of creating a program.

As you are working through the material in this chapter, you should keep in mind the Microsoft exam objectives. To pass this part of the exam you need to know how to link an ADODC with information in a database. You then need to be able to link the ADODC to other controls to display and edit the information.

Setting Up the ADO Data Control

The ADODC is the key element to creating data access applications with a minimum of programming. The ADODC handles two key functions for you: creating the link to the database and providing database navigation capabilities to the user. The controls that are bound to the ADODC then automatically handle the display and editing functions for you; there is no need to write code for displaying data. In fact, you need to write code for only a few functions if you are using the ADODC:

- Adding new records
- Deleting a record
- Finding a specific record
- Validating the user input
- Handling database errors, such as multi-user conflicts

A typical data entry program created with the ADODC is shown in Figure 7.1. The figure also indicates the navigation buttons that the ADODC provides to let the user move through the records of the database.

FIGURE 7.1

A data entry program can be easily created with the ADODC and bound controls.

Basic Setup

Before you can work with the ADODC, you need to add it to the toolbox. You can do this by choosing the Components item from the Project menu and adding the Microsoft ADO Data Control 6 component to your project. After the control is added to your toolbox, you can use it just like other controls, that is, you place an instance of the control on your form and set its properties.

Though the ADODC does provide you with a great deal of functionality, it is easy to set up. For example, to use the ADODC with an Access (Microsoft Jet) database, you need to set only two properties of the control: the Connection-String and the RecordSource properties.

You typically should set the Name and Caption properties of the ADODC, as you would for any other control you use.

The ConnectionString property specifies the type and location of the database that you are trying to access. In addition, if you are working with a secured database, the ConnectionString also specifies the security information such as user ID and password. The easiest way to set up the ConnectionString property is through the property pages of the ADODC. To access the property pages, click the ellipsis button next to the Custom property in the Properties window. The General tab of the property pages is shown in Figure 7.2.

FIGURE 7.2

The property pages make it easy to set up the ConnectionString.

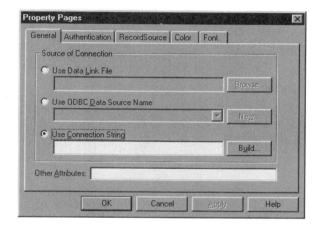

From the property pages, you can use the ConnectionString Builder to set the property. This Builder walks you through the process of creating the ConnectionString. Exercise 7.1 shows you the steps of the process.

EXERCISE 7.1

Setting the ConnectionString Property

1. Start a new project.

2. Add the ADODC to your toolbox; then place an instance of the control on the form.

3. Click the button next to the Custom property to bring up the property pages shown in Figure 7.2.

4. Select the Use Connection String option and click the Build button.

5. From the dialog box shown below, select the data provider. The dialog shows a list of all providers available on your machine. For Access databases, select the Microsoft Jet 3.51 OLE DB Provider.

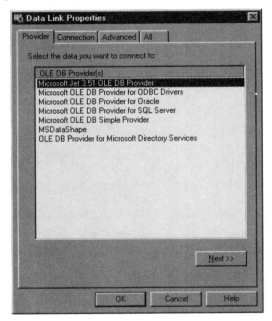

6. Click the Connection tab of the dialog box to specify the database that you will be accessing. You need to fill in the name of the database or select it from the open dialog accessed by clicking the ellipsis button. After specifying the database name, you need to specify a user name and password if the database is secured. For the sample project, select the Nwind.mdb database from the VB directory. The completed dialog is shown below.

7. Click the OK button of the Data Link Properties dialog, then the OK button of the property pages to accept the connection information.

EXERCISE 7.1 (CONTINUED)

Data Link Properties

Provider | Connection | Advanced | All

Specify the following to connect to Access data:

1. Select or enter a database name:

    rogram Files\Microsoft Visual Studio\VB98\Nwind.mdb | ...

2. Enter information to log on to the database:

    User name: Admin

    Password:

    ☑ Blank password   ☐ Allow saving of password

[Test Connection]

[OK]   [Cancel]   [Help]

WARNING The database location specified in the ConnectionString property may use path information specific to your machine. If you are distributing your application to others to use, you need to specify the location of the database by setting the ConnectionString property in code, in the Load event of the form containing the ADODC.

After you set the ConnectionString property, you can set the Record-Source property to determine the specific information in the database that you want to access. You can set the RecordSource property to the name of a table or query in the database, or you can enter an SQL statement to access specific data. The simplest way to set the RecordSource property is to use the RecordSource tab of the property pages shown in Figure 7.3.

F I G U R E 7.3

The property pages
help you set up
the RecordSource
property of the
ADODC.

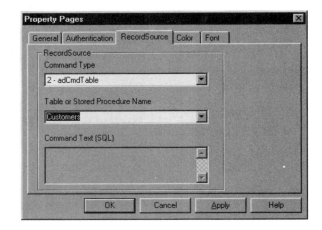

On the RecordSource tab, you can choose to enter the name of a table, the name of a query (or stored procedure), or an SQL statement to access data. The first step is to choose the command type from the drop-down list in the dialog. A command type of adCmdUnknown or adCmdText enables you to specify an SQL command in the box marked Command Text. If you choose a command type of adCmdTable, the drop-down list labeled Table or Stored Procedure Name is populated with the names of all the available tables in the database. You can then select the desired table from the list. Likewise, if you choose a command type of adCmdStoredProc, the list is populated with all the available queries or stored procedures available in the database.

If you are unfamiliar with tables, queries, or SQL statements, check out Sybex's *Mastering Visual Basic 6,* by Evangelos Petroutsos, for more information on database programming.

If you are working with an access database, an easy way to create SQL statements is to create your query in Access and then cut and paste the statement into the RecordSource property or your code. To learn more about using Access to create SQL statements, read Sybex's *Mastering Access 97,* by Alan Simpson and Elizabeth Olson.

To illustrate how easy it is to set up an ADODC, Exercise 7.2 shows you how to set up the ADODC as the first step of creating a data access program.

EXERCISE 7.2

Setting Up an ADODC to Access a Jet (Access) Database

1. Open a new project.

2. Add an ADODC to your form (remember to add the ADODC to your toolbox first).

3. Set the Name and Caption properties of the ADODC to identify the control to the user and in the program. (Note: Typical naming conventions use the *ad* prefix for naming the ADODC.)

4. Click the ellipsis button next to the ConnectionString property to set up the database connection as described in Exercise 7.1. For this example, use the Northwind sample database that comes with Visual Basic, `Nwind.mdb`.

5. After setting the ConnectionString property, click the ellipsis button next to the RecordSource property to select the data that you will be accessing. For the example, choose a command type of adCmdTable, then select the Products table from the drop-down list.

6. Save the project to use later in the chapter. You can save it as `Ch7a.vbp`.

Working with Cursor Types

Setting up the ADODC as you did in the previous section creates a cursor of the default type. The default is a static cursor. A static cursor provides a snapshot of the data in the RecordSource. The information in a static cursor cannot be modified, nor can additions or deletions be made to the cursor. Obviously, a static cursor is of limited use in a data entry program. However, you can create two other types of cursors with the ADODC:

- Dynamic

- Keyset

A dynamic cursor enables you to modify the information in the cursor as well as add new records and delete existing records. In addition, any changes made by other users in a multi-user environment are reflected in the cursor.

This type of cursor should be used in a multi-user environment when each user needs to immediately see changes made to the database by other users. However, the dynamic cursor comes with a penalty of increased memory usage and network traffic when compared to the keyset.

A keyset cursor is similar to a dynamic cursor, except that changes, additions, and deletions by other users are not visible to you in the keyset until the keyset is specifically refreshed. This type of cursor should be used in a multi-user environment when changes to the database made by the users will have little or no impact on each other.

For a single user application, the keyset and dynamic cursors can be used interchangeably.

You determine the type of cursor to use by setting the CursorType property of the ADODC. You will use the keyset type for most applications, but sometimes you will want to use one of the other types.

Other Key Properties of the ADODC

Up to this point, you have covered the major properties of the ADODC. Several other properties, however, control the behavior of the ADODC. The following list summarizes these properties. For a more detailed discussion of the properties, you can look them up in Visual Basic's online help. Using these properties is optional, as they are not required to connect an ADODC to the information in a database.

BOFAction   Determines what the ADODC does when the user moves to the beginning of the file. The options are to set the BOF flag for the cursor or move to the first record of the cursor.

EOFAction   Determines what the ADODC does when the user moves to the end of the file. The options are to set the EOF flag for the cursor, move to the last record of the cursor, or add a new record.

LockType   Determines whether to use optimistic or pessimistic locking. Optimistic locking locks records only when the actual data updates are being written to the database. Pessimistic locking locks records as soon as the user starts the process of editing the data. The LockType property can also be used to specify that the cursor be accessed as read-only.

Binding Controls to the ADODC

The ADODC can provide you access to the information in a database, but it cannot display that information on a form. For that, you need to use the bound controls. Bound controls are directly linked to the ADODC and handle the tasks of retrieving values from specific fields in the database and displaying the values to the user. Also, for those controls that allow user interaction, the controls handle the editing of the information. These bound controls let you create the applications with which a user can view and modify data. The exam objectives state that you need to be able to use the ADODC and the bound controls to access data. The ADODC sets up a cursor for use, but without the bound controls, you have no access to display or edit the information.

What the Controls Can Do

Visual Basic comes with several controls that enable you to handle data in the recordset of the ADODC. Eight of the controls in the standard Visual Basic toolbox are capable of being bound to the ADODC. Each of these controls retrieves the value of a field and assigns it to a property of the control. These eight controls and their associated properties are listed in Table 7.1.

TABLE 7.1 Standard controls that can be bound to the ADODC	Control Name	Property
	Picture Box	Picture
	Label	Caption
	Text Box	Text
	Check Box	Value
	Combo Box	Text
	List Box	List
	Image	Picture
	OLE Control	N/A

In addition to the standard controls, Visual Basic ships with six other controls that can be bound to the ADODC:

- DataGrid
- DataCombo
- DataList
- Hierarchical Flex Grid
- Masked Edit
- RichTextBox
- Chart

The standard controls and the Masked Edit and RichTextBox controls work equally well with the ADODC and the DAO-based Data control. The DataGrid, DataCombo, DataList, and Hierarchical Flex Grid controls work only with the ADODC. Visual Basic contains related controls (DBGrid, DBCombo, DBList, and FlexGrid) that work with the DAO Data control.

You cannot use the ADO controls with the DAO Data control, nor can you use the DAO-based controls with the ADODC.

In addition to the built-in controls, many third-party controls enable you to bind to the data control and ADODC to retrieve and manipulate data.

Using Simple Data Bound Controls

The simplest data bound controls are also the ones that you will use most often in your applications—the Text Box, Label, and Check Box controls. You bind each of these three controls to the ADODC by setting two properties, the DataSource and DataField properties. The steps for setting up these controls are shown in Exercise 7.3.

EXERCISE 7.3

Binding Controls to the ADODC

1. Open a project.

2. Set up an ADODC on the form as described in Exercise 7.2. If you saved your project from that exercise, open it and you are ready for the next step.

3. Add a text box to the form.

4. Click the arrow button next to the DataSource property in the Properties window to bring up a list of all the data controls (ADO and others) on the current form, as shown in the next graphic. Select the data control that contains the information you want to display.

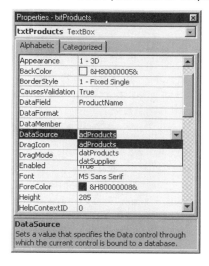

5. Click the arrow button next to the DataField property to display a list of all the fields in the cursor of the selected ADODC. This list is shown in the following graphic. Select the field that you want displayed in the text box.

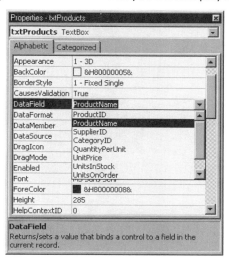

EXERCISE 7.3 (CONTINUED)

6. Run the program and click the navigation buttons on the ADODC. You will see how the information for each record is displayed as it is accessed.

7. You can use this same process to set up bound Label and Check Box controls.

Like other lists in the Properties window, you can cycle through the lists of the DataSource and DataField properties by double-clicking the mouse on the property name.

The Text Box control enables you to display and edit text information of any kind and is useful for handling numbers and dates as well. The Label control can be used to display any of the same information as the Text Box, but is used where you don't want the user to be able to edit the data. The Check Box control is used to handle Yes/No choices in a program. The Check Box must be bound to a logical or Yes/No field in a database. These three controls can be used to create a large number of data access programs. A sample data entry program using only these controls is shown in Figure 7.4.

FIGURE 7.4

Sample data entry program

Products	
CategoryID:	1
Discontinued:	☐
ProductID:	1
ProductName:	Chai
QuantityPerUnit:	10 boxes x 20 bags
ReorderLevel:	10
SupplierID:	1
UnitPrice:	18
UnitsInStock:	39
UnitsOnOrder:	0

Add   Update   Delete   Refresh   Close

|◀ ◀ Record: 1   ▶ ▶|

Working with Lists and Combo Boxes

The Text Box, Label, and Check Box controls can handle the bulk of the interface for most data access applications; however, many times you want to allow the user to select items from a list—to make the data input easier for the user and to limit the user's data input to specified values. Visual Basic provides two basic types of list-handling controls: the List Box and the Combo Box. You are probably already familiar with the operation of these controls in their normal (unbound) mode. They operate in a similar fashion in bound mode but have the added capability of displaying and editing data directly in a database.

In addition to the standard list and combo boxes, Visual Basic has Data-List and DataCombo controls that are specifically designed for database operations. Their purpose is similar to the standard controls, but how you set them up is quite different. Therefore, you will look at these controls separately.

Working with the Standard List and Combo Boxes

The standard List Box and Combo Box controls enable you to display the data from a field in the ADODC. In the case of the list box, the data field is bound to the selected item of the List property. The list that is used in the list box is input either through the Properties window or by adding items with the AddItem method in code. To modify the value of a field, the user selects an item in the list box. This item is stored in the field specified by the DataField property when the record is saved. The combo box binds the field of the ADODC to the Text property of the combo box, enabling the user to select items from a list or to enter new items. As with the list box, the data is stored in the field specified by the DataField property when the record is saved. Exercise 7.4 shows you how to set up a standard list box for data entry purposes.

EXERCISE 7.4

Using a List Box to Enter Data in a Database

1. Open a project containing an ADODC, or set up an ADODC as described in Exercise 7.2.

2. Add a list box to the form.

3. Add items to the List property of the list box. These items are the choices for the data field that you will link the list box to.

4. Set the DataSource property of the list box to the ADODC containing the data to be accessed.

5. Set the DataField property to the name of the field that contains the data represented by the items in the list.

6. Run the program. As you move from record to record, the selected item in the list changes to correspond to the data in the bound field.

If you are setting up a bound list box for use with an existing table, make sure your list includes all the values that are presently in the field in the table to avoid inadvertently changing the data or causing an error.

Working with DataList and DataCombo Controls

The standard List Box and Combo Box controls enable you to handle simple list processing for your database applications. Most times, however, you will want to use the more robust capabilities of the DataList and DataCombo controls. These controls not only link the information in the list to a field in the database, but they can also derive the list choices from the database itself.

The following example illustrates how these controls are set up and operate. In a normalized database, you would store information about suppliers in one table and information about products in another table. You then link each product to a specific supplier by storing a supplier ID in the product table. You do not store the supplier name and other information in each record of the product table, as this would lead to redundant data. Setting up data this way is a standard part of database design.

The problem with this normalized database occurs when the user enters a new product. You want the user to be able to enter the supplier ID by selecting an item from a list, but you want to show the supplier's name, not the ID, in the list. (This type of interface is illustrated in Figure 7.5.) Because the items in the List property of a standard list box are the ones that are bound to the database field, creating this type of interface is not possible with the standard control, which is why the DataList and DataCombo controls were created.

F I G U R E   7.5

Using a DataList to facilitate data entry

The DataList and DataCombo controls are not part of the standard toolbox for Visual Basic. These are custom controls that must be added to the toolbox using the Components dialog box. This dialog box can be accessed by choosing the Components item of the Project menu. You can also access the dialog box by pressing Ctrl+T or by using the pop-up menu in the toolbox.

Depending on your setup, the DataList and DataCombo controls may be included as part of your standard project.

Both of these controls enable you to use one ADODC as the source of the items in the list, and another ADODC as the destination of the information.

To set up the controls, you need to specify values for five properties, as described below:

BoundColumn   Specifies the field from the RowSource ADODC that is used as the value for the DataField information when a record is saved

DataField   Specifies the field from the DataSource ADODC that is the destination for information entered through the control

DataSource   Specifies the ADODC that provides the connection to the database that is the destination for edits or additions

ListField   Specifies the field that contains the values to be shown to the user in the list of the control

RowSource   Specifies the ADODC that provides the connection to the information that is the source of the list items

Exercise 7.5 shows you how to set up a Product/Supplier data entry screen like the one shown in Figure 7.6. A DataCombo control is used as a drop-down list to provide the list of suppliers.

FIGURE 7.6

Product Infor-
mation form

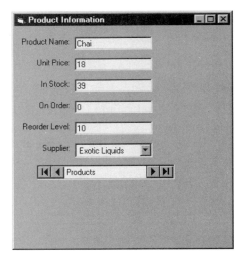

EXERCISE 7.5

Creating an Application with DataList or DataCombo Controls

1. Start a new project.

2. Add the DataList and DataCombo controls to the project by selecting the Microsoft DataList Controls 6.0 in the Components dialog box (if they are not already present).

3. Add an ADODC named **adProducts** to the form and link it to the Products table of the Nwind.mdb database. (See Exercise 7.2 for setting up an ADODC.)

4. Add a second ADODC named **adSuppliers** to the form and link it to the Suppliers table in the Nwind.mdb database.

5. Add bound text boxes to the form, linked to the adProducts ADODC, for the ProductName, UnitPrice, UnitsInStock, UnitsOnOrder, and ReorderLevel fields of the Products table.

6. Add a DataCombo control to the form and name it **dcSupplier**.

7. Set the Style property of the DataCombo to dbcDropDownList to allow the user to select only items that are already in the Suppliers table.

8. Set the RowSource property of dcSupplier to adSuppliers to specify the source of the list items.

9. Set the ListField property to **CompanyName**, the name of the field containing the names of each supplier.

10. Set the BoundColumn property to **SupplierID**, the field that is one end of the link between the tables.

11. Set the DataSource property to adProducts, the ADODC containing the destination table.

12. Set the DataField property to SupplierID, the other end of the link between the two tables.

13. Run the program. As you move through the Products table, you see the supplier name for each product appear in the DataCombo list. If you change the name in the list, that new supplier ID is assigned to the product you are currently editing.

This sample program is supplied as *Lists.vbp* on the companion CD-ROM.

Beyond Editing

So far, you have looked at displaying data in bound controls and using them to edit existing data in a database, but most database programs also need other capabilities, including:

- Adding records
- Deleting records
- Finding specific records

The ADODC, on its own, is not capable of handling these functions. These functions are not among the built-in methods of the control; however, they are easy to add to your program using the Recordset object of the ADODC and three of its methods—AddNew, Delete, and Find.

Adding and Deleting Records with the ADODC

When you add a new record to the database, the ADODC clears the bound controls to prepare them for the addition of new information. As the user enters information in the controls, the data is stored in the properties of the controls. The new record is not added to the database until you move to another record or exit the form. Either of these actions tells the ADODC to save the information to the database.

When you delete a record using the Delete method of the ADODC's recordset, the record is removed from the database, but the information from the record is still displayed in the bound controls. Therefore, it is important for you to reposition the record pointer to another record. Otherwise, if the user tries to edit the information in the deleted record, an error occurs.

Exercise 7.6 continues the project created in Exercise 7.5 by adding record addition and deletion capabilities to the project. Figure 7.7 shows how the project looks after the addition of these capabilities.

EXERCISE 7.6

Setting Up for Record Addition and Deletion

1. Open the Product/Supplier data entry project created in Exercise 7.5.

2. Add two command buttons to the form, one named **cmdAdd** and one named **cmdDelete**. Set the Caption properties of the buttons to Add Record and Delete Record respectively.

3. In the Click event of the cmdAdd button, place the following line of code:

```
adProducts.Recordset.AddNew
```

4. In the Click event of the cmdDelete button, place the following code segment:

```
With adProducts.Recordset
    .Delete
    If Not .EOF Then
        .MoveNext
    Else
        .MoveLast
    End If
End With
```

5. You can now run the program to see how these capabilities work.

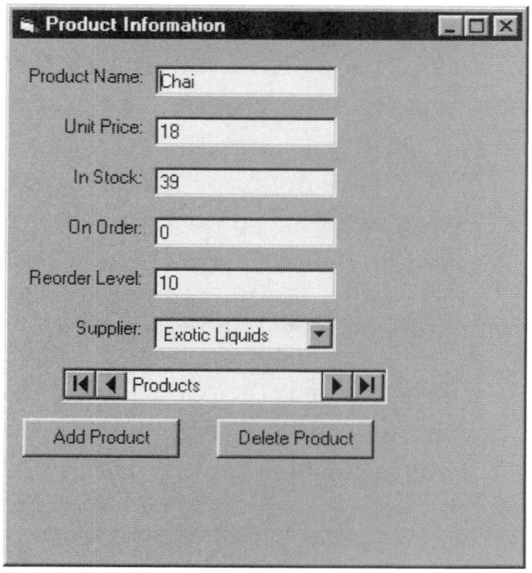

FIGURE 7.7

Your program can now add and delete records.

Because the ADODC does not verify that a user wants to delete a record, you may wish to add the following code in the cmdDelete button's Click event prior to the line that deletes the record:

```
Dim iReturn As Integer
iReturn = MsgBox( _
"Do you really want to delete this record?", _
vbYesNo)
If iReturn = vbNo Then Exit Sub
```

Finding Specific Records

Finding specific records in a recordset is a little more complex than adding new records or deleting existing ones. Finding a record requires invoking the Find method of the recordset and specifying the criteria of the record you wish to find.

The basic setup of the Find method consists of calling the method of the recordset and passing it the criteria for which you are searching. This criteria consists of three items:

- The field name to be searched

- The comparison operator, such as >, <, =, Like, or Between

- The value to which the field contents are compared

The field name item is the name of the field as it is listed in the recordset. The power of the Find command lies in the proper use of the comparison operator and the comparison value. Simple comparisons use a single value and use an operator such as <, >, or =. You are probably familiar with these comparisons from handling logical operations in your programs. The comparison operators Like and Between, however, require a little more discussion.

The Like operator enables you to compare a text field to a text pattern. For example, if you want to find the first record that has a product name beginning with S, you can use the Like operator as follows:

```
adProducts.Recordset.Find "ProductName Like 'S*'"
```

The S* string is the pattern to be matched, with * being a wild card operator that indicates any string of characters. You can also use the ? wild card to match a single character. These wild cards can be used in front of or after any literal characters that you want to match. The following list shows a few sample patterns:

Search for	Sample pattern
Contains the string 'SQL'	*SQL*
Names starting with 'St'	St*
Products ending with 'board'	*board
Four letter names starting with 'M'	M???

The * wildcard is used for Jet databases. Other database engines may use other characters for the wildcard. You should check the SQL documentation for your database.

The Between operator, unlike the other operators, takes two values for comparison. The Between operator is usually used to find records with a value in a specific numeric or date range. For example, the following line searches for shipment dates that occurred in a particular month:

```
adProducts.Recordset.Find "ShipDate Between"& _
"#12/01/97# And #12/31/97#"
```

In the sample, the two comparison values follow the Between operator and are separated by the And operator. The dates are enclosed in # signs, which are required for all literal dates used in code. Several other requirements must be met when setting up the criteria for the Find method:

- The criterion for the Find method must be a literal string or string variable.

- For criteria that are literal strings, the criteria must be enclosed within double quotes.

- The comparison value must be of the same type (text, numeric, date) as the field being searched. Otherwise, an error occurs.

- Text values, including patterns, must be enclosed within quotes (single or double) in the criteria.

- Date values must be enclosed within # signs.

If you are familiar with the Where clause of an SQL statement, the criteria for the Find method is essentially a Where clause without the Where keyword.

To illustrate the Find method in action, Exercise 7.7 shows how to add the capability of finding a particular product to the sample Product data entry program created in previous exercises.

EXERCISE 7.7

Adding Search Capabilities to the Program

1. Open the project containing the Product data entry screen.

2. Add a text box to the form with the name **txtProdSearch**. Also, clear the Text property of the text box.

3. Add a command button to the form with the name **cmdProdSearch**.

4. Add the following code to the Click event of the cmdProdSearch button:

```
Dim sSearchText As String
sSearchText = txtProdSearch.Text
adProducts.Recordset.FindFirst "ProductName >= '" & _
sSearchText & "'"
```

5. Run the program and try searching for product names. The following illustration shows the addition of the search capability.

Notice that in the preceding code, single quotes are embedded in the criteria to surround the text contained in the sSearchText variable, because all text comparison values must be contained within quotes. If there is a possibility that a search string will contain an apostrophe, you need to replace the single quotes with double quotes, as shown in the following line:

```
adProducts.Recordset.FindFirst "ProductName >= " Chr(34) & _
sSearchText & Chr(34)
```

The preceding search routine assumes that a record will be found. You should include code to return to the original record from which you started because a record might not be found. This enhancement is covered in Chapter 8.

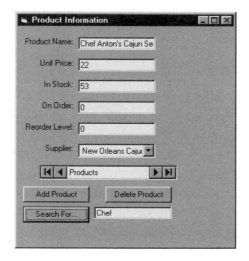

Summary

This chapter has shown you how to create data access programs using the ADODC and a variety of bound controls. You saw how to use the data bound capabilities of some standard controls to create the bulk of a program. You also saw how to extend the capabilities of the ADODC by adding a little code to the program, enabling the program to add new records, to delete existing records, and to find specific records. You also saw that you can build robust data access/data entry programs using the ADODC and bound controls. Because the ADODC does so much work for you, the biggest challenge in creating a program with the ADODC is handling the Addition, Deletion, and Search capabilities. The most important thing to remember in creating these capabilities is that you will be working with the Recordset object of the ADODC. In the next chapter, you will see how you can use the ActiveX Data Objects and program code to accomplish the same tasks without the use of the ADODC.

Now, it is time to test your knowledge based on the following exam objectives covered in this chapter:

- Access and manipulate a data source by using ADO and the ADO Data control.

- Use data binding to display and manipulate data from a data source.

Review Questions

1. In setting up the ADODC, which property do you use to specify the database that the control will link to?

   A. ConnectionString

   B. RecordSource

   C. LockType

   D. CursorType

2. What is a valid setting for the RecordSource property? Check all that apply.

   A. The name of a Table in the database

   B. The name of a Query in the database

   C. A valid SQL Select statement

   D. The name of another ADODC

3. Which CursorType setting would you use if you wanted to create a read-only cursor?

   A. Dynamic

   B. Keyset

   C. Static

   D. Read-only

4. In setting up a text box as a bound control, which property specifies the field of the recordset to be displayed?

   A. Name

   B. DataSource

   C. DataField

   D. Text

5. Which list controls let you create the selection list from a table in a database? Check all that apply.

A. Standard ListBox

B. DataList

C. Standard Combo Box

D. DataCombo

6. Which property of the DataList specifies the display field for the list?

A. RowSource

B. ListField

C. DataSource

D. DataField

7. Which property of the DataList control specifies where the list information comes from?

A. RowSource

B. ListField

C. DataSource

D. DataField

8. How do you handle adding and deleting records in a database program using the ADODC?

A. Set the appropriate properties of the ADODC (AllowAddNew, AllowDelete).

B. Write program code to invoke recordset methods (AddNew, Delete).

C. Either A or B can be used.

D. Neither A nor B is correct.

9. Which items must be specified as part of the criteria for the Find method?

A. Field name, comparison operator, comparison value

B. Field name, database name, comparison value

C. ADODC, bound control name, comparison value

D. Field name, comparison operator, bound control name

10. What must you do with literal dates in a search criteria for the Find method?

A. Enclose the date in single quotes.

B. Enclose the date in double quotes.

C. Enclose the date in # symbols.

D. No special treatment is required.

CHAPTER

8

Creating Programs
with the ActiveX Data Objects

Microsoft Exam Objectives Covered in This Chapter:

- Access and manipulate a data source by using ADO and the ADO Data control.

Visual Basic provides a variety of ways to accomplish any given task, and creating database applications is no exception. In Chapter 7, "Accessing Data with the ADO Data Control," you saw how you could create a database application using the ActiveX Data Objects Data control (ADODC). With the ADODC, you set up the data control, then bound standard controls such as text boxes to it to handle displaying the data. This use of the data control and bound controls provides a means to quickly and easily create an interface for viewing and editing data.

Another approach to creating database applications is to use the ActiveX Data Objects (ADO) in code. This method requires more effort than using the ADODC, but there are some advantages to using pure code. Some of these advantages are:

- You can more easily validate all the information entered by the user before it is saved to the database.

- You reduce the possibility of locking conflicts in multi-user systems because your program controls when the record is locked.

Access and many other databases use page locking, meaning an entire page of data on which the record is located is locked.

- You can handle locking conflicts and other database errors more easily using standard error-trapping techniques.

- You can use SQL statements to make changes to multiple records at a time.

- You can use batch updates to handle modifying several records at once.

- You can use transaction processing to speed up data storage and to help preserve data integrity.

- You can create database applications that do not require a visual interface. The data control is only good for handling programs that have a visual component.

Actually, using ADO in code and using the ADODC are not all that different. The ADODC is actually a wrapper around the ADO objects. For example, when you click one of the navigation buttons of the ADODC, you are invoking one of the Move methods of ADO. Also, when you used code to add and delete records with the ADODC, you were actually writing ADO code.

This chapter shows you how to create the various ActiveX Data Objects, how to retrieve information using the objects, and how to store new or changed information to the database.

Understanding the ActiveX Data Objects

The ActiveX Data Object model provides Visual Basic with a robust environment for creating database applications. Each of these objects contains methods and properties that control their behavior and enable them to perform certain data manipulation tasks. The ADO objects are designed to work equally well with Microsoft Jet databases and SQL databases such as SQL Server or Oracle. ADO also works with almost any Open Database Connectivity (ODBC) compatible database.

Many objects are contained within the ActiveX Data Objects. However, you will look closely at three of them in this chapter. These objects are:

Connection   This object provides the link between your program and a data source. The data source can be a Jet database, an ODBC database, or a SQL Server data source. When you create the Connection object, you are performing the same function that the ADODC does when you set the ConnectionString property. Each Connection object can support multiple lower-level objects, such as recordsets or commands. The Connection object manages the collections of recordsets, commands, and other objects. The Connection object is also where transaction processing is handled in the ADO model.

You may notice that collections play an important role in the ADO model. You can learn more about manipulating collections in Chapter 6, "Working with Collections."

Recordset   This object is the link with the actual data in the database. The recordset will typically be of one of the four types described in Chapter 7—dynamic, keyset, forward-only, or static. It is through the Recordset object that you navigate through database records, retrieve values from fields, and update information in the database.

Command   This object is an SQL statement that can be run from your program. The Command object can contain an SQL command that was created within your program, or it can refer to a stored procedure in the database.

These three objects are the main ones used to access data in an existing database.

Creating a Recordset with Code

Before you can begin to display, edit, or otherwise manipulate data in a database, you need to create the connection to the information through the ActiveX Data Objects. This involves two main steps—opening a connection to the database and creating a recordset for the desired information. Each of these steps requires you to create an object reference for use in your program.

Before you can create the ADO objects, however, you have to tell Visual Basic that your program will be using ADO by setting a reference to the ADO library in the References dialog box. This dialog box, shown in Figure 8.1, is accessed by choosing the References item from the Project menu.

When you create an application with the ADODC, the reference to the ADO library is handled automatically for you.

The References dialog box lets you tell Visual Basic the object libraries that your program requires.

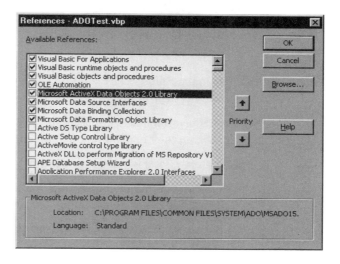

Opening a Connection

The first step to gaining access to the information in a database is to create a Connection object and establish the link to the database. As you write the code to handle creating the connection, you need to perform three steps:

1. Declare a variable to hold the instance of the connection.

2. Set the properties of the Connection object.

3. Use the Open method to create the link to the data source.

As you create the Connection object, you need to set two key properties—the Provider property and the ConnectionString property. The Provider property identifies the type of database with which you will be working. The property must be set to the name of an OLE DB provider. The ConnectionString property specifies the name of the database or data source that you will be accessing. This can be a Jet database or an SQL Server data source depending on your application.

Exercise 8.1 shows you how to get started creating a database program and how to create the Connection object for the program. This exercise shows you how to connect to a Jet database.

EXERCISE 8.1

Opening a Connection in Code

1. Open a new project in Visual Basic.

2. Open the References dialog box by choosing the References item from the Project menu.

3. Add the reference to the Microsoft ActiveX Data Objects 2.0 Library by checking the box next to the item in the References dialog box.

4. Open the Code window for the form.

5. In the Declarations section of the Code window, declare a Connection object variable as shown in the following code:

```
Dim cnMainData As New Connection
```

6. In the Load event for the form, set the properties of the Connection object and open the connection using the code shown below:

```
With cnMainData
    .Provider = "Microsoft.Jet.OLEDB.3.51"
    .ConnectionString = "D:\VB98\Nwind.mdb"
    .Open
End With
```

As an alternative to the method used in Exercise 8.1, you can specify the Provider, the Data Source, and other information in the ConnectionString as shown in the following code:

```
.ConnectionString = _
"Provider=Microsoft.Jet.OLEDB.3.51;
Data Source=D:\VB98\Nwind.mdb"
```

The ConnectionString property used in Exercise 8.1 specifies a literal string for the path and database name. If you are distributing your program, you need to have a method to retrieve the user's path for the database. You can do this by using Registry settings or by using the App.Path information if the database is in the same folder as the application.

Opening the Recordset

After you have opened a connection, the next step is to create a recordset containing the information that you want out of the data source. The recordset can contain the entire contents of a table, a few fields and records from a table, combined information from several tables, or even a single item of summary data. What is contained in the recordset depends on how you create it.

To create any recordset using the ADO, use the Open method of the Recordset object. To use this method, you need to specify the source of the records for the recordset, the name of an open Connection object, the type of recordset to create, and the type of locking that the recordset will use. Take a look at these items one at a time.

The source of the records for the recordset can be the name of a table in the database or the name of a stored procedure (query) in the database. You can also use an SQL statement to specify the records to be used.

The connection information for the recordset needs to be the name of a Connection object that you created in your code. This object associates the recordset with a particular database or data source. Exercise 8.1 showed you how to create a Connection object.

Recordset types are described in Chapter 7.

The recordset type specifies how the information can be handled by your program. You can specify one of four recordset types:

Static Provides a snapshot of the data in the recordset. The information in a static cursor cannot be modified, nor can additions or deletions be made to the cursor.

Dynamic Enables you to modify the information in the cursor as well as add new records and delete existing records. In addition, any changes made by other users in a multi-user environment are reflected in the cursor.

Keyset Similar to a dynamic cursor, except that changes, additions, and deletions by other users are not visible to you in the keyset until the keyset is specifically refreshed.

Forward-only Similar to a static recordset except that you can only move forward through the data. This type of recordset can be used to improve performance where only a single pass of the data is required, such as in reporting.

The final parameter is the lock type. This setting determines how ADO locks records while the user is editing data. You can use four lock types:

Pessimistic   Locks the record when the user starts the edit of the data in the record, usually through the AddNew or Edit methods of the recordset

Optimistic   Locks the record only when the changes to the data are saved to the database using the Update method

Read-only   Specifies that the data in the recordset cannot be modified

BatchOptimistic   Handles batch updates of multiple records in the recordset

Displaying the Data from a Recordset

Microsoft ✓ *Exam* *Objective*	**Access and manipulate a data source by using ADO and the ADO Data control.**

After you have created the recordset, you are ready to display the information from the recordset on your form or to perform calculations with the data. To do this, you first need to access the fields of the recordset. Then, if you are displaying the data, you need to assign the contents of the field to the appropriate control on your form. Figure 8.2 shows a typical data entry form created with ADO. As you can see, it is similar to a form that you would create with the ADODC.

The simplest and most efficient way to retrieve the information from a field is to use what is known as the bang operator (!). This operator works in the same manner as dot notation; you specify the name of the Recordset object, insert the bang operator, and specify the name of the field to be retrieved. If the name of the field to be retrieved contains spaces, the name must be enclosed in

FIGURE 8.2

A typical data
entry form

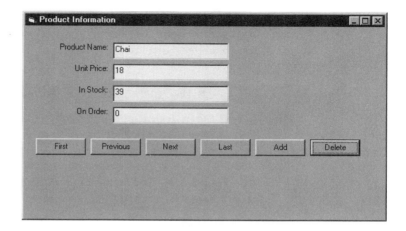

brackets []. The following code shows how the bang operator is used to assign
the contents of the ProductName field to a variable.

```
sProdName = RSProducts!ProductName
```

You can use two alternate methods to specify the field from which values
should be retrieved. Both methods use the Fields collection of the Recordset
object. The first method enables you to specify the field using the field name,
which is similar to using the bang operator. The advantage of this method is
that you can use a variable to specify the name of the field, which is useful if
you develop a generic routine for handling multiple fields. The second method
uses the index of the field in the fields collection. This method requires that you
know the order in which the fields appear in the collection so that you can
select a specific field. Both methods are shown in the following code.

```
sProdName = RSProducts("ProductName")
sProdName = RSProducts.Fields(1)
```

Both of these statements produce the same results as the original statement
using the bang operator.

If you use the field index in the fields collection, you need to make sure that
your statement for creating the recordset always places the same number of
fields in the same order. Otherwise an error or unpredictable results occur.

Figure 8.2 showed a sample data entry form for handling product information using ADO. Exercise 8.2 shows you how to create the display portion of this form. Figure 8.3 shows the Code window for the form with all the necessary code to display the information from the first record.

EXERCISE 8.2

Displaying Data from a Recordset

1. Start a project and open the Code window for the main form.

2. Declare a Connection object and Recordset object in the Declarations section of the form. The statement is shown below. Be sure to set the proper reference to the ADO library before creating these objects.

```
Dim cnMainData As New Connection
Dim rsProducts As New Recordset
```

3. Open the connection and the recordset, using the following statements placed in the Load event of the form.

```
With cnMainData
    .Provider = "Microsoft.Jet.OLEDB.3.51"
    .ConnectionString = "D:\VB98\Nwind.mdb"
    .Open
End With
With rsProducts
    .Open "Products", cnMainData, adOpenKeyset, _
adLockBatchOptimistic
End With
```

4. Place several text controls on the form to hold the following items: product name, unit price, quantity in stock, and quantity on order. Name the text boxes **txtProdName**, **txtUnitPrice**, **txtInStock**, and **txtOnOrder** respectively. Place several label controls next to the text boxes to identify the information.

5. Create a Sub procedure named **ShowData**. You can create a procedure using the Procedures dialog box accessible by choosing the Add Procedure item from the Tools menu.

EXERCISE 8.2 (CONTINUED)

6. Place the following code in the ShowData procedure. This code retrieves the contents of the database fields and places the information in the appropriate text box.

```
txtProdName.Text = RSProducts!ProductName
txtUnitPrice.Text = RSProducts!UnitPrice
txtInStock.Text = RSProducts!UnitsInStock
txtOnOrder.Text = RSProducts!UnitsOnOrder
```

7. Call the ShowData procedure from the Activate event of the form by placing the following statement in the event procedure.

```
ShowData
```

8. Run the program. You should see the information for the first record in the Products table of the database.

FIGURE 8.3

The complete code for opening a recordset and showing the first record

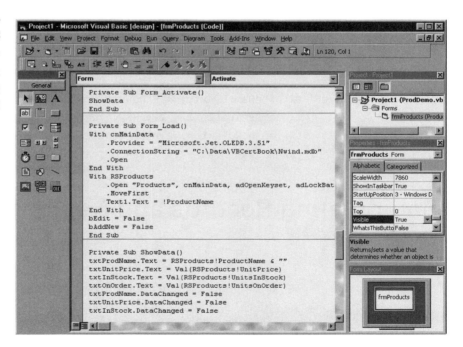

In the preceding exercise, you will need to specify a different directory as the location of your database file if your directory structure is different from the one indicated.

Exercise 8.2 showed you the basics of displaying information from a database using ADO. However, you need to perform several tasks in addition to the basic retrieval in the exercise. When you create a database application using the ADODC, the bound controls automatically handle functions for you such as type conversions and null values. When you use ADO, you have to handle these functions yourself. One of the most common errors that you will encounter is trying to assign a null value that exists in one of the database fields to a text box. Because the text box does not know how to handle this task, an error occurs. Therefore, you should ensure that the values passed to the text box will be handled correctly. How you do this depends on the type of information that is in the data field. For a text field, you can simply append a zero-length string to the end of the field value. If the field contains a text string, this action has no effect, but if the field contains a null value, a zero-length string instead of a null value is passed to the text box. For a numeric field, you can use the Val function to ensure that a numeric value is passed to the text box. Implementing these changes yields the following code for the ShowData procedure.

```
txtProdName.Text = RSProducts!ProductName & ""
txtUnitPrice.Text = Val(RSProducts!UnitPrice)
txtInStock.Text = Val(RSProducts!UnitsInStock)
txtOnOrder.Text = Val(RSProducts!UnitsOnOrder)
```

Manipulating Records and Navigating the Recordset

At this point, you can display the information from the first record of the recordset. Obviously, you need to add more capabilities to the program to make it really useful. First, you need a way to move to other records in the database. Then you need to be able to edit existing records, add new records, and delete records. You will see how to add these capabilities in this section.

Moving through the Recordset

You move from one record to another by using one of the Move methods of the Recordset object. When you use the ADODC, these commands are issued automatically when you press one of the navigation buttons on the ADODC. In your program, you have to handle these functions yourself. There are five Move methods that you can use in your program:

MoveFirst   Positions the record pointer at the first record of the recordset

MovePrevious   Positions the record pointer at the record prior to the current one

MoveNext   Positions the record pointer at the record after the current one

MoveLast   Positions the record pointer at the last record of the recordset

Move   Enables you to specify a number of records forward or backward of the current position that you want to move

In addition to invoking the Move methods, your program also needs to be able to detect whether the record pointer has been moved to the beginning or the end of the recordset. If you are beyond the first or last record of the recordset and try to display data, you will encounter an error. Fortunately, the Recordset object has BOF (beginning of file) and EOF (end of file) properties to let you know whether you are at the beginning or end of the recordset. Exercise 8.3 continues the example started in Exercise 8.2 by adding the capability of moving from one record to another. The exercise assumes that there is at least one record in the recordset. You will need to add code to handle an empty recordset.

EXERCISE 8.3

Navigating through the Recordset

1. Add a command button to the form and name it **cmdFirst**. Set the Caption property of the button to **First**.

2. Add the following code to the Click event of the cmdFirst button.

   ```
   RSProducts.MoveFirst
   ShowData
   ```

3. Add a command button to the form and name it **cmdPrevious**. Set the Caption property of the button to **Previous**.

4. Add the following code to the Click event of the cmdPrevious button.

```
With RSProducts
    .MovePrevious
    If .BOF Then .MoveFirst
End With
ShowData
```

5. Add a command button to the form and name it **cmdNext**. Set the Caption property of the button to **Next**.

6. Add the following code to the Click event of the cmdNext button.

```
With RSProducts
    .MoveNext
    If .EOF Then .MoveLast
End With
ShowData
```

7. Add a command button to the form and name it **cmdLast**. Set the Caption property of the button to **Last**.

8. Add the following code to the Click event of the cmdLast button.

```
RSProducts.MoveLast
ShowData
```

9. Run the program. You can now move through the recordset and see the various products.

You can also use a control array of command buttons to place all the code for recordset navigation in a single event procedure.

Notice that you included a call to the ShowData procedure in each of the event procedures for the command buttons. By placing the code to display the data in a procedure, you avoided having to repeat this code in each of the event procedures. Figure 8.4 shows the data entry form as it exists after the addition of the navigation buttons.

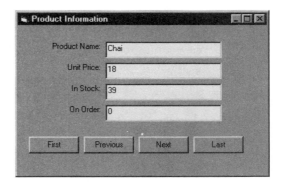

Exercise 8.3 used four of the Move methods. These are the ones that are most typically used in a data entry program. If you need to use the other Move method to handle moving the record pointer more than one record at a time, you simply list the name of the recordset, the Move method, and the number of records you want to move. Because you can potentially move the pointer past either the beginning or the end of the file, the routine you use to invoke the Move method should also include checks for these conditions and take the appropriate action. A sample Move routine is shown below:

```
lNumRecords = Val(txtMove.Text)
With RSProducts
    .Move lNumRecords
    If .BOF Then .MoveFirst
    If .EOF Then .MoveLast
End With
ShowData
```

By including the checks for the ends of the file, you assure that a record is available for display.

Editing and Adding Records

The previous section showed you how to display information in a form using ActiveX Data Objects. However, data entry programs are of little use if the user has no way of editing existing records or adding new ones. As you would expect, there is an easy method of accomplishing these tasks. To edit or add a record, you need to perform three simple tasks:

1. Prepare the recordset to receive data changes.

2. Post the new values of the field in the recordset.

3. Post the changes to the record in the database.

This section shows you how to implement these steps for the tasks of editing and adding records.

Editing Records

As with everything else in creating a data entry program with code, you have to handle the editing of data within your code; it is not handled automatically for you. After displaying the information from a record on the form, the user has the capability to change the information in the display (assuming that the controls allow changes). Your job in setting up the edit function consists of three tasks:

1. Determine that a change in the data has occurred.

2. Prepare the record for editing.

3. Commit the changes to the database.

You can perform the first task (determining that the data has been changed) in several ways:

- You can set a form-level flag to indicate that the data has been changed. To implement this, you need to write code in the Change or Click event of each control to set the flag, and then you need to reset the flag after the data is changed. Although this sounds like a lot of work, using control arrays makes it quite manageable. The advantage of using this method is that you can visually indicate that changes have been made by changing the color of the controls or displaying a Save button as soon as any changes are made.

- If your program is using only controls that can be bound to a data control (even though they are operating in unbound mode), you can use the DataChanged property of the controls to determine if the data was changed. In this case, you need to set the DataChanged property of each control to False after the information is displayed for the current record. Then, before you allow the user to move to another record, you check the DataChanged property of each record to determine if a change has occurred. If so, save the changes to the database.

- Finally, you can write code to compare the current contents of the controls to the fields from which the data was retrieved. Again, you would perform the check prior to allowing the user to move to another record. This is probably the slowest method of determining that a change has been made. However, it does have the advantage of not requiring you to save data if the user made a change, then reversed it.

After you use one of the above methods to determine that the user made a change, you have to handle making the changes to the record, then saving the changes to the database. You first assign the values of the controls to the appropriate fields in the recordset. Then, you use the Update method to tell the recordset to commit the changes to the database. An example of the code for this task is shown below:

```
With RSProducts
!ProductName = txtProdName.Text
    !UnitPrice = Val(txtUnitPrice.Text)
    !UnitsInStock = Val(txtInStock.Text)
    !UnitsOnOrder = Val(txtOnOrder.Text)
    .Update
End With
```

Adding Records

The process for adding records is similar to the process for editing records. To add a record to the database, you need to:

1. Clear the controls to allow the user to enter new information.

2. Tell the recordset to add a new record.

3. Assign the values to the fields.

4. Commit the information to the database.

In the first step of this process, you simply set the text property of a text box to a blank or default value and perform a similar function with any other controls used for data input. Next, you use the AddNew method of the Recordset object to tell the recordset to prepare to receive the information for a new record. Then, assigning the values and committing the changes is handled the same way as it was for editing a record. In fact, because adding a record and editing a record are so closely related, you can put both functions in the same routine.

Adding Modification Capabilities to a Program

Now that you have looked at the concepts involved in editing or adding a record, it is time to put them into practice. Exercise 8.4 shows you how to add the Edit and Add capabilities to the sample project. The techniques shown in the exercise are relatively simple, but there are other ways to modify records, and you should feel free to experiment.

EXERCISE 8.4

Modifying Records

1. To the existing project, add three command buttons. One of these buttons should be named **cmdSave**, with the Caption property set to **Save**. The second button should be named **cmdCancel**, with the Caption property set to **Cancel**. Both of these command buttons should have their Visible property set to False. The third command button should be named **cmdAdd**, with the Caption property set to **Add**.

2. Declare two logical variables in the Declarations section of the form. The variables should be named **bEdit** and **bAddNew**.

3. In the Load event of the form, set the value of the bEdit and bAddNew variables to False.

4. Create a procedure called SetEditMode. In this procedure, add code to hide the visible command buttons and display the cmdSave and cmdCancel buttons. This code is shown in the following graphic.

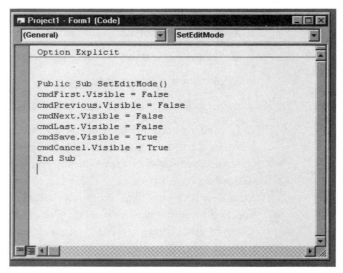

5. Create a second procedure called SetDisplayMode that resets the command buttons to their original configuration.

6. In the Change event of each text box, place the following code. This code sets the value of the Edit flag and displays the appropriate buttons.

```
bEdit = True
SetEditMode
```

7. In the Click event of the cmdAdd button, add code to clear all the text boxes and set the Edit flag (bEdit) and Add Record flag (bAddNew) to True.

8. In the Click event of the cmdCancel button, you need to place code to redisplay the original record information, reset the Edit and Add Record flags to False, and reset the command buttons using the following code:

```
ShowData
bEdit = False
bAddNew = False
SetDisplayMode
```

9. In the Click event of the cmdSave button, place the code to handle the editing or adding of records. This code consists of statements that assign values to the fields of the database. If you are adding a new record, the AddNew method needs to be invoked prior to assigning values. After the field values have been assigned, the Update method is used to commit the changes to the database. Finally, the Edit and Add Record flags are set to False and the command buttons are reset to their original configuration. The code for this event is shown in the next graphic.

10. You can now run the program to test the new changes. Figure 8.5 shows the form with the Add record button, and Figure 8.6 shows the form in the editing mode with the Save and Cancel buttons displayed.

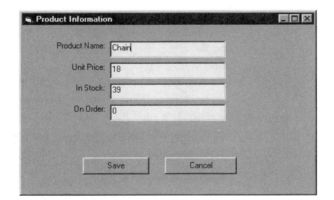

Deleting Records

The last data modification capability to be added is to allow the user to delete the current record. This capability requires the use of the Delete method of the Recordset object. In most programs you will want to verify that the user really wants to delete the record. To do so, you invoke the Delete method and then move the record pointer to another record to display its data. You do not want to leave the information from a deleted record displayed, as the user might try to edit it, and an error may occur. Exercise 8.5 shows you how to add deletion capabilities to your program.

> **EXERCISE 8.5**
>
> ### Deleting Records
>
> 1. Add a command button to the form with the name **cmdDelete** and set the Caption property to **Delete**.
>
> 2. In the Click event of the cmdDelete button, add the following code to determine whether the user really wants to delete the record:
>
> ```
> Dim iDelConfirm As Integer
> iDelConfirm = MsgBox _
> ("Are you sure you want to delete this record?", _
> vbYesNo)
> If iDelConfirm = vbNo Then Exit Sub
> ```
>
> 3. After the confirmation routine, add the following line to delete the record:
>
> ```
> RSProducts.Delete
> ```
>
> 4. Finally, add the code to move to another record and display its data. This code is shown below:
>
> ```
> With RSProducts
>     .MoveNext
>     If .EOF Then .MoveLast
> End With
>     ShowData
> ```

Summary

This chapter covered how to create a database program using the methods and properties of the ActiveX Data Objects. You have seen how to display data, navigate through a recordset, add, edit, and delete records. The specific exam objective covered was:

- Access and manipulate a data source by using ADO and the ADO Data control.

The review questions are similar to the questions you might expect to find on the MCSD Visual Basic 6 exam. If the questions do not seem familiar to you, refresh your memory by reviewing the exercises in this chapter.

Review Questions

1. Which object handles the link to a specific database?

    A. Connection

    B. Command

    C. Database

    D. Recordset

2. Which object provides the link to specific data?

    A. Connection

    B. Command

    C. Database

    D. Recordset

3. Which object is responsible for handling transaction processing?

    A. Connection

    B. Command

    C. Database

    D. Recordset

4. Which of the following is a valid data source for the Open method of the Recordset object? Check all that apply.

    A. The name of a table

    B. The name of a stored query

    C. An SQL statement

    D. The name of a data control

5. What is the proper method of referring to a field in a recordset in order to retrieve the value of the field? Check all that apply.

A. RSProd!ProductName

B. RSProd(ProductName)

C. RSProd("ProductName")

D. RSProd.Fields(3)

6. Which statement is valid for setting the ProductName field to a new value?

A. Set ProductName = "Syrup"

B. RSProducts!ProductName = "Syrup"

C. SetFieldValue "ProductName", "Syrup"

D. RSProducts.Fields(3).Set "Syrup"

7. To modify the value of a field, what is the proper sequence of commands?

A. Assign the value of the field and then invoke the Edit and Update methods.

B. Invoke the Edit method and then assign the value of the fields. The Update method is not needed.

C. Invoke the Edit method, assign the values of the fields, and then invoke the Update method.

D. Invoke the Edit method, assign the values of the fields, and then invoke the Commit method.

8. What is the proper method to use to add a record to the recordset?

A. Edit

B. NewRecord

C. Add

D. AddNew

CHAPTER

9

Working with the
Data Environment

Microsoft Exam Objectives Covered in This Chapter:

- Use data binding to display and manipulate data from a data source.

F or a long time, the majority of applications created with Visual Basic have been database-related applications. Recently, it has been estimated that over 90% of all Visual Basic applications will have data access capabilities. This means that more and more developers are using Visual Basic to create the user interfaces (or front ends) for programs that need to view and manipulate information in a database.

Microsoft has recognized this trend and has put more database tools in each successive version of Visual Basic. Version 6 is no exception to this improvement in database tools. In Chapters 7 and 8, "Accessing Data with the ADO Data Control" and "Creating Programs with the ActiveX Data Objects," you saw how ActiveX Data Objects and the associated Data control could be used to build database applications. However, these are not the only new tools in Visual Basic 6 that enable you to quickly and easily create database applications. Two significant tools are the Data Environment and the Data Reports. These tools are the subject of this chapter. Although there are no specific references to these tools in the Microsoft exam objectives, it is likely that you will see questions about them, particularly the Data Environment, on the certification exam.

Using the Data Environment Designer

T he Data Environment provides a way for you to handle multiple Connection objects that are associated with your programming project. The Data Environment Designer (DED) provides you with a visual interface for managing an instance of the Data Environment. Through the DED you can add, modify, and delete the connections to data sources within the project. In addition, the DED provides an easy method of creating the Command objects that provide the links to specific sets of records in the data sources identified by the Connection objects. Also, the DED provides the simplest way of creating the parent/child queries that are necessary for use with the Hierarchical Flex Grid and with master/detail data screens.

The first step in using a Data Environment in your program is to add an instance to your project. You do this by selecting the Data Environment item from the More ActiveX Designers submenu of the Project menu. (You can also select this option from the Add button on the main toolbar.) This menu item adds an instance of the Data Environment to your project and opens the DED window, as shown in Figure 9.1.

FIGURE 9.1

The Data Environment Designer

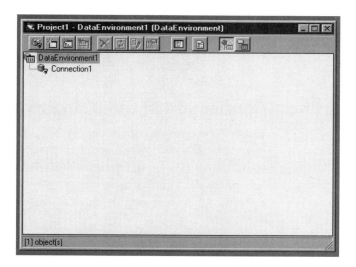

If you are starting a new project, the easiest way to add the Data Environment and all the necessary libraries is to start a Data Project.

If you look at the project references for your project, you will notice that adding the Data Environment adds a reference to the Microsoft Data Environment Instance 1.0 and to the Microsoft ActiveX Data Objects 2.0 Library, as shown in Figure 9.2. The Data Environment is based on ADO, and you will need some ADO code in many of your applications.

F I G U R E 9.2

ADO and Data Environment references are automatically added to your project.

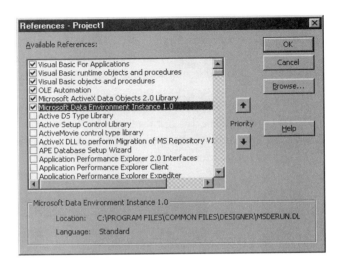

Creating a Connection in the Data Environment

The DED starts out with a single Connection object in the Data Environment. This Connection object enables you to create a link to a single data source, such as a Jet database or SQL Server data source. You set up the link to the data source by setting properties of the Connection object. Exercise 9.1 walks you through the process of creating the link to a Jet database.

The examples shown in the exercises are geared to Jet databases. However, the DED is equally adept at creating links to SQL data sources from Microsoft SQL Server or Oracle.

EXERCISE 9.1

Creating a Connection to a Data Source

1. Start a new Data Project in Visual Basic.

2. Open the instance of the Data Environment in the project by double-clicking the object in the Project window.

3. Right-click the Connection1 object in the DED and select Properties from the pop-up menu to bring up the Data Link Properties dialog box for the connection, as shown in the following graphic.

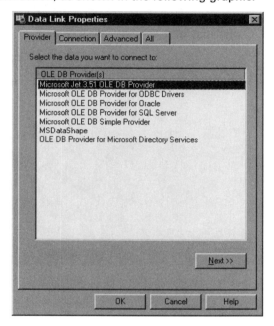

4. On the first page of the properties, select the OLE DB provider for the connection. For this example, select the Microsoft Jet 3.51 OLE DB Provider.

5. After selecting the provider, click the Connection tab of the Data Link Properties dialog box. This page of the dialog, shown below, enables you to select the specific source of the data for the connection. The content of this page varies depending on the data provider that you select. For the Jet data provider, you select the name and path of the database to which you are connecting. You may also need to provide

the security information for the database if it is secured. For this example, select the Nwind.mdb database that comes with Visual Basic.

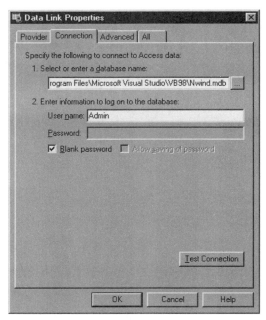

6. After selecting the database name, test the connection by clicking the Test Connection button on the dialog. This creates a temporary connection to the database to ensure that all necessary parameters have been specified correctly. If everything is OK, you should receive the "Test connection succeeded" message. Otherwise, you receive an error message describing the problem.

7. Close the dialog by clicking the OK button. Your connection to a database is now set up.

You will probably notice that the DED gives the first connection a default name of Connection1. To change this name, click the connection in the DED and type a new name, or change the Name property of the connection in the Properties window in Visual Basic.

Creating Command Objects

The Connection object provides a link to a database or a data source. However, the Connection object itself does not provide a link to specific tables or sets of records in the database. For this, you need to create Command objects. Command objects are child objects of the Connection object. Each Command object can reference a table in a database, a stored procedure, a database view, or an SQL statement to modify or retrieve records.

Each Command object provides a link to the specific information in a database. Many Command objects return a recordset. It is this recordset that you will use to create data entry or data viewing forms.

To add a command to a Connection object, you need to click the Add Command button on the DED and specify the properties of the command. Exercise 9.2 shows you how to create a command to retrieve order information from the Nwind.mdb database.

EXERCISE 9.2

Creating a Command

1. Starting with the project created in Exercise 9.1, click the Add Command button of the DED. (This button is the second from the left on the toolbar.) Clicking the button adds a Command object to the DED as shown below. (You can also add a command by choosing the Add Command item from the pop-up menu, which is accessed by right-clicking the Connection object.)

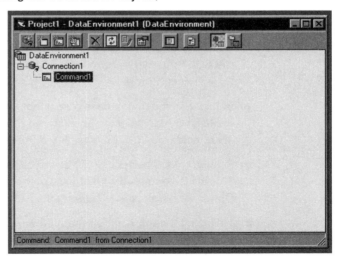

2. Open the Properties window for the Command object by right-clicking the object and selecting Properties from the pop-up menu. You can also access the properties by selecting the Command object in the DED and clicking the Properties button on the toolbar. Either action displays the Properties dialog box shown below.

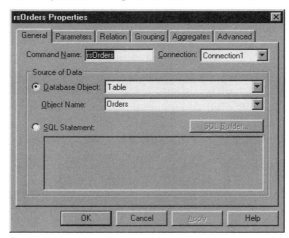

3. Set the name of the command in the text box to **rsOrders**.

4. Select the name of the Connection object for the command from the drop-down list. In this example, you have only one connection. However, if more than one connection is present, you may choose which connection to use from the list.

5. Select the source of the data that you are retrieving. If you are using a table or a stored procedure, you should select the Database Object option button. If you need to enter an SQL statement, you have to select the SQL Statement option button. For this example, select the Database Object button.

6. Select the type of database object that you will be working with. From the list, you can select a table, stored procedure, or view. (Jet queries are considered View objects.) For this exercise, select the Table object.

7. Finally, select the specific database object from the Object Name list. This list is populated with objects of the type specified in the Database Object box. Select the Orders table from the list.

8. This is all the information that you need for most of the Command objects that you will create. When you have completed the information on the General page of the Properties dialog, click the OK button.

After you set up the Command object, the DED displays the object with a plus sign (+) to the left of the object name. Clicking the plus sign expands the object view to show you the fields of the recordset that you created. Figure 9.3 shows this expanded view.

FIGURE 9.3

Showing the fields of the Command object

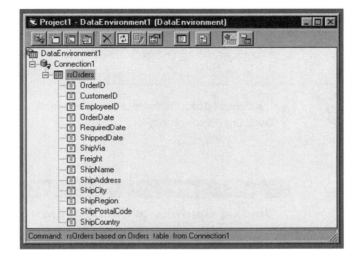

Binding the Data to Controls on a Form

Microsoft ✓ *Exam* *Objective*

Use data binding to display and manipulate data from a data source.

After you have created the Command object, you can start creating the data entry form to view or edit the information in the recordset. Creating a data entry form from objects in the Data Environment is very similar to creating data entry forms using the ADO Data control as discussed in Chapter 7.

The key difference between binding controls to a Data control and binding controls to a Data Environment is the setting of the DataSource and the Data-Member properties of the control. As you recall from Chapter 7, when binding a control to a Data control, you had to set only the DataSource property to the name of the Data control; you did not have to set a value for the Data-Member property. This is because both the database and recordset information were set when you set up the Data control.

When binding a control to the Data Environment, you first have to set the DataSource property to the name of the Data Environment. Then, you have to set the DataMember property to the name of the command that contains the recordset you are binding to. This is because the Command object sets up the link to the records in the database. Exercise 9.3 shows you how to bind fields in a recordset to controls on a form.

If a control does not have a DataMember property, it cannot be bound to a Data Environment object.

EXERCISE 9.3

Binding Controls to the Data Environment

1. Start with the project that you created in Exercise 9.2.

2. Open the Form window of the project.

3. Add a text box to the form.

4. Set the DataSource property of the text box to **DataEnvironment1** (or the name of the Data Environment that you created).

5. Set the DataMember property of the text box to rsOrders. This is the Command object that returns the orders recordset.

6. Set the DataField property of the text box to the name of a field in the recordset. For the example, use the ShipName field.

7. If you run the program, you will see the information for the first record displayed in the text box.

You can see that this method of binding controls to the Data Environment is easy to use. However, Microsoft has made it even easier for you to create data entry programs. The Data Environment supports drag-and-drop capabilities for adding controls to a form. This means that you can select a field from a Command object and drop it onto a form in your project. Doing this places a control, typically a text box, on the form and automatically binds it to the field in the Data Environment. You will also see that a Label control, containing the name of the field, is added to the form. This is illustrated in Figure 9.4.

F I G U R E 9.4

Adding controls via
drag-and-drop

Also, if you want to add all the fields from a recordset to the form, you can simply drag the Command object from the Data Environment to the form. Visual Basic then creates a Label/bound control pair for each of the fields, as shown in Figure 9.5.

F I G U R E 9.5

Adding controls for
all fields

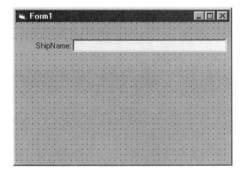

The only feature lacking from the forms created in this manner is a way to navigate between records. However, you can add a series of command buttons to your form and use the Move methods discussed in Chapter 8 to handle the navigation.

One other point of interest: If you right-click and drag the Command object onto the form, you are presented with a pop-up menu that enables you to choose among a DataGrid, a Hierarchical Flex Grid, and bound controls for displaying the data.

Creating Child Command Objects

One of the great new features available with ADO 2 is the capability to create hierarchical recordsets. In simple terms, a hierarchical recordset is one that handles master/detail information in a single recordset. This capability makes it easier to create data entry forms that show, for example, general information about an order, along with the item details of the order. Although it is difficult to create this type of recordset in code, the DED makes the process easy.

The key to creating hierarchical recordsets with the DED is the capability to create child commands attached to any Command object. A child Command object opens a second recordset that is linked by a key field to a parent Command object and its recordset. Exercise 9.4 walks you through the process of creating a child command from the rsOrders Command object created in Exercise 9.2.

EXERCISE 9.4

Creating a Child Command

1. Using the project you created in Exercise 9.2, open the Data Environment Designer.

2. Select the rsOrders Command object.

3. Click the Add Child Command button (the fourth button from the left). This adds a Command object under the rsOrders object. (You must have the outline expanded to see the child object.)

4. Select the child Command object and open the Properties dialog box by clicking the Properties button on the toolbar.

5. On the General page of the dialog, set the name of the command to rsDetails. Then set the Database Object property to Table and set the Object Name to the Order Details table.

6. Click the Relation tab of the dialog to set the properties of the command that will create the link between the two tables. The dialog is shown in the following graphic.

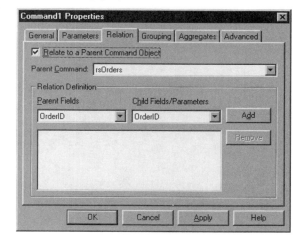

7. Most of the information for the relation is already set for you. The Relate to Parent Command Object check box is checked, and the Parent Command is set to rsOrders. The only requirement is for you to set the fields that define the relation. The dialog makes a guess at the fields in each recordset that relate the two. After you select the correct fields, click the Add button to add this definition to the relation. You can add multiple definitions if the relation between the two tables is based on more than one field.

8. After setting the relation between the two tables, you can close the dialog by clicking the OK button.

After you have created a hierarchical recordset using child Command objects, you can create the detail section of the data entry form by placing a data grid or hierarchical flex grid on your form, and then setting the Data-Source property to the name of the Data Environment and the Member property to the name of the child command containing the detail information. An example of this is shown in Figure 9.6.

FIGURE 9.6

Handling the master/
detail relation with
child commands

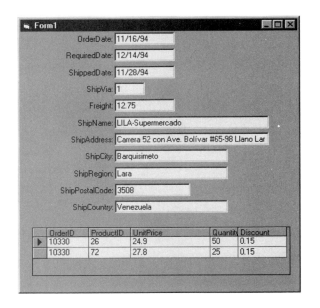

 Setting up the entire data form, including the grid, is handled for you if you drag the parent Command object to the form.

Using Data Reports

One other addition to the data-handling capabilities of Visual Basic is the new Data Reports Designer. This designer works like the report designer in Access to enable you to quickly and easily create reports for your database applications. Although the designer is not as robust as the one in Access or in Crystal Reports, it is a good first implementation.

One of the key advantages to using the Data Reports Designer is that it works hand in hand with the DED. This enables you to create reports by dragging and dropping fields from a Command object in the DED to the report designer. You can even drag and drop an entire Command object and allow the report designer to set up the fields for you. Figure 9.7 shows you a simple report in the design view, while Figure 9.8 shows you the same report as it would look in a Preview window run from your program.

FIGURE 9.7

Designing a simple report

After you create the report in the designer, you display the report using the Show method of the DataReport object. The Show method previews the report, as shown in Figure 9.8. The user can then view portions of the report on the screen, and print the report by clicking the Print button at the top of the Preview window. To print the report directly to the printer, you can use the PrintReport method of the DataReport object.

FIGURE 9.8

Previewing the report
from the application

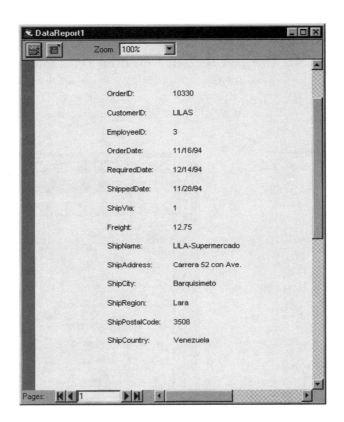

FIGURE 9.8

Previewing the report
from the application

Summary

In this chapter you have seen how the Data Environment Designer makes it easy for you to create data entry forms. The DED enables you to create connections to databases and links to particular recordsets with ease. You have even seen how to create a master/detail (hierarchical) recordset using child Command objects. Finally, you have seen how the Data Reports Designer makes quick work of simple database reports.

The Microsoft exam objective covered in this chapter is:

- Use data binding to display and manipulate data from a data source.

Review Questions

1. Which object provides a link to a database or data source?

   A. Connection

   B. Command

   C. Recordset

   D. Data Environment

2. Which object provides a link to a particular set of records in a database?

   A. Connection

   B. Command

   C. Recordset

   D. Data Environment

3. What are valid sources of data for a Command object? Check all that apply.

   A. A database table

   B. A Data control

   C. A stored procedure

   D. An SQL statement

4. Which properties must be set to bind a control to a Data Environment?

   A. DataSource and DataField

   B. DataField and DataFormat

   C. DataMember and DataField

   D. DataSource, DataMember, and DataField

5. What does a child Command object do?

   A. Provides clarification of the parent command.

   B. Handles the master records of a master/detail recordset.

   C. Handles the detail records of a master/detail recordset.

   D. There are no child command objects.

6. Which method of the DataReport enables the user to preview the report information?

   A. PrintReport

   B. PrintForm

   C. Preview

   D. Show

PART

III

Developing
and Using
COM Objects

CHAPTER

10

Creating COM Components

Microsoft Exam Objectives Covered in This Chapter:

- Create a COM component that implements business rules or logic. Components include DLLs, ActiveX controls, and active documents.

- Compile a project with class modules into a COM component.
  - Set properties to control the instancing of a class within a COM component.
  - Implement an object model within a COM component.

- Debug a COM client written in Visual Basic.

- Register and unregister a COM component.

- Create callback procedures to enable asynchronous processing between COM components and Visual Basic client applications.

I n Chapter 5, "Creating Classes in a Program," you learned that you can create a class to encapsulate data and code for a particular function. This capability to place the data and code into a single object made it easier to reuse code than was possible with procedures alone. Classes, such as the ones you created in Chapter 5, are the basis of Component Object Model (COM) components. COM components provide a means of reusing code not only within other Visual Basic programs, but also within any programs that can use COM components.

COM components include Automation servers (also known as ActiveX servers), ActiveX controls, and active documents. Chapter 12, "Creating ActiveX Controls with Visual Basic," examines how to create your own controls, and Chapter 13, "Creating Documents for the Web," shows you how to create programs that run inside a Web browser. The focus of this chapter is to demonstrate how to create the ActiveX server type of COM component.

ActiveX servers take the use of classes a step further than just including the classes in multiple programs. By compiling the classes and placing them in an ActiveX server, either DLL or EXE, you make the objects (and their associated properties, methods, and events) available to multiple projects. You can use the objects without adding the class itself to the project on which you are working. In addition, other programs can make use of the classes that you have written.

Using ActiveX Servers

ActiveX servers let you make functions and objects that you create in classes available to other programs. By compiling these functions and objects into a server, the other applications can use the server objects without being able to modify them. In a client-server environment, this means that many applications can use the same server objects for database access, information validation, and other tasks. When the tasks need to be modified, only the server has to be changed; the client applications can be left alone, and the new or modified functionality is automatically available.

What Is an ActiveX Server?

An ActiveX server is a collection of objects that can be used by your program. For example, Excel is an ActiveX server that exposes spreadsheet objects that you can use in your programs. You can create instances of these objects and then load and manipulate spreadsheets from within your Visual Basic program.

When you create an ActiveX server, you are creating objects that can be used in other programs. These objects can be used to handle complex math functions, retrieve data from a local or remote database, provide messaging capabilities within a company, or perform any number of other tasks.

Visual Basic gives you the capability to create two types of servers:

- In-Process servers
- Out-of-Process servers

In-Process Servers

In-Process servers are created as `.dll` files. When your program accesses one of the objects of the `.dll`, the object is linked to your program and runs in the same process space (area of memory) as your program. When your program is finished with the object, the link is closed and the `.dll` is no longer active for your program. A `.dll` cannot be run by itself.

The key advantage of using an In-Process server is speed. Because the component object and your program are in the same process space, the transfer of information between them is much faster than is possible with an Out-of-Process server. The key disadvantage of the In-Process server is that it cannot be run on a machine separate from the client application (your program). This limitation means that you cannot take advantage of the speed of a server to run parts of your application, such as data retrieval, in which the data typically resides on a server.

Out-of-Process Servers

Out-of-Process servers are stand-alone programs that expose objects to other programs. The Out-of-Process server can be started on its own or can be started by a client application. When your application finishes with an object from an Out-of-Process server, the server can continue running, able to provide objects to other client programs or to perform tasks of its own.

The key advantage of Out-of-Process servers is that the objects run in a separate process space than the client applications. This setup makes Out-of-Process servers useful for client-server applications in which processes such as data retrieval and storage can be run on the server machine, close to the data. The disadvantage of Out-of-Process servers is that communication between your application and the server objects is slower than with In-Process servers because the information has to cross process boundaries.

What Is the Benefit of Using a Server?

The key benefit of using ActiveX servers is to make objects and their properties and methods available to multiple programs. For example, because Excel is an ActiveX server, you do not need to write functions such as regression analysis for your applications; you can simply create an instance of a spreadsheet object and use the regression analysis capabilities built into Excel.

There are two typical uses for ActiveX servers that you may write:

- Supplying business objects to an application
- Supplying custom functions to an application

Using Business Objects

Database applications are a major part of the computing needs of many companies. Companies use databases to handle payroll, customer support, billing, and business analysis. Typically, the data for a company is stored in central databases that can be accessed by several applications. However, companies have rules about who can access the data and how they can access it. In addition, there are typically business rules that must be met before any data can be posted to the database. These rules might include:

- Hours worked by an employee cannot exceed 45.

- A pay raise cannot be greater than 15% of the current salary.

- If the posting of an invoice fails, all invoice line items should be removed from the database. (This is an example of transaction processing.)

- Managers may view payroll data only for employees in their own department.

As programmers write applications that access the corporate databases, these rules must be enforced. To make sure all these rules make it into every application would be almost impossible. Business objects provide an alternate means of handling all the necessary tasks for enforcing the business rules. By placing the rules in business objects and placing the objects in a server, programmers need to know only how to access the object. They don't even have to know what the rules are.

This centralized containment of the business rules and objects provides another major benefit—when the rules change, only one program, the ActiveX server, needs to be changed. All programs that access the server remain unaffected, reducing the cost of program maintenance.

Making Functions Available to Multiple Programs

The other major use of ActiveX servers is to make libraries of custom functions available to multiple programs. For example, if you work for an engineering firm, many complex math functions are required for engineering calculations. By placing these functions in a single ActiveX server, any programmer who needs a function merely calls it from the server. The function does not have to be rewritten in every program.

As with business objects, a key benefit of placing functions in a server is program maintenance. If a function needs to be modified, it has to be modified only in a single place.

Creating an ActiveX Server

Whether you are creating an In-Process or an Out-of-Process server, the key steps to building the server are the same:

1. Start the appropriate type of project.

2. Build the classes that define the objects of the server.

3. Set up the object model of the server.

4. Create any supporting routines needed by the server.

5. Test the server.

6. Compile the server and make it available for use.

Microsoft ✓ *Exam* *Objective*

Create a COM component that implements business rules or logic. Components include DLLs, ActiveX controls, and active documents.

In this section, you will examine each one of these steps in detail. Where appropriate, this section points out the differences between working with an In-Process and an Out-of-Process server. Otherwise, you can assume that the steps shown do not depend on the type of server you are creating. To illustrate the concepts of creating an ActiveX server, the exercises in this section create and test a server that handles payroll calculations. Information about employees is stored in a database and is accessed through the server. You can find the sample database on the CD-ROM as *Payroll.mdb*.

Starting a Server Project

When you begin to create an ActiveX server, first you must choose which type of server to create. Earlier in this chapter, the section entitled "What is an ActiveX Server?" discussed the two types of servers, In-Process and Out-of-Process. An In-Process server runs in the same process space as the client application. You create In-Process servers by creating an ActiveX DLL project. An Out-of-Process server is a stand-alone program that runs in a separate process space from the client application. To create an Out-of-Process server, you choose the ActiveX EXE project.

To start a new project, you can start Visual Basic or select the New Project item from the File menu. You are presented with the New Project dialog box shown in Figure 10.1. From this dialog box, you can choose the type of project to create. After you have chosen the project type, a project and a class are created for you and you are placed in the Code window of the class. You will probably want to rename the project and the class to names that indicate what the server and objects will be doing.

FIGURE 10.1

Project selection
dialog box

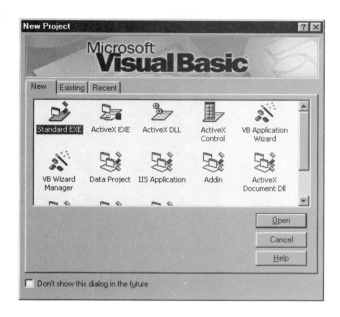

After you are in the project, you can add more classes, .bas modules, and forms to the project to handle all the tasks the server needs to accomplish. If you are working with an ActiveX EXE project, you may want to add a module and create a Sub Main procedure to initially set up the server when it loads. Exercise 10.1 shows you how to set up the basic project for the Payroll server.

EXERCISE 10.1

Creating the Payroll Server

1. Start a new project and select ActiveX EXE as the project type.

2. Select the project in the Project window and change the name of the project to **Payroll** to identify the server to other applications. For now, skip the class module. It will be covered in the next section.

3. Because the Payroll project will be working with a database, you need to provide a reference to the database library. Open the References dialog box from the Project menu and select the Microsoft DAO 3.51

Object Library, as shown in the next illustration. (If you are using a version of Jet other than 3.51, also known as Access 97, you need to set the appropriate reference.)

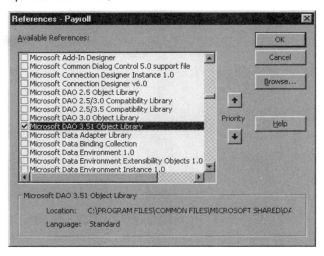

4. Add a .bas module to the project to handle the initialization of the server. You can add a module by choosing the Add Module item from the Project menu. Name the module **DataAccess**.

5. Place the following code in the Declarations section of the DataAccess module. This code creates two database objects and makes them available to other routines in the server.

   ```
   Public EmpRset As Recordset, EmpData As Database
   ```

6. Create a procedure entitled Sub Main. This procedure handles the start-up of the server and makes a connection to the database. You can use the Add Procedure dialog box available from the Tools menu to create the procedure or type **Sub Main** in the Code window of the .bas module.

7. Add the following code to the Sub Main procedure. This code connects to the database.

   ```
   Dim sMainData As String
   sMainData = App.Path & "\Payroll.mdb"
   Set EmpData = _
   DBEngine.Workspaces(0).OpenDatabase(sMainData)
   ```

8. Set Sub Main as the Startup Object for the Payroll project. You do this by selecting the Properties item from the Project menu and then selecting the Sub Main procedure from the list of Startup Objects, as shown in the following illustration.

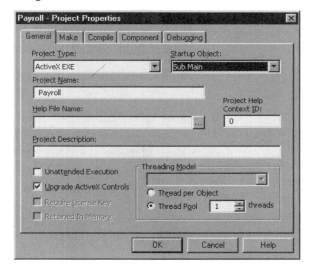

9. Select the Class module in the Project window and delete it from the project. Don't worry, you will add another one later.

10. Save the project.

Controlling the Operation of the Server

As you are creating an ActiveX server, you set properties of the project and properties of the classes in the server while you are in the design environment. However, several properties that control the behavior of the server can be set only at run time. These properties are part of the App object. The App object is an internal Visual Basic object that is used by an application to refer to itself. For standard programs, the properties of the App object are used to determine the name of the program, the path of the executable file, and whether another copy of the program is running.

When you are creating server applications, several properties determine the server's response to an application's request for objects while the server is busy with other requests. These properties are defined as follows:

OLEServerBusyTimeout   Specifies the number of milliseconds that an application can retry a request before the Component Busy dialog box is shown.

OLEServerBusyMsgText   Specifies the text to be displayed in the Component Busy dialog box when a request times out.

OLEServerBusyMsgTitle   Specifies the text to be shown in the title bar of the Component Busy dialog box when a request times out.

OLEServerBusyRaiseError   Determines whether an error is raised when the component request times out. If the property is set to True, an error is raised. If the property is set to False, the default Component Busy dialog box, or a dialog box with the custom message, is displayed on a time-out.

If you use any of these properties in your application, the values of the property are typically set in the Sub Main procedure. (The Sub Main procedure starts the server.)

Creating the Classes of the Server

After you have created the ActiveX server project and set the necessary project properties, you are ready to start creating the objects that will be provided by the server. Each object that you want to provide from the server is defined as a class in the server. Chapter 5 covered the creation of classes in detail, but you will review some of the key points here and then create the class for the Payroll server.

To start creating a class, add a new class to your project by selecting the Add Class Module item from the Projects menu. You can then set the two properties of the class: Name and Instancing. The Name property should reflect what is represented by the class and should be preceded by the letter *c*. For example, a class that represents an invoice could be named cInvoice, whereas a class that represents the detail items of the invoice could be named cInvoiceDetail.

Choosing the Instancing Property Setting.

Microsoft *Exam* *Objective*

Compile a project with class modules into a COM component.

- Set properties to control the instancing of a class within a COM component

The setting of the Instancing property is the key to how a server provides objects to client applications. There are six possible settings of the Instancing property, as defined below for an ActiveX server:

Private   The class can be used only within the server. It is not available to client applications.

PublicNonCreatable   The class can be used by client applications, but only if it has already been created by the server. Client applications cannot create an instance of the class using the New keyword or the CreateObject function.

SingleUse   Other applications can create and use objects of the class; however, each time a client application creates an object from the class, a new instance of the class is started by the server.

GlobalSingleUse   Similar to SingleUse, but an application does not have to specifically create the object to use its methods and properties. The methods and properties are treated as global functions.

MultiUse   Similar to SingleUse, but the server creates only a single instance of your class, no matter how many clients create objects from the class. All objects from the class are generated from the single instance.

GlobalMultiUse   Similar to MultiUse except that the methods and properties are treated as global functions, which means that applications do not have to specifically create an instance of the class.

Depending on the type of server you are creating, all these options may not be available to you. An ActiveX EXE server can use any of the settings of the Instancing property; however, the ActiveX DLL server cannot use the SingleUse or the GlobalSingleUse settings. Fortunately, you don't have to remember this because Visual Basic provides you with only the choices that are available for your type of project.

In addition to the Instancing property of a class, you may want to set the value of the Persistable property. This property determines whether the object created from the class can persist data between one instance of the object and another. The only two settings of the Persistable property are Not Persistable (the default setting) and Persistable. Persisting the properties of an object is similar to persisting information about an ActiveX control. Chapter 12 covers this process in detail.

Creating Elements of the Class

After setting the basic properties of the class, you are ready to start creating the elements of the class. These elements are the properties, methods, and events that are exposed by the class to client applications. Again, the following sections provide a quick review of creating these elements. For more detailed information, you should review Chapter 5.

Creating Properties   Properties are the elements of a class that store information. This information can be, for example, an invoice ID, the number of hours worked by an employee, or the dimensions of a room. Properties are defined for a class by Property procedures. As you recall, you can create three types of Property procedures:

Property Let   Sets the value of a property of a standard data type

Property Get   Retrieves the value of a property

Property Set   Sets the value of a property containing an object

You create the shell of the property using the Add Procedure dialog box. In the dialog box, you set the name of the procedure, select the procedure type, and specify the scope of the procedure. Figure 10.2 shows the Add Procedure dialog box for a Property procedure.

You can also create procedures by typing **Public Property Let** (or **Set** or **Get**) along with the property name directly in the Code window.

You can also create a property by typing the declaration statement in the Code window of the class.

F I G U R E 10.2

Creating a Property
procedure from the
Add Procedure
dialog box

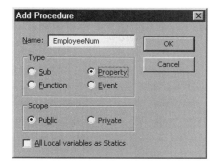

After you create the shell of the Property procedure using the dialog box, you enter code to handle the setting or retrieving of values from the class. The data of the class is stored in variables that are private to the class and are accessible through the Property procedures. The Property procedures can simply set or retrieve the values of these private variables, or they can provide additional functionality, such as data verification.

Creating Methods Methods are the elements of a class that perform a task—anything from retrieving data to printing a report or performing a complex calculation. Methods are simply Sub or Function procedures that have been declared Public to make them available outside the class. When you are creating methods, you typically create a Function procedure whenever you need to return a value to the client program. If you do not need to return a value, you usually create a Sub procedure.

In the same way that you create a Property procedure, you can create a Sub or Function procedure by using the Add Procedure dialog box or by typing in the declaration statement for the procedure. In addition to the Public procedures that are used as methods of the class, you can create Private procedures that can be used only in the class itself. You can also create Friend procedures that are available within the project that defines the class but are not available to client applications.

Creating Events The final element of the class is an event. An event is used to notify a client application that something is happening in the class. You can use an event to let a client know that a database record has been retrieved or that a statement has finished printing.

There are two parts to creating an event in a class. First, you must declare the event procedure using a declaration statement that specifies the name of the event and any arguments that are passed by the event to the client program. The following code shows an example of a declaration statement:

```
Public Event PrintFinished(ByVal Pages As Integer)
```

The second part of creating an event is to trigger the event from code in your class. You handle this with the RaiseEvent statement. This statement specifies the name of the event and the values of the parameters to be passed to the client application. An example of the RaiseEvent statement is shown in the following code:

```
RaiseEvent PrintFinished(iNumPages)
```

Creating the Employee Class for the Payroll Server

For the Payroll server, you need to create a class that handles the employee data and employee pay calculations. This class will be accessed by client applications that are processing payroll information. Exercise 10.2 takes you through the steps of creating the class.

EXERCISE 10.2

Creating the Employee Class

1. Add a new class to the project by choosing the Add Class Module item from the Project menu. Name the class **cEmployee**.

2. Set the Instancing property of the class to MultiUse.

3. You will be creating three Public properties of the class and several internal variables to hold information such as gross pay, tax withheld, social security taxes, Medicare taxes, net pay, and hours worked. The first step in setting up the properties is to create the Private variables that will hold the data. To do this, place the following code in the Declarations section of the class module:

```
Dim m_lEmpID As Long, m_iMaxHours As Integer, _
m_iHours As Integer
Dim m_sLastName As String, m_sFirstName As String
Dim m_sngPayScale As Single, m_sngOvertime As Single
Dim m_sngTaxRate As Single
Dim m_sngPay As Single, m_sngSocial As Single, _
m_sngNetPay As Single
Dim m_sngTax As Single, m_sngMedicare As Single
```

4. You need to provide initial values for several of these variables. You handle this in the Initialize event of the class with the following code:

```
m_iMaxHours = 0
m_iHours = 0
m_sLastName = " "
m_sFirstName = " "
```

5. The first Property is the EmployeeNum property, a write-only property that enables the user to enter the employee ID to be processed by the class. To create a write-only property, use the Property Let procedure as shown in the following code:

```
Public Property Let EmployeeNum(ByVal lNewID As Long)
m_lEmpID = lNewID
End Property
```

6. The second property is the HoursWorked property, also a write-only property, which enables the user to input the number of hours worked for the week. Notice in the following code that the Property procedure checks the input hours against the maximum allowable hours for the employee.

```
Public Property Let HoursWorked(ByVal iWklyHours As _
Integer)
If iWklyHours > m_iMaxHours Then
    m_iHours = m_iMaxHours
Else
    m_iHours = iWklyHours
End If
End Property
```

7. The final property is the EmpName property, a read-only property that enables the user to see the name of the employee that was retrieved using the EmployeeNum property. This property lets the user make sure that the correct employee is being processed. To create a read-only procedure, you use only a Property Get procedure, as shown below:

```
Public Property Get EmpName() As String
EmpName = m_sLastName & ", " & m_sFirstName
End Property
```

8. After creating the properties of the class, you can create the methods of the class. The Employee class has two methods: GetEmployee and CalcTax. The GetEmployee method takes the information in the EmployeeNum property and attempts to retrieve the employee information. If the procedure is successful, it returns True to the client application. Otherwise, it returns False. Because it returns a value, the GetEmployee method is implemented as a function. The code for the GetEmployee method is:

```
Public Function GetEmployee() As Boolean
Dim sSQLSearch As String
If m_lEmpID <= 0 Then
    GetEmployee = False
    Exit Function
End If
On Error Resume Next
Set EmpRset = Nothing
sSQLSearch = "Select * From Employee Where EmpID = " _
& m_lEmpID
Set EmpRset = EmpData.OpenRecordset(sSQLSearch, _
dbOpenDynaset)
If EmpRset.RecordCount = 0 Then
    GetEmployee = False
    Exit Function
End If
With EmpRset
    m_sLastName = !LastName & ""
    m_sFirstName = !FirstName & ""
    If IsNull(!Payscale) Then
        m_sngPayScale = 0
    Else
        m_sngPayScale = !Payscale
    End If
    If IsNull(!MaxHours) Then
        m_iMaxHours = 40
    Else
m_iMaxHours = !MaxHours
        End If
```

```
        If IsNull(!OvertimeRate) Then
            m_sngOvertime = 1
        Else
            m_sngOvertime = !OvertimeRate
        End If
        If IsNull(!TaxRate) Then
            m_sngTaxRate = 0
        Else
            m_sngTaxRate = !TaxRate
        End If
    End With
    GetEmployee = True
    End Function
```

In the above code, double quotes are appended to the end of any database field that returns a text value. This is to avoid errors that occur when the field contains a null value.

9. The final method is the CalcTax method, a Sub procedure that calculates gross pay; social security, Medicare, and federal tax withholding; and net pay. The code for the CalcTax method is:

```
Public Sub CalcTax()
Dim iNormHours As Integer, iOverHours As Integer
If m_iHours > 40 Then
    iNormHours = 40
    iOverHours = m_iHours - 40
Else
    iNormHours = m_iHours
    iOverHours = 0
End If
m_sngPay = Int(100 * (iNormHours * m_sngPayScale + _
iOverHours * m_sngPayScale * m_sngOvertime)) / _
100
m_sngSocial = Int(100 * m_sngPay * 0.062) / 100
m_sngMedicare = Int(100 * m_sngPay * 0.0145) / 100
m_sngTax = Int(100 * m_sngPay * m_sngTaxRate / 100) _
/ 100
```

```
        m_sngNetPay = m_sngPay - m_sngSocial - _
          m_sngMedicare - m_sngTax
        End Sub
```

In the above code, numbers are multiplied by 100, then divided by 100 to avoid round-off error after the second decimal place.

10. After creating the properties and methods of the class, you need to save the project. The default name for the .cls file is cEmployee, the class name.

Displaying a Form from a Class

Objects created from classes are not the only components that can be exposed by the server. An ActiveX server can have a visual interface for some of its tasks. This visual interface is created using forms, like you would use in a standard executable file. There is, however, a difference in the way that these forms are exposed to the client applications. From a client, you cannot reference a form in a server directly. Instead, the server uses a class method to create an instance of the form and display it.

The technique for creating an instance of a form is basically the same as creating an instance of a class. You use a Dim statement to create a form object. You can then manipulate the properties of the form and use its methods like a regular form, which is very similar to creating multiple forms in a Multiple Document Interface (MDI) program. The Dim statement to create a form object is shown below:

```
Dim frmCheck As New frmPaycheck
```

Of course, the form that you are creating must exist as a form within the ActiveX server project. To create the form in the project, you add a form to the project and use the same visual design tools that you would use for a form in a standard program. Exercise 10.3 shows you how to create a form for previewing a paycheck before it is printed.

NOTE   You should use caution when displaying forms from a server. If the server application is located on a machine other than the one where the client application is located, the form will appear on the machine that is running the server application.

EXERCISE 10.3

Creating and Displaying a Form from an ActiveX Server

1. Open the Payroll project.

2. Choose the Add Form item from the Project menu to add a new blank form to the project. Name the form **frmPaycheck**.

3. Set the Caption property of the form to Paycheck Preview.

4. Add seven label controls to the form with the following captions: **Name:**, **Hours Worked:**, **Gross Pay:**, **Social Security:**, **Medicare:**, **Federal Tax:**, and **Net Pay:**.

5. Add a label control array to the form. Name the labels **lblPayroll** and set the BorderStyle property to Fixed Single. These labels will be used to display the payroll information. (If you do not remember how to create a control array, refer to Chapter 4, "Advanced Design Features.") You need to have seven elements of the control array, numbered zero to six.

6. Add two command buttons to the form named **cmdPrint** and **cmdCancel**. Set the Caption properties to &Print Check and &Cancel respectively. After you have added the command buttons, the form will look like the following illustration.

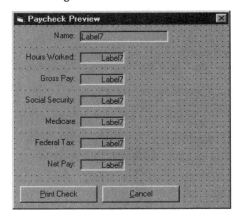

7. To the Click event of each command button, add the statement Unload Me to close the form. If you want to print a check, that is left as an exercise for you.

8. Now that the form has been designed, you need a way to display it. Select the cEmployee class in the Project window and bring up its Code window.

9. Add another method named **PreviewCheck** to the class. This method creates an instance of the form, populates the label controls with the current data, and shows the form.

10. Create an instance of the form in the method using the following declaration statement in the PreviewCheck method:

```
Dim frmCheck As New frmPaycheck
```

11. Set the values of the label controls using the following code. Notice the use of the With statement to avoid having to type the object name for each label setting.

```
With frmCheck
        .lblPayroll(0) = m_sLastName & ", " & m_sFirstName
        .lblPayroll(1) = m_iHours
        .lblPayroll(2) = m_sngPay
        .lblPayroll(3) = m_sngSocial
        .lblPayroll(4) = m_sngMedicare
        .lblPayroll(5) = m_sngTax
        .lblPayroll(6) = m_sngNetPay
End With
```

12. Finally, show the form using the following statement. The form is shown modal because you want the user to examine the information before the check is printed.

```
frmCheck.Show vbModal
```

13. Save the project.

Setting Up the Object Model

Microsoft ✓ *Exam* *Objective*

Compile a project with class modules into a COM component.

- Implement an object model within a COM component.

As you are creating the classes that comprise your COM component, you may notice that some classes have a greater importance than other classes or that a particular class may need to manage multiple instances of another class. This hierarchy of classes is formalized in the object model of the COM component. The object model defines the relationship between multiple objects within a component.

As an example of an object model, consider an application designed for tracking attendance and grades in an elementary school. As you might expect, the application would use several objects: school, teacher, student, subject, and classroom. You can almost immediately see how these objects are related. A school object would need to be able to manage a collection of teacher objects and classroom objects. Each teacher object would have a collection of student objects, and each student object would have a collection of subject objects.

The object model of the school component is created as you create the properties and methods of the classes used to define the objects. The Class Builder add-in can be very useful in creating the object hierarchies that make up the object model. The Class Builder lets you easily add collections to a class and automatically creates the Add and Remove methods needed for managing the collection. Figure 10.3 shows the layout of the school object model. Because building this entire model is a long process, the classes of the school component are included on the companion CD-ROM.

FIGURE 10.3

Using the Class Builder to facilitate creating an object model

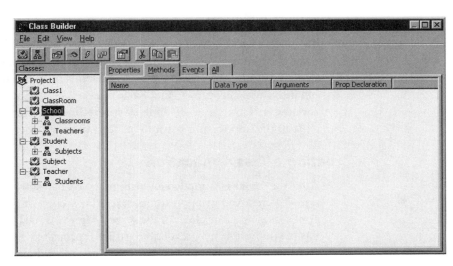

Testing the Server Components

Debug a COM client written in Visual Basic.

After you have designed all the components (classes) of the server, you need to test each component carefully. The design of Visual Basic enables you to use all the debugging tools of the development environment in the testing of your server. Using the debugging tools enables you to watch the values of variables, set breakpoints, and step through the code to determine the path of code execution. This type of debugging capability makes it much easier to find and fix errors in a server than was previously possible.

To test the components of the server, you need to do three things:

1. Start the server.

2. Start a second instance of Visual Basic.

3. Create and run a test application in the second instance of Visual Basic.

Starting the Server

To start the server, you need to click the Run button on the toolbar. Visual Basic then compiles the initialization part of the application, and the server will be running. Another, better approach is to press the Ctrl+F5 key combination, which causes Visual Basic to compile the entire application before running it. This approach enables you to find any compiler errors that may exist in the application before you start the test process.

Creating a Test Application

After the server is compiled and running, you can start creating a test application. To create a test application, start a new copy of Visual Basic to test the application as a true client of the server. After you start the new copy of Visual Basic, you need to create a Standard EXE project as the client application.

After starting the project, open the References dialog box from the Project menu to set a reference to the server that you created. The server is listed in the References dialog box by the project description you provided, or by the project name if no description was entered. The References dialog box indicating the Payroll server is shown in Figure 10.4.

F I G U R E   10.4

References for the test
application

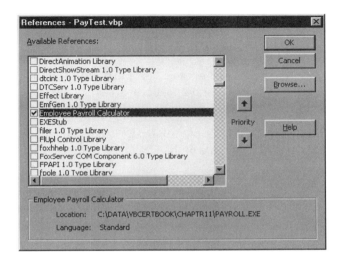

If you have not started the server, you cannot set a reference to it.

At this point, you can design the forms, modules, and classes of the test application as you would for any other program that you create. To effectively test a server, you need to create an instance of each public class in the server and access each property, method, and event of each class. Exercise 10.4 shows you how to create a test application for the Payroll server.

EXERCISE 10.4

Creating a Payroll Test Application

1. Start the Payroll server by pressing Ctrl+F5.

2. Start a second copy of Visual Basic and select the Standard EXE project type.

3. Open the References dialog box and set a reference to the Payroll server.

4. Set the name of the Project to **PayTest**.

5. Select the main form of the project and name it **frmPayInput**. Set the Caption property of the form to **Payroll Input Form**.

6. Add three labels to the form and set the Caption properties to **Employee ID:**, **Name:**, and **Hours Worked:**.

7. Add two text boxes to the form and name them **txtEmpID** and **txtHours**. Clear the Text properties of both text boxes.

8. Add another label to the form and name it **lblName**. Set the Border-Style of the label to Fixed Single. This label will be used to display the name of the employee retrieved from the server.

9. Add four command buttons to the form and name them **cmdGet-Employee**, **cmdCalculate**, **cmdShowPay**, and **cmdExit**. Set the Caption properties to **&Get Employee**, **&Calculate Pay**, **&Show Paycheck**, and **&Exit** respectively. When you are finished, the form should look like the one in the following illustration.

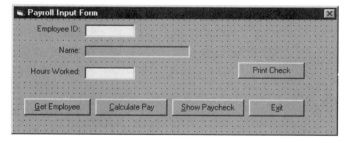

10. You first need to create an instance of the cEmployee class that is accessible to all the procedures of the form. You do this by placing the following statement in the Declarations section of the form:

    ```
    Dim oEmployee As New cEmployee
    ```

11. The first task of the test application is to retrieve employee information, which uses the GetEmployee method of the cEmployee class. To execute this method, place the following code in the Click event of the cmdGetEmployee button. The code passes the input employee ID to the property of the class and invokes the appropriate method. If the method is successful, the name of the employee is returned.

    ```
    With oEmployee
        .EmployeeNum = txtEmpID.Text
    ```

```
            If .GetEmployee Then
                lblName.Caption = .EmpName
            Else
                MsgBox "Employee not found"
            End If
        End With
```

12. The next step is to calculate the employee's pay based on the number of hours worked. Place the following code in the Click event of the cmdCalculate button. The code passes the hours worked as entered by the user to the class, then invokes the CalcTax method to handle the payroll calculations.

    ```
    oEmployee.HoursWorked = Val(txtHours.Text)
    oEmployee.CalcTax
    ```

13. After the calculation is made, you should verify the calculations. Use the following code in the Click event of the cmdShowPay button to display the Paycheck Preview form that exists in the ActiveX server.

    ```
    oEmployee.PreviewCheck
    ```

14. Place the following code in the Click event of the cmdExit button. The code destroys the instance of the class and unloads the test application.

    ```
    Set oEmployee = Nothing
    Unload Me
    ```

15. Save the test project.

16. Run the test project and enter **2** as the employee ID and **45** as the number of hours worked. Then click the Get Employee button. The test application returns the name of the employee, as shown in the next illustration.

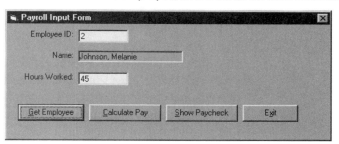

17. Continue testing the application by clicking the Calculate Pay button. Then click the Show Paycheck button to calculate all the payroll information and display the paycheck preview, as shown in the following illustration.

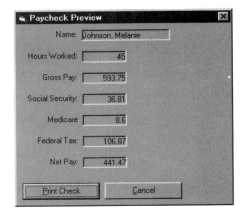

18. You can repeat the process for other employee ID values. If you are using the sample database provided on the CD-ROM (*Payroll.mdb*), there are four employees, numbered one to four. If you enter a number above four, the server does not find the employee, and a message to this effect is displayed.

Compiling the Server

After testing is complete, it is time to compile the server so it can be used by others. The process of compiling the server is the same as compiling standard programs, except that the process has a few more options.

Multithreading Objects in the Server

The key option in creating a server is the Multithreading option. Multithreading enables several processes to run simultaneously on the server, which means that one client application does not have to wait for a process of another client application to be completed before its process is started. Multithreading enables a program to make good use of multiple processors on a server computer.

Visual Basic supports a multithreading model known as the Apartment model. In this model, each thread contains its own copy of the global data of the object, and each thread is unaware of any objects that are parts of other threads. This model provides a "safe" multithreading environment that is less likely to cause problems than other more sophisticated models.

To set up a server to use multithreading, you specify options in the properties of the project. ActiveX DLL servers and ActiveX EXE servers have different multithreading options, as described in the following sections.

Multithreading with In-Process Servers   Two multithreading options are available for ActiveX DLL servers :

- One Thread of Execution

- Apartment Threading

You can select these options from the General page of the Project Properties dialog box, as shown in Figure 10.5.

FIGURE 10.5

Multithreading options for ActiveX DLL servers

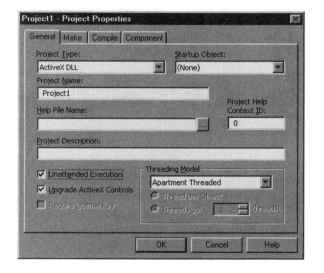

One Thread of Execution means that all objects created by the server run on a single thread, resulting in no multithreading of the objects. You can choose this option by selecting Single Threaded from the drop-down list in the Threading Model options.

Apartment Threading enables the clients of the ActiveX DLL to use multithreading. The use of multiple threads is controlled by the client. Also, to use multithreading, the Unattended Execution option must be checked, which means that the server cannot have forms or message boxes displayed that require user interaction. To use this multithreading model, select Apartment Threaded from the drop-down list in the Threading Model options.

Multithreading with Out-of-Process Servers   For ActiveX EXE servers, you can use three multithreading models:

- One Thread of Execution

- Thread Pool with Thread Sharing

- One Thread per Object

You can select the multithreading option from the General page of the Project Properties dialog box, as shown in Figure 10.6.

F I G U R E   10.6

Multithreading
options for an ActiveX
EXE server

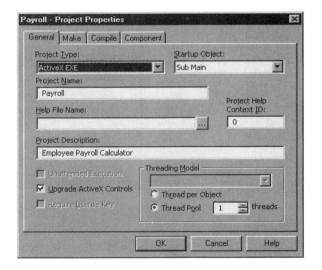

The One Thread of Execution model means that all the objects handled by your server will execute in a single thread. In essence, there is no multi-threading with this model of execution. To select one thread of execution, choose the Thread Pool option in the Threading Model options of the Project Properties dialog box and set the number of threads to one.

The Thread Pool model enables you to specify the number of threads that are available on the server for handling objects. As you create new objects, each object is assigned to a thread. When you have reached the last thread in the pool, the next object is created on the first thread and the process repeats. This process is similar to teller lines in a bank. If a bank has three tellers, the first three customers can each go to a different line and be handled simultaneously. The fourth customer lines up behind one of the original three customers and waits a turn to handle their transactions. To implement thread pooling, choose the Thread Pool option and specify the number of threads you want to have in the pool. You can specify any number of threads for the process, but a general rule of thumb is to have one thread for each processor on the computer.

The final model is One Thread per Object. This model creates a new thread for each object that is created by the server. The advantage of this model is that each object operates in an independent thread and is not waiting on other objects to finish. A major drawback to this model is that you cannot control the number of threads that will be created. If you have an application that uses a large number of objects, many threads will be created and will eventually slow down the system performance. If you do want to choose the thread per object model, select the Thread per Object option button in the Threading Model options.

Setting Other Compiler Options

Because an ActiveX server provides components to other applications, there are other compiler options you can set that were not available for standard programs. These options are contained on the Component page of the Project Properties dialog box, as shown in Figure 10.7. The options are described below.

FIGURE 10.7

Component options for the project

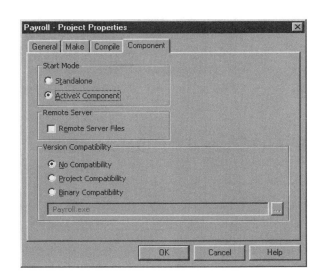

Start Mode   Determines whether the server can be started in stand-alone mode (running tasks on its own) or only as a component server. This option is not available for ActiveX DLL servers.

Remote Server Files   Determines whether Visual Basic creates a .vbr file that is required for the server to be run on a remote computer. This option is available for ActiveX EXE and ActiveX DLL servers, but is available only with the Enterprise Edition of Visual Basic.

Version Compatibility   Determines whether new versions of the project will be forced to be compatible with previous versions. This option has three settings:

No Compatibility   Version compatibility is not enforced.

Project Compatibility   The current version will be compatible with the project specified in the file location box.

Binary Compatibility   The current version will be compatible with compiled programs that used a previous version of the server.

Finishing the Compilation

After you have set the Multithreading options and the Component options for the server, you can complete the compilation by choosing the Make item from the File menu. The Make Project dialog box enables you to specify the name and location of the .exe or .dll file that you are creating. Also, the Options button provides you access to the Project Properties dialog box in case you want to make any last-minute changes to the properties before compilation is finished.

When you select the OK button on the Make Project dialog box, Visual Basic compiles the project, checking for any compiler errors, and writes the .exe or .dll file to the specified location.

Registering Components

Microsoft ✓ *Exam* *Objective*	**Register and unregister a COM component.**

After you have created a COM component, you must register it before it can be used. This must occur whether the component is on your development machine or on a client machine that will be using the component. On your development machine, the component will be registered as it is compiled. There are several methods of registering a COM component on a client machine:

- Run the component (if it is capable of being run by itself). This action automatically registers the component.

- Use the Regsvr32.exe program to register the component. With this method, you specify the path and the name of the component as a command line argument of the Regsvr32 program.

- Use a setup program to register the component as your program is being installed on another computer. You will look at setup programs in Chapter 18, "Deploying an Application."

Of course, at some point, there will come a time when a component is no longer needed and you will want to remove the information about the control from the system Registry. How you unregister a component depends on the type of component with which you are working. If the component is an EXE server, you can run the .exe with the UnRegserver parameter as illustrated in the following line of code:

```
Payroll.exe /UnRegserver
```

If you are working with a DLL server, you need to use the Regsvr32 utility and specify the /U parameter. This is shown in the following code:

```
Regsvr32.exe /u C:\Automation\Payroll.dll
```

Running Asynchronous Processes

Microsoft ✓ *Exam* *Objective*

Create callback procedures to enable asynchronous processing between COM components and Visual Basic client applications.

In the normal course of operations, a call to a procedure on the server must finish before the next step in the client application can be executed. This process is known as synchronous operation. Synchronous operation works well for short operations; a long operation on the server could tie up the client application, preventing the user from performing other tasks within the application. A better method is to use asynchronous operation, which enables the client to spawn a process, and then have the server notify the client when the operation is finished. Asynchronous operations can be set up between a client and a server using either events created by the server object or by using callback functions.

The easiest way to set up asynchronous operations is through the use of an event. You create an event on the server object using an event declaration and the RaiseEvents statement. Then the client uses a procedure to respond to the event. Exercises 10.5 and 10.6 show you the steps in setting up asynchronous operations.

Setting Up the Server for Asynchronous Operation

The server side of the asynchronous operation requires only the creation and triggering of an event, as illustrated in Exercise 10.5.

EXERCISE 10.5

Setting Up an Event for Asynchronous Operation

1. Open the Payroll project created in Exercises 10.1 through 10.3.

2. Add an event declaration to the cEmployee class using the following code:

   ```
   Public Event PrintFinished(ByVal iNumPages As Integer)
   ```

3. Add a new method to the cEmployee class to raise the event. Call the method **PrintCheck** and place the following code in the method. In a real setting, you would perform a Print operation and report the number of pages printed.

   ```
   Public Sub PrintCheck()
   RaiseEvent PrintFinished(15)
   End Sub
   ```

4. Save the project. Then run the server to make it available to the client application.

Setting Up the Client for Asynchronous Operation

Setting up the client requires that you specify a variable using the WithEvents keyword, to let your program know that you will be expecting events from an object on the server. Because you cannot use the New keyword with the WithEvents keyword, you have to declare the variable and then set it to an instance of the cEmployee class. After creating the variable, you need to write an event procedure to respond to the event triggered by the server. Exercise 10.6 shows you how to accomplish this.

EXERCISE 10.6

Allowing the Client to Respond to Server Object Events

1. Start a second copy of Visual Basic and open the PayTest project created in Exercise 10.4.

2. Change the declaration statement for the oEmployee object to the following to enable the object to capture and respond to events.

   ```
   Dim WithEvents oEmployee As cEmployee
   ```

3. Add the following code to the Load event of the Form to create an instance of the cEmployee object:

   ```
   Set oEmployee = New cEmployee
   ```

4. In the Code window, select the oEmployee object and place the following code in the PrintFinished event of the object:

   ```
   MsgBox "Printer has printed " & Str(iNumPages) & _
   " pages."
   ```

5. Add a command button to the form and name it **cmdPrint**. Set the Caption to **Print**. Place the following code in the Click event of the button to start the PrintCheck method of the oEmployee object:

   ```
   oEmployee.PrintCheck
   ```

6. Save the project and run the program. When you click the Print button, the PrintCheck method is called and program execution is immediately returned to the next line of code. When the method finishes, the Print-Finished event is triggered. The client application then responds to the event by displaying a message box with the number of pages printed.

Summary

This chapter has covered a lot of information about the creation of ActiveX servers, but is by no means an in-depth study of the topic. I could write another book about creating and using ActiveX servers. However, working through the material of this chapter should help you meet the following Microsoft exam objectives.

- Create a COM component that implements business rules or logic. Components include DLLs, ActiveX controls, and active documents.

- Compile a project with class modules into a COM component.

  - Set properties to control the instancing of a class within a COM component.

  - Implement an object model within a COM component.

- Debug a COM component written in Visual Basic.

- Register and unregister a COM component.

- Create callback procedures to enable asynchronous processing between COM components and Visual Basic client applications.

Review Questions

1. Which of the following is not true of In-Process servers?

   A. An ActiveX DLL is an In-Process server.

   B. They are faster than Out-of-Process servers.

   C. They can run as a stand-alone application.

   D. They run in the same process space as the client.

2. Which of the following is an advantage of an Out-of-Process server? Check all that apply.

    A. It can run as a stand-alone application.

    B. An Out-of-Process server has more multithreading options than an In-Process server.

    C. It can handle more objects in a single project than an In-Process server.

    D. It is faster than an In-Process server.

3. Which of the following settings of the Instancing property apply only to Out-of-Process servers? Check all that apply.

    A. Private

    B. Public Not Creatable

    C. MultiUse

    D. SingleUse

4. What is the advantage of multithreading?

    A. It enables a single object to execute on more than one processor.

    B. It significantly speeds up any server operations.

    C. Multiple objects can run in separate threads and avoid blocking each other.

    D. There is no advantage to multithreading.

5. Which of the following multithreading models uses the most resources?

    A. Apartment model

    B. Single Threaded

    C. Thread Pool

    D. Thread per Object

6. Which setting of the Instancing property creates all client objects from the same instance of the server object?

A. Private

B. Public Not Creatable

C. MultiUse

D. SingleUse

7. How do you create a property for a server object?

A. Declare a variable as Public.

B. Use Property procedures.

C. Create a Friend variable.

D. Use a Sub procedure.

8. What statement is used to trigger an event?

A. LoadEvent

B. Trigger

C. RaiseEvent

D. Event.Raise

9. How do you display a server form from a client application?

A. Use the Show method and specify the form name.

B. Call a method of the server object that creates and displays an instance of the form.

C. Use a server event to show the form.

D. You cannot create forms in a server project.

10. What is the advantage of asynchronous processing?

    A. There is no advantage.

    B. The server can accomplish other tasks while the requested task is running.

    C. The client can accomplish other tasks while the requested task is running.

    D. It enables the client to display a server form.

11. What keyword must be used in a declaration statement to enable an object to respond to events?

    A. Notify

    B. New

    C. WithEvents

    D. UseEvents

CHAPTER

11

Creating a COM
Client Application

In Chapter 10, "Creating COM Components," you learned how to create a COM component to provide business objects and other functions to other programs. COM client applications are the counterpart to COM components. COM client applications are the programs that create instances of the objects and use them to perform tasks.

COM client applications are not limited to using objects from components that you create. Client applications can work with objects from any program that provides COM components, including Microsoft Word, Microsoft Excel, and many others. All that you need to create a COM client application is a connection to a component and an understanding of the objects of the component.

In this chapter, you will look first at the fundamentals of creating COM client applications. Then, you will create some specific applications that use objects from COM components.

COM Client Fundamentals

When you create a COM client, you are using the objects that are made available by the component(s) that you are accessing. Therefore, it is important to understand object models in general as well as the object model of the particular component with which you are working.

After you have an understanding of the objects of the component, you can follow three basic steps to create a COM client:

1. Set a reference to the component you are accessing.

2. Create object variables for the objects that you will be using.

3. Write code to use the properties, methods, and events of the objects.

Understanding Object Models

From working with Visual Basic, you should have a basic understanding of how object models work. All the forms and controls in Visual Basic are objects, and you create your own objects by defining classes in a program. (If you are unfamiliar with the creation of classes, review Chapter 5, "Creating Classes in a Program.") Each time you create a new form or a new control on a form, you are creating an instance of a form or control object.

Unlike the form and control objects, many of the objects that you use from COM components will not have a visual component; they will be handled only in code. If you are familiar with writing code for the forms and controls of Visual Basic, however, you are already familiar with the process of writing code with objects. Each object can have properties, methods, and events, as the forms and controls do. To access these elements of the objects, you write code using dot notation as shown in the following code:

```
oEmployee.EmployeeNum = txtEmpID.Text
If oEmployee.GetEmployee Then
    lblName.Caption = oEmployee.EmpName
Else
    MsgBox "Employee not found"
End If
```

In this code example, you specify the variable that contains the instance of the object, followed by a period (or dot) and the name of the property or method. You can see that setting a property of the object (shown in the first line) uses the same type of notation and statement as setting the property of a control (shown for the label control in the third line). As this sample illustrates, your knowledge of working with Visual Basic's objects translates to any other objects that you may use from COM components.

How to Find Help for Object Models

Now that you have seen how to access the properties and methods of an object, you need to find out what properties and methods are available for a given object. Fortunately, several sources of help are available to you. In many commercial applications, such as Microsoft Word, help files are available that describe the objects and help you work with the properties and methods. Figure 11.1 shows you the object model for Microsoft Word. This information is contained in the VbaWrd8.hlp help file that comes with Word.

FIGURE 11.1

Microsoft Word's
object model

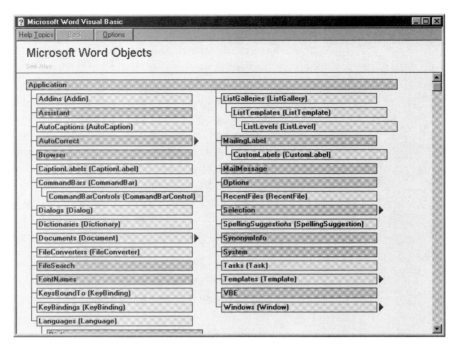

If you are working with a component created by another programmer, you need to look for documentation of the component's objects in either printed or help file form. By the same token, if you create a COM component, make sure that you document it well so others can use it.

How Visual Basic Helps You with Object Models

Two other sources of help for working with object models are contained within Visual Basic itself. The first source of information is the Object Browser. The Object Browser enables you to look at any objects that are part of the references for the project. The Browser shows you the objects and the properties, methods, and events of each object. This information may not necessarily tell you the purpose of each of the objects, but it gives you information about the following:

- Which properties are contained in the object and which are read-only

- The data type of each property

- Which arguments are required for a method call and which arguments are optional

- The return data type of a method that is a Function procedure
- Which parameters are passed by an event of the object
- Any constants defined for the object
- A brief description of each of the methods, properties, and constants (if provided by the developer)

To access this information, you need to have set a reference to the COM component in the References dialog box for your project. Then, you can invoke the Object Browser by clicking the Toolbar button, selecting the Object Browser item from the View menu, or pressing the F2 key. Figure 11.2 shows the Browser contents for Microsoft Word.

F I G U R E 11.2

Viewing objects in the Object Browser

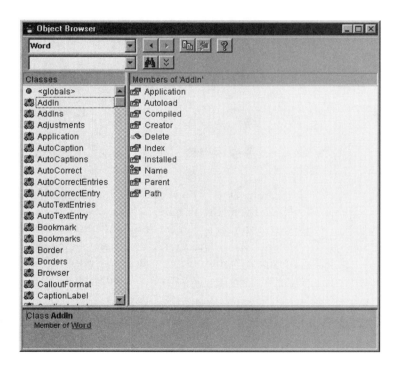

Visual Basic's second form of help comes from its Auto List Members and Auto QuickInfo tools. As you are writing code, Auto List Members displays a drop-down list of an object's properties and methods when you type the period (dot) after an object variable name. This list is shown in Figure 11.3.

FIGURE 11.3

Auto List Members
displaying properties
and methods

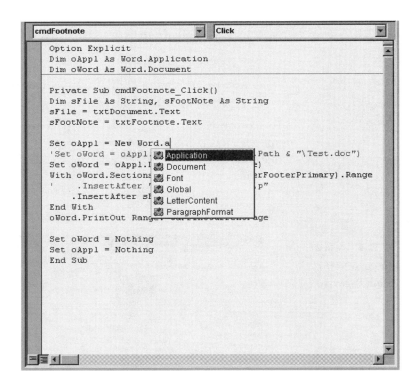

Auto QuickInfo shows you the method's syntax as a ToolTip when you enter the method's name. This tool provides a quick reference of the required and optional arguments of the method as well as the data types of the arguments. The Auto QuickInfo tool also provides a drop-down list of valid property values if the values have been defined for the property. The Auto QuickInfo tool is shown in Figure 11.4.

Creating Objects in a Program

When you create objects in a program, you are creating variables that hold an instance of the object. You create the object variables using a declaration statement, as you would for a variable of any other data type. You can use Dim, Private, or Public keywords in creating object variables. You can then assign an object to the variable using a Set statement or the CreateObject function.

When you create an object variable, you have two options. You can create a variable to hold a specific type of object, such as a Word application or Excel spreadsheet, or you can create a generic object variable that can work with any object. This situation is somewhat analogous to using a specific

FIGURE 11.4

Auto QuickInfo displaying method syntax

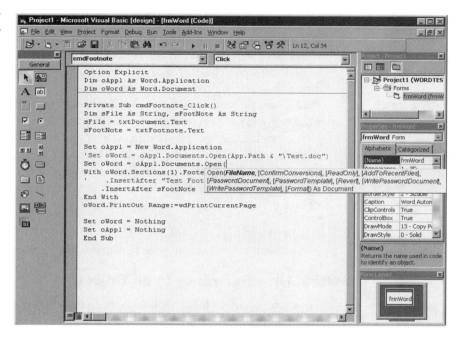

FIGURE 11.4

Auto QuickInfo displaying method syntax

data type or the Variant data type for other variables. Declaring a specific object type is known as early binding of the object. Declaring a generic object variable is known as late binding of the object.

Using Early Binding versus Late Binding

Whenever possible, you should use early binding of objects in your code. There are several advantages of early binding, including:

- Objects are created faster because a specific object type is known.

- Information about the properties and methods of the object are known at design time, which enables Visual Basic's tools (Auto List Members and Auto QuickInfo) to provide you with information about the properties and methods of the object.

Early binding occurs when you specify the object type in the declaration statement for the object variable, as shown in the following statements:

```
Dim oWord As Word.Document
Dim oAppl As Word.Application
Dim oSheet As Excel.Worksheet
```

The only real advantage to late binding is that it gives you the flexibility of defining the object type while the program is running (in contrast to early binding, where you specify the object type in design mode). One example for using late binding is in the creation of a program where you allow the user to pick the tool to be used. For example, you might write a program that uses either Word or WordPerfect to open and print a document. The application that is used depends on which is available on the user's machine. You would need to write your program to handle Word and WordPerfect, and allow the user to pick the appropriate one. When you need to use late binding, you declare a variable as simply Object, then use the CreateObject function to assign an object to the variable. Only when the object is assigned to the variable is the type of the object known. The following code shows an example of late binding:

```
Dim oWord2 As Object
Set oWord2 = CreateObject("Word.Application")
```

Setting Up a Reference to an Object

For many of the COM components that you will work with, you can specify the component in the References dialog box of the project. Specifying the component enables you to identify the specific object type in your declaration statements to enable early binding. To set up a reference to a component, choose the References item in the Project menu and select the COM component in the dialog box. If the component is not listed, you can click the Browse button to look through the available .dll, .tlb, and .exe files available to your computer and find the particular component. After the component is identified, specific object information is available through the Object Browser or the Auto List Members and Auto QuickInfo tools of Visual Basic. Figure 11.5 shows the References dialog box for a typical project using the Microsoft Word Object Library.

Creating an Object Instance

When you declare an object variable, you are specifying only a placeholder for the object. An instance of the object is not created in the declaration statement. The creation of the object instance occurs later in code through one of the three methods discussed below.

Using the New Keyword   The first method of creating an instance of an object is to use the New keyword in the declaration statement of the object variable. The New keyword tells Visual Basic that a new instance of the specified object is to be created. This instance is not created when the declaration

FIGURE 11.5

References dialog box

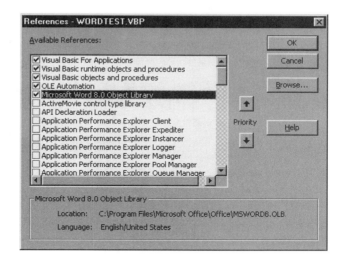

statement is executed. Rather, the instance is created when the object variable is first used, either in setting a property or calling a method. The following code illustrates the use of the New keyword:

```
'An object variable is defined here. The object
' is not created here.
Dim oAppl As New Word.Application
'The object is actually created here.
oAppl.Documents.Open "Test1.Doc"
```

Using the Set Command The second method of creating an instance of an object is to use the Set command. This command assigns an object to an object variable. You can use the Set command to assign an existing object to a variable. You can also use the Set command with the New keyword to create a new instance of an object. When you use the Set command to assign an object to an object variable, the declaration statement for the object variable cannot use the New keyword.

The Set command creates an instance of an object when the command is executed. The following code shows how the Set command is used to assign existing objects and to create new objects:

```
'Object variables are defined here
Dim oWord As Word.Document
Dim oWord2 As Word.Document
```

```
'An existing object is assigned to a variable
Set oWord = oAppl.Documents(0)
'A new object is created and assigned to a variable
Set oWord2 = New Word.Document
```

Using the CreateObject Function   The final method of creating an instance of an object is with the CreateObject function. This function is typically used to create a specific object type with a generic object variable. That is, you typically use this function only when the object type is unknown at design time. When using the CreateObject function, the object variable is declared as simply Object. The object is then created with the Set command and the CreateObject function. The following code shows the use of the Create-Object function to create an instance of an Excel spreadsheet:

```
'Declare an object variable
Dim oSpread As Object
'Create an Excel object
Set oSpread = CreateObject("Excel.Sheet")
```

Some programs provide objects that do not support early binding. These objects can be created only with the CreateObject function.

Destroying an Instance of an Object

One final bit of information: When you create objects in your program, each object uses memory and other system resources. These resources are held until the object is destroyed or until your program finishes. The object instance should be destroyed when the object variable goes out of scope or when the program ends, but this is not always the case. Therefore, it is a good practice to specifically destroy each object instance when you are through with it. You destroy an instance of an object by setting the object variable to the special value of Nothing. The following code illustrates how to do this:

```
Set oWord = Nothing
Set oAppl = Nothing
Set oSpread = Nothing
```

Using the Nothing value destroys an object instance no matter how the object was created.

Creating a Client for Microsoft Programs

One of the most common uses of COM client applications is to automate tasks using the components of Microsoft Office. To create these types of clients, follow these steps:

1. Set a reference to the proper object library for the task.

2. Create an object of the proper type.

3. Use the methods and properties of the object to accomplish the task.

4. Destroy the object.

In the next two sections, you will perform exercises that illustrate how to accomplish a task in Microsoft Word and Microsoft Outlook. These two exercises show you the basics of automating Microsoft Office tasks.

Working with Microsoft Word

Microsoft ✓ *Exam* *Objective*	**Instantiate and invoke a COM component.** • Create a Visual Basic client application that uses a COM component.

With a client application created in Visual Basic, you can automate almost any task that can be performed in Word. Exercise 11.1 shows you how to open a document, add a footnote to the document, and print the first page of the modified document.

EXERCISE 11.1

Creating a Microsoft Word Client

1. Start a new project in Visual Basic.

2. Using the References dialog box, add a reference to the Microsoft Word 8.0 Object Library. (If you are using an older version of Word, you need to add the appropriate reference. Also, you may need to modify the code presented in the exercise.)

3. Add two label controls to the form and set the Caption properties to **Document to be Modified** and **Footnote to be Added**.

4. Add two text boxes to the form and name them **txtDocument** and **txtFootnote**. Clear the Text property of each text box.

5. Add a command button to the form and name it **cmdFootnote**. Set the Caption property of the button to **Add Footnote**. The completed form is shown in the following illustration.

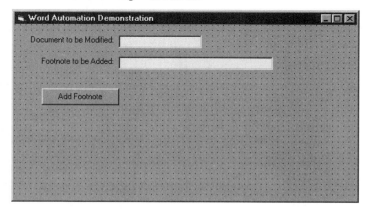

6. Add the following code to the declarations section of the form. This code declares the object variables to hold instances of the Word Application and Document objects.

   ```
   Dim oAppl As Word.Application
   Dim oWord As Word.Document
   ```

7. In the Click event of the cmdFootnote button, add the code to open a document and set the footnote for the document. The code first retrieves the document and footnote information from the text boxes. It then creates the appropriate Word objects. The objects are then used to invoke the methods that set the footnote and print the page. Finally, the objects are destroyed by setting them to Nothing. The code for the command button is shown below:

   ```
   Dim sFile As String, sFootNote As String
   sFile = txtDocument.Text
   sFootNote = txtFootnote.Text
   Set oAppl = New Word.Application
   ```

```
Set oWord = oAppl.Documents.Open(sFile)
With _
oWord.Sections(1).Footers(wdHeaderFooterPrimary).Range
.InsertAfter sFootNote
End With
oWord.PrintOut Range:=wdPrintCurrentPage
Set oWord = Nothing
Set oAppl = Nothing
```

8. Save the project. Then, run the program. If you specify the name of a file (including the full path to the file) and a footnote, then click the command button, the first page of the modified document prints.

Linking Your Program to Microsoft Outlook

Microsoft ✓ ***Exam Objective***

Instantiate and invoke a COM component.

- Create a Visual Basic client application that uses a COM component.

Microsoft Outlook is a contact manager, e-mail client, and scheduler that comes as part of Microsoft Office. Outlook has its own forms that enable you to work with contacts; create, send, and receive e-mail messages; and handle appointment scheduling. However, you may have occasion to create custom applications that access, add to, or modify the information that is handled by Outlook. By using the Outlook object model and a COM client program, you can do just that. Exercise 11.2 shows you how to add a new contact to Outlook from a Visual Basic program. This example comes from a program that managed loan applications. The client wanted to have the contact information placed in Outlook for follow-up calls.

EXERCISE 11.2

Creating an Application that Links to Microsoft Outlook

1. Start a new Visual Basic project.

2. In the References dialog box, set a reference to the Microsoft Outlook 8.0 Object model.

3. On your form, add six label controls with the following captions: **First Name:**, **Last Name:**, **Address:**, **City:**, **State:**, **Zip:**.

4. Add six text boxes to the form with the following names: **txtFirst**, **txtLast**, **txtAddress**, **txtCity**, **txtState**, and **txtZip**. Clear the Text property of each of the text boxes.

5. Add a command button to the form with the Caption **Add Contact**. Name the command button **cmdAdd**. The completed form should look like the following illustration.

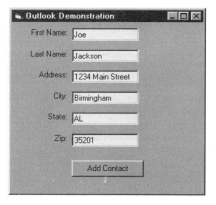

6. Add the following code to the declarations section of the form. This code sets up the variable for the Outlook application object.

   ```
   Dim oOutlook As New Outlook.Application
   ```

7. Add the following code to the Click event of the command button. This code takes information from the text boxes, creates a new contact item in Outlook, and sets the contact information.

   ```
   Dim oContact As Outlook.ContactItem
   With oOutlook
   Set oContact = .CreateItem(olContactItem)
       With oContact
   ```

```
                    .FirstName = txtFirst.Text & ""
                    .LastName = txtLast.Text & ""
                    .HomeAddressStreet = txtAddress.Text & ""
                    .HomeAddressCity = txtCity.Text & ""
                    .HomeAddressState = txtState.Text & ""
                    .HomeAddressPostalCode = txtZip.Text & ""
                    .Save
                End With
            End With
        Set oContact = Nothing
```

8. Place the following code in the Unload event of the form to destroy the object instance created by the program:

    ```
    Set oOutlook = Nothing
    ```

9. Save the project. When you run the program, you can enter information in the form and click the command button to add the data to Outlook. The following illustration shows Outlook with the contact information added.

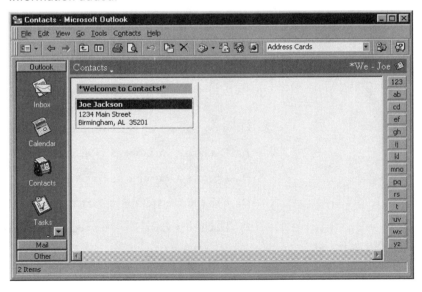

Summary

This chapter has shown you how to create COM client programs that enable you to access the objects of COM components. You have seen how to declare object variables and to create the objects. You have seen specific examples of creating applications that use Microsoft Word or Microsoft Outlook as the COM component. The information in this chapter should help you meet the following certification exam objectives:

- Instantiate and invoke a COM component.

  - Create a Visual Basic application that handles events from a COM component.

  - Create a Visual Basic client application that uses a COM component.

Review Questions

1. Which statement or function do you use to declare an object variable?

   A. Dim oWord As Word.Application

   B. Set oWord = Word.Application

   C. Set oWord = CreateObject("Word.Application")

   D. Dim oWord As String

2. How do you set up early binding in an application?

   A. Declare a variable as Object.

   B. Declare a variable as Variant.

   C. Use the CreateObject Function.

   D. Declare a variable as a specific object type.

3. How do you declare an object variable for late binding?

   A. Declare a variable as Object.

   B. Declare a variable as Variant.

C. Use the CreateObject Function.

D. Declare a variable as a specific object type.

4. Which of the following statements creates an instance of an object? Check all that apply.

A. Dim oWord As Object

B. Dim oWord As New Word.Document

C. Set oWord = New Word.Document

D. Set oWord = CreateObject("Word.Document")

5. What are advantages of early binding? Check all that apply.

A. Objects are created faster.

B. You can use an early bound variable with any object.

C. Information about properties and methods is available while you program.

D. There are no advantages.

6. What are advantages of late binding? Check all that apply.

A. Objects are created faster.

B. You can use a late bound variable with any object.

C. Information about properties and methods is available while you program.

D. There are no advantages.

7. Which of the following statements show the proper use of the New keyword? Check all that apply.

A. Dim oWord As New Object

B. Dim oSheet As New Excel.Sheet

C. Set New oSheet = CreateObject("Excel.Sheet")

D. Set oWord = New Word.Document

CHAPTER

12

Creating ActiveX
Controls with Visual Basic

- Create ActiveX controls.
  - Create an ActiveX control that exposes properties.
  - Create and enable property pages for an ActiveX control.
  - Use control events to save and load persistent properties.
  - Test and debug an ActiveX control.
  - Enable the data binding capabilities of an ActiveX control.
  - Create an ActiveX control that is a data source.
- Design Visual Basic components to access data from a database.
- Use Visual Component Manager to manage components.

V isual Basic has always had the capability to use custom controls to extend its functionality. This capability has created a thriving third-party control market and has made it easy for Visual Basic developers to find controls that they need to perform a task, instead of having to write tons of code. Until version 5 of Visual Basic came out, however, VB developers lacked one capability—writing their own controls. You could learn C++ and write a control, but there was no easy way to create that one perfect control for your application.

What started in version 5 of Visual Basic has been enhanced in version 6. You can now write controls using Visual Basic, employing the same techniques and code you are familiar with for writing standard programs. You can even set up your controls to enable binding to a data source and can allow the control to be a data source itself. The ActiveX controls you create can be used not only in your Visual Basic applications, but also in Office 97 applications, Web pages, or any other environment that supports ActiveX controls. For the average developer, this means tremendous benefits in the reuse of code and custom controls. For the more ambitious, this means a large potential market for a commercial control to be developed.

This chapter focuses on the techniques for creating ActiveX controls in Visual Basic. To prepare for the Visual Basic certification exam, this chapter covers in detail how to create the basic interface of a control; how to add properties, methods, and events to a control; and how to test a control. After you finish the chapter, you will understand the relevant exam objectives, have a basic knowledge of control creation, and have a couple of controls to use in your own applications.

Learning the Basics of Control Creation

Creating an ActiveX control is closely related to writing class modules in Visual Basic. Like a class, you create the Public interface of the ActiveX control by coding Property procedures to create properties, writing Sub and Function procedures to create methods, and using declarations and the Raise-Event statement to create events. If you have a good understanding of creating classes, you are well on your way to understanding the creation of ActiveX controls.

NOTE   Creating classes is covered in Chapter 5, "Creating Classes in a Program."

One key difference between an ActiveX control and a class is that the control has a visual interface. This interface provides a means for the developer and users to interact with the control. Creating the user interface is similar to creating a form with which a user would interact. You either place Visual Basic controls on the user control or you draw components on the control using Line, Circle, and Print methods (the same techniques you use for creating forms).

The other key difference between an ActiveX control and a class is that instances of an ActiveX control can be used and manipulated in the design environment of Visual Basic. Objects created from classes are available only at run time.

The methods you use for creating the user interface depend on the type of control that you want to create. There are three basic categories of ActiveX controls that you will create with Visual Basic:

An extension of an existing control   You take a standard control and add capabilities to it. For example, you might create a text box that accepts only numeric input or a list box that can sort items in descending order.

A new control created from constituent controls   You use several standard controls working together to create a control for a specific task. You may wish to create a command button array for recordset navigation or a single control that handles all the tasks associated with a two-column pick list.

A user-drawn control   You create the entire interface of the new control with drawing methods and the Print method. This is the most difficult method of creating a control. An example of this type of control is a round command button.

No matter which type of control you are going to create, you need to approach the creation of the control in the same way that you approach any other programming project. You need to have a well-planned design for creating the control and a test plan for making sure the control works.

Creating an ActiveX Control

Microsoft ✔ *Exam* *Objective*

Create ActiveX controls.

• Create an ActiveX control that exposes properties.

The simplest way to create the user interface of an ActiveX control is to use controls that already exist. This is known as creating from constituent controls. (Even when creating an extended standard control, you are using a constituent control.) To illustrate the techniques for creating a control, you are going to create a simple Security control that enables the user to enter a user ID and password. If you handle logins for your applications or have to pass user information to a database, you have had to ask for a user ID and password. Typically, you place a couple of labels and text boxes on a form and do a little bit of text processing. This is a simple enough task, but wouldn't it be nice if all you had to do was draw a single control on the form and then access its properties to get all the needed information? This is what the Security control does.

Starting the Project

The first step in creating an ActiveX control is to start the project by choosing New Project from the File menu. This brings up the New Project dialog box shown in Figure 12.1. This dialog box lists all the project types you can create with your version of Visual Basic. (This dialog is also typically displayed when you first start Visual Basic.)

FIGURE 12.1

Selecting the
project type

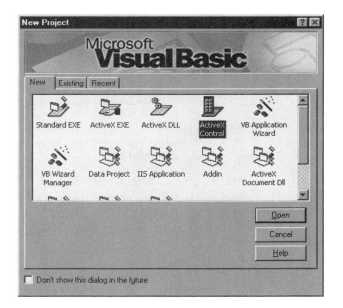

From the Project dialog box, select the ActiveX Control project to start your new control. After you have selected the project type, Visual Basic opens a new UserControl design form, shown in Figure 12.2. Notice that this User-Control looks similar to a standard form without the borders. After the project is created, you need to set the Name property of the control; otherwise, your control will go through life with the generic name UserControl1 (or User-Control2, and so on).

If you look closely at Figure 12.2, (if you are following along on your computer, look at the Properties window) you will see that a number of properties are associated with the UserControl object.

FIGURE 12.2

A UserControl
design form

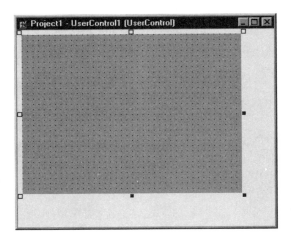

Many of these properties are the same as properties for a form, and a couple deserve special mention:

BackStyle   Determines whether the form behind the control is visible through the blank areas of the UserControl. This is the same as the Back-Style property of a Label control. For most controls you create, you should set this property to Transparent (0), especially if you are creating a control from multiple constituent controls. (You can also leave the setting of the control up to the developer who is using your control.)

ToolboxBitmap   Determines the image that is displayed for your control in the toolbox of anyone who is using the control. If you do not specify a value for this property, the control is shown in the toolbox with the default image, meaning that there is nothing to distinguish your control from any other using the default value. The bitmaps used for this property must be 16×15 pixels, and icon files are not usable.

Adding Constituent Controls

The next step in creating your control is to add the constituent controls to the UserControl object. Two steps are involved in handling the constituent controls:

1. Setting the initial appearance of the controls

2. Handling the position of the controls as the UserControl object is resized

This second step is extremely important. Unless you are going to restrict the size of the control to a single value (as you do for the timer or other invisible

Visual Basic controls), you need to change the size and/or position of the constituent controls in response to the user resizing the UserControl object.

Setting the Initial Appearance

Placing controls on a UserControl object is like placing them on a standard form. You simply select the control from the toolbox and draw an instance of the control on the object. After drawing the control, you need to set the basic properties of the control, such as its name, or the Caption property for a label or command button. However, one difference between creating a standard form and a UserControl is that you typically draw the constituent controls to fill the entire UserControl. You start the controls in the upper left corner of the UserControl and then, after placing all the controls, set the size of the UserControl to enclose only the constituents. To illustrate the creation of a UserControl, Exercise 12.1 walks you through the steps of creating the initial interface of the Security control. The completed control is contained on the CD-ROM as *Security.ctl*.

EXERCISE 12.1

Starting to Create the Security Control

1. Start a new ActiveX control project by selecting the appropriate project type from the New Project dialog box.

2. Change the Name property of the UserControl to **Security**, change the BackStyle property to Transparent, and set the ToolboxBitmap to an appropriate icon. (I used a modified version of the Key.bmp file found in the Graphics folder of Visual Basic.)

3. Add a Label control to the UserControl. Place the label in the upper left corner of the UserControl. Change the Name of the label to **lblSecurity**, set the Caption property to **User Name:**, set the Alignment property to Right Justified, and set the BackStyle property to Transparent. Also, because you will be using multiple Label controls, make this label the first element of a control array by setting the Index property to zero.

4. Copy the existing label and place a second copy on the UserControl below the first instance of the control. Change the Caption property to **Password**.

5. Add a text box next to the first Label control. Set the Name property of the text box to **txtUserName** and delete the information in the Text property.

6. Add a second text box to the UserControl. Place this one below the first text box and next to the second Label control. Set the Name property to **txtPassword**, delete the information in the Text property, and set the PasswordChar to * to keep the information typed by the user from being visible to others.

7. Resize the UserControl to enclose only the constituent controls. When you are finished, your UserControl form should look like the one in the next illustration.

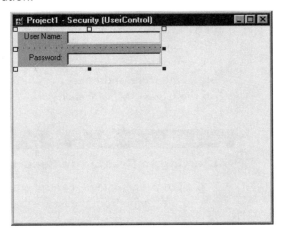

8. Save the project.

The appearance of the UserControl in the preceding graphic is the initial appearance if a developer creates a default instance of the control by double-clicking the control in the Toolbox of a project. If the developer draws the control on a form, the size of the UserControl will be different from what you designed. Figure 12.3 illustrates three instances of the Security control on a form, showing the default size and two other sizes. Notice how the appearance of the control is changed by changing the size. These different appearances show why you have to accommodate size changes for the control.

Handling the Resizing of the Control

As a developer draws an instance of your control on a form, the Resize event of the UserControl is fired. Using this event, you can change the size and position of the constituent controls to allow for different sizes of the UserControl.

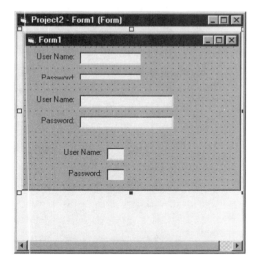

FIGURE 12.3

Several sizes of the
Security control

You can also include code in the event, which limits the size of the control to a particular minimum or maximum value. In Exercise 12.2, you add the code to handle the resizing of the Security control.

EXERCISE 12.2

Accommodating the Changing Size of the Security Control

1. Start with the Security control project.

2. Open the Code window for the UserControl object.

3. Place the following code in the Initialize event to set the initial position of the constituent controls:

```
lblSecurity(0).Top = 1
lblSecurity(0).Left = 1
lblSecurity(1).Top = lblSecurity(0).Top + _
lblSecurity(0).Height + 225
lblSecurity(1).Left = 1
txtUserName.Top = lblSecurity(0).Top
txtUserName.Left = lblSecurity(0).Left + _
lblSecurity(0).Width + 105
txtPassword.Top = lblSecurity(1).Top
```

```
txtPassword.Left = lblSecurity(1).Left + _
lblSecurity(1).Width + 105
```

4. Place the following code in the Resize event to make sure the control meets a minimum size requirement and to expand the text boxes to fill the width of the UserControl:

```
If UserControl.Width < txtUserName.Left + 800 Then
    UserControl.Width = txtUserName.Left + 810
Else
    txtUserName.Width = UserControl.Width - _
txtUserName.Left - 10
    txtPassword.Width = UserControl.Width - _
txtPassword.Left - 10
End If
If UserControl.Height < 810 Then UserControl.Height _
= 810
```

5. At this point, you are ready to try the control in a project. Close the Code and Design windows of the UserControl. Be sure not to exit the project.

6. Select Add Project from the File menu to add a Standard project to the Project group. Notice that the Toolbox of the new project contains the UserControl that you have created, as shown in the next illustration.

7. Select the Security control and add an instance of the control to the form of your standard project. Notice that the control allows you to size it down only to a certain minimum. This is due to the code in the Resize event.

8. Save the project.

Creating the Control's Interface

After you have created your control's visual interface, you need to create your control's programming interface. The programming interface is made up of the properties, methods, and events of the control. These elements are used by developers to set the appearance of your control in their programs and to work with your control from the code in their programs. As you create an ActiveX control, there are two categories of properties, methods, and events that your control may use:

Custom properties, methods, and events   The controls you create through code in Property, Sub, Function, and event procedures

Properties, methods, and events of constituent controls   Part of the controls you use to create the user interface, but they need to be assigned to elements accessible by the user of your control

Adding Your Own Properties, Methods, and Events

As stated earlier, creating ActiveX controls is similar to creating class modules. This is particularly true in the case of creating properties, methods, and events. In this section, you will learn the general process of creating these elements of your controls and then you will look at adding particular elements to the Security control that you are creating as a sample.

Adding Properties to the Control   You add properties to a control by creating Property procedures in the code of your control. There are two basic types of Property procedures:

Property Let   For setting the value of a property

Property Get   For retrieving the value of a property

A third type of Property procedure is the Property Set, which is the same as the Property Let procedure but is used with objects instead of standard data types.

The easiest way to create a property is to use the Add Procedure dialog box accessible from Visual Basic's Tools menu. In the Add Procedure dialog box, shown in Figure 12.4, you identify the procedure as a Property type and set a name for the property. The dialog box creates the shell of a Property Let and Property Get procedure. You then add the necessary code to the procedure to set or retrieve the property values or handle any other appropriate tasks.

FIGURE 12.4

Add Procedure
dialog box

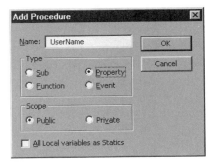

As you are writing the code for the Property procedures, keep a few things in mind:

- You need to specify the data type of the Property Get function. The default type is Variant.

- You need to specify the data type of the variable passed to the Property Let procedure. This data type should match the one set for the Property Get function.

- If you want to create a read-only property, delete the Property Let procedure.

- If you are working with an object, change the Property Let procedure to a Property Set procedure.

Adding Methods to the Control   Methods, as you know, enable the control to perform a function. The methods you create for a control are Sub or Function procedures that are declared as Public. As such, you can write methods to perform any task that you want. For example, you can write a routine to sort the items in a list box in descending order. By making the procedure

Public, the routine becomes a method that is accessible to a program using the control.

To create a method for the control, you can use the same Add Procedure dialog box you used to create Properties. In the case of a method, you specify the procedure type as either a Sub or a Function procedure. You use a Function if your procedure should return a value. Otherwise, you use a Sub procedure. After you fill out the information in the dialog box, Visual Basic creates the procedure declaration statement and the skeleton of the procedure.

Creating Events   The basic steps of creating an event are:

1. Use the Add Procedure dialog box to create the Event declaration.

2. Add to the declaration statement the names of the arguments that will be passed by the event to a program using the control. These arguments will show up in the header for the event procedure in code.

3. Use the RaiseEvent statement to trigger the event and pass information to the calling program.

Creating events is only a little more difficult than creating properties or methods. You still use the Add Procedure dialog box to create the shell of the event. However, you have to do a little more work to implement the event.

Creating the Code Interface of the Security Control   Continuing with the creation of the sample control, Exercise 12.3 shows you how to add properties, methods, and events to the Security control. The exercise shows you how to create the following:

UserName property   Sets and retrieves the username entered in the control

Password property   Sets and retrieves the password information entered in the control

MaxNameLength property   Limits the size of the username

MaxPassLength property   Limits the size of the password

EncryptPass method   Applies a simple encryption to the password

Change event   Notifies the calling program that either the UserName or Password property was changed

Creating the Public Interface of the Control

1. Open the project created in Exercises 12.1 and 12.2.

2. Use the Add Procedure dialog box to create the UserName property.

3. Change the data type of the Property Get statement and the argument of the Property Let statement to String.

4. Add code to the procedures as shown below:

```
Public Property Get UserName() As String
UserName = txtUserName.Text
End Property
Public Property Let UserName(ByVal vsUser As String)
txtUserName.Text = vsUser
End Property
```

5. Create the Password property using the Add Procedure dialog box and the following code:

```
Public Property Get Password() As String
Password = txtPassword.Text
End Property
Public Property Let Password(ByVal vsPassword As String)
txtPassword.Text = vsPassword
End Property
```

6. Create the MaxPassLength and MaxNameLength properties using the following code:

```
Public Property Get MaxNameLength() As Integer
MaxNameLength = txtUserName.MaxLength
End Property
Public Property Let MaxNameLength(ByVal viMaxLen As _
Integer)
txtUserName.MaxLength = viMaxLen
End Property
Public Property Get MaxPassLength() As Integer
MaxPassLength = txtPassword.MaxLength
End Property
```

```
Public Property Let MaxPassLength(ByVal viMaxLen As
Integer)
txtPassword.MaxLength = viMaxLen
End Property
```

7. Create a Sub procedure named **EncryptPass** and add the following code to the procedure. This code simply reverses the order of the letters in the txtPassword text box. You can create a more sophisticated routine if you desire.

```
Dim sOriginal As String, sEncrypt As String
Dim iPassLen As Integer, I As Integer
sOriginal = txtPassword.Text
iPassLen = Len(sOriginal)
sEncrypt = ""
For I = iPassLen to 1
    sEncrypt = sEncrypt & Mid(sOriginal, I, 1)
Next I
txtPassword.Text = sEncrypt
```

8. Create an event declaration statement for the Change event using the Add Procedure dialog box. The declaration statement looks like the following line of code:

```
Public Event Change()
```

9. You will want to activate the Change event whenever a change occurs to either text box in the control. Therefore, you need to add the following statement to the Change events of the txtUserName and txtPassword text boxes:

```
RaiseEvent Change
```

10. Save the project and exit the Code window. If you have another project loaded with a copy of the control on the form, the properties, methods, and events will now show up when you write code for the control.

Using the Control Interface Wizard

The custom elements you create are only part of the programming interface of your control. You may want to give your users access to several of the more standard properties, methods, and events, such as Font, ForeColor, BackColor, and so on. Although you could code each of these by hand, Visual Basic provides an easier method.

Selecting the Members of the Interface Visual Basic comes with the Control Interface Wizard to facilitate creating the interface for your control. To use the Control Interface Wizard, you must first add it to the list of Visual Basic's add-ins using the Add-In Manager. Then, to start the wizard, select it from the Add-Ins menu of Visual Basic. The wizard starts by displaying a start-up screen. After clicking the Next button on the start-up screen, you start the process of creating Public properties for your control. Figure 12.5 shows this second screen of the wizard.

FIGURE 12.5

Selecting members of the Public interface

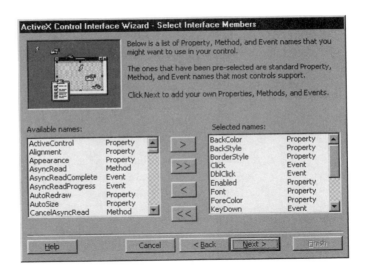

The second page of the wizard, the Select Interface Members page, contains two lists. The first list indicates members that you might want to include in the interface of your control. The second list shows those members that you have selected or members that have been made Public through code that you have already created. You can select members by highlighting them and using the buttons on the wizard or by double-clicking the name. After you have selected all the desired items, click the Next button to move to the next step.

Managing Custom Properties and Methods The next page of the wizard, the Create Custom Interface Members page, shows you the custom elements that you have created in code. This page, shown in Figure 12.6, also enables you to create new elements or edit or delete existing elements. Creating new elements accomplishes the same function as the Add Procedure dialog box; only the shell of the procedure is created. You still have to add the code for the procedure after the wizard has finished its work. When you are satisfied with the custom elements of the control, you can move to the next page of the wizard.

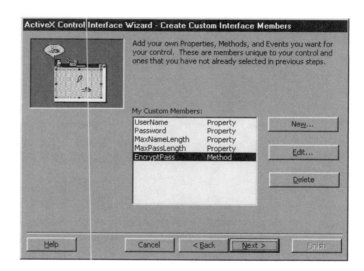

Assigning Properties to the Proper Constituent On the next page of the Control Interface Wizard, you specify what the Public properties and methods of the control will do. This part of the wizard enables you to assign a Public property or method to a property or method of one of the constituent controls. This process of assigning Public interface members is called mapping. As an example of mapping, suppose you specified BackColor as one of the Public properties to create. This page lets you assign the property to the BackColor property of the UserControl. When the wizard creates the Public property, it creates a set of procedures like the following:

```
Public Property Get BackColor() As OLE_COLOR
Attribute BackColor.VB_Description = "Returns/sets the" _
& " background color used to display text and graphics" _
& " in an object."
    BackColor = UserControl.BackColor
End Property
```

```
Public Property Let BackColor(ByVal New_BackColor As OLE_
COLOR)
    UserControl.BackColor() = New_BackColor
    PropertyChanged "BackColor"
End Property
```

To map Public members to the properties or methods of a constituent, select the member to be assigned from the list at the left of the page. (The wizard's Set Mapping page is shown in Figure 12.7.) Then, select the constituent control (or the UserControl) and the specific property from the combo boxes on the right of the page. Repeat this process for each Public member you need to map.

F I G U R E   12.7

Mapping properties to
constituents

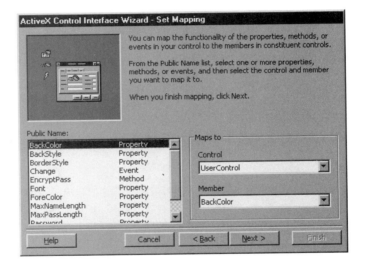

Setting Property Attributes   The final step in using the wizard is to set the attributes of the properties, methods, and events of your control. The Set Attributes page, shown in Figure 12.8, makes it easy for you to create read-only properties and to specify the arguments of methods and events. The attributes that you can set are determined by the type of member you are creating. The specific attributes for each member are:

Properties   You can specify the data type, default value, design-time accessibility, and run-time accessibility of a property. The accessibility options determine whether the property is read/write, read-only, write-only, or not available.

Methods   You can specify the data type of the return value. If you specify a data type, a Function procedure is created; otherwise, a Sub procedure is created. You can also specify the arguments of the procedure.

Events   You can specify the arguments of the event that determine the information that is passed to the calling program.

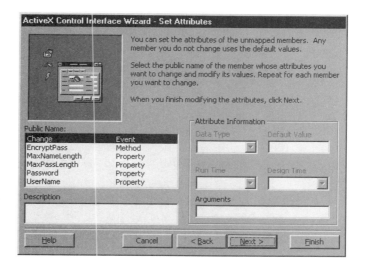

FIGURE   12.8

Specifying the attributes of the members

After you have specified the attributes, you can complete the creation of the Public interface by pressing the Finish button in the wizard. The wizard then creates the code for all the properties, methods, and events that you have defined. Figure 12.9 shows you a sample of the code that is created. As you can see, the wizard does a lot of work for you. You can find the complete code for the Security control on the CD-ROM (in the file *Security.ctl*).

Creating the Members of the Security Control   As always, working through the process of a task is better than only reading about it. Exercise 12.4 continues the process of creating the Security control by using the Control Interface Wizard to create additional parts of the Public interface of the control.

EXERCISE 12.4

Creating the Public Members of the Security Control

1. Add the Control Interface Wizard to your Add-Ins menu by using the Add-In Manager.

EXERCISE 12.4 (CONTINUED)

2. Start the Control Interface Wizard and proceed to the second page of the wizard.

3. Select the following properties to add to the Public interface: Back-Color, BackStyle, BorderStyle, Font, ForeColor.

4. Select the following events as well: KeyDown, KeyPress, KeyUp. After selecting the properties and events, skip to the Set Mapping page of the wizard.

5. Map each of the properties and events selected in steps 3 and 4 to the corresponding properties and events of the UserControl object. Do this by selecting all the properties and events listed in steps 3 and 4 in the Public Name list. Next, select the UserControl object in the Control drop-down list.

6. Click the Finish button to tell the wizard to write the code for you.

FIGURE 12.9

Code generated by the Control Interface Wizard

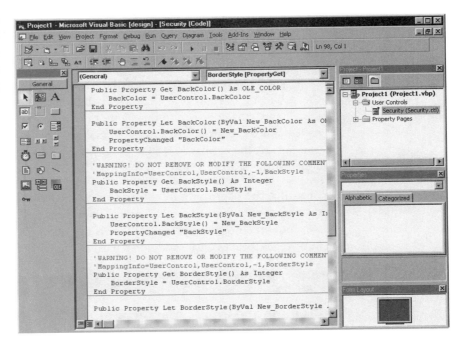

Developing a Property Page

Microsoft
Exam
Objective

Create ActiveX controls.

- Create and enable property pages for an ActiveX control.

You have probably noticed that many of the controls in Visual Basic have a way for you to easily work with the properties of a control. Of course, you have the Properties window that can be organized alphabetically by property name or by categorized groups of properties. But many controls also have a Custom property, which gives you access to property pages. These pages, like the one shown for the TreeView control in Figure 12.10, organize the properties of the control into functional groups and present these groups on pages of a dialog box. The properties typically display default values and enable you to choose other values through drop-down lists, option buttons, or check boxes. The property pages make it easy for you to see all the related properties of a control at the same time.

F I G U R E   12.10

Property pages for
modifying a control

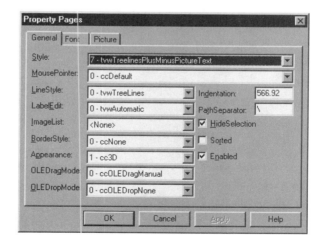

Setting Up the Property Page Wizard

I wouldn't be talking about property pages here if you didn't have the capability to create property pages for your own controls. Visual Basic version 6 makes it easy for you to create and implement property pages for your control. The Property Page Wizard does most of the work for you. To use the Property Page Wizard, you have to access Visual Basic's Add-In Manager by choosing the Add-In Manager item from the Add-Ins menu. From this dialog box, you can load the Property Page Wizard for use in your project. After closing the Add-In Manager, the Property Page Wizard becomes available as one of the options of the Add-Ins menu.

Running the Property Page Wizard

To begin creating the property pages for your control, start the Property Page Wizard by selecting it from the Add-Ins menu. You will see a title page that tells you a little about the wizard. Clicking the Next button takes you to the first page where you start the creation process.

Defining the Pages of the Dialog Box

The first working page of the wizard, shown in Figure 12.11, lets you define the pages that you want to include in your Property Pages dialog box. The wizard inserts a couple of standard pages for you, StandardColor and Standard-Font. You can keep these pages or remove them by clearing the check box next to the name of the page. If you wish to add more pages, click the Add button, which brings up an input dialog box where you can enter the name of a new page.

As you add pages to your dialog box, the page names appear in the list of pages for your dialog box. In addition to being able to add or remove pages, you can also control the order of the pages by changing the order of the names in the list. To move a page, select it in the list and use the arrow keys to the right of the list to change its position. When you have finished defining the pages for your dialog box, you can move to the next step of the wizard.

Assigning Properties to a Page

The next step in the process is to assign the properties that you have created to the pages of the dialog box. The Add Properties page of the wizard, shown in Figure 12.12, makes it easy for you to create these assignments. Simply select the tab that represents the page where you want the properties to go. Then, select the properties to be placed on the page and use the arrow buttons to move the properties from the selection list to the desired page. You will see that if you used the default property pages, the properties for these pages are already assigned for you.

F I G U R E 12.11

Creating the pages of your Property Pages dialog box

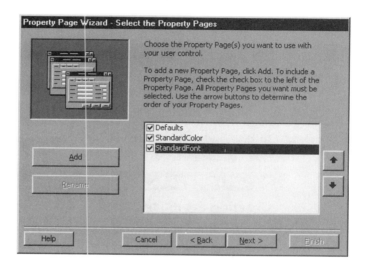

F I G U R E 12.12

Assigning properties to a page

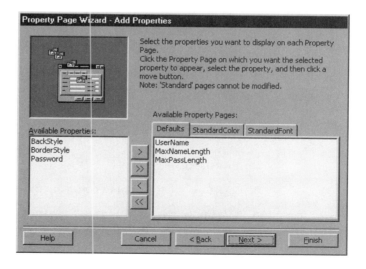

You cannot add new properties to the StandardColor or StandardFont pages, nor can you remove the properties assigned to these pages. These defaults are set by the wizard and cannot be changed. You can assign properties only to the pages you create.

After you have finished assigning properties, click the Finish button to create the property pages for your control.

Creating the Property Pages for the Security Control

Now that you have seen the basics of creating property pages, put this information into practice by creating pages for the Security control. Exercise 12.5 shows you how to do this.

EXERCISE 12.5

Creating Property Pages

1. Start the Security control project if you do not already have it open.

2. Start the Property Page Wizard by selecting its option from the Add-Ins menu.

3. Move to the second page of the wizard to create additional pages.

4. Click the Add button and type **Defaults** in the input dialog box. Click OK on the dialog box to add the page to the list.

5. Using the arrow buttons, move the new Defaults page to the top of the list. Then click the Next button to move to the next page of the wizard.

6. From the Available Properties list, select the UserName, MaxName-Length, and MaxPassLength properties to be included on the Defaults page. You can use the arrow buttons or drag and drop the properties onto the page.

7. Click the Finish button to complete the process.

8. If you have a test form loaded, create a new instance of the Security control and look at the Properties window. You will see a Custom property located at the top of the Properties list. Clicking the ellipsis button next to this property displays the property pages for the Security control, shown in the next illustration.

EXERCISE 12.5 (CONTINUED)

Saving Developer Information for the Control

Microsoft ✓ **Exam Objective**

Create ActiveX controls.

- Use control events to save and load persistent properties.

$\mathbf{A}$s developers work with your control, they will probably change the settings of several of the control's properties. After the project containing your control is saved, they will expect to be able to reopen the project and have the control appear as it was left. Unfortunately, no automatic mechanism exists for saving the property information that developers use. With a little code, however, you can save and restore settings of the control so developers do not have to reset the values each time.

Two key events are involved in storing developer information:

WriteProperties   Used to save the information

ReadProperties   Used to retrieve the information

Each of these events works with an object called the PropertyBag, a storage device for the design-time properties of the control.

Saving the Developer Information

Two steps are involved in saving the property information for your control. First, you must notify Visual Basic that the property value has changed. Second, you must write the property information to the PropertyBag.

To notify Visual Basic of a property change, you use the PropertyChanged function in the Property Let procedure of each property. This function specifies the name of the property and sets a flag that triggers the WriteProperties event when the instance of the control is closed. The PropertyChanged function for a typical property is shown in the following line of code:

```
PropertyChanged "BackStyle"
```

The PropertyChanged function only notifies Visual Basic that a property value needs to be saved. You must write the code in the event procedure of the WriteProperties event to save the information. For each property to be stored, you need to use the WriteProperty method of the PropertyBag object. This method specifies the property name, the current value of the property, and the default value of the property. The WriteProperty method is illustrated below:

```
Private Sub UserControl_WriteProperties(PropBag As _
PropertyBag)
PropBag.WriteProperty "BackColor", UserControl.BackColor, _
&H8000000F
PropBag.WriteProperty "BackStyle", UserControl.BackStyle, 0 _
PropBag.WriteProperty "BorderStyle", _
UserControl.BorderStyle, 0
PropBag.WriteProperty "ForeColor", UserControl.ForeColor, _
&H80000012
End Sub
```

Retrieving Property Settings

Of course, if you save the setting information, you will want to retrieve it as well. The ReadProperties event of the UserControl is triggered whenever the project containing your control is loaded, enabling you to retrieve the property information stored in the PropertyBag object. To retrieve the values, you use the ReadProperty method of the PropertyBag object. This method specifies the name of the property and the default value, in case a value had not been saved. The following code shows the use of the ReadProperties event and the ReadProperty method:

```
Private Sub UserControl_ReadProperties(PropBag As _
PropertyBag)
UserControl.BackColor = PropBag.ReadProperty("BackColor", _
&H8000000F)
UserControl.BackStyle = PropBag.ReadProperty("BackStyle", 0)
UserControl.BorderStyle = _
PropBag.ReadProperty("BorderStyle", 0)
UserControl.ForeColor = PropBag.ReadProperty("ForeColor", _
&H80000012)
End Sub
```

If you use the Control Interface Wizard to create the Public interface of your control, most of the code for saving and retrieving properties is written for you. You need to handle this task manually only for properties that were not created through the Control Interface Wizard.

Exercise 12.6 shows you how to handle saving and retrieving the property information for the Security control.

EXERCISE 12.6

Saving and Retrieving Developer Settings

1. Select the Property Let procedure for the MaxNameLength property.

2. Add the following line of code to the procedure:

   ```
   PropertyChanged "MaxNameLength"
   ```

3. Repeat this process for the MaxPassLength and UserName properties. Be sure to use the appropriate name in the PropertyChanged function.

4. Place the following code in the WriteProperties event of the User-Control to save the information about the properties of the control:

```
PropBag.WriteProperty "MaxNameLength", _
txtUserName.MaxLength, 0
PropBag.WriteProperty "MaxPassLength", _
txtPassword.MaxLength, 0
PropBag.WriteProperty "UserName", txtUserName.Text, ""
```

5. Place the following code in the ReadProperties event of the User-Control to retrieve the saved property information:

```
txtUserName.Text = PropBag.ReadProperty _
("UserName", "")
txtUserName.MaxLength = PropBag.ReadProperty _
("MaxNameLength", 0)
txtPassword.MaxLength = PropBag.ReadProperty _
("MaxPassLength", 0)
```

Testing the ActiveX Control

Microsoft ✓ *Exam* *Objective*

Create ActiveX controls.

- Test and debug an ActiveX control.

After you have created the ActiveX control, you need to test it to make sure that all the procedures work as you think they should. You can use all the standard debugging techniques that are available in Visual Basic to debug your control. Only a few steps are involved in setting up a test for your ActiveX control.

1. Add a standard project to your development environment to create a project group, which is the mechanism used for testing ActiveX controls and servers.

2. Close the UserControl window of your control project. If the User-Control (form) window is open, Visual Basic assumes that you are still working on the design of the control and will not allow you to create an instance of the control in another form.

3. Create an instance of the control on your test form. Then you can test the properties of the control and write code to test its methods.

You can learn more about debugging techniques in Chapter 15, "Debugging Your Application."

If you must make changes to the design of the ActiveX control, delete the instance of the control from your test form and re-create it after you have made the design changes. Otherwise, the changes will not appear in the test.

Letting Your Control Work with Data

Microsoft ✓ *Exam* *Objective*	**Design Visual Basic components to access data from a database.**

The ability to create ActiveX controls in Visual Basic was introduced in version 5. The key significant enhancement in version 6 is the capability of the ActiveX controls to work with data. You can now set up your ActiveX controls to be bound to a Data control or to even serve as a data source. This increases the flexibility and usability of your controls even more.

Using the Security control, you will look first at how to bind your control to a data source. Then, you will create a new control that can serve as a data source itself.

Binding to a Data Source

Microsoft ✔ *Exam* *Objective*

Create ActiveX controls.

- Enable the data binding capabilities of an ActiveX control.

The data-bound ActiveX controls that you create will behave in a manner similar to Visual Basic's intrinsic data-bound controls, such as the text box or label. Setting up your ActiveX control to be data bound is relatively easy and requires only a few steps. Of course, as in the case of many features in Visual Basic 6, Microsoft has included several dialogs to make the task as easy as possible. To enable your ActiveX control to be bound to data, you must perform three key steps:

1. Indicate that the control is to be bound.

2. Select the properties that can be bound.

3. Designate one property that will be the default bound field.

Exercise 12.7 illustrates how to set up the Security control to be data bound.

EXERCISE 12.7

Enabling Data Binding

1. If it is not already open, open the project containing the Security control.

2. Set the DataBindingBehavior property of the control to 1 – vbSimpleBound. This enables the control to interface with a data source.

3. Open the Code window of the UserControl object.

4. From the Tools menu, choose the Procedure Attributes item to bring up the Procedure Attributes dialog box.

5. Click the Advanced button to show the Data Binding portion of the dialog box, as shown in the following illustration.

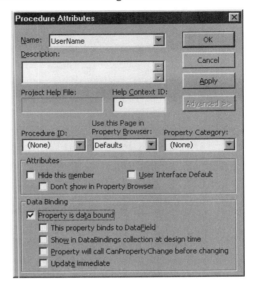

6. For the exercise, use the UserName property of the control as the bound property. To do this, first select the UserName control in the Name dropdown list. Then, check the "Property is data bound" check box in the dialog. As you check this box, notice that several other check boxes are enabled.

7. Check the box marked "This property binds to DataField" in the dialog. This marks the UserName property as the default property for data binding.

8. Click the OK button to accept the changes to the control.

Only one property of your control can be bound to the DataField property of the control. However, you can bind other properties of the control to a data source through the DataBindings collection. This collection holds the names of all the properties that are enabled as data bound. When the control is used in a project, you can access a dialog box that enables you to assign fields of a data source to any properties in the DataBindings collection.

After you have set up the control for data binding, you should test the control. To do this, you create an instance of the control in a project and create a data source from a Data control or ADO Data control. (A data-bound ActiveX control can work with either of these controls.) As you set the properties of the ActiveX control, notice that there is a DataSource property for selecting the Data control and a DataField property for selecting the field to be bound to the default property. These properties are set the same way as you would set them for one of Visual Basic's built-in controls. Exercise 12.8 continues with the Security control example to show how this works.

EXERCISE 12.8

Using a Data-Bound Control

1. While still in the project containing the Security control, close the Code window and Design window of the control.

2. Add a Standard EXE project to the project group to use as the test project.

3. Add a Data control to the form of the new project. Set the DatabaseName and RecordSource properties of the control to point to the Authors table of the Biblio.mdb database that comes with Visual Basic.

4. Add an instance of the Security control to the form.

5. Set the DataSource property of the control to the name of the Data control created in step 3. Then set the DataField property of the control to the Author field of the table. These settings are shown in the following illustration.

EXERCISE 12.8 (CONTINUED)

6. Run the program and step through the records with the Data control. Notice that the User Name box in the Security control displays the name of the currently selected author, as shown in the following illustration.

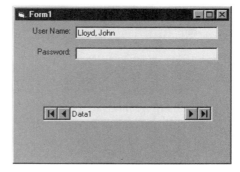

If you specified multiple properties to bind to a data source, you can set up the bindings of these properties through the Data Bindings dialog box shown in Figure 12.13. This dialog is accessed by clicking the ellipsis button next to the DataBindings property in the Properties window. For each bound property, the Data Bindings dialog enables you to select the data source, data field, data member, and data format for the information to be bound to the property.

FIGURE 12.13

Binding properties to a data source

Creating a Data Source

Microsoft
✓ ***Exam***
Objective

Create ActiveX controls.

▪ Create an ActiveX control that is a data source.

The other piece of working with data is creating a control that can act as a data source. Creating this type of control is more involved than creating a control that simply binds to a data source. Most of the work for this type of control is handled in the code of the control.

If you are going to create a data source control, you need to become very familiar with the workings of ActiveX Data Objects 2. A user control must use ADO to create a data source; it cannot be done with DAO code.

To create a data source control, you must perform the following steps:

1. Set the DataSourceBehavior property to enable the control to function as a data source.

2. Write code to set up the recordset that the data source will access.

3. Write navigation code to enable the data source control to perform a function.

Exercises 12.9 and 12.10 illustrate how to respectively create and use a data source control.

EXERCISE 12.9

Creating a Data Source Control

1. Start a new ActiveX control project.

2. Set the Name of the control to DataTest.

3. Set the DataSourceBehavior property of the control to 1 – vbDataSource.

4. Using the References dialog box, set a reference to the ActiveX Data Objects 2.0 Library.

5. Add the following code to the Declarations section of the Code window. This code sets up the Connection and Recordset variables.

```
Private rsAuthors As Recordset
Private cnMain As Connection
```

6. Add the following code to the Initialize event of the control. This code sets up the control to access the Authors table of the `Biblio.mdb` database. (You may have to specify a different path to the database.)

```
Dim sConnStr As String
sConnStr = "Provider=Microsoft.Jet.OLEDB.3.51;"
sConnStr = sConnStr & "Persist Security Info=False;"
sConnStr = sConnStr & "Data Source=C:\data\Biblio.mdb"
Set cnMain = New Connection
cnMain.Open sConnStr
Set rsAuthors = New Recordset
rsAuthors.Open "Select * From Authors", _
cnMain, adOpenKeyset
```

7. Add the following line of code to the GetDataMember event of the control. This event provides the link between the recordset that you create and the controls that will access the data.

```
Set Data = rsAuthors
```

8. Add two command buttons to the UserControl form and name the buttons **cmdPrevious** and **cmdNext**. Set the Captions of the buttons to **Previous** and **Next** respectively.

9. Resize the UserControl to contain only the two command buttons. When you are finished, your control should look like the following illustration.

10. Place the following code in the Click event procedures of the command buttons. This code enables the user to navigate through the recordset.

```
Private Sub cmdNext_Click()
rsAuthors.MoveNext
If rsAuthors.EOF Then rsAuthors.MoveLast End Sub
Private Sub cmdPrevious_Click()
rsAuthors.MovePrevious
If rstAuthors.BOF Then rsAuthors.MoveFirst
End Sub
```

The If statements in the above code prevent the user from moving past the beginning or end of a file and generating an error.

11. Save the project and close the Code and Design windows of the control.

At this point, you are ready to test the data source control that you created. To test the control, you need to create a second project, add an instance of the control to the form, and bind a control to the data source control. Exercise 12.10 shows you how to do this.

EXERCISE 12.10

Using a Data Source Control

1. Starting with the project created in Exercise 12.9, add a Standard EXE project to the project group.

2. Add an instance of the data source control to the form of the new project. Set the Name property of the control to **udsAuthor**.

3. Add a text box to the form.

4. Set the DataSource property of the text box to the Data control that you created.

5. Set the DataField property of the text box to the Author field of the recordset.

6. Run the project and press the command buttons to move through the data set. The completed form is shown in the following graphic.

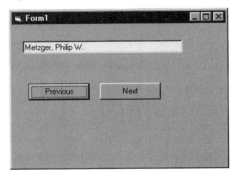

Managing Components

Microsoft ✓ *Exam* *Objective*

Use Visual Component Manager to manage components.

After you have created a number of controls (or classes, form templates, servers, or other components) you will find that it is somewhat difficult to manage all the components so that you can use them in multiple projects. If you are like me, you tend to have your projects scattered over a number of directories on your system.

Microsoft helps solve this problem with the Visual Component Manager. This tool provides a repository for you to store your components and to catalog information about them. This makes it easier to determine what a component does and to know whether it is the appropriate component for your current project.

Using the Visual Component Manager requires two steps: 1) adding components to the manager, 2) retrieving components for use in other projects. Exercise 12.11 shows you how to add a control to the repository of the Visual Component Manager.

EXERCISE 12.11

Adding a Component to the Visual Component Manager

1. Open the Visual Component Manager by selecting it from the toolbar or from the View menu. The Visual Component Manager is shown below.

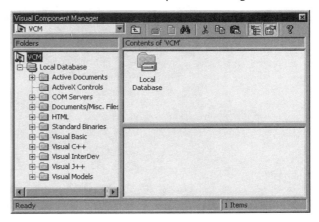

EXERCISE 12.11 (CONTINUED)

2. Select the ActiveX Controls folder.

3. Click the Publish New Component button on the toolbar of the Visual Component Manager. This brings up the Publish Wizard.

4. Skip the introductory screen of the wizard and enter the component name and primary file for the control. The following graphic shows these settings for the DataSource control created in Exercise 12.9.

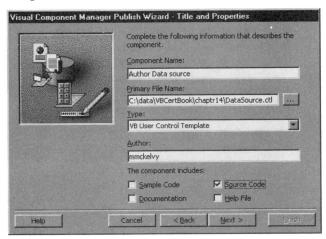

5. On the wizard's next page, titled More Properties, you can enter a description of the control and provide a series of keywords to help in locating the control when you want to use the control in another project. This is shown below.

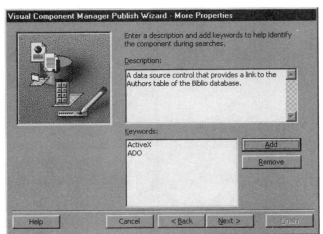

EXERCISE 12.11 (CONTINUED)

6. The next page of the wizard enables you to specify any additional files that need to be published with the component. After you have specified any files, you may click the Finish button to publish the component.

If you are working with a new project and need to add components that you have created, follow these simple steps:

1. Open the Visual Component Manager.

2. Locate the component that you need in the manager.

3. Double-click the icon representing the component.

Summary

This chapter has shown you how easy it can be to create your own ActiveX controls using Visual Basic. You have seen how wizards in Visual Basic can do most of the interface work for you, leaving you to focus on the visual design and functionality of the control. Along the way you have learned how to use constituent controls to create the user interface and how to create properties, methods, and events to create the Public programming interface of the controls. By now, you should also realize how powerful the capability to produce controls is. These controls enable you to reuse components not just in other Visual Basic applications, but in any application that supports ActiveX controls, including some Web browsers.

In addition to creating basic controls, you have seen how you can use the data enabling capabilities of the UserControl to enable your controls to be bound to a data source, or even to function as a data source. You have also seen how to use the Visual Component Manager to manage all the components that you create.

After completing this chapter, you should be ready for the following objectives of the Microsoft certification exam:

- Create ActiveX controls.

  - Create an ActiveX control that exposes properties.

  - Create and enable property pages for an ActiveX control.

- Use control events to save and load persistent properties.
- Test and debug an ActiveX control.
- Enable the data binding capabilities of an ActiveX control.
- Create an ActiveX control that is a data source.
- Design Visual Basic components to access data from a database.
- Use Visual Component Manager to manage components.

Review Questions

1. Which of the following statements is true about creating ActiveX controls?

   A. You must create the control completely from scratch.

   B. You can use only a single standard control in the creation of an ActiveX control.

   C. You cannot add properties to a standard control to enhance its capabilities.

   D. You can use multiple standard controls as well as drawing methods to create the interface of your control.

2. What statement is used to trigger an event in your ActiveX control?

   A. LoadEvent

   B. RaiseEvent

   C. FireEvent

   D. Trigger

3. Which property statement is required for a read-only property?

   A. Property Get

   B. Property Let

   C. Property Set

   D. Property Read

4. How do you create a method of a control?

    A. Use a Method declaration statement.

    B. Create a Sub or Function procedure and declare it as Public.

    C. Create a Sub or Function procedure and declare it as Private.

    D. Creation of the method is automatic because all procedures in a control are public.

5. What does the Control Interface Wizard do for you? Check all that apply.

    A. Designs the visual interface of your control

    B. Helps you create properties, methods, and events for your control

    C. Lets you assign properties of the control to properties of the constituent controls

    D. Handles the code for storing property changes

6. What is the purpose of property pages?

    A. To make it easier for you to create properties of your control

    B. To provide a developer with easy access to the properties of your control

    C. To automatically test the property settings of your control

    D. To link the properties of your control to the properties of its constituent controls

7. Which of the following programs can use ActiveX controls that you create? Check all that apply.

    A. Visual Basic

    B. Microsoft Office

    C. Microsoft Visual FoxPro

    D. Internet Explorer 3 or higher

8. Which event is used to store developer settings for your control?

   A. WriteSettings

   B. StoreProperties

   C. WriteProperties

   D. Save

9. What is a PropertyBag?

   A. Another name for property pages

   B. An object used to store developer settings for a control

   C. A made-up term

   D. A list of properties that can be included in a UserControl

10. What method is used to retrieve developer settings for your control?

   A. The Read method of the UserControl object

   B. The Retrieve method of the PropertyBag object

   C. The ReadProperty method of the PropertyBag object

   D. The ReadProperty method of the UserControl object

CHAPTER

13

Creating
Documents for the Web

Microsoft Exam Objectives Covered in This Chapter:

- Create an active document.
  - Navigate to other active documents.
  - Use code within an active document to interact with a container application.

- Create a Web page by using the DHTML Page Designer to dynamically change attributes of elements, change content, change styles, and position elements.

With Visual Basic, you have long been able to create great stand-alone programs and programs that access network data. Visual Basic also gives you the capability to write multi-tier, client-server programs. But wouldn't it be great if you also had an easy way to create Internet applications? After all, the Internet is the next frontier for computer programs.

A way to use Visual Basic to write Internet programs has arrived. Visual Basic now has ActiveX documents, programs that run in containers that support ActiveX, such as Internet Explorer. With ActiveX documents, you can easily write programs that run across the Internet or on your corporate intranet. These programs can have most of the capabilities of standard Visual Basic programs but with fewer hassles in distributing the programs and with a wider audience.

This chapter takes you through the process of creating ActiveX documents. You will learn how to create an ActiveX document from scratch and how to leverage your current programming efforts by converting projects to ActiveX documents. Along the way, you will learn several facts about ActiveX documents that you need to know to meet several of the certification exam objectives.

Understanding ActiveX Documents

ActiveX documents have a dual personality. On one hand, they are programs that users can run to accomplish all kinds of tasks, from a simple calculator to a program that accesses database information and displays it in a grid. On the other hand, the documents have the characteristics of a Word document or Excel spreadsheet in that they cannot stand alone. ActiveX documents can be used only within a container that supports them. In fact, the term *document* comes from this similarity to Word and Excel documents.

One of the key containers for using ActiveX documents is Microsoft's Internet Explorer. IE's support of ActiveX documents gives you the capability to easily create Internet applications. This ease of creation is what makes ActiveX documents so exciting.

Advantages of Using ActiveX Documents in Internet Programs

Just as Visual Basic made it easy for programmers to develop Windows applications, the introduction of ActiveX documents makes programming for the Internet easier. With ActiveX documents, you can apply all the skills you have learned in creating Visual Basic programs to the development of Internet or intranet programs. Therefore, you face no steep learning curve for understanding a new language. You simply change the "container" for your program and dive right in. The only caveat is that the browser used by you and your users must be capable of supporting ActiveX components.

For the types of programs that you can create with ActiveX documents, your main alternative is to use HTML pages with embedded objects such as text boxes, lists, command buttons, and so on. Being able to use ActiveX documents provides you with a number of advantages over using these methods:

- Your knowledge of Visual Basic can be directly applied to creating the programs that you want to create for the Internet.

- Laying out forms is much easier in Visual Basic's design environment than is possible when you must code tags and then run the program to verify that controls are where you want them.

- You can debug an ActiveX document using the tools of Visual Basic's development environment.

- ActiveX documents support the Hyperlink object, which makes it easy to move from one document to another or even to another Web page.

- ActiveX documents can persist data between sessions.

Convinced? If you need to write programs for the Internet, ActiveX documents can make the job a whole lot easier.

Comparison of ActiveX Documents to Visual Basic Forms and ActiveX Controls

ActiveX documents are designed to work with the Internet, but there are many similarities between creating ActiveX documents and creating forms for standard programs. An ActiveX document starts with a UserDocument object, shown in Figure 13.1, which is very similar to a form without a border. The border is not needed because the document will be contained within Internet Explorer or some other container.

FIGURE 13.1

UserDocument for creating an ActiveX document

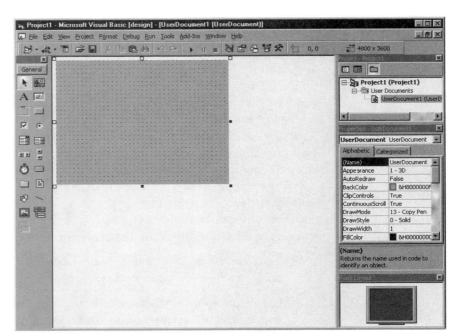

Although Internet Explorer is the most common container for ActiveX documents, other containers also support ActiveX documents. These containers include the Office Binder and the Visual Basic integrated development environment (IDE).

When you are creating an ActiveX document, you design the interface just as you would a form's interface. You select controls from the toolbox and draw instances of the controls on the UserDocument. To write code, you open the Code window and enter the necessary program lines in the event procedures of the controls. Also, as you do with a form, you can create custom properties and methods by using Property procedures and publicly declared Sub and Function procedures.

There are, however, a few differences between a form and a User-Document object. Some of the key differences are:

- The UserDocument does not support the Load or Unload events, which means that you cannot use these events to initialize information for the UserDocument.

- You cannot use the Load method to start a UserDocument or Unload to terminate it. Displaying a UserDocument object is handled by directly opening the file in the container or by using the Hyperlink object.

- You cannot use the OLE container control on a UserDocument, nor can you create links to other applications, such as Word or Excel.

The UserDocument may have many similarities to the Form object, but in one way it is closer to the UserControl object that you use to create ActiveX controls. Both the UserDocument and the UserControl can use an object called the PropertyBag to store data about the properties of the UserDocument or UserControl. You will look more closely at the PropertyBag as it relates to the UserDocument later in this chapter. If you want to know more about creating ActiveX controls, refer to Chapter 12, "Creating ActiveX Controls with Visual Basic."

Creating ActiveX Documents

Creating an ActiveX document is similar to creating a standard program in Visual Basic. As with a standard program, you follow a sequence of steps to create the document:

1. Start the project.

2. Create the user interface of the document.

3. Write the code to handle the tasks required of the document.

4. Test the document program.

5. Compile the document and prepare it for distribution.

You will look at each of these steps in detail in this section.

Creating the ActiveX Document Project

The first step in creating an ActiveX document is to start an ActiveX document project. You can start the project by choosing the ActiveX Document EXE option from the New Project dialog box shown in Figure 13.2. You open the dialog box by choosing the New Project item from the File menu of Visual Basic.

F I G U R E   13.2

New Project
dialog box

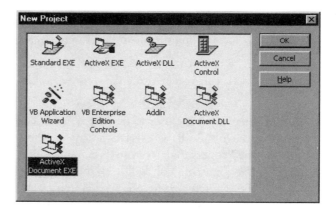

There are two types of ActiveX document projects, EXE and DLL. The DLL type of document can be used only as a subprogram of another project. To create documents that can be used in Internet Explorer, you must choose the EXE type of ActiveX document.

The new project starts with a single UserDocument object created for you. Typically, the UserDocument automatically opens to enable you to begin your design. If not, you can click the UserDocuments folder in the Project window, then double-click the UserDocument object to display it. Like a form, a UserDocument has a default name, in this case UserDocument1. The first thing that you need to do is to set the name to something meaningful. The name you assign is also the default name of the document file that you create when you compile the document and the name that you will use to retrieve the document using Internet Explorer. After setting the Name property, you can set any of the other properties that you wish to change.

Creating the User Interface

After you have the UserDocument object open, you can start placing controls on the document. Just as with the form of a standard program, these controls provide the user interface for the document. You can use almost any control available in Visual Basic, except the OLE container control. You can even use custom controls obtained from third parties (be sure to check licensing requirements) or ActiveX controls that you have created.

After you have added the controls to the UserDocument and set their properties, you can start writing the code for the document. To access the Code window, double-click the document or any control, or click the Code button in the Project window. You can write code to handle almost any task from the document, including connecting to databases, reading and writing information in files, and printing. The statements that you use are the same ones that you would use for a standard program.

To illustrate the creation of an ActiveX document, you will create and test a sample application. This application can be used to print trip requests for a corporate intranet. To keep it simple, the design of the sample application prints the request on paper. If you were developing this application for your company, you might want to connect directly to the e-mail system to send the request to the proper person for approval. Exercise 13.1 starts the process of creating this application.

EXERCISE 13.1

Creating an ActiveX Document

1. Start a new project and select the ActiveX Document EXE option from the New Project dialog box.

2. Open the UserDocument object by double-clicking UserDocument1 in the Project window.

3. Change the name of the UserDocument object to **TravReq**.

4. Add four labels to the UserDocument to indicate the information that will be entered in the document. These labels have the captions **Name:**, **Destination:**, **Trip Dates:**, and **Purpose of Trip:**. Align all the labels, make them the same width, and set the Alignment property of all the labels to Right Justify.

5. Add four text boxes to the UserDocument. Name the text boxes **txtName**, **txtDestination**, **txtDates**, and **txtPurpose**. Clear the Text property of each of the boxes. For the txtPurpose text box, set the MultiLine property to True and set the ScrollBars property to Vertical. Also, make the box large enough to hold several lines of text.

6. Add a command button to the UserDocument. Name the command button **cmdPrint** and set the Caption property to **Print Request**. The final appearance of the UserDocument should be something like the following illustration.

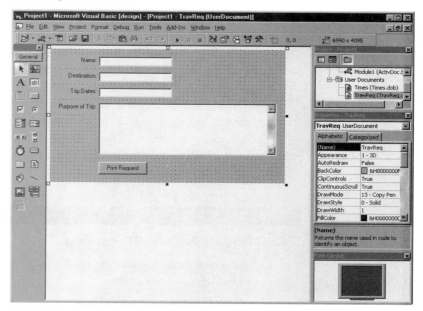

7. Open the Code window for the command button by double-clicking the button. Enter the following code in the Click event of the command button. This code prints the travel request.

```
Printer.Print "Name: " & txtName.Text
Printer.Print "Destination: " & txtDestination.Text
```

```
Printer.Print "Trip Dates: " & txtDates.Text
Printer.Print "Purpose: " & txtPurpose.Text
Printer.EndDoc
```

8. Save the document by clicking the Save button on Visual Basic's toolbar. You can use the default name of TravReq for the User-Document.

When you saved the project containing the UserDocument, you created a file with the extension .dob. This file contains the information about the UserDocument in text form, as the .frm file contains information about a form. If you have graphical controls on the UserDocument, information about them is contained in a .dox file, similar to the .frx file for forms.

Running and Testing the ActiveX Document

After you have created the user interface and the program code for the ActiveX document, you are ready to run and test the document. This is where some key differences exist between working with standard programs and ActiveX documents. In a standard program, you can simply click the Run button or press the F5 key to run your program, and the results show up instantly on the screen. This is not the case with an ActiveX document.

With an ActiveX document, clicking the Run button compiles the program and creates a file containing the working version of the document. This file has the same name as your UserDocument and an extension of .vdb and is placed in the same subdirectory as your project. To view the document, you must open it with an application that is capable of working with ActiveX documents, such as Internet Explorer.

While you are working with the document in a browser, the document remains active in the Visual Basic development environment—which means that you can still use all of Visual Basic's debugging tools to check the values of variables, step through the program, and set breakpoints to pause the execution of the program at specified locations. Figure 13.3 shows the execution of the TravReq document paused in the development environment. To learn more about debugging, check out Chapter 15, "Debugging Your Application."

F I G U R E   13.3

Using debugging tools
with an ActiveX
document

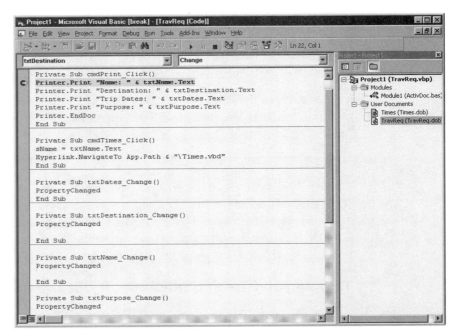

To demonstrate how to run and test an ActiveX document, Exercise 13.2 continues where Exercise 13.1 left off, with running the TravReq document.

EXERCISE 13.2

Running and Testing the TravReq Document

1. If it is not already open, open the TravReq project created in Exercise 13.1.

2. Click the Run button to start the ActiveX document. Then minimize Visual Basic. Visual Basic automatically starts Internet Explorer and displays the page as shown in the following graphic.

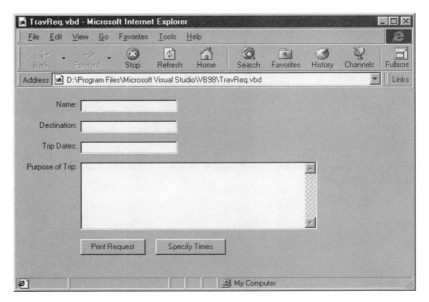

3. You can now enter information in the text boxes of the document and click the command button to print the information.

4. When you have finished, you need to close Internet Explorer or move to another page before terminating the program in Visual Basic.

Storing Data Created in ActiveX Documents

If you have the users of your document entering data, you need a way to store the information. Because you can perform almost any programming task with an ActiveX document, you can save the information in a file or save it in a database. However, you may want to save the information only between times that the user accesses the document. For example, you may want to save the name of the person so that the name will appear the next time that person uses the document. It is also helpful to save all the information in the document in case the user closes the browser before having an opportunity to finish the form.

ActiveX documents support the PropertyBag object, like the ActiveX controls described in Chapter 12. The PropertyBag is a storage device that enables you to write and read property information for the document. The Property-Bag has two methods that you use for handling information: ReadProperty and WriteProperty. When you issue the ReadProperty method, you specify the property to be retrieved and a default value, in case the desired property cannot be located. With the WriteProperty method, you specify the property to be written, the value to use, and a default value. The following lines of code show examples of these two methods.

```
txtName.Text = PropBag.ReadProperty("Name", "")
PropBag.WriteProperty "Name", txtName.Text, ""
```

The PropertyBag works like the Registry or .ini files. You do not have to have properties in your document to use it. You can store any information by specifying a key and a value.

To use these methods, you need to know when a property has changed. You notify the UserDocument that a property value has been changed by issuing the PropertyChanged method. You do not have to specify a particular property with this method; the method is merely used to trigger the WriteProperties event of the UserDocument.

The two events of the UserDocument object that are used in storing and retrieving properties are the ReadProperties event and the WriteProperties event. The ReadProperties event is triggered when the document is first loaded from a file, which enables you to retrieve the property information from the PropertyBag and set the initial values of properties or controls. The WriteProperties event is triggered when the document is unloaded, if the PropertyChanged method has been used in the program. Exercise 13.3 shows you how to use these events and methods to create persistent data in the TravReq document.

EXERCISE 13.3

Reading and Writing Information for the Document

1. Open the project created in Exercise 13.1.

2. In the Change event of each of the text boxes, place the following code statement:

```
PropertyChanged
```

3. In the ReadProperties event of the UserDocument, place the following code to read the information to be placed in the text boxes. Note that you must specify a default value for each of the ReadProperty calls. Also, note that the code uses the Format function to set a default date of the current date.

```
txtName.Text = PropBag.ReadProperty("Name", "")
txtDestination.Text = _
PropBag.ReadProperty("Destination", "")
txtDates.Text = PropBag.ReadProperty("Dates", _
Format(Date, "Short Date"))
txtPurpose.Text = PropBag.ReadProperty("Purpose", "")
```

4. In the WriteProperties event of the UserDocument, place the following code to write the new values of the information in the text boxes. Note that you should also specify a default value for the WriteProperty method.

```
PropBag.WriteProperty "Name", txtName.Text, ""
PropBag.WriteProperty "Destination", _
txtDestination.Text, ""
PropBag.WriteProperty "Dates", txtDates.Text, ""
PropBag.WriteProperty "Purpose", txtPurpose.Text, ""
```

Your document is now capable of storing and retrieving information entered by the user.

The first time you open the document, no properties will be read because the PropertyBag has not been created.

Working with Multiple Documents

Like a single form program, a single document program is of limited usefulness. There are only so many controls that you can place on a single form.

However, you are not limited to working with just a single document. ActiveX documents are capable of navigating to other documents through the use of the Hyperlink object, which enables you to use as many documents as you need to achieve your program goals.

Adding Documents to a Project

If you are creating multiple documents to work together, you can add more documents to the project. Choose the Add User Document item from the Project menu to place a second (or third, and so on) document in the project. You can now design the interface for the second document and add code to its events as well. There is no limit to the number of documents that you can have in a single project.

In addition to adding documents, you can also add standard forms to the project. These forms can be used for any purpose that you wish. Forms in an ActiveX document project can be called using the standard Show method.

Navigating Between Documents

Microsoft
✓ *Exam*
Objective

Create an active document.

- Navigate to other active documents.

When you start working with more than one document, you need a way to move between the documents. This capability is provided by the Hyperlink object. The Hyperlink object has no properties, but contains three methods:

NavigateTo Tells the container to move to a specific file or URL specified as an argument of the method

GoForward Tells the container to move to the next item in the History list

GoBack Tells the container to move to the previous item in the History list

Also, if you are working with multiple documents, you need a way to pass information between them. Unfortunately, UserDocuments do not enable you to create properties that can be set from another UserDocument object. Therefore, you have to use global variables to pass data. Global variables must be declared in a .bas module that is part of the project. Exercise 13.4 shows you how to add multiple documents and navigate between them. The exercise adds a second page to the TravReq document you created previously.

Working with Multiple Documents

1. Open the TravReq project that you created in Exercise 13.1.

2. Add a second document to the project by selecting the Add User Document item from the Project menu.

3. Name the second document **Times**.

4. Add three labels and three text boxes to the document. The labels should have the captions **Name:**, **Departure:**, and **Return:**. The text boxes should be named **txtName**, **txtDeparture**, and **txtReturn**.

5. Add a command button to the document and name it **cmdReturn**. When you have finished, your form should look like the next illustration.

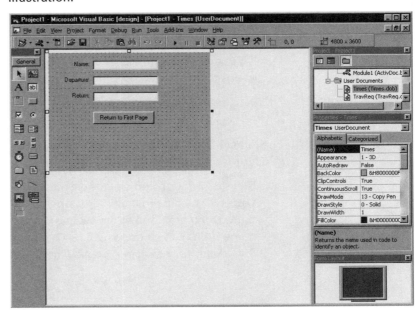

6. Place the following code in the Click event of the command button. This code uses the Hyperlink object to return to the previous page of the project:

```
Hyperlink.GoBack
```

7. Add a module to the project to hold a global variable. Add the module by selecting the Add Module item from the Project menu.

8. Place the following code in the module to declare a global variable:

```
Public g_sName As String
```

9. Place the following code in the Show event of the Times document. This code places the name of the user in the txtName text box when the document is displayed:

```
txtName.Text = g_sName
```

10. Go to the TravReq document and add a command button to the document. The command button should have the name **cmdTimes** and the caption **Specify Times**.

11. Place the following code in the Click event of the cmdTimes button. This code places the name of the user in the global variable and navigates to the second page of the document.

```
g_sName = txtName.Text
Hyperlink.NavigateTo "D:\VB\Times.vbd"
```

The directory you specify may be different because of your directory structure.

12. Run the program and open the document in Internet Explorer. After you enter a name in the first document and click the Specify Times button, you are taken to the second document. You will see that the name from the first document has been transmitted to the second document, as shown in the following illustration.

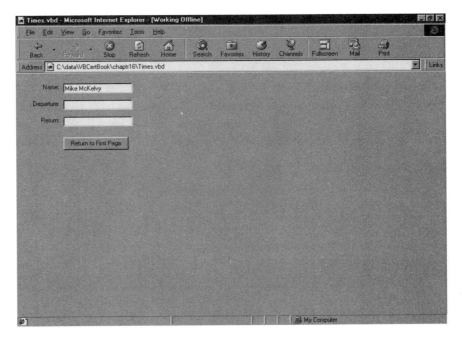

You may have noticed when you moved to the second document in Internet Explorer that the Back button of Explorer became enabled. You can use the navigation buttons of Internet Explorer to move between documents, but it is better to use the Hyperlink object to specify an exact document to use.

When you compile your document, you need to change the line that contains the specific navigation path to one that reads: Hyperlink.NavigateTo App.Path & "\Times.vbd".

Automatically Creating ActiveX Documents

You probably have a lot of work invested in programs that you have created over the years. ActiveX documents provide you with an easy way to create programs that are ready for the Internet. In addition, Microsoft included the Document Migration Wizard to help you convert your existing programs to ActiveX documents. The wizard handles a large part of the work for you, but it cannot handle all the conversion. Some items that you need to do by hand are:

- Move or remove code that is in the Load or Unload events of your forms.

- Remove OLE container controls and their associated code.

- Set up code in the Initialize and Terminate events of the documents to handle the tasks that would have been performed in the Load and Unload events.

- Set up global variables to pass information between user documents.

- Remove references to form names.

As always, an example makes things easier to understand. Exercise 13.5 shows you how to convert the Calc program from the Visual Basic samples to an ActiveX document.

EXERCISE 13.5

Converting an Existing Program to an ActiveX Document

1. Open the Calc.vbp program in the Visual Basic samples directory.

2. If the Document Migration Wizard is not in the Add-Ins menu, add it using the Add-In Manager. Then open the Document Migration Wizard.

3. Skip the opening page of the wizard to move to the Form Selection page, shown in the next illustration. Select the Calculator form and click the Next button.

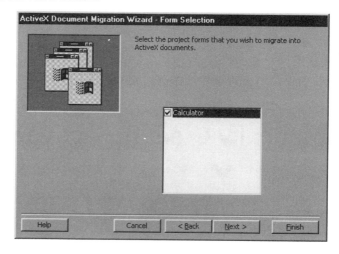

4. Click the Finish button to complete the process. The wizard then displays a report that tells you what you have to do to finish the migration.

When you are finished with the document migration, you can run your document in Internet Explorer. Figure 13.4 shows the Calculator program running inside Internet Explorer.

FIGURE 13.4

Running the Calculator in Internet Explorer

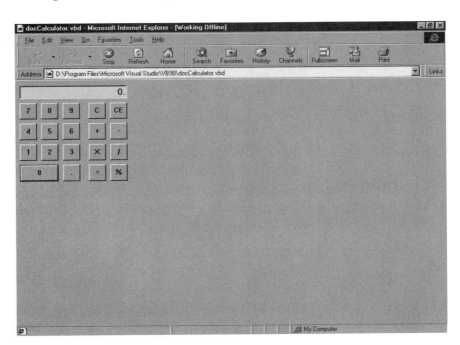

Using ActiveX Documents with Internet Explorer

Microsoft Exam Objective

Create an active document.

- Use code within an active document to interact with a container application.

After the ActiveX document is programmed, tested, and compiled, you can distribute it and run it in any browser or other container that supports ActiveX documents. One such container is, of course, Internet Explorer. When you are working with Internet Explorer, you run your ActiveX document by creating an HTML page that points to the ActiveX document.

Embedding ActiveX Documents in a Web Page

The other alternative for using ActiveX documents with Internet Explorer is to embed the document in a Web page, the only method that you can use to distribute your documents over the Internet. Embedding the ActiveX document in a Web page requires two steps: downloading the document and running the document.

To cause Internet Explorer to download the ActiveX document, you need to specify an HTML object that indicates:

- The class ID of the document

- The name of the .cab file containing the document

- Version information for the document

Fortunately, Visual Basic's Setup Wizard creates a sample HTML file for you that contains this information. The OBJECT tag information for the TravReq document is shown in the following code:

```
<OBJECT ID="TravReq"
CLASSID="CLSID:B044F674-B017-11D1-BCCD-0000C051F6F9"
CODEBASE="TravReq.CAB#version=1,0,0,0">
</OBJECT>
```

The code in the OBJECT tag tells Internet Explorer to download the document and register it in the Windows Registry.

The second step to running the document from a Web page is to set up HTML code to activate the document. You can do this with VBScript using the following code:

```
<SCRIPT LANGUAGE="VBScript">
Sub Window_OnLoad
Document.Open
Document.Write "<FRAMESET>"
```

```
Document.Write "<FRAME SRC=""TravReq.VBD"">"
Document.Write "</FRAMESET>"
Document.Close
End Sub
</SCRIPT>
```

This code is also created for you by the Setup Wizard.

Creating Internet Documents with DHTML

Microsoft Exam Objective

Create a Web page by using the DHTML Page Designer to dynamically change attributes of elements, change content, change styles, and position elements.

ActiveX documents provide you one method of creating documents for use on the Internet or on an intranet. Another method of creating Web documents is through the use of Dynamic Hypertext Markup Language (DHTML). DHTML enables you to provide dynamic content on Web pages, based on user actions and requests. As with many other new technologies, Visual Basic provides a way to quickly and easily create DHTML documents.

With the DHTML Page Designer, you can create interactive Web pages using tools and code similar to the controls and code you use to create a form-based application. After you create the pages, you compile the application and place it on a server where users can access it. At present, only an Internet Explorer 4 (or higher) Web browser can use the DHTML pages created in Visual Basic.

To demonstrate the capabilities of the DHTML Page Designer, Exercise 13.6 walks you through the steps of creating a simple DHTML page.

Creating a DHTML Page

1. Start a new project in Visual Basic and select the DHTML Application option from the New Project dialog box. The project starts with a single page designer and a code module. If your application requires multiple DHTML pages, you can add them to the project, just as you would add a form to a standard project.

2. Open the default page designer by double-clicking it in the Project window. The initial appearance of the page designer is shown in the following graphic.

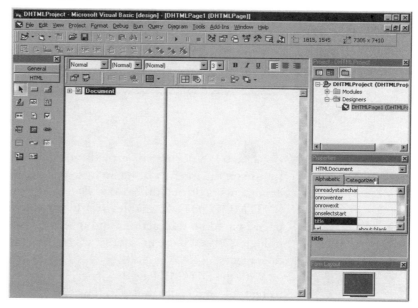

3. Click the + sign next to the Document item in the Design window. This displays the Body element of the DHTML page. Each element, such as the Body, has an ID associated with it. This ID is contained in the Id property. Select the Body element and change the Id property to **bdTest**.

4. Click the right pane of the Design window and type **Web Site sign-in:**. Then press the Enter key and type **Enter your user name:**. As you do this, you will see that two paragraph elements are created under the Body element of the document. Name the paragraph elements **paTest1** and **paTest2** respectively.

5. From the toolbox, select a TextField control and draw an instance of the control on the designer, under the second paragraph. Change the Id property to **txtUser**.

6. Select a Button control from the toolbox and draw an instance on the designer below the TextField. Change the Id property of the button to **cmdSignin**. Also, change the Value property of the button to **Sign-In**. This changes the caption that is shown on the button. At this point, your designer should look like the one in the following graphic.

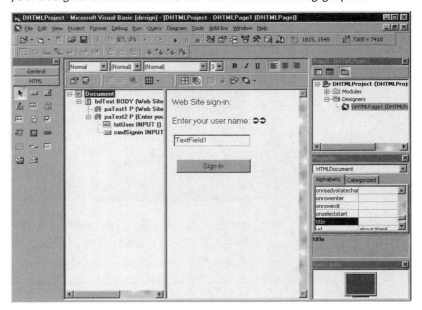

7. Double-click the Sign-In button to bring up the Code window associated with the page designer. Add the following code to the OnClick event of the button:

```
Dim sName As String
sName = txtUser.Value
paTest1.innerText = "Hello, " & sName
paTest2.innerText = ""
```

8. Save your project.

9. You can now run your DHTML page by clicking the Run button on the Visual Basic toolbar. Your page will be opened in Internet Explorer as shown below.

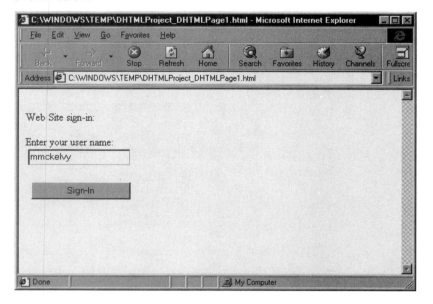

10. Enter a name in the TextField control and click the Sign-In button. This runs the code you placed in the OnClick event and displays the name that you entered.

Summary

As you can see, ActiveX documents open up a whole new frontier for programming. With these documents, you can easily create applications for the Internet. You can even convert some of your existing programs to ActiveX documents with the help of the Document Migration Wizard. In this chapter, you have covered the following certification exam objectives:

- Create an active document.
  - Navigate to other active documents.
  - Use code within an active document to interact with a container application.
- Create a Web page by using the DHTML Page Designer to dynamically change attributes of elements, change content, change styles, and position elements

Review Questions

1. What is the primary object used in creating ActiveX documents?

A. UserControl

B. Form

C. UserDocument

D. Class Module

2. How many documents are allowed in a single project?

A. Maximum of 5.

B. There is no set limit.

C. Maximum of 10.

3. Which of the following is not allowed in an ActiveX document?

A. Custom controls

B. User-created controls

C. OLE container control

D. Database controls

4. How do you store information from an ActiveX document so it is available when the document is reloaded?

   A. Write the information to a file.

   B. Use the methods of the PropertyBag object.

   C. It cannot be done.

   D. Specify the initial settings in the Hyperlink object.

5. What does the Document Migration Wizard do for you?

   A. Helps you move documents to another folder

   B. Helps you create an ActiveX document from an existing program

   C. Creates a file that lets you distribute your document over the Internet

   D. Lets you move from one document to another

6. Which of the following can run an ActiveX document? Check all that apply.

   A. Internet Explorer

   B. Visual Basic development environment

   C. Windows Explorer

   D. Office Binder

7. Which file do you load to run an ActiveX document?

   A. .dob

   B. .vbd

   C. .cab

   D. .vbp

8. How do you display one document from another?

   A. Use the Show method of the document.

   B. Use the NavigateTo method of the Hyperlink object.

   C. Use the Display method of the document.

   D. Use the Navigate method of the UserDocument object.

9. How do you pass information from one document to another?

   A. Set the value of a property in the target document.

   B. Use a global variable to contain the data.

   C. Use the PropertyBag.

   D. You cannot pass data between documents.

PART

IV

Dealing with Errors and Bugs

CHAPTER

14

Handling and Logging
Errors in Visual Basic Programs

N o matter how well you create your program or how carefully you test it, run-time errors can always occur in your program. A run-time error can occur when the user forgets to put a disk in the floppy drive and tries to read the disk. Or an error can occur when you expected that a user would know to enter a number, but they enter a string instead. In any case, a run-time error can stop your program dead in its tracks.

Visual Basic does not handle errors automatically. It simply notifies your program of the error. If your program has been set up to handle errors, you can retry an operation, allow the user to correct a value, or exit the program. If you do not have an error handler in your program, your program terminates with error messages like those shown in Figure 14.1. These types of messages are something that you never want your user to see.

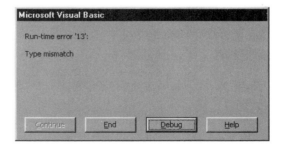

FIGURE 14.1

Error messages you get from Visual Basic

There are several processes that you need to understand in handling errors. The importance of these processes is indicated by the Microsoft exam objectives. To handle errors well in your program and to pass the exam, you need to:

- Have a good understanding of the Err object.

- Be able to create an error-handling routine using the On Error statements.

- Know how to use proper error-trapping options.

If you are creating ActiveX servers, you also need to know how to raise an error. Raising an error is the only way to communicate a problem to an ActiveX client. Raising errors is also one of the exam objectives.

Understanding Errors

Before you get into the mechanics of handling errors, take a moment to review what program errors are. As you are developing programs, you can encounter three classes of errors:

Syntax errors   You have incorrectly entered a line of code.

Logic errors   Your program does not produce the correct output but runs OK.

Run-time errors   A condition in your program causes a problem.

Visual Basic provides you with tools to track down syntax errors. These tools are discussed in detail in Chapter 15, "Debugging Your Application." Finding logic errors requires meticulous testing and tracking of the code's execution. Chapter 15 also discusses tools that help you with this function. The final category, run-time errors, is the focus of this chapter.

Causes of Errors

Run-time errors occur when something unexpected happens in your program, or when a statement in your program cannot be correctly resolved. Some examples of run-time errors are:

- Trying to open a file that does not exist

- Trying to assign a string to a numeric variable

- Dividing a number by zero

- Saving a database record that is locked by another user

Some of these errors can be avoided, but many times the causes of the errors are beyond your control. For example, if a user deletes a file that your program needs, an error will occur, even though it is not your fault. Likewise, two users trying to save the same database record will cause an error, because both are not allowed to write to the same record at the same time. There is no way to avoid these errors, but you must take appropriate action when the errors occur.

Avoiding Errors

Your program will need an error handler for many tasks. There are also ways to avoid certain types of errors. For example, you can trap a division-by-zero error, but it is easier to avoid the error in the first place. The following code illustrates how you can avoid such an error:

```
If Y = 0 Then
    MsgBox "Enter a non-zero value for Y"
    Z = 0
    Exit Sub
Else
    Z = X / Y
End If
```

Likewise, you can check for the existence of a file before you try to open it. If the file does not exist, you can give the user the option of specifying an alternate location or even an alternate file. Careful planning of your programs enables you to avoid many errors, leaving your error handler to take care of the errors that are unavoidable.

Working with the Err Object

The Err object is the centerpiece of Visual Basic's error notification and handling capabilities. Using the Err object, you can determine which error occurred, get a description of the error, and find out where the error occurred. You can even use the Err object to raise your own errors from code. Raising your own error is the recommended way to report errors in an ActiveX server that you create.

Like most objects in Visual Basic, the Err object provides information to the program and takes action through the properties and methods of the object. The Err object has no events. The following sections provide a good overview of the properties and methods of the error object. You will also look at how to use the information in the Err object to display detailed error messages. Then, in the section "Trapping Errors in Your Program," you will see how to use the Err object to write error-handling routines for your programs.

Using the Properties of the Err Object

When an error occurs in Visual Basic, the program populates the properties of the Err object to provide information about the error to you and your program. These properties tell you the kind of error encountered and give you an indication of the location where the error occurred. This information enables you to determine the appropriate action to take to recover from the error and provides descriptions of the error that you can display to your users or can log to a file.

Determining Which Error Occurred

The most important property of the Err object is the Number property. This property tells you which of Visual Basic's hundreds of possible errors has occurred. This number is used in error-handling routines to determine which action to take. For example, in the following code, if an error occurs during a Save operation for a database program, the type of error is used to determine whether to retry the Save operation or report the error and continue with the next line of code.

```
Select Case Err.Number
    Case 3046, 3158, 3186, 3187, 3188, 3189, 3218, 3260
        'Record is locked by another user
        iTriesCnt = iTriesCnt + 1
        If iTriesCnt > 10 Then
            iErrReturn = MsgBox( _
"Record is locked by another user. Try again?", _
vbExclamation + vbYesNo)
            If iErrReturn = vbYes Then
                iTriesCnt = 0
                Resume
            Else
                bUpdateOK = False
                Resume Next
            End If
        Else
            fPauseTime = Timer
            Do Until Timer > fPauseTime + 0.1
            Loop
            Resume
        End If
End Select
```

In looking at this code, two questions probably arise in your mind:

- How do I find out what the error codes are?
- How do I know which errors to check for?

The answer to the first question is easy. Visual Basic's help file provides a comprehensive list of error codes that can occur in your program. This list tries to group some of the errors into logical sets. For each error number, you will find a description of the error and some information about why the error occurred. Figure 14.2 shows an example of the help file for one of the database errors listed in the above code.

FIGURE 14.2

Database error
descriptions

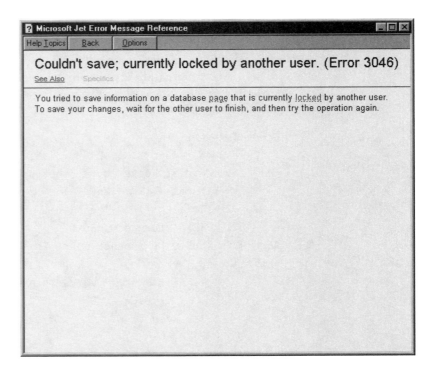

The answer to the second question is a little more difficult. It is obvious that if you are not working with database functions, you do not need to look out for database errors; however, the only way to determine which errors to look for is through experience and testing. Also, it helps to have your programs create an error log so that users can easily report errors that occur after you have distributed your program.

The counterpart of the Number property is the Description property of the Err object. The Description property provides you with a brief description of the error that occurred. This information is more useful for error messages displayed to the user or messages that are written to an error log. For example, the following code produces an error:

```
X = 5
Y = 0
Z = X / Y
```

If you check the properties of the Err object after the error occurs, you will see that the Number property is 11. This is great for the error handler in your program, but doesn't tell you much, unless you have memorized the complete error list for Visual Basic. If you check the Description property, however, you will find the text "Division by Zero," which tells you immediately what has happened and what action can be taken to avoid the error in the future or to recover from the error.

Determining Where the Error Occurred

Microsoft ✓ *Exam Objective*   **Fix errors and take measures to prevent future errors.**

Another property of the Err object is the Source property. This property gives you a general idea of where the error occurred. General, because if an error occurs in a standard module or form of your program, the Source property contains only the name of your project, which could give you a fairly large area to search for the occurrence of the error. The Source property is most useful when an error occurs in a class module or an object in an ActiveX server. When this is the case, the Source property contains the name of the class or object. For example, if you were linked to an instance of Microsoft Word and an error occurred in one of the Word commands, Source would contain the string Word.Application, telling you that one of the commands in a Word document or one of the Word commands passed by your program created the error.

Errors in DLLs

One final property to mention for the Err object is the LastDLLError property. This property is used only when DLL calls are made from your Visual

Basic program. When your program makes a DLL call, the DLL typically returns a value to indicate whether the DLL ran successfully or failed. If the DLL failed, the error causing the failure is stored in the LastDLLError property. Like regular Visual Basic error messages, knowing the cause of the error lets you determine whether to retry an operation or simply log the error and continue on.

One key difference between standard Visual Basic errors and DLL errors is that a DLL error does not raise an exception that can be trapped by your error handler. Therefore, your code must check the success status of the DLL call and immediately check the LastDLLError property if the operation failed.

Using the Methods of the Err Object

In addition to its properties, the Err object has two methods that you can use in your programs: the Clear method and the Raise method.

The Clear method of the Err object is used to reset all the property values of the object. You typically use this method after an error has occurred and been processed using deferred error handling (described later in this chapter). After the Clear method has been called, all information about the last error is deleted. Visual Basic automatically calls the Clear method when a Resume statement is used, when an On Error statement is used, or when your program leaves a Sub, Function, or Property procedure.

The Raise method is used to generate an error in Visual Basic. You might ask why you would want to generate an error when your code will probably generate enough on its own. The Raise method enables you to indicate that an error has occurred in a class module or other part of your program (an error that you determine, not one of the built-in errors of Visual Basic). By using the Raise method, you cause the error to be generated so that it can be handled by an error handler elsewhere in your program. This is particularly useful for class modules, especially if you will be compiling them into a DLL or ActiveX server. You will look more closely at raising errors in the section "Raising Errors from Your Program."

Displaying Errors Using the Err Object

Microsoft ✓ **_Exam_** **_Objective_** | **Implement error handling for the user interface in desktop applications.**
- Identify and trap run-time errors.

Now that you have some information about the Err object, it is time to put the information to use. Exercise 14.1 shows you how to display an error message using the Err object.

Displaying an Error Message

1. Start a new Visual Basic project.

2. Place a command button on the form of the project.

3. Open the Code window and place the following code in the Click event of the command button:

```
Dim X As Single, Y As Single, Z As Single
X = 5
Y = 0
Z = X / Y
```

4. Run the program and you will see that an error is generated, as shown in the next illustration. You will also see that Visual Basic terminates the program when the error occurs. After checking out the message, go back to the design environment.

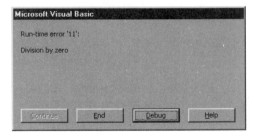

5. Place the following line of code immediately after the Dim statement. This statement tells Visual Basic to continue processing after an error has occurred.

```
On Error Resume Next
```

6. After the assignment statement for *Z*, place the following code to display an error message:

```
If Err.Number > 0 Then
    MsgBox "The following error has occurred: " & _
Err.Description
End If
```

7. Run the program again and notice that the new error message is displayed and Visual Basic does not terminate the program. The error message you receive should look like the one in the following illustration. The process shown in these steps is the essence of error handling, albeit a simple example.

Trapping Errors in Your Program

Understanding the Err object is only part of the equation for providing effective error handling in your programs. To handle the errors, you must capture from Visual Basic the fact that an error has occurred— known as trapping the errors. After you trap an error, you can take appropriate action based on the type of error that occurs and often on a decision you allow the user to make regarding the error. For example, if the user forgets to insert a disk in the disk drive, you would want to give the user the option of retrying or aborting the operation. In other cases, you would handle the error automatically, or log the error and give the user the option of continuing or terminating the program.

In designing your error-handling routines, you need to choose between two methods of trapping and handling the errors. Each method has merit, and in many cases you may use both methods in the same program but not in the same routine.

The first method is immediate handling. In this case, you force your code to branch to the error-handling routine immediately after the error occurs. You typically use this method if you intend to retry an operation. The second method is known as deferred handling. In this case, you tell Visual Basic to proceed to the next statement when an error occurs. Then, later in your procedure, you check the contents of the Err object and take any necessary action. This chapter covers both methods of trapping and handling errors. But first, you will take a look at the statements that you use to trap and handle errors. You will use these statements regardless of the method of error handling you choose.

Defining the Error-Handling Statements

When you are handling errors in your program, you use two basic statement types:

On Error statements   To tell Visual Basic where to go when an error occurs

Resume statements   To tell the program what to do after the error is handled

These two types of statements form the basis of Visual Basic's error-handling capabilities. Each statement has several forms that are described in the next sections.

Working with the On Error Statement

The On Error statement tells Visual Basic what to do in the event of an error. This statement can be used in one of three ways:

On Error GoTo line   Tells Visual Basic to branch to the line number or line label specified in the command whenever an error occurs. This line number or label corresponds to the beginning of the error-handling routine in the procedure. This form of the On Error statement is used with immediate error processing. The following code shows an example of using this form of the On Error statement.

```
On Error GoTo CaptureErrE
'This procedure copies the contents of a grid cell or text
'box
If TypeOf ActiveControl Is SSDBGrid Then
    CrRow = ActiveControl.Row
    CrBkMrk = ActiveControl.RowBookmark(CrRow)
    CrCol = ActiveControl.Col
    HoldCell = ActiveControl.Columns _
(CrCol).CellText(CrBkMrk)
End If
Clipboard.SetText HoldCell

Exit Sub
CaptureErrE:
LogError "Capture", "CopyVal", Err.Number, Err.Description
Resume Next
```

On Error Resume Next   Tells Visual Basic to move to the next line in the code if an error occurs. If the error is in the current procedure, the next line of code is executed. If the error occurs in a Sub procedure called from the current procedure, execution continues on the next statement after the procedure call. This form of the On Error statement is used with deferred error processing or when you want to ignore any errors that might occur. This type of error statement was illustrated in Exercise 14.1.

On Error GoTo 0   Tells Visual Basic to disable the error handlers in the current procedure. If an error occurs, the error is passed up the call stack to determine if an error handler can be found. If there are no error handlers, a Visual Basic run-time error is generated and your program terminates. Typically, you use this statement only to allow higher level procedures to handle the errors.

Using the Resume Statement

The second piece of the error-handling function tells Visual Basic what to do after an error is encountered. The Resume statement can be used in any of three forms to allow the program to continue execution after an error has been trapped and handled:

Resume   Tells Visual Basic to retry the statement that caused the error. If the statement is a Sub procedure call, the call is repeated and the Sub procedure is run from the beginning.

Resume Next   Tells Visual Basic to continue execution on the line following the one where the error occurred. If the error occurred in a Sub procedure, the line following the procedure call is the next one executed.

Resume line   Tells Visual Basic to continue execution at the line number or line label specified in the Resume statement. The line number or label must be in the same procedure as the Resume line statement. Using the Resume line statement enables you to redirect the execution of a program if an error occurs. You use the Resume line statement to branch around statements that would cause additional errors after the first one has occurred.

Any of the Resume statement's forms can be used only inside an error-handling routine like the one shown in the following code. Using the statement outside an error-handling routine causes an error.

```
EdtCopyErr:
Select Case Err.Number
    Case 524
        Resume Next
```

```
    Case Else
        LogError "Capture", "Edit Copy", Err.Number, _
Err.Description
        Resume Next
End Select
```

Placement of Error-Handling Statements

Before you begin creating the error-handling routines, you may wonder where these routines need to be placed. Some programming languages enable you to set one On Error-type statement and create a single procedure for handling any error that occurs in your code. Visual Basic does not support this type of centralized error handling directly. To properly handle errors in your Visual Basic programs, you need to place error-handling code in each procedure where an error may be encountered, in other words, in almost every procedure.

Now, the error handling can be simple. For some procedures, you may wish to include only the On Error Resume Next statement to cause Visual Basic to ignore any errors in the procedure. Also, the error handling can branch to a section of code that makes a call to a central error routine, which is how centralized error handling is accomplished in Visual Basic.

But, what if you don't have an error handler in a particular routine? In this case, Visual Basic moves up the call stack to the procedure that called the one containing the error. If the calling procedure contains error-handling code, the error is handled there. If the calling procedure contains no error-handling code, Visual Basic continues up the call stack until the top-level procedure is encountered. If no error-handling code has been found to that point, Visual Basic generates a run-time error. The following code shows a modification of the division-by-zero example shown in Exercise 14.1. In this case, the error occurs in the DivideError procedure, but the error is handled in the Click event procedure of the command button. This modified code shows how the search for error handling proceeds up the call stack.

```
Private Sub DivideError()
Dim X As Single, Y As Single, Z As Single
On Error GoTo 0
X = 5
Y = 0
Z = X / Y 'Error occurs here
End Sub
```

```
Private Sub Command1_Click()
On Error Resume Next
DivideError
If Err.Number > 0 Then 'Error is handled here
    MsgBox "The following error has occurred: " & _
Err.Description
End If
End Sub
```

 For more information on the call stack, refer to Chapter 15, "Debugging Your Application."

Deferred Handling of Errors

The beginning of this section discussed deferred and immediate handling of errors. In the case of deferred handling, Visual Basic is told to ignore the error when it occurs, but your code comes back and checks the error later in the procedure. This method of error handling is useful for some types of errors, such as division by zero. The error-handling code can be used to reset the value of variables, to enable processing to continue. However, there are drawbacks to using this method of deferred error handling:

- You must place error-handling code in several places in your procedure, that is, wherever an error that needs to be handled might occur.

- The Err object stores information only about the last error that occurred. If the error handling is very far removed from the source of the error, additional errors may occur prior to the error-handling routine, and you lose the information about the original error.

To use deferred error handling in a procedure, you need to start the procedure with the On Error Resume Next statement, which tells Visual Basic to continue execution of the program after an error has occurred. Then you must create the error-handling routine itself. For deferred error handling, the routine always starts with a statement that checks the Number property of the Err object. If the property is greater than zero, an error has occurred. Finally, the error-handling routine typically ends by clearing the Err object properties using the Clear method, which sets up the Err object for the next possible error. Exercise 14.2 shows you how to use deferred error processing to handle possible errors in the division of two variables.

Microsoft ✓ *Exam* *Objective*

Implement error handling for the user interface in desktop applications.

- Handle inline errors.

EXERCISE 14.2

Deferred Error Handling

1. Start a new project.

2. Add three text boxes and three labels to the form to serve as the input and output areas for the addition function. Also, add a command button to the form.

3. In the Click event of the command button, declare three variables to be used and enter the division equation as shown in the following code. This code allows the possibility of several errors, including division by zero and assigning a string to a numeric variable.

```
Dim X As Single, Y As Single, Z As Single
X = Text1.Text
Y = Text2.Text
Z = X / Y
```

4. After the Dim statement, add the On Error Resume Next statement to indicate that deferred processing will be used.

5. After the statement that assigns a value to Z, place the error-handling code. This code, shown below, checks for the occurrence of an error and then takes action depending on the error number. For division by zero, the code sets the result to zero. For other errors, a message is displayed. The code ends with the Clear method to reset the Err object.

```
If Err.Number > 0 Then
    If Err.Number = 11 Then
        Z = 0
    Else
        MsgBox "Invalid input."
        Exit Sub
    End If
    Err.Clear
End If
```

6. After the error-handling routine, enter a statement that displays the results of the calculation to the third text box:

```
Text3.Text = Z
```

7. Run the program and try several errors such as using zero for the second value and entering a string in the text box. Note the actions of the program. You may notice that if you enter a string in the text box, the result still displays zero because Visual Basic encounters the second error of dividing by zero before the error-handling routine is run, which means that the contents of the Err object indicates a division-by-zero error.

Immediate Handling of Errors

The immediate method of handling errors causes your program to branch to an error-handling routine as soon as the error occurs. This method of handling errors begins with an On Error GoTo line statement that tells Visual Basic the location of the error-handling routine in the procedure. The actual error-handling routine starts with a line label that corresponds to the line identifier given in the On Error statement. The error handler then evaluates the error, takes the appropriate action, and returns the execution of the program to the proper point, either the line where the error occurred or the line immediately following. You can also handle the error by simply exiting the current procedure or ending the application depending upon the severity of the error.

One other key piece of an immediate error-handling routine is that a line of code is required immediately prior to the routine to exit the procedure. This line is needed to prevent the error handler from being run if no errors exist. The code to exit a procedure is:

```
Exit Sub
```

If your procedure is a function or property procedure, you need to use the Exit Function or Exit Property statement instead of the Exit Sub statement.

The advantage of using immediate error handling is that all errors are handled as soon as they occur. Also, all the error handling for a procedure can be located in a single place instead of being spread throughout the procedure. Exercise 14.3 shows how to implement immediate error handling for the same project as Exercise 14.2.

EXERCISE 14.3

Using Immediate Error Handling

1. Create a new project with three text boxes, three labels, and a command button, as you did in Exercise 14.2.

2. Place the following code in the Click event of the command button to perform the calculation.

```
Dim X As Single, Y As Single, Z As Single
X = Text1.Text
Y = Text2.Text
Z = X / Y
Text3.Text = Z
```

3. Place the following statement immediately after the Dim statement in the procedure. This statement tells Visual Basic where to go when an error occurs.

```
On Error GoTo DivError
```

4. Place an Exit Sub statement immediately after the last statement of the procedure to prevent the error code from being run if no errors are encountered.

5. Place the following code after the Exit Sub statement. This code is the error handler for the procedure. If the error is divide by zero, a default value of *Z* is set. Otherwise, a message is displayed and the program exits the procedure.

```
DivError:
If Err.Number = 11 Then
    Z = 0
    Resume Next
Else
    MsgBox "Invalid input."
    Exit Sub
End If
```

6. Run the program and try different values of input, including strings. Notice that the program responds differently under this type of error handling because each error is trapped as it occurs.

You can have more than one error handler in a single procedure. However, you need to ensure that the code for each error handler is separated from the others so that you do not run code that is not needed.

Creating a Common Error-Handling Procedure

Because Visual Basic requires you to place error-handling code in most procedures of your program, you can imagine that there could be a lot of code duplication. For example, if you have several routines that handle saving information to a database, you could repeat the same error-handling code in each of these procedures. There are several ways around this type of problem:

- Create a class that handles all the database activities and include the error-handling code in the procedures of the class.

- Create a procedure that is called whenever database information needs to be saved and include the error-handling code in the procedure.

- Create a central procedure for handling all database errors.

The last option still requires you to add error-handling code to all your procedures, but the code required to determine the type of error and to determine the appropriate action is located in only one place. As an example, the following function could be used to determine the type of error that occurred and to indicate to the procedure whether to retry the operation, resume execution with the next statement, or exit the procedure.

```
Public Function DataError(ByVal iErNum As Integer) As _
Integer
Select Case iErNum
    Case 3046, 3158, 3186, 3187, 3188, 3189, 3218, 3260
        'Record is locked by another user
        iTriesCnt = iTriesCnt + 1
        If iTriesCnt > 10 Then
            iErrReturn = LabMessage(751, vbExclamation + _
```

```
vbYesNo, 752)
            If iErrReturn = vbYes Then
                iTriesCnt = 0
                DataError = 1
            Else
                bUpdateOK = False
                DataError = 2
            End If
        Else
            fPauseTime = Timer
            Do Until Timer > fPauseTime + 0.1
            Loop
            DataError = 1
        End If
    Case 3167
        bUpdateOK = False
        DataError = 2
    Case 3020
        DataError = 2
    Case Else
        LogError "Capture", "Change SubArchive", Err.Number, _
Err.Description
        bUpdateOK = False
        DataError = 3
End Select

End Function
```

The error-handling code in your database procedure would then be reduced to the following code:

```
ErrOccur:
Select Case DataError(Err.Number)
    Case 1
        Resume
    Case 2
        Resume Next
    Case 3
        Exit Sub
End If
```

You can use this same technique to create an error log that writes the contents of the error message to a database or text file.

Raising Errors from Your Program

One major objective of the Microsoft certification exam is for you to be able to raise errors from a server. When you create an ActiveX server, you are creating class modules that provide objects for other programs to use. In these modules, situations that you would want to inform a calling program about might occur. For example, if you were unable to open a recordset in the class, you would want to inform the calling program to avoid additional operations that required access to the database. Or, if you lost the database connection in the middle of an operation, you would want to inform the calling program.

One method of informing a calling program is to set properties that indicate whether a condition exists; however, this method makes it difficult to notify the calling program when the condition changes. To handle changes that create problems, you raise an error in the server component. To raise an error, you use the Raise method of the Err object.

When you use the Raise method, you can include one required argument and four optional arguments. These arguments set the properties of the Err object in the calling program. The required argument of the Raise method is the Number argument. The Number argument is a long integer that identifies the error to the calling program. Visual Basic supports error numbers between 0 and 65535; however, these numbers are for Visual Basic's internal errors as well as for errors you generate. To be sure that you do not conflict with Visual Basic's internal numbers, you should add the constant vbObjectError to any error number you wish to indicate. The following line of code shows you how to raise error number 101 from a class module.

```
Err.Raise 101 + vbObjectError
```

In addition to the required argument, there are four optional arguments that you can specify with the Raise method. These arguments provide additional information to the Err object for the calling program to use in determining the error. The optional arguments are:

Source   Identifies the name of the object that generated the error. If you omit this argument, Visual Basic uses the programmatic ID of your project.

Description   Provides text that describes the type of error that occurred. If this is omitted, Visual Basic uses the message "Application-defined or object-defined error" as the description.

Helpfile   Specifies the help file that contains more information about the error, if such a file exists.

Helpcontext   Specifies the specific context ID of the help file topic that contains more information about the error.

When using the optional arguments, you must enter the arguments in the following order: Number, Source, Description, Helpfile, and Helpcontext. You must also separate the values with commas. The following code shows how several of the arguments are used to generate an error.

```
Err.Raise 39 + vbObjectError, "Command", "Division Error"
```

You can also enter the value of arguments using named arguments, as shown in the following line of code:

```
Err.Raise Number:=39 + vbObjectError, _
Description:="Division Error"
```

Displaying Errors During Testing

As you are testing your program, your error handler traps any errors that occur in a procedure that has an error handler. Sometimes, however, you need to avoid having errors trapped. For example, if your error handler logs errors to a file, it may be able to tell you what error occurred and in which procedure it occurred, but it cannot tell you on which line the error occurred. Often, though, this information is crucial in determining why the error occurred and how to fix it.

To help you identify errors while you are testing your program, Visual Basic provides several error-trapping options. These options, shown in Figure 14.3, can be accessed from the Options item of the Tools menu. The error-trapping options are located on the General tab of the Options dialog box in the Error Trapping frame.

You can choose any of the following three options for breaking the execution on errors in your code:

Break on All Errors   Causes Visual Basic to pause on any error, even if the error is handled by an error handler in your code.

Break in Class Module Causes Visual Basic to pause on unhandled errors that occur anywhere in your program, even if in a class module.

Break on Unhandled Errors Causes Visual Basic to pause only for errors that are not handled by an error handler in your code. The difference between this option and the Break in Class Module option is that the Break on Unhandled Errors option will only show the line of code that references a class if an error occurs in the class.

If you want to see the errors in a procedure with an error handler, you need to select the Break on All Errors option.

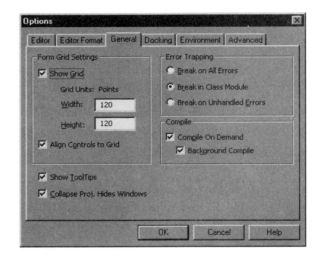

F I G U R E 14.3

Error-trapping options for testing programs

Summary

This chapter has delved into the creation of error-handling code for your program. Error handling is often overlooked but is an extremely important part of any good program. You don't want your users to see a default error message and then have your program terminate.

Knowing about error handling is also important for successfully passing the Microsoft certification exam. The exam objectives specify the following concepts you need to know about handling errors:

- Fix errors and take measures to prevent future errors.

- Implement error handling for the user interface in desktop applications.
  - Identify and trap run-time errors.
  - Handle inline errors.

Review Questions

1. Which of the following statements is used to turn off error handling in a procedure?

  A. On Error GoTo line

  B. On Error Resume Next

  C. On Error GoTo 0

  D. Error Off

2. Which of the following statements tells Visual Basic to retry the statement that caused the error?

  A. Resume Next

  B. Resume

  C. Retry

  D. Resume line

3. Which statement is used with deferred error handling?

  A. On Error GoTo line

  B. On Error Resume Next

  C. On Error GoTo 0

  D. On Error Defer

4. Which of the following are drawbacks of deferred error handling? Check all that apply.

   A. It runs slower than immediate error processing.

   B. Errors may occur between the original error and your error handler.

   C. Your error code is spread throughout your procedure instead of being located in a single place.

   D. If multiple errors occur, your program will crash.

5. What does the Clear method of the Err object do?

   A. Transfers error handling to the next higher procedure.

   B. Generates a run-time error.

   C. There is no Clear method.

   D. Resets the properties of the Err object.

6. Which of the following is a required argument of the Raise method?

   A. Description

   B. Number

   C. Source

   D. Helpfile

7. What is the purpose of the Raise method?

   A. To transfer error handling to the next higher procedure

   B. To generate a run-time error

   C. To trap errors that occur in your program

   D. To reset the properties of the Err object

8. What happens if you use a Resume statement outside of an error-handling routine?

   A. Your program retries the statement that generated the error.

   B. Nothing happens.

   C. An error occurs because the Resume statement cannot be used outside an error handler.

   D. Your error handler enters an infinite loop.

9. What are some ways that you can centralize error handling? Check all that apply.

   A. Write a class to encapsulate functions and include the error handling in the class.

   B. Place an On Error GoTo procedure statement as the first line of your program and write an error procedure.

   C. Have the error-handling code in each procedure call a function that identifies the error and indicates the appropriate action.

   D. Place your function in a Public procedure that includes error-handling capabilities.

CHAPTER

15

Debugging Your Application

Microsoft Exam Objectives Covered in This Chapter:

- Monitor the values of expressions and variables by using the Immediate window.
  - Use the Locals window to check or change values.
  - Use the Immediate window to check or change values.

- Set watch expressions during program execution.

- Given a scenario, define the scope of a watch variable.

- Implement project groups to support the development and debugging processes.
  - Test and debug a control in process.
  - Debug DLLs in process.

Unless you are writing very small applications, it is almost impossible to write perfect code the first time through. You will almost always find some errors in your programs. These errors can be anything from a simple typographical error to a logic error that causes the code to do something that you didn't intend for it to do.

The next best thing is to have a solid understanding of debugging techniques and a good suite of debugging tools at your disposal. Visual Basic provides a good suite of tools for finding errors in your program, and, because the debugger is integrated with the programming environment, the tools make it easy to correct these errors on the fly. This chapter gives you some of the understanding that you need for using Visual Basic's debugging tools.

Learning Techniques for Debugging

The certification exam will test your ability to apply the mechanics of debugging, using Visual Basic's debugging tools. But, to successfully use the tools available to you, you need to have some understanding of what is involved in tracking down and eliminating bugs in a program. Numerous types of errors can creep into your programs, but most of them can be grouped into one of three categories:

Syntax errors   You incorrectly type a statement or use a variable that has not been defined.

Invalid value errors   You assign a string value to an integer variable, or try to load a file that does not exist.

Logic errors   Your program runs fine but produces incorrect results.

For the first two groups of errors, Visual Basic notifies you when the error has occurred and helps you locate the line that caused the error. For logic errors, Visual Basic does not find the errors for you but does provide you with a means to determine what is wrong with the logic of the program.

The only hard and fast rule for creating a truly bug-free program is test, Test, TEST! Testing is the only way to find bugs. Beyond this one rule, there are several good practices that you can follow to make debugging a program easier and more successful:

- Create a test plan with sets of inputs and expected outputs from the program.

- Test the program on multiple machines, not just your development machine, to help find errors such as hard-coded file paths.

- Try to write and test your code in modules. Working with smaller program components makes it easier to find a bug.

- Place plenty of comments in your code so that you can come back to the program later and still know what a particular module is designed to do.

Checking Out Visual Basic's Debugging Tools

The key component of Visual Basic that enables you to easily debug programs is the integrated development environment (IDE). The integrated development environment enables you to run your programs in the development environment instead of having to compile the program, run it, and then try to determine what went wrong. By running your program in the integrated development environment, you have the capability to watch the values of variables as they change, step through your program line by line, and even make changes to the program on the fly.

As part of the integrated development environment, Visual Basic provides you with tools to make it easier for you to find and correct errors. These tools can be grouped into three broad categories:

- Tools for avoiding errors

- Tools for watching the value of variables and watching program calls

- Tools for pausing the program and for executing one or a few lines of code at a time

Tools for Avoiding Errors

The best place to start eliminating errors is to avoid them in the first place. Visual Basic gives you four tools to help you avoid errors. The use of these tools is not specifically covered in the certification exam, but you should know what these tools are and how to use them. You can avoid many programming headaches by using these four tools :

- Auto Syntax Check

- Require Variable Declaration

- Auto List Members

- Auto Quick Info

The tools can be turned on or off using the Options dialog box. You can access the dialog box, shown in Figure 15.1, by choosing the Options item from the Tools menu, then choosing the Editor tab in the dialog box. You turn on an option by checking the box next to the option. You turn off the option by clearing the box. Now, take a closer look at what these options do for you.

Using Automatic Syntax Checking

The Auto Syntax Check option tells Visual Basic to check the syntax of each statement as you type it. Using this option prevents you from making simple typing mistakes such as forgetting to include the Then keyword at the end of an If statement or forgetting to enter a value on the right side of an assignment statement. If you make this type of error, Visual Basic notifies you of the mistake as soon as you try to move to another line in your code. Figure 15.2 shows a sample of this error message.

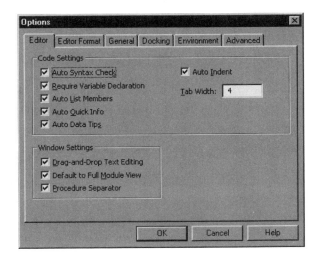

F I G U R E 15.1

Setting the Editor
options for debugging

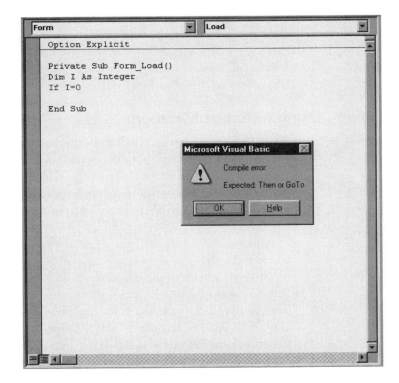

F I G U R E 15.2

An error caught by
automatic syntax
checking

Using Required Variable Declaration

Another common typographical error is mistyping the name of a variable in your code, which is easy to do but often hard to find. For example, you might create a variable named sLastName and accidentally refer to it later as sLst-Name. The code looks fine on an initial read-through, but will not work correctly because the two variable names represent different values. By choosing to require variable declaration, Visual Basic places the following statement as the first line in each form or module of your program:

```
Option Explicit
```

The Option Explicit statement is added only to new forms and modules, not ones that have already been created. If you are working with existing forms, you can force the variable declaration by manually placing the statement at the beginning of the code in a form or module.

This statement requires that you define a variable using a declaration statement before you can use it in code. Visual Basic does not give you any messages while you are editing code but gives you an error if it encounters an undefined variable when you try to run the program. Figure 15.3 shows how this works for the sLastName/sLstName example stated above.

Using Auto List Members

If you have worked with Visual Basic much at all, you know that hundreds of properties and keywords are used in creating programs. Often it is difficult to remember which properties belong with which controls or to remember the exact spelling of a keyword. With the Auto List Members feature, Visual Basic presents you with a drop-down list of appropriate properties or keywords as you type.

For example, if you enter the name of a text box on your form, as soon as you type the dot (period) after the name of the box, a list of properties appears. As you type a letter of the property, the selected item in the list moves to the first item that matches the letters you have typed. When the desired property is selected, you can accept it by pressing the Tab, spacebar, Enter, or equals (=) key. Visual Basic then enters the entire property name in your code, saving you keystrokes and helping you avoid typographical errors. Figure 15.4 shows an example of this feature.

FIGURE 15.3

Finding undeclared
variables

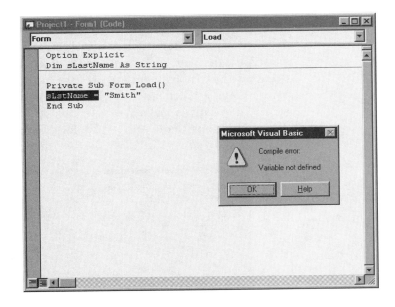

FIGURE 15.3

Finding undeclared
variables

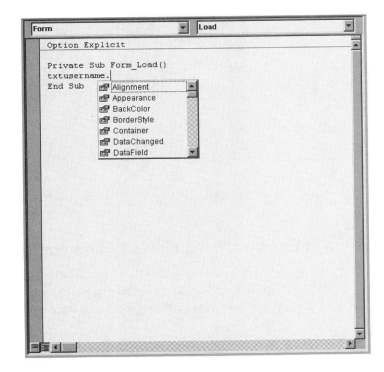

FIGURE 15.4

Letting Visual Basic
complete your code

Using Auto Quick Info

The last feature mentioned is Auto Quick Info. This feature displays the required syntax of a function as a ToolTip. The ToolTip is enabled as soon as you type in the name of the function you are calling. The ToolTip displays the required and optional parameters of the function and what information is returned by the function. The main benefit of Auto Quick Info is that it saves you a lot of trips to the help files to look up information about a function. Figure 15.5 shows how Auto Quick Info works for the MsgBox function.

F I G U R E 15.5

Getting help with command syntax

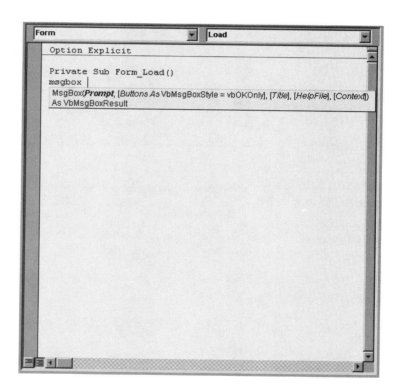

How the Environment Finds Errors for You

After you have done all you can to avoid errors, the real work of finding the remaining errors and eliminating them begins. Now the power of Visual Basic's integrated development environment and debugging tools comes into play.

The first thing that Visual Basic does for you when finding errors is tell you where they occur. When you are running your program from the development environment, you can have Visual Basic stop the execution of the program when an error occurs and show you the line of code where the error occurred. This capability gives you a starting point for determining why and how the error occurred. When the error occurs, Visual Basic displays a message that tells you the type of error. If you click the Debug button on this message dialog box, Visual Basic places you in Break mode, displays the Code window for the current form or module, and highlights the line of code where the error occurred, as shown in Figure 15.6.

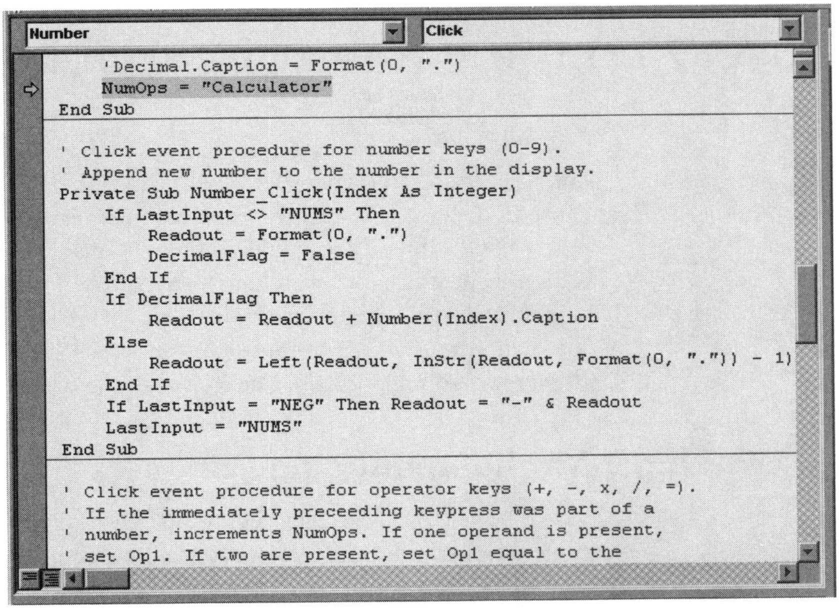

FIGURE 15.6

Visual Basic shows you where an error occurs.

Visual Basic also enables you to specify which types of errors will cause the program to pause. You can set the Error Trapping option from the General Tab of the Options dialog box. There are three options for trapping errors:

Break on All Errors   Causes Visual Basic to pause on any error, even if the error is handled by an error handler in your code.

Break in Class Module   Causes Visual Basic to pause on unhandled errors that occur anywhere in your program, even if in a class module.

Break on Unhandled Errors Causes Visual Basic to pause only for errors that are not handled by an error handler in your code. The difference between this option and the Break in Class Module option is that the Break on Unhandled Errors option will only show the line of code that references a class if an error occurs in the class.

The other part of taking care of errors is the creation of error-handling routines in your code. Creating error handlers is the topic of Chapter 14, "Handling and Logging Errors in Visual Basic Programs."

Observing the Values of Variables

After you have determined that you have an error in your program and have found out where the error occurred, you can start looking into the cause of the error. One of the most common causes of errors is an invalid or unexpected value of a variable. Therefore, Visual Basic includes a number of tools for observing (or "watching") the values of variables in your code. Using these tools, you can find the value of a variable at any point in your code. You can also use some of these tools to watch how the value of the variable changes as you move from line to line in the program.

Working with the Debugging Windows

Visual Basic contains four tools specifically designed to let you determine the value of a variable while your program is running:

- Watch window
- Locals window
- Quick Watch dialog box
- Auto Data Tips

Two of these tools, the Watch window and the Locals window, enable you to create a permanent view of variables while you are in the development environment. Using these tools enables you to observe the values of a variable or expression as the program executes, so that you can see the value at any time and determine where the value is changing. In addition, the Watch window and the Locals window enable you to change the values of variables as your program is running.

Displaying Information in the Watch Window

Microsoft ✓ ***Exam Objective***

Monitor the values of expressions and variables by using the Immediate window.

The most versatile of the variable observation tools is the Watch window. The Watch window lets you track the value of any variable or expression anywhere in your program. The Watch window displays the following information for each watch that you create:

- The variable or expression being observed

- The current value of the expression

- The data type of the expression

- The context of the expression (or where the expression is currently being used)

Figure 15.7 shows a typical Watch window in use.

FIGURE 15.7

The Watch window shows you the value of variables.

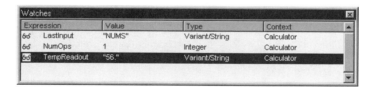

Microsoft ✓ ***Exam Objective***

Set watch expressions during program execution.

Adding a Watch to Your Program   To observe the value of a variable in your program, you need to add a watch to the Watch window. You add a watch by choosing the Add Watch item from the Debug menu to bring up the Add Watch dialog box shown in Figure 15.8. In the dialog box, you specify:

- The name of a variable that you want to watch. You can also specify an expression instead of a single variable.

- The context in which the expression should be viewed. You can specify that the expression be observed only in a single procedure, within a module, throughout the program, or any scope in between.

- The type of watch. You can choose three types of watches, depending on the purpose for setting the watch:

Watch Expression   Simply evaluates the expression and shows its value.

Break When Value Is True   Causes the program execution to stop when the value of the expression is True. This watch can be used only for a logical expression or a Boolean variable.

Break When Value Changes   Causes the program execution to stop when the value of the expression changes.

F I G U R E   1 5 . 8

To add a watch, specify the expression, scope, and type of watch.

After specifying the information for the watch, you click the OK button to add the watch to the Watch window. Exercise 15.1 shows you how to add several watches to the Watch window and lets you see how this process works.

EXERCISE 15.1

Creating Watches in a Program

1. You will use one of Visual Basic's sample applications to write a program to set watches. Open the `Calc.vbp` program in the `Samples\ Pguide\calc` folder under the VB folder on your computer.

2. Open the Code window of the main form for the calculator.

3. Open the Add Watch dialog box by choosing the Add Watch item from the Debug menu.

4. For the first watch, enter **Op1** as the variable name and set the watch type to Break When Value Changes. Then click the OK button on the dialog box.

5. Using the Add Watch dialog box, set another watch for the program. This time, enter **NumOps** as the variable name and set the watch type to Watch Expression.

6. For the last watch, set the expression to **NumOps = 0** and set the watch type to Break When Value Is True.

7. Run the program. Notice that the program stops in several places as you access different parts of the program. Each time the program stops, you can look at the values of the variables. To continue the program after it stops, press F5 or click the Run button again.

Editing a Watch   After you have initially created a watch, you often find that you need to make changes to the watch. You may need to change the expression, modify the scope, change the type of watch, or even delete the watch completely. Editing the watch is as easy as creating it. To edit a watch, highlight the watch in the Watch window, then right-click the mouse to bring up the pop-up menu for the watch. From here you can delete the watch or call up the Edit dialog box. This dialog box is the same as the Add Watch dialog box. After making any necessary changes, you can save the edited watch by clicking the OK button on the dialog box.

Changing a Variable   The Watch window displays expressions (variable names, logical expressions, or the results of a calculation) that you define. The information shown for each expression is the expression itself, its value, and its scope. If the expression is simply a variable name, you can change the value of the variable from within the Watch window. To do this, simply highlight the current value in the Watch window and enter the new value.

Microsoft
✓ *Exam*
Objective

Monitor the values of expressions and variables by using the Immediate window.

Using the Quick Watch Feature Sometimes when you are checking variables in your programs, you need to check only the current value of a single variable or expression. While the program is paused, either due to an error condition or another watch, you can use the Quick Watch feature to check the current value. To use this feature, highlight a variable or expression in the Code window of a form or module and call up the Quick Watch dialog box by choosing the Quick Watch item from the Debug menu or by pressing Shift+F9. The dialog box, shown in Figure 15.9, shows you the chosen expression, its context, and its current value. After viewing the value of the expression, you can close the dialog box by clicking the Cancel button, or you may choose to add the expression to the Watch window by clicking the Add button.

FIGURE 15.9

Quick Watch gives you a way to determine the value of a single expression.

Another way to check the value of a single variable is through the use of a feature called Auto Data Tips. This feature enables you to determine the value of a variable by resting the mouse cursor on the variable while the program is paused. The value of the variable appears as a ToolTip beneath the mouse cursor, as shown in Figure 15.10. Exercise 15.2 illustrates the use of Quick Watch and Auto Data Tips.

You activate Auto Data Tips by choosing the option on the Editor tab of the Options dialog box of Visual Basic.

EXERCISE 15.2

Using the Quick Watch and Auto Data Tips Features

1. Using the program from Exercise 15.1, make sure that you have the same watches set for the program.

2. Run the program.

3. When the program pauses, highlight an expression in the Code window, then activate the Quick Watch dialog box from the Debug menu. Examine the contents of the dialog box.

4. After closing the dialog box, rest the mouse cursor on several variables in the Code window. Notice how the value of the variable is displayed in a data tip.

5. Stop the execution of the program.

FIGURE 15.10

Auto Data Tips provides quick access to the value of variables.

```
Operator                          ▼   Click                                    ▼
   ' Click event procedure for operator keys (+, -, x, /, =).
   ' If the immediately preceeding keypress was part of a
   ' number, increments NumOps. If one operand is present,
   ' set Op1. If two are present, set Op1 equal to the
   ' result of the operation on Op1 and the current
   ' input string, and display the result.
   Private Sub Operator_Click(Index As Integer)
       TempReadout = Readout
       If LastInput = "NUMS" Then
           NumOps = NumOps + 1
       End If
⇨    Select Case NumOps
           Case 0
           If Operator(Index).Caption = "-" And LastInput <> "NEG" The
               Readout = "-" & Readout
               LastInput = "NEG"
           End If
           Case 1
           Op1 = Readout
           If O  Readout = "56."  ex).Caption = "-" And LastInput <> "NUMS" An
               Readout = "-"
               LastInput = "NEG"
           End If
           Case 2
```

You can also access most of the debugging functions from the Debug toolbar, which can be displayed from the Toolbars item of the View menu.

Using the Locals Window

Microsoft
✓ *Exam*
Objective

Monitor the values of expressions and variables by using the Immediate window.

- Use the Locals window to check or change values.

The Watch window enables you to specify the individual variables and expressions that you want to observe. However, sometimes you need to check out all the variables in a particular procedure. Although you could add each variable to the Watch window, there is an easier method. Visual Basic also has a Locals window. This window shows the value of all the variables that are local to the current procedure. In addition, the window shows the properties of the current form and all its controls. The properties are presented in a hierarchical view that you can expand or collapse to show as much detail as you wish. Exercise 15.3 walks you through the use of the Locals window.

EXERCISE 15.3

Using the Locals Window

1. Open the Mouse.vbp project in the Visual Basic samples directory.

2. Open the Code window of the frmMain form.

3. Move to the Click procedure for the mnuInstructions menu option.

4. Place the cursor on the line that starts CR =.

5. Press the F9 key to create a program breakpoint. (You will learn more about breakpoints shortly.)

6. Run the program and choose the Instructions item from the menu.

7. When the program pauses, choose the Locals window item from the View menu of Visual Basic. At this point, you can see the value of locally defined variables and the properties of the form and any of its

EXERCISE 15.3 (CONTINUED)

controls. The next illustration shows you an example of the Locals window.

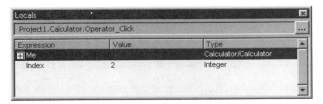

8. To see how the values of the variables change as you move through the program, press the F8 key to move through the program one line at a time.

9. When you have finished viewing variables, exit the program.

Changing a Value   As with the Watch window, the Locals window gives you the ability to change the value of a variable. Simply highlight the current value and enter the new value.

Understanding the Scope of Watch Variables

Microsoft
Exam
Objective

Given a scenario, define the scope of a watch variable.

As you were creating watches, you saw that you could specify the context of the watch variable, which is similar to the scope of a variable but with a key difference. The context setting of a variable tells you only where the watch expression will be evaluated. It does not affect the usage scope of a variable. For example, you can create a global variable in your program, but if you set a watch for the variable with a context of a single procedure, the Watch window displays only the value of the variable while that procedure is running. All other times, the watch is out of scope. A watch can also be out of scope if you are trying to watch a local variable and you are outside of the procedure in which the variable was defined.

Using the Immediate Window to Check or Change a Value

Up to this point, you have concentrated on viewing the values of variables. As you are debugging a program, however, you often need to change the value of a variable during program execution—for example, after you determine that you have an invalid value, but want to make sure that the rest of the program works correctly if a proper value is used.

Microsoft ✓ *Exam Objective*

Monitor the values of expressions and variables by using the Immediate window.

- Use the Immediate window to check or change values.

Another method of viewing or changing the values of variables is through the use of the Immediate window. The Immediate window lets you enter any valid line of code and execute it, enabling you to change values as well as determine the values of variables. To determine the value of a variable, you can use a question mark followed by the variable name in the Immediate window, as shown in the following line of code:

```
? Op1
```

To change the value of the variable, you use an assignment statement, like you would in your program, as shown in the following code:

```
Op1 = 5
```

Figure 15.11 shows the appearance of the Immediate window after the value of a variable has been checked and then changed.

FIGURE 15.11

Changing values in the Immediate window

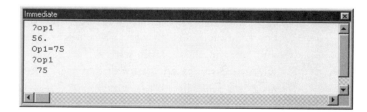

```
Immediate
?op1
 56.
Op1=75
?op1
 75
```

The Immediate window is typically displayed at the bottom of the screen when the program is paused. If the window is not visible, you can display it by selecting the Immediate window item from the View menu. You can also display the window by pressing Ctrl+G. Exercise 15.4 shows you how to use the Immediate window in a program.

EXERCISE 15.4

Changing the Value of a Variable

1. Open the Calc.vbp project from the Visual Basic samples.

2. Add a watch to the program using the variable **Op1** as the expression, and set the watch type to Break When Value Changes, pausing the program when a value is assigned to the variable.

3. Run the program. Enter a couple of digits in the calculator and press the key to start any math function (for example, the + key).

4. With the program paused, press the Ctrl+G key combination to display the Immediate window.

5. Enter the code **?Op1** in the Immediate window and press Enter. The value of the variable appears below the code.

6. Change the value of Op1 using an assignment statement.

7. Check the value of the variable again using the ?Op1 statement. The program should return the new value of the variable.

8. Stop the execution of the calculator program. (You can, if you wish, continue to prove that the new value is the one used in further operations. To do this, press the F5 key to finish running the program.)

Stepping through the Program

So far, you have learned how to stop the program for an error or in response to a specific condition occurring with a watch variable. These procedures enable you to evaluate a variable at a certain time or to change the value. This, however, is only part of the task of debugging a program. Unless the bug is a simple one, you need to see how the values of variables change as the program progresses. You also need to see which statements and procedures in the program are executed. Watching the progression of the program is also crucial in determining the cause of logic errors. Often a logic error is caused when a program takes an unexpected branch.

Stopping at a Specific Line of Code

You have seen how you can pause the execution of a program based on a certain condition. You do this by setting a watch to break when an expression is true or when its value changes. You also know that the program pauses automatically when it encounters an error. But what if you want to pause at a particular line in your program? Fortunately, Visual Basic provides a tool for this as well.

Visual Basic enables you to set what is called a breakpoint in your program. You set a breakpoint in your code by placing the cursor on the line of code where you want to pause, then pressing the F9 key. You can also set the breakpoint by clicking in the margin to the left of the program line. Either action toggles the breakpoint for the line. In other words, if a breakpoint is not set, the action sets one; and if the breakpoint is set, it will be cleared. When a breakpoint is set, the program line becomes highlighted and a dot appears in the left margin, as shown in Figure 15.12. If you wish to clear all the breakpoints in a code, you can press the Ctrl+Shift+F9 key combination.

WARNING You cannot set a breakpoint on a declaration statement for a variable or on a comment line. Most other statements can be used as a breakpoint.

Another way to pause the execution of your program is through the use of the Stop statement. The Stop statement is placed directly in code to pause the execution of the program at the statement. The statement is used without any additional arguments or parameters. The Stop statement has an effect on your program only when you are running in the development environment. The statement is ignored when your program is compiled.

The Stop statement pauses your program whenever the line is encountered. You can also use another tool to pause the program execution if certain conditions are met. This tool is the Assert method of the Debug object. The Assert method enables you to specify a criteria, such as the value of a variable. If this criteria is met, your program ignores the statement and continues on. If the criteria is not met, program execution pauses at the line containing

FIGURE 15.12

Setting breakpoints in
your code

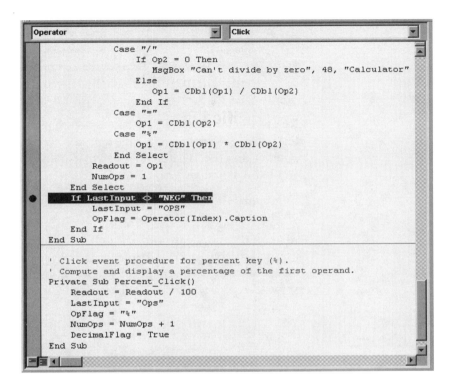

```
                    Case "/"
                        If Op2 = 0 Then
                            MsgBox "Can't divide by zero", 48, "Calculator"
                        Else
                            Op1 = CDbl(Op1) / CDbl(Op2)
                        End If
                    Case "="
                        Op1 = CDbl(Op2)
                    Case "%"
                        Op1 = CDbl(Op1) * CDbl(Op2)
                End Select
                Readout = Op1
                NumOps = 1
            End Select
            If LastInput <> "NEG" Then
                LastInput = "OPS"
                OpFlag = Operator(Index).Caption
            End If
        End Sub

' Click event procedure for percent key (%).
' Compute and display a percentage of the first operand.
Private Sub Percent_Click()
        Readout = Readout / 100
        LastInput = "Ops"
        OpFlag = "%"
        NumOps = NumOps + 1
        DecimalFlag = True
End Sub
```

the Debug.Assert statement. As an example, the following statement causes program execution to pause whenever the value of iInputNum is zero.

```
Debug.Assert iInputNum <> 0
```

Continuing the Program

After you have paused the program, you can set watches or view and set the values of variables using the Immediate window. At some point, though, you will want to continue the execution of the program. You can either have the program continue running until it encounters the next breakpoint, or you can step through the program in one of several ways. The methods for stepping through the program (along with the keyboard shortcuts for the commands) are:

Step Into (F8) Executes the next line of code in the program. If the execution point (indicated by a yellow highlight on the line) is a procedure call, the Step Into command moves to the first line of the procedure and executes the procedure one line at a time as you continue to issue the command.

Step Over (Shift+F8)   Works the same as Step Into, except that when a procedure call is encountered, the procedure is run in its entirety, and the execution pauses again on the line following the procedure call.

Step Out (Ctrl+Shift+F8)   Causes the execution of the current procedure to run to the end; then the program pauses on the line following the procedure call.

Run to Cursor (Ctrl+F8)   Enables you to place the cursor on the next line where you want to pause the program execution and then runs to that point of the code. This enables you to skip loops or sections of code that you know work correctly.

Continue (F5)   Causes the program to run as normal until the next breakpoint is encountered.

All these commands are available as key combinations. They are also available from the Debug menu and from the Debug toolbar shown in Figure 15.13. You can display the Debug toolbar by choosing it from the Toolbars item in the View menu. Exercise 15.5 takes you through the use of some of the continuation commands.

F I G U R E   15.13

The Debug toolbar holds all your debugging tools in one place.

EXERCISE 15.5

Stepping through a Program

1. Open the `Calc.vbp` project from the Visual Basic samples.

2. Open the Code window of the form and go to the Click procedure of the Operator button.

3. Place the cursor on the first executable line after the procedure declaration.

4. Press the F9 key to set a breakpoint on this line.

5. Run the program. Then enter a couple of digits and click a math operator button. The program pauses at the breakpoint in the Click event.

6. Open the Watch window and set watches for the TempReadout and NumOps variables.

7. Place your cursor on the line that starts with Select Case and press the Ctrl+F8 key combination. You will see that execution proceeded from the original breakpoint to where the cursor was located. Also notice that the values of variables in the Watch window changed.

8. Press the F8 key several times to observe the execution of the program one line at a time. Notice that this enables you to easily determine which branch of a conditional programming structure is executed.

9. When you are ready to continue execution without interruption, press the F5 key.

Working with the Call Stack

Sometimes you need to know why a particular procedure was called in order to determine why an error occurred. Visual Basic also provides you with a tool for determining how you got to a particular place in the code. This tool is the Call Stack window.

When your program pauses, you can display the Call Stack window by choosing the Call Stack item from the View menu. The Call Stack window, shown in Figure 15.14, displays all the procedures that lead up to the call to the current procedure. The calls are listed in order from the top of the window to the bottom, with the current procedure listed at the bottom. From the Call Stack window, you can highlight a procedure and click the Show button to display the line that called a subsequent procedure.

FIGURE 15.14

Determining where the call came from

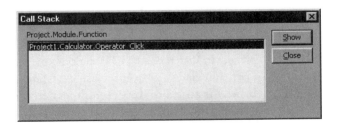

Debugging Servers and Controls

Version 4 of Visual Basic introduced the capability to create servers in Visual Basic, but these programs were difficult to debug. To debug a server, you had to start a second instance of Visual Basic and write a program to call the server. Even then, it was difficult to trace the execution of the program in the server.

Since then, versions of Visual Basic not only enable you to create COM servers (DLLs and executables), but also give you the capability to create your own controls. Fortunately, Visual Basic also provides a new tool for testing these elements—the project group. Using a project group enables you to create a control or a server and then, in the same Visual Basic session, create a program to test the component. With both programs in the same session, it is much easier to trace the progress of the program through the calls to the server or control and to determine the cause of errors in the component.

Creating a Project Group

The first step to debugging a COM component is creating the component itself. You looked at creating ActiveX servers in Chapter 10, "Creating COM Components." You also looked at creating ActiveX controls in Chapter 12, "Creating ActiveX Controls with Visual Basic."

Microsoft ✓ *Exam* *Objective*	**Implement project groups to support the development and debugging processes.**

After you have created the component that you want to test, the next step is to create a project group and create the project that will be used to call the component. Fortunately, you can accomplish all this in one simple step. While you have your server or control project loaded, choose the Add Project item from the File menu of Visual Basic to bring up the Add Project dialog box (which is the same as the New Project dialog box that you use to create a new project in Visual Basic). This dialog box enables you to create a new project or open an existing project for use in testing your COM component. When the project is added to the development environment, you can see information about both projects shown in the Project window. You can also see that the caption of the Project window changes to indicate that you are now working with a project group. The caption also shows the name of the project group file after it has been saved. Figure 15.15 shows an example of a project group.

FIGURE 15.15

Project groups are used to test ActiveX components.

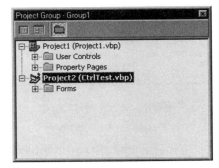

When you save the project group, each project is saved in its own .vbp file. One other file is created with a .vbg extension—the group file that contains information about which projects are included in the group. Exercise 15.6 shows you briefly how to create a project group to test an ActiveX control.

When you have multiple projects in a group, you need to specify which project is the startup project. The startup project is the one that is in control when you run the program. By default, the startup project is the first one that is added to the group. You can set the startup project by right-clicking the desired project in the Project Window and selecting the Set as Start Up option from the pop-up menu.

EXERCISE 15.6

Creating a Project Group

1. Create a new User Control project in Visual Basic.

2. Add a control to the User Control to give Visual Basic something to display in the test project.

3. Close the form of the User Control.

4. Choose the Add Project item from Visual Basic's File menu; then add a standard executable.

5. You can see that the Project window now contains two projects and has Project Group in the caption. Also notice that the User Control is one of the controls in the toolbox of the new project.

6. You can now place instances of the User Control on your form.

Executing the DLL or Control

After you have created the project group, you need to create a client application as your test project. This client application is the one that you execute in the testing. In turn, the client application causes the program code of the DLL or control to run as needed. As the code is run, you can use the standard debugging techniques to find and eliminate errors in the program.

Microsoft
✓ *Exam*
Objective

Implement project groups to support the development and debugging processes.

- Test and debug a control in process.

If you are working with a User Control, you can debug the control without ever running the test program, because the User Control's program is running while you are creating instances of the control in the test project. As you edit the properties of a User Control, you are running the code associated with the Property procedures of the control. You will, however, have to run your test program to test the methods of the User Control, because methods are called by your program code, and this code will not be executed until the program is run. As you are setting properties or running your test program, you can use the standard debugging tools to check variables. Visual Basic enables you to set breakpoints and watches in the User Control as you would in a standard program.

Microsoft
✓ *Exam*
Objective

Implement project groups to support the development and debugging processes.

- Debug DLLs in process.

If you are working with an ActiveX DLL, you can test the DLL only by running your test program. The test program creates objects from the classes of the DLL. As the properties and methods of these objects are used, the program code in the DLL is run. As with the User Control, you can set breakpoints in the DLL and set watches to observe the values of variables.

In working with either User Controls or DLLs, you should make sure that your test program checks all the properties and methods of the components. You should also be sure that all optional code is executed, which gives you the best opportunity of discovering all the errors in the code before someone else uses the component and stumbles across a problem.

Summary

After working through this chapter, you should have a good understanding of Visual Basic's debugging tools. You have seen how you can observe the values of variables and how you can change their values while the program is executing. You have also seen how you can pause the program and step through it one line or a few lines at a time. Finally, you have seen how using a project group makes it relatively easy to handle the debugging process for an ActiveX control or server.

Working though the text and exercises of this chapter should prepare you for the following objectives of the Microsoft certification exam:

- Monitor the values of expressions and variables by using the Immediate window.

  – Use the Locals window to check or change values.

  – Use the Immediate window to check or change values

- Set watch expressions during program execution.

- Given a scenario, define the scope of a watch variable.

- Implement project groups to support the development and debugging processes.

  – Test and debug a control in process.

  – Debug DLLs in process.

Review Questions

1. Which of the following tools helps you avoid errors in your programs? Check all that apply.

   A. Auto Syntax Check

   B. Require Variable Declaration

   C. Call stack

   D. Immediate window

2. Which of these tools displays the value of a variable? Check all that apply.

   A. Immediate window

   B. Watch window

   C. Call Stack window

   D. Locals window

3. Which of these tools shows you the properties of a form and its controls?

   A. Watch window

   B. Immediate window

   C. Auto Data Tips

   D. Locals window

4. Which of these tools enables you to change the value of a variable? Check all that apply.

   A. Watch window

   B. Immediate window

C. Auto Data Tips

D. Locals window

5. How can you cause a program to pause execution? Check all that apply.

A. Set a breakpoint in code.

B. Set a watch to break when the value changes.

C. Insert the Stop command in your program.

D. Right-click the mouse on the program while it is running.

6. How are the scope of a variable and the scope of a watch related?

A. The scope of the variable determines the scope of the watch.

B. The scope of the watch determines the scope of the variable.

C. The scope of the watch and scope of the variable are set independently and are, therefore, unrelated.

7. Which command do you use to pause execution after a procedure when you are stepping through a program?

A. Step Into

B. Step Out

C. Run to Cursor

D. Step Over

8. What Visual Basic element must you use to debug an ActiveX DLL?

A. Call stack

B. Immediate window

C. Project group

D. Compiler

9. When is the program code of a User Control running and able to be tested? Check all that apply.

   A. When the control is being built

   B. When the control is being added to another project and the properties are being set

   C. When a project containing the control is running

   D. During compilation of the control

PART

V

Distribution
Implementation

Compiling
Your Visual Basic Program

n versions of Visual Basic before version 4, compiling your program was a simple task. You chose the Make Exe option of the File menu and let Visual Basic do the rest. Visual Basic created an .exe file that you could distribute along with the VB run-time libraries. These libraries provided the support routines that were necessary for other people to use your program.

The task of compiling a program started changing a little in version 4 of Visual Basic. In version 4, you had the capability to create not only regular programs, but also ActiveX servers (though they weren't called that at the time). You had two options for compiling your programs: create an .exe file or create an OLE .dll file. Both options were accessible from the File menu. Programmers still weren't completely happy, however; one major complaint was the slow speed of some programs. The other complaint was that Visual Basic lacked a native code compiler, a feature that was available with other programming languages.

In version 5 (and continuing in version 6), things changed again. Not only could you create a standard program or an ActiveX DLL, now you could create ActiveX server .exe files, ActiveX documents, and ActiveX controls. In addition to giving you more types of programs that you could create, Visual Basic now had a multitude of compiler options available to let you optimize your code. These choices, as well as the ability to conditionally compile your project, are the subject of this chapter.

Choosing the Correct Options

The first decision you have to make in compiling your program is whether to use P-code or native code compilation. The main difference between the two is the size of the executable file and the speed of some parts of the program. Contrary to what many people might think, compiling to native code does not create a stand-alone application that does not need run-time libraries. With either a native code or a P-code program, you have to distribute the Visual Basic run-time libraries in order for your program to work. You also have to distribute any custom control .ocxs that your program uses.

Also, compiling to native code does not guarantee a major improvement in speed over the use of P-code. The speed improvements that you see depend on what your program is designed to do and how it is written. If your program performs extensive number crunching, native code may give you a speed advantage. If, however, your program is designed to access a database and display information, the speed bottlenecks will most likely be the retrieval speed of the database engine, something that you cannot significantly control in your program.

To determine which compilation option is right for you, take a closer look at P-code and native code.

Understanding P-Code

The term P-code derives from pseudo-code. Original versions of BASIC were interpreted. That is, an interpreter read a line of code in your program and created instructions for the computer's processor on the fly. By comparison, native code is the language that the processor uses, so native code instructions can be run directly by the processor in the computer. In the earlier days of PC programming, native code was typically written in Assembler, then later in C.

As Basic became more complex, and Visual Basic came on to the scene, purely interpreted code was too slow to be effective. A better way was needed to run the code in order to achieve better speed. With the use of P-code, instructions written in your programs are translated into a tokenized code that already contains instructions for performing operations and links to run-time libraries that are required for many functions. Although still not directly executable by the processor, P-code is much faster than the original interpreted code—in some cases, almost as fast as native code.

Deciding between P-Code and Native Code

Making a decision between P-code and native code requires considering the trade-offs. Each type of compilation has its own advantages and disadvantages.

If you compile your program to P-code, you get the following advantages: faster compile times and smaller .exe file sizes. The key disadvantage of P-code is that your program runs slower than one compiled to native code. Compiling to native code gives you the advantage of faster program execution, at the expense of slower compile times and larger .exe files.

The best way to determine which compilation is best for your program is to try compiling and running the code both ways. If native code gives your particular program a speed boost, and that boost is needed, compile to native code. If you are looking for small distribution sizes, compile to P-code.

Most people find P-code acceptable for the majority of their programs.

To tell Visual Basic which compilation method to use, you need to specify an option in the Compile options of the project. You can get to the Compile options by choosing the Properties item of the Project menu or by clicking the Options button from the Make Project dialog box. Either way, you are presented with a dialog box with several tabs. The Compile tab of the dialog box is shown in Figure 16.1. From this dialog box, you choose whether to use P-code or native code compilation.

FIGURE 16.1

Compile options for your project

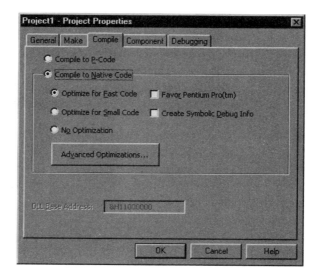

Choosing Native Code Compiler Options

If you choose to compile to native code instead of P-code, you have a variety of other options available to you for compiling the program. As you can see in Figure 16.1, these options are enabled when you select the Compile to Native Code option in the Compile dialog box. This section covers two sets of options: basic and advanced.

Basic Options

The basic native code compilation options are shown on the main part of the Compile page of the Project Properties dialog box. There are five options broken into two groups. The first group of three options determines the type of optimization that is performed during compilation:

Optimize for Fast Code   Causes the compiler to produce the fastest possible code. The compiler does this by examining all the program structures in your code and changing some of them to equivalent faster structures. For example, if you had a For loop whose function was to simply count from one to ten, the compiler could set the value of the variable to ten and eliminate the loop. The following code illustrates the equivalence of these two structures:

```
'The ultimate result of this loop is to set J
'    equal to 10.
For I = 1 To 10
    J = I
Next I
'This statement performs the same task and is faster
J = 10
```

Optimize for Small Code   Causes the compiler to create the smallest possible executable file. Sometimes, the optimizations that make a program faster increase the size of the executable file. With this option set, an optimization that increases the size of the executable would not be made.

No Optimization   Causes the compiler to simply create an executable file without trying to optimize for either size or speed.

The three optimization options of the compiler are mutually exclusive. As you can see from the use of option buttons in the dialog box, only one of these options can be selected at any given time. The other two basic options can be used separately or together, and can be used with any of the three optimization options. These other two options are:

Favor Pentium Pro™   Causes the compiler to optimize the code to take advantage of features of the Pentium Pro processor. This option should be used only if you know that your target machines will all have this processor. A program compiled with this option will run on other processors, but the performance will not be as good as if the program were compiled with the option turned off.

Create Symbolic Debug Info   Causes the compiler to create a separate file (with the extension .pdb) that contains symbolic debugging information. This information is not needed to debug your program in Visual Basic, but several more sophisticated debuggers such as Microsoft's Code-View or BoundsChecker by NuMega use the information to handle debugging chores. These programs can help you find difficult errors such as memory leaks.

Advanced Options

In addition to offering basic options for compilation, the native code compiler enables you to specify a number of advanced options. These options are for programmers who want to wring every last bit of performance out of their programs. You can access the advanced options by clicking the Advanced Optimizations button on the Compile options dialog box. The Advanced Optimizations dialog box is shown in Figure 16.2.

F I G U R E   16.2

Advanced compiler optimizations

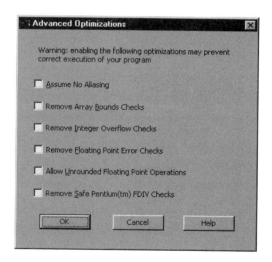

For most of your programs, you will not use any of these advanced optimizations; however, if you decide you want to try them, here is what each of the six options can do:

Assume No Aliasing   Aliasing enables you to use more than one variable name to reference a specific variable location, which typically occurs when you pass arguments to a subroutine by reference. Selecting this option tells the compiler that your program does not use aliasing. Typically, this option should be left off.

Remove Array Bounds Checks   Whenever Visual Basic accesses an element of an array, it checks to make sure that the index it is using is within the bounds of the array. If the index is out of bounds, an error occurs. With this option turned on, Visual Basic does not perform the bounds check and does not generate errors; removing the bounds checking can cause your program to retrieve a value from an invalid memory location and can result in crashes or strange behavior of your program. You should use this option only if you are sure that all array indexes are within bounds or if you perform your own bounds checking.

Remove Integer Overflow Checks   This option causes Visual Basic to bypass the normal checks that make sure a value will fit in the data type defined. When the checks are in place, an error occurs if the number you are storing is larger than the capacity of the variable that you created. When this option is on, the checks are removed and no overflow error occurs, but you may get incorrect results from some of your calculations.

Remove Floating Point Error Checks   Similar to the checks performed for integers, Visual Basic checks floating point operations to determine whether the value will fit in the declared variable and to verify that there is no division by zero. With this option turned on, these checks are bypassed, eliminating the reporting of overflow errors and division-by-zero errors. If these conditions occur, however, the results of your program may be incorrect.

Allow Unrounded Floating Point Operations   This option keeps the compiler from forcing floating point operations to be rounded to a particular size. The benefits of using this option are:

- Floating point registers are used more efficiently.

- Some memory operations associated with rounding are avoided.

- Floating point number comparisons are performed more efficiently.

Remove Safe Pentium™ FDIV Checks   Some time back, a floating point division error was reported in some versions of the Pentium processor chip. This error produced floating point results that were off in one of the last decimal places, but this was not a problem for most programs. By default, Visual Basic produces code that is not affected by this bug, but at the expense of size and speed of the program (minor effects). With this option set, floating point calculations are faster and your executable may be smaller, but there is the possibility that the Pentium bug will cause an incorrect result. As more computers are using later versions of the Pentium chip and using the Pentium Pro or Pentium II chip, this option can be safely used with most programs.

It is left to you and the user to determine which of these options you use for compiling your programs. The one caveat to using any of the options is to test your program completely to ensure that the compiler options do not create problems for you. Also, testing should always be done on multiple machines, particularly if you are using options that treat one processor preferentially.

Compiling Only Parts of the Program

Microsoft ✓ Exam Objective

Control an application by using conditional compilation.

Another important aspect of compiling your program is determining which parts of the program to compile. Visual Basic does not give you the option of compiling only a single module or a single form. Each time you compile the program, each file in your project is compiled. Rather, Visual Basic provides you with a means to choose whether to compile a specific code segment in a form or module, known as conditional compilation.

Understanding Conditional Compilation

You should be familiar with the If...Then...Else...End If programming structure. This structure is used in most programs to determine whether to run a particular segment of code based on whether the condition in the If statement is True or False. The following code segment illustrates a typical If construct:

```
If Len(FileStr) > 0 Then
    Set ErrDb = OpenDb(ErrPath & "ErrorLog.Mdb")
    Set LogErrSet = OpenRSet(ErrDb, "ErrorLog", 1)
Else
    Set ErrDb = CreateDb(ErrPath & "ErrorLog.Mdb")
    CreateErrTable ErrDb
    Set LogErrSet = OpenRSet(ErrDb, "ErrorLog", 1)
End If
```

Conditional compilation uses a similar construct to determine whether the compiler should include a particular segment of code. Before you look at the specifics of how conditional compilation works, take a look at why you might want to use conditional compilation.

Maintaining Multiple Versions of Code

One of the primary reasons for using conditional compilation is to maintain multiple versions of a program. In version 4 of Visual Basic, you could produce an executable file for 16-bit or 32-bit systems from the same code base. This capability made it easier to create and maintain programs that had to work on different operating systems.

However, you are probably aware that several programming elements, specifically application programming interface (API) declaration statements, must be coded differently for 16-bit and 32-bit systems. Using conditional compilation enables you to keep both sets of code in the same module and to compile the correct code based on the value of the condition. The following code shows one such use of conditional compilation:

```
#If Win16 Then
    Public glbValid As Integer, glbWinDir As String
    Public lpReturnString As String, Size As Integer
#Else
    Public glbValid As Long, glbWinDir As String
    Public lpReturnString As String, Size As Long
#End If
```

Using Conditional Compilation for Debugging

Another typical use of conditional compilation is for debugging your programs. As you are going through the debugging process, you may need to write the contents of variables to the Immediate window, or to keep a detailed log of the progress of the program. This information may be crucial for finding bugs, and you may want to keep the code in your program for maintenance purposes. However, you don't want the code to be running in the released version of your program. By surrounding the debug code with conditional compilation statements and setting the proper conditional values, you can compile your program with the debug code during development and without the code for the commercial release. The following code segment shows this possibility:

```
#If InDebugMode Then
    Debug.Print I, J, "Form_Load Routine"
    LogRun "Form_Load", Date
#End If
```

Using Conditional Compilation for Other Tasks

You can probably think of many other uses for conditional compilation of your programs. A few possible uses are:

- Creating demonstration versions of a program. You can use conditional compilation to include only key features, such as printing, in the full version of the program.

- Creating different versions of a program for different user levels. For example, if you have several related programs for managing different nonprofit organizations, these programs can use a common code base, but implement different features depending on the organization type.

- Creating single-user and network versions of a program.

Determining What to Compile

Now that you have covered what conditional compilation is and why you might want to use it, you are ready to learn how to implement conditional compilation. Implementing conditional compilation requires two steps:

1. Setting up the areas of code to be compiled

2. Setting the values of the conditions

Defining the Code Segments

The construct for setting up conditional compilation is simple. It is a variation of the standard If…Then…End If construct that you probably use extensively in your programs. The only difference is that for the conditional compiler statements you precede the If, ElseIf, Else, and End If keywords in the code with a pound (#) sign. This format instructs Visual Basic that the code is a compiler directive instead of a program statement. The rest of the statement is like the standard If statement. You specify the name of a variable or expression to be evaluated as the condition. If the condition is True, the segment of the code following the If statement is compiled. Otherwise, the code segment is ignored. Exercise 16.1 shows you how to set a conditional compilation to include a print feature only in the production version of a program.

NOTE The variables that you specify with compiler directives look the same as standard variables and are named the same way. These variables have no use in the normal course of your program, however, and are evaluated only as the program is being compiled.

EXERCISE 16.1

Conditional Compilation of Code Segments

1. Start a new project.

2. Add a command button to the form and set its Caption property to **Print**. Set the Name property of the command button to **cmdPrint**.

3. In the Click event of the command button, place the following code:

```
#If Production Then
    Printer.Print _
"General Report for Membership Program"
#Else
    MsgBox "Print functions are not available in" _
& "the demonstration version."
#End If
```

The exercise shows a simple two-level condition. If you are compiling the production version, the printer functions are enabled. Otherwise, a message is displayed telling the user that the functions are not available. Like a standard If statement, you can have multiple conditions using ElseIf statements as shown in the following code:

```
#If YouthMode Then
    'Enable youth group functions
    mnuYouth.Enabled = True
#ElseIf FinancialMode Then
    'Enable contribution menus
    mnuGifts.Enabled = True
#Else
    'Enable membership menus
    mnuMember.Enabled = True
#End If
```

Setting Conditions for Conditional Compilation

After you have defined the segments of code to be compiled and specified the variables or expressions to be used as conditions, you must set values for the conditions. One set of conditions is handled by Visual Basic. The other conditions are those that you define, and you must set the values of the variables prior to running the compilation process.

Creating Your Own Variables   You are not required to declare variables that are used in conditional compilation. Therefore, the variables are defined as you use them in the conditions of the #If statements. When you compile your code, you need to provide values for these variables. If you fail to provide values, Boolean variables default to False, numeric variables default to zero, and string variables default to a null string.

You can use three methods to provide values for the variables that are used in the conditional compilation:

- Set the variable in code using the #Const directive.

- Use the Project Properties dialog box.

- Use command line switches.

The first method of setting the value of a variable is to use the #Const directive. To use this method, simply specify the directive, the name of the variable (now a constant), and the value that you want to assign. The following line of code illustrates this method:

```
#Const InDebugMode = True
```

Setting the value of a conditional variable using the #Const directive sets only the value for the module in which the directive is used. You have to set the value in each module that uses the variable in order to use it. Using this method also makes it more difficult to change values, because you need to make sure that you make the appropriate change in each required location.

The best method for setting the value of conditional variables is through the use of the Project Properties dialog box. You can open the Project Properties box by choosing the Properties item from the Project menu. After opening the dialog box, click the Make tab to display the dialog box shown in Figure 16.3.

FIGURE 16.3

Setting the conditional
compilation arguments

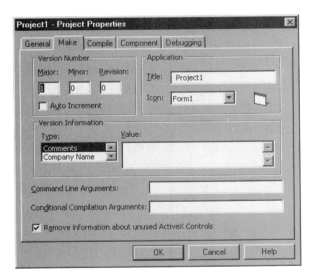

In the dialog box, you set the value of the variables by entering the name of the variable and its value in the Conditional Compilation Arguments box at the bottom of the dialog box. If you need to specify more than one variable, you need to separate the assignment statements with a colon, as shown in the following program line:

```
InDebugMode=True:Production=True
```

Exercise 16.2 illustrates the steps for setting the compiler arguments.

EXERCISE 16.2

Setting Conditional Compilation Arguments

1. Start with the project created in Exercise 16.1.

2. Choose the Properties item from the Project menu.

3. Select the Make tab in the dialog box.

4. Place the cursor in the Conditional Compilation Arguments text box and enter the following text:

   ```
   Production=True
   ```

5. Close the dialog box.

 NOTE You can access this same dialog box by pressing the Options button on the Make Project dialog box shown in Figure 16.4.

F I G U R E 16.4

Make Project dialog box

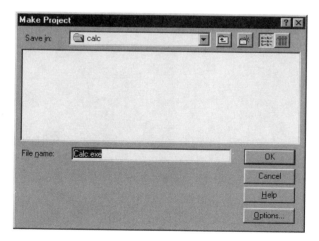

The final method of setting the conditional compilation arguments is through the use of command line switches. These switches are used when Visual Basic is started to set certain parameters of the program. The compilation arguments are set with the /d command line switch. The arguments and their values follow the /d switch. As with the arguments in the Project Properties dialog box, multiple arguments are separated by colons. The following command line could be used to start Visual Basic and set the compilation constants:

```
vb5.exe /make DemoProject.vbp /d
InDebugMode=False:Production=False
```

Creating the Executable File

After you have set the compiler options and specified values for all the conditional compilation arguments, you are ready to compile your program to an executable file. To start the compilation process, simply choose the Make item from the File menu to display the Make Project dialog box shown in Figure 16.4. In this dialog you specify the name of the executable file that will be created. You can also select the Options button to change any options that you previously selected. When you are ready, click the OK button to start the compilation process. Visual Basic compiles each form, module, and class module in your program and notifies you of any compilation errors that it encounters. After each component is compiled, Visual Basic writes the executable file. When this process is completed you are returned to the development environment.

If you look closely at the Make tab of the Project Properties dialog box, shown in Figure 16.5, you will see that there is other information that you can set for your project prior to compilation. This information provides details about your program and about the specific version of the program that you are compiling. This information is stored in the properties of the App object and can be retrieved by your program when it is running. Table 16.1 specifies the information that is contained in the dialog box and the corresponding property of the App object.

One other bit of information that can be specified in the dialog box is the icon to be used to represent the program. This icon must be one that is assigned to a form in the program. A list of all forms is shown next to the property, enabling you to easily choose which form's icon you wish to use.

FIGURE 16.5

Details provided on the Make tab of the Project Properties dialog box

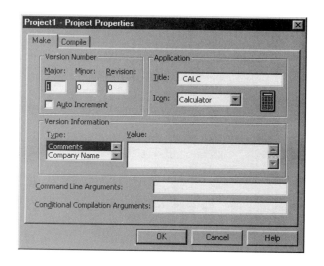

TABLE 16.1

Properties of the App Object

Make Dialog Information	App Object Property
Major version number	Major
Minor version number	Minor
Revision number	Revision
Program title	Title
Comments about the program	Comments
Your company name	CompanyName
Copyright information	LegalCopyright
Trademark information	LegalTrademarks
Description of the executable file	FileDescription
Name of the product	ProductName

Summary

Although compiling your program is one of the last steps of the development process, you can see that the options you select can have a significant impact on the performance of your code. You have also seen in this chapter how you can use the same code base to handle multiple versions of a program by using conditional compilation.

The information in this chapter should prepare you for the following Microsoft exam objectives:

- Given a scenario, select the appropriate compiler options.

- Control an application by using conditional compilation.

Review Questions

1. Which compilation option typically produces the smaller executable file?

   A. Compile to native code.

   B. Compile to P-code.

   C. Both options produce the same size file.

2. Which compilation option typically produces the faster executable?

   A. Compile to native code.

   B. Compile to P-code.

   C. Both options produce equally fast programs.

3. Which compiler options would be a benefit for a program to be run on a Pentium Pro machine? Check all that apply.

   A. Favor Pentium Pro™

   B. Create Symbolic Debug Information

   C. Assume No Aliasing

   D. Remove Safe Pentium™ FDIV Checks

4. How can you set the value of conditional compilation arguments? Check all that apply.

   A. Use the #Const directive.

   B. Use the Const statement.

   C. Use an assignment statement in your program.

   D. Use the Project Properties dialog box.

5. What are reasons for using conditional compilation? Check all that apply.

   A. To maintain multiple versions of a code

   B. To incorporate debug information

   C. To compile a single module for testing

   D. To create demonstration programs

6. What compiler options can lead to unexpected results from your program? Check all that apply.

   A. Remove Integer Overflow Checks

   B. Remove Floating Point Error Checks

   C. Create Symbolic Debug Info

   D. Favor Pentium Pro™

7. How can you access version information about your program that is input in the Make dialog box?

   A. It is unavailable while your program is running.

   B. Through the properties of the App object.

   C. Through the properties of the Program object.

   D. Read the header information in your code files.

CHAPTER
17

Adding Help
to Your Application

Microsoft Exam Objectives Covered in This Chapter:

- Implement online user assistance in a desktop application.

    - Set appropriate properties to enable user assistance. Help properties include HelpFile, HelpContextID, and WhatsThisHelp.

    - Create HTML help for an application.

One of the most overlooked aspects of any programming project is the documentation. This neglect occurs whether the documentation is in the form of hard-copy manuals or online help files. As the cost of producing printed documentation rises, however, many firms have begun the practice of including only online help with their products. For the programmer, this means that users have come to expect a help file associated with every program they run. Moreover, users expect the help to be easy to use and to be context sensitive; they expect specific help to pop up when they need it.

Fortunately, Visual Basic provides tools that make it easy for you to associate a help file with your application and to reference specific topics on demand. Unfortunately, for those who hate writing documentation, no one has invented a simple way for the program to document itself; programmers still have to write the text for the help files and create the files.

This chapter focuses primarily on how to incorporate an existing help file into your Visual Basic application. In addition, you will look briefly at how to create help files for your application and will examine some of the alternatives to help files for providing information to your users.

Understanding Help Basics

If you have worked with Windows for any length of time, you are probably familiar with the Help system that is used in most Windows applications. For most programs, simply pressing the F1 key brings up a dialog box that contains either general information about the program or information specific to the task you are trying to perform. A typical Help window is shown in Figure 17.1.

As you can see in the figure, the Help dialog box typically includes three tabs—Contents, Index, and Find. The Contents page works like the table of

FIGURE 17.1

A typical Help
dialog box

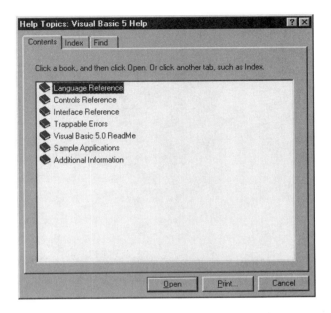

contents in a book, showing you the overall structure of the information in the help file. The great advantage of the online Contents page is that it enables you to move directly to the topic of interest with the click of the mouse, which is much easier than finding a specific page in a book. The contents that are shown on this page are determined by the contents information that you build into your help file. If you do not include contents information, this page is not be displayed when the user invokes the Help dialog box.

The Index page of the Help dialog is similar to the index in the back of a book. It contains a list of every topic included in the help file, organized in alphabetical order. You can access individual topics by scrolling through the list or by entering the topic of interest in the text box at the top of the page. As you type the topic name, the list of topics scrolls to the first topic that matches the letters you have typed. A typical Index page of a Help dialog box is shown in Figure 17.2. The topics that are shown in this index are the names of the individual topics that you create in the help file.

The final tab of the Help dialog is the Find page. When first accessed for a help file, this page invokes a wizard that helps you create a database of information in the help file. This database contains almost every word that occurs anywhere in your help file. This feature makes it easier for users to find specific information in the event that they do not remember the topic name. The Find page of Visual Basic's Help dialog is shown in Figure 17.3.

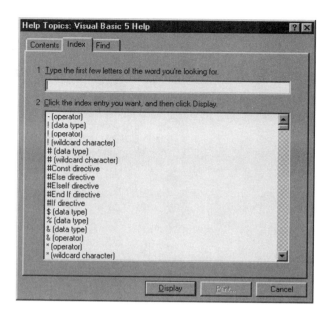

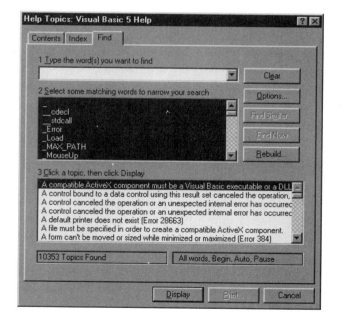

The organization of information in a help file is not a topic specifically covered in the Microsoft certification exam, but it is important that you understand the concepts in order to successfully create and implement a good help system.

Help Components

The Contents, Index, and Find pages of the Help dialog are only the initial part of the interface to the information in the help file. Like a book, the real information is contained in the pages of the help file. The pages of a help file contain text and graphics that describe a particular topic or function of your program, very much like the pages of any reference book that you read. A typical page from a help file is shown in Figure 17.4.

FIGURE 17.4

Help pages contain the actual information needed by the user.

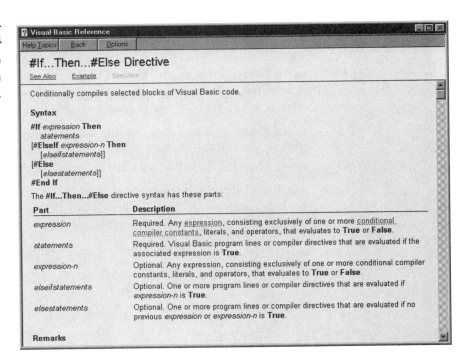

In addition to the text information that you find, Help pages have a few special elements that can make them far more useful than their printed counterparts:

Jump   A direct link to another page in the help file. A jump is indicated on the Help page by green text underlined with a single solid line.

Pop-up   A small window containing additional information about a specific key word or phrase. A pop-up is indicated by green text underlined with a single dashed line.

See Also   A collection of related topics that might be of interest to the user. The topics are accessible through the See Also list at the upper left corner of the Help page.

Each of these features can be included in your help system by creating the proper structures in your help files.

Characteristics of Good Help Files

You know that you will find help files with almost every program that you encounter. You have probably also seen that some of the help files in programs are not very helpful. Help file design is a major topic unto itself, but the following tips will assist you in creating files that are easy for your users to use and provide helpful information in a concise manner.

Use short pages   The text for a single help topic should be contained on one or two screens, if possible, to avoid making users scroll through pages of information to find what they want. If a topic is too long, consider breaking it into multiple topics or placing some of the information in a pop-up.

Make it well organized   You should use a Contents page with sufficient detail to cover the major topics of the program. Also, make judicious use of jumps and See Also lists to enable the user to quickly find related information.

Make sure all the links work   Like a good program, a good help file should be thoroughly tested. Users can get annoyed if they click on a link and get the message "Topic does not exist."

This is far from an exhaustive list of the considerations that should go into creating a good help file, but these tips should help to get you started in the right direction.

Getting Help with F1

The primary means by which most people access the help system is by pressing the F1 key. For simple programs, such as a game, pressing F1 accesses the Contents page of the help system. For more complex programs, users expect to be able to click a particular function or control and press F1 to get help specific to the current control or function. You receive this kind of help when you click a control and press F1 to get information about the properties, methods, and events of the control.

Like many other parts of the programming adventure, Visual Basic makes it relatively easy to provide not only help, but also context-sensitive help for your programs. You must do two things to provide the context-sensitive help for a program:

1. Identify the help file that will be used with the program.

2. Assign context IDs to the controls that will access context-sensitive help.

Determining Which Help File to Use

After you have created a help file for your application, you need to link the file to your program to make the file available to your users. The easiest means of linking the help file to the program is through the Project Properties dialog box. The General page of the dialog box, shown in Figure 17.5, lets you enter the name of the help file to be associated with your program. If you are not sure of the name, you can click the Browse button to open a File dialog box that lets you look for the file and select it. Exercise 17.1 walks you through the steps of associating a help file with a project.

F I G U R E 17.5

The Project Properties dialog box lets you identify the help file for your project.

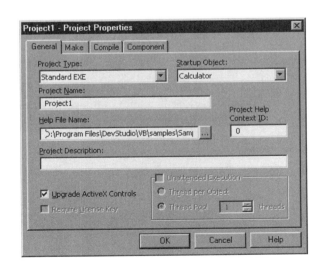

EXERCISE 17.1

Linking a Help File with a Project

1. Start a new project.

2. Open the Project Properties dialog box by choosing the Properties item from the Project menu.

3. Click the General tab of the Project Properties dialog box to get to the desired page.

4. Click the Browse button on the General page to open the File dialog box so you can select the file.

5. Select the *Test.hlp* file that is located on the enclosed CD-ROM.

6. Close the Project Properties dialog box.

7. Run the program and press the F1 key. The Index page of the help system should appear.

You may have noticed as you worked through Exercise 17.1 that the Project Properties dialog box specifies the full path to the help file. The full path may work fine on your machine, but can cause problems for your users if they do not have the same directory structure as you do (and it is safe to assume that they don't). Therefore, you need another method to set the help file for your project.

You can enter the name of the help file without the path information, and Visual Basic will default to the current path (typically the folder where the application is located).

Microsoft ✓ *Exam Objective*

Implement online user assistance in a desktop application.

- Set appropriate properties to enable user assistance. Help properties include HelpFile, HelpContextID, and WhatsThisHelp.

The best method of setting the HelpFile property for your program is through code placed at the start of your program. All Visual Basic programs support the App object, which enables you to set and retrieve information about the currently running program. The specific property that identifies the help file for your application is the HelpFile property. Using the App object, you can specify the help file in a line of code such as the following:

```
App.HelpFile = App.Path & "\Test.hlp"
```

This code specifies that the application should use the Test.Hlp file located in the same directory as the application. Using this technique, the directory structure of your user does not matter, as long as the executable and the help file are located in the same directory. You can make sure that they are located in the same place through the setup routine for your program.

Setting Up Context-Sensitive Help

Setting the HelpFile property, or identifying the help file in the Project Properties dialog box, allows you access to the help file but does not allow the user to get context-sensitive help. For context-sensitive help, you need to identify the topic within the help file to be associated with each form or control in your program.

You do not have to link every control in your program to a specific topic. You need to link only those controls for which you wish to provide context-sensitive help. However, it is a good idea to have a help topic for each form in your program.

Setting the Help ID for a Control or Form

Each topic that you create in a help file is identified by a specific tag. This tag is a numeric ID that enables you to associate the topic with a specific item in your program. The corresponding ID in your program is the HelpContextID property of a control or a form. By setting this property, either in the design mode or through code statements, you create a link between the control and the specific help topic.

For forms and most controls, the easiest way to set the HelpContextID is through the Properties window in the design mode. Figure 17.6 shows the setting of the HelpContextID property for a form.

FIGURE 17.6

Setting the Help-
ContextID in the
Properties window

Controls such as the Label, Timer, Shape, and Line do not have a HelpContextID property. Because the user cannot place the focus on these controls while the program is running, there is no way to get context-sensitive help for them, nor should there be a need for it.

If you want to set the HelpContextID from code in your program, you can do it by using an assignment statement to set a value for the property. The following code statement sets the property for a text box:

```
txtName.HelpContextID = 220
```

Exercise 17.2 shows you how to set the HelpContextID to enable context-sensitive help.

If you are creating help files in a word processor, you specify the Context IDs in the document used to create the file. If you are using an automated help tool, these Context IDs are usually created for you.

EXERCISE 17.2

Creating Context-Sensitive Help

1. Start with the project you created in Exercise 17.1.

2. Add two command buttons to the form. Name the buttons **cmdFile** and **cmdAnalyze**. Set the Captions of the buttons to **Open File** and **Analyze Database** respectively.

3. Set the HelpContextID property of the cmdFile button to **220**.

4. Set the HelpContextID property of the cmdAnalyze button to **240**.

5. Run the program.

6. Move the focus to the Open File button and press F1. The Help page shown in the next illustration should appear. Close the Help window.

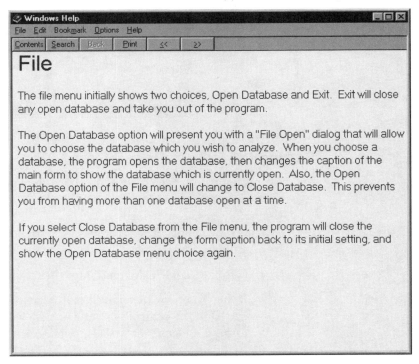

7. Move the focus to the Analyze Database button and press F1. You will see that a different Help page is displayed.

One other element of your programs that you might want to associate with specific help topics is the menu. You can assign a help topic to each item in your menu. Like the other controls on your form, you can use an assignment statement to set the HelpContextID for the menu item, or you can set the value while you are in the Menu Builder, as shown in Figure 17.7.

FIGURE 17.7

Setting the Help-
ContextID for a menu

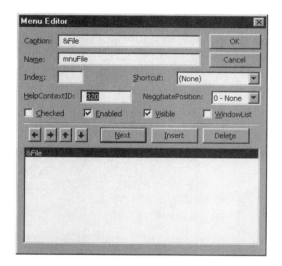

Setting the Default Help Topic

At this point, you can create context-sensitive help for your programs. But what happens if the user presses the F1 key on a control for which no HelpContextID has been defined?

The user will not get an error message. When the user presses F1 on a control, Visual Basic does the following search:

1. Check for a HelpContextID for the control and if found, use it.

2. If there is no HelpContextID for the control, check the HelpContextID of the control's container, such as a frame, picture box, or form. If a HelpContextID is found, use it.

3. Repeat step 2 until the top-level container has been accessed.

4. If no HelpContextID is found, display the Index page of the help system.

WARNING If you specify a HelpContextID that does not exist in your help file, the user encounters an error.

Displaying Help with the Common Dialog

Using the F1 key is the primary method through which users access the help system, but most programs also have Help options as part of the main menu. These options enable the user to view the Help contents and the Help index. The functionality for implementing these menu choices is not an integral part of Visual Basic, but it is a capability of one of Visual Basic's controls, the Common Dialog.

The Common Dialog control provides you with a means of using a variety of dialog boxes that are used in all Windows programs:

- File Open
- File Save
- Font Selection
- Color Selection
- Printer Control
- Printer Setup
- Help

The key dialog box you are concerned with in this chapter is the Help dialog box. Using the Common Dialog, you can invoke help from anywhere in your program, allowing your users to access help using menu choices or command buttons on dialog boxes that you build.

Accessing help from the Common Dialog requires the completion of three tasks—setting the HelpFile property, setting the HelpCommand property, and invoking the ShowHelp method. The HelpFile property of the Common Dialog is the same as the HelpFile property of the App object. The name of the file can be set using an assignment statement. The HelpCommand property determines what action will be taken when the ShowHelp method is run; therefore, this property must be set before the method is invoked. The Help-Command property has a variety of settings, as summarized in Table 17.1.

TABLE 17.1	Help Action	Common Dialog Constant
HelpCommand Property Settings	Execute a Help macro.	cdlHelpCommand
	Display the Contents page of the help system.	cdlHelpContents
	Display a specific topic. (You must also set the HelpContext property.)	cdlHelpContext
	Display a topic in a pop-up Help window.	cdlHelpContextPopup
	Display help for a particular keyword.	cdlHelpKey
	Display help for a keyword starting with a specific letter.	cdlHelpPartialKey

There are other settings of the HelpCommand property; however, the preceding settings are the most commonly used values. You can find the description of all the settings in Visual Basic's help system.

To run a specific help command, you enter two lines of code in your program. The first line specifies the action to be taken, and the second line invokes the ShowHelp method. The following code illustrates how to perform this task:

```
getfile.HelpFile = App.Path & "\ArcHelp.hlp"
getfile.HelpCommand = cdlHelpContext
getfile.HelpContext = 220
getfile.ShowHelp
```

Displaying Help Contents

As mentioned above, the Contents page of the help file is typically accessed from a menu item on your form. Exercise 17.3 takes you through the process of creating the menu and setting it up to access help.

EXERCISE 17.3

Accessing the Contents of Help with the Common Dialog

1. Start a new project.

2. Add the Common Dialog to your Visual Basic toolbox by adding the control in the Components dialog box. You can access the Components dialog box by choosing the Components item from the Project menu.

3. Add an instance of the Common Dialog box to your form. Name the control **cdlHelp**.

4. Open the Menu Editor of the form. Create a top-level menu named **mnuHelp** and set the Caption of the menu to **&Help**. As a submenu of the Help menu, create an item named **hlpContents** and set the Caption property to **Help &Contents**.

5. Close the Menu Editor to build the menu.

6. Open the Click event of the Help Contents menu item.

7. Place the following code in the Click event procedure:

```
cdlHelp.HelpFile = "C:\Data\VB6Guide\Test1.hlp"
cdlHelp.HelpCommand = cdlHelpContents
cdlHelp.ShowHelp
```

8. Run the program and choose the Help Contents menu item. Your program should display the Contents page of Visual Basic's help system.

Displaying the Help Index

The other item that is typically on a Help menu is the Search item. This item is usually coded to bring up the Index page of the help system to enable the user to search for a particular topic. Exercise 17.4 extends Exercise 17.3 by adding another menu item and setting up the code to display the Help index.

EXERCISE 17.4

Adding a Menu Item and Displaying the Help Index

1. Start with the project created in Exercise 17.3.

2. Open the Menu Editor and add another item under the Help menu. Name the item **hlpIndex** and set the Caption property to **Help Topics**.

3. Close the Menu Editor and open the Code window for the Click event of the Help Topics menu.

4. Add the following code to the Click event procedure:

```
cdlHelp.HelpFile = " C:\Data\VB6Guide\Test1.hlp "
cdlHelp.HelpCommand = cdlHelpKey
cdlHelp.HelpKey = ""
cdlHelp.ShowHelp
```

5. If you run the program and select the Help Topics item, you will see the Index page of Visual Basic's help system, as shown in the following illustration.

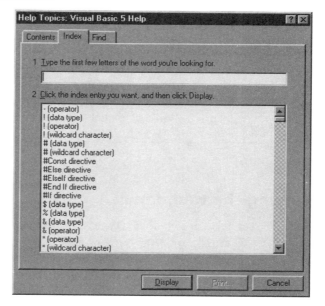

Creating Help Files

In this chapter's exercises, you have used help files that already existed on your system or were supplied on the CD-ROM that accompanies this book. For your programs, you will need to create your own help files—a very tedious task, but much easier than it used to be. Microsoft has introduced some new tools to help you create the files, and several third-party programs exist that provide complete solutions for creating help files.

To create a help file for your program, you need to perform four tasks:

1. Create the Help Topic information files.

2. Create the help project file that maps the help file information.

3. Create the Help Contents file.

4. Compile the help file from the text files and the help project file.

After you create the help file and know all the context IDs for the topics, you need to insert the topic IDs in the HelpContextID properties of the appropriate forms and controls.

Using the Help Workshop and a Word Processor

To make it easier for you to create help files for your applications, Microsoft includes the Help Workshop with Visual Basic. The Help Workshop is located in the \Common\Tools folder of the Visual Basic CD-ROM as HCW.exe.

The Help Workshop, shown in Figure 17.8, helps you organize the topics of your help file. The program also creates the help project file and the contents file, and helps you compile and test the actual help file.

The main effort in building the help file for your program is creating the topic files. A detailed discussion of this task is beyond the scope of this book, but to create help topic files on your own, you need to use a word processor that can create Rich Text Format (RTF) files. You also need to understand several formatting options of the word processor that are required to encode the help topic jumps, pop-ups, and context IDs. You can find more information about creating help files in Visual Basic's help system and VB Books Online.

FIGURE 17.8

Help Workshop for
creating help files

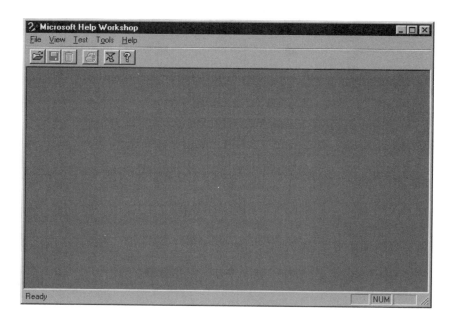

Using Other Help Products

Programmers try to find tools that help them to be more productive so they can concentrate on creating the unique routines and interfaces for their programs, particularly in the case of creating help files. Fortunately for VB programmers, several products make it fairly easy to create help files without having to worry about all the custom formatting required when using a word processor.

Several of these products are also designed to work specifically with Visual Basic. These products search your forms for any control that has a HelpContextID and use this control as the first cut at the topics for the help file. When you have finished creating the help file, these same products go back through your project and set the correct values of the HelpContextID properties for the forms and controls. Several of these products are:

- WinHelp Office by Blue Sky Software

- ForeVB by ForeFront Technologies

- VB HelpWriter by Teletech Systems

Creating HTML Help

Microsoft
✓ **Exam**
Objective

Implement online user assistance in a desktop application.

▪ Create HTML help for an application.

T he Windows help files have long been the standard for providing online help in your applications. However, many products are starting to provide help in the form of HTML pages. The advantage of using HTML help is that it uses a browser interface similar to the browsers used for surfing the Web. This interface is familiar to most users and makes navigating through help files more intuitive. Microsoft is adopting HTML help as the standard for online help for all of its products. You can see an example of HTML help in the Visual Basic help example shown in Figure 17.9.

F I G U R E   17.9

HTML help in
Visual Basic

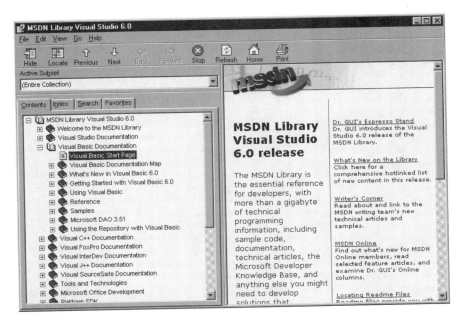

As was the case for Windows help files, Microsoft provides a tool to help you create HTML help files. The HTML Help Workshop is one of the extra tools on the Visual Basic CD. The HTML Help Workshop is not installed as part of the standard Visual Basic installation; you have to install it separately.

The HTML Help Workshop assists you with the two main tasks of creating HTML help:

1. Creating HTML files for each help topic.

2. Compiling the HTML files into a single help file.

Exercise 17.5 shows you how to create a simple HTML help file for an application.

EXERCISE 17.5

Creating HTML Help

1. Start the HTML Help Workshop. Click the New button on the toolbar and choose HTML File from the pop-up menu. You are prompted to enter a name for the file. After you name the file, the HTML Help Workshop creates a basic HTML file as shown in the following graphic.

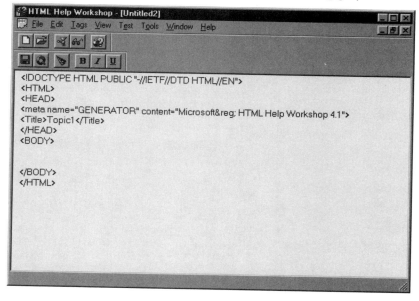

EXERCISE 17.5 (CONTINUED)

2. Enter the text you want for the help topic in the BODY section of the HTML file. You can use the bold, italic, and underline buttons of the editor to help you with basic formatting. You can handle other formatting with standard HTML tags.

3. Save the HTML file.

4. Click the New button of the toolbar and choose Project from the pop-up menu. This starts a wizard that creates an HTML Help project.

5. On the Destination page of the wizard, specify the name of the project file and the folder where you want to save the file. Then, click the Next button.

6. On the Existing Files page of the wizard, click the box next to HTML Files to indicate that you want to include existing HTML files in the project. Click the Next Button.

7. On the HTML Files page, shown below, you use the Add button to add files to the project. Add the HTML file that you saved in step 3.

8. After adding the HTML files, click the Next button. Then click the Finish button on the Finish page of the wizard. This creates the project file and displays the project management view of the HTML Help Workshop, as shown below.

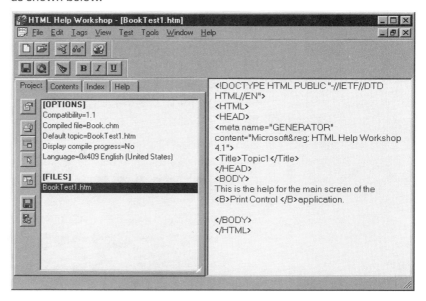

9. Add other HTML files as needed.

10. After you have added all the HTML files for the individual help topics, compile the HTML Help project by choosing the Compile option from the File menu. This creates the actual HTML help file that will be used by your application.

11. View the finished help file by choosing the Compiled File option from the View menu. This brings up the help browser and displays the first page of your HTML help file as shown in the following graphic.

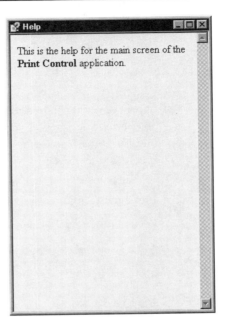

Providing Help in Other Ways

The help system is, of course, the main method of providing help to your users; however, there are several other means of providing timely information about the tasks users are performing:

ToolTips   The little boxes that pop up when the user rests the mouse on a control for a few seconds. Typically, these tips are used to provide a brief description of the function of a control. You can include ToolTips for many controls by entering a string of text in the ToolTipText property of the control.

Status bars   The status bar at the bottom of a form is often used to provide information to the user about a particular task. The status bar is particularly useful in a data entry application where it can be used to describe the information that should be input into the current control. To learn more about the StatusBar control, refer to Chapter 2, "Working with ActiveX Controls."

Message boxes These boxes are usually reserved for warnings or confirmation of an action, but you can use a message box to provide help to a user on demand or when a problem occurs.

Summary

This chapter covered the two main means of displaying help in your Visual Basic programs. Specifically, you learned how to create context-sensitive help and how to use the Common Dialog box to display help items.

The review questions cover the following exam objectives that were discussed in this chapter:

- Implement online user assistance in a desktop application.

  - Set appropriate properties to enable user assistance.

  - Help properties include HelpFile, HelpContextID, and WhatsThis-Help. Create HTML help for an application.

Review Questions

1. HelpFile is a property of which object? Check all that apply.

   A. Form

   B. Common Dialog

   C. Project

   D. App

2. How do you make a specific topic appear when the user presses F1 on a control?

   A. Pass the control name to the Common Dialog.

   B. Set the value of the HelpContextID property of the control.

   C. Set the value of the Index property of the control.

   D. Set the ToolTipText property of the control.

3. What happens if there is no specific topic for a control when the user presses F1?

   A. The Topic not Found error is displayed in the help file.

   B. Help is not accessed.

   C. The HelpContextID of the control's container is used.

   D. Windows 95/NT help is shown.

4. What happens if the topic assigned to a control is not in the help file?

   A. The Topic not Found error is displayed in the help file.

   B. Help is not accessed.

   C. The HelpContextID of the control's container is used.

   D. Windows 95/NT help is shown.

5. Which two properties of a Common Dialog must be set before trying to display help?

   A. HelpFile

   B. HelpContext

   C. HelpCommand

   D. HelpKey

6. Which method of the Common Dialog is used to display help information?

   A. Help

   B. OpenHelp

   C. ShowHelp

   D. Assist

7. Which files are created by the Help Workshop? Check all that apply.

   A. Help Topic files

   B. Help file (.hlp extension)

   C. Help Project file

   D. Help Contents file

8. Which groups of controls can be linked to a specific help topic?

   A. Any control that is visible on the screen

   B. Only controls with a HelpContextID property

   C. All controls

   D. Only menu items

CHAPTER

18

Deploying an Application

Microsoft Objectives Covered in This Chapter:

- Use the Package and Deployment Wizard to create a setup program that installs a desktop application, registers the COM components, and allows for uninstall.

- Deploy application updates for desktop applications.

- Plan and implement floppy disk-based deployment or compact disc-based deployment for a desktop application.

- Plan and implement network-based deployment for a desktop application.

- Plan and implement Web-based deployment for a desktop application.

The application is finally finished. You have written the program, debugged it, tested it on multiple machines; you have even written a great help file to go along with your program. Just one final task remains for you to perform—creating the setup routine that will enable other people to install your application on their machines.

Like all the other parts of the programming process, this final task requires some thought and preparation. For example, do you want to distribute the application over a network, have your users download it from the Web, or distribute the application on floppy disks or a CD-ROM? Also, you need to determine if you have special requirements for the installation. For example, will you support multiple installation types or a one-size-fits-all approach? Will all the files be copied to the user's hard drive or can some be left on the CD-ROM or network? The answers to these questions will determine, in part, the type of setup program you create.

After you have decided how you want to distribute your application, you will find that Visual Basic comes with a great tool for helping you create the setup program and the distribution media for your application. This tool is the Package and Deployment Wizard. This wizard lets you create the type of setup package you need and helps you deploy the application either onto disk media or to a Web site.

Creating Setup Programs

Microsoft
✓ *Exam*
Objective

Use the Package and Deployment Wizard to create a setup program that installs a desktop application, registers the COM components, and allows for uninstall.

When you begin to create setup programs and distribution disks (or files) for your programs, you need to accomplish several tasks:

1. Compile your program.

2. Determine the files that must be distributed with the program. These files include the VB run-time libraries, any other required .dll files, and any files required by your program (help files, databases, documents, or ReadMe files).

3. Create a setup program for copying files to the user's machine and uncompressing the files.

4. Compress the files that will be included on the distribution disks. Compression is necessary to minimize the number of disks needed for a standard installation or to minimize download time for an Internet installation.

5. Identify the location where files should be installed on the user's machine. For example, most .dll or .ocx files should be installed in the Windows\System or Winnt\System32 folder on the user's machine. Other files should be installed in an application directory specified by the user.

6. Create the disks or download files that will be used to distribute the program.

7. Test the setup program. A setup program is like any other program; it must be tested to ensure that it works correctly. Nothing turns a user off faster than an installation program that doesn't work. Preferably, you should test the program on a machine other than your development machine to make sure all the proper components have been installed.

You can get help with all these steps, except the testing, from the Package and Deployment Wizard. The wizard contains the following tools to help you distribute your applications:

- A setup program for copying and expanding compressed files from the setup disks to the user's hard drive

- A compression program for compressing the files to be distributed with your application

- A program for making cabinet files for Internet distribution

- Dependency files for determining which components are needed with specific applications, such as Data Access Object files

A dependency file simply lists all the files required for your application. This file is useful if you are using another installation program, such as InstallShield, to create your installation routine.

The Package and Deployment Wizard is one of the Visual Basic/Visual Studio tools that is installed with Visual Basic. For any type of installation routine that you are creating, you need to start the Package and Deployment Wizard from the Windows Start menu. This brings up the first screen of the wizard, shown in Figure 18.1.

FIGURE 18.1

Initial screen of the Package and Deployment Wizard

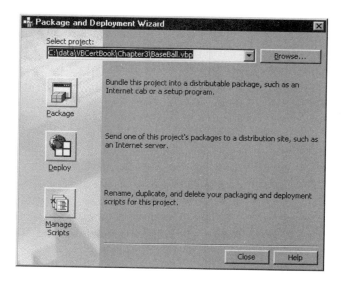

The Package and Deployment Wizard can also be run as an add-in from inside the Visual Basic development environment.

You can create three main types of installations with the wizard: 1) disk-based, 2) network-based, and 3) Internet- or Web-based. You will look at each of these installation types and will go through an exercise that familiarizes you with the steps for each installation.

Microsoft
✓ *Exam*
Objective

Deploy application updates for desktop applications.

As you create any of installation types mentioned above, you have the option of creating packaging and deployment scripts. These scripts enable you to quickly recreate the installation program when you make changes to your applications and need to deploy the updates.

Creating a Disk-Based Installation Program

Microsoft
✓ *Exam*
Objective

Plan and implement floppy disk-based deployment or compact disc-based deployment for a desktop application.

For a large number of your applications, you will be creating a disk-based installation program. This type of installation places all the necessary files for your program on a CD-ROM or on a series of floppy disks. When creating this type of installation, you need to make sure that all the components necessary for your program are placed on the disk(s). These components include:

- The executable file (the program itself)
- Required .dll files
- Required server components
- Custom controls

- Data files

- Private initialization files (.ini)

- Help files

After you determine the files that are required (the wizard helps you with file dependencies), the wizard takes care of most of the rest of the work. Exercise 18.1 walks you through creating an installation program for a simple application.

EXERCISE 18.1

Creating a Disk-Based Installation Program

1. Start the Package and Deployment Wizard.

2. Select the project file of the application you wish to distribute. (For the exercise, I am using the BaseBall.vbp project created in Chapter 2, "Working with ActiveX Controls.")

3. After selecting the project file, click the Package button of the wizard to start the packaging process. The wizard examines your project to determine which files are required for your application. The wizard then displays the Package Type page of the dialog box where you determine the type of package to create. This page is shown in the graphic below. (If you are starting from a Visual Basic 5 project or if any of the project's files have been saved since your last compilation, the wizard notifies you that it is an older program and offers to recompile the program for you.)

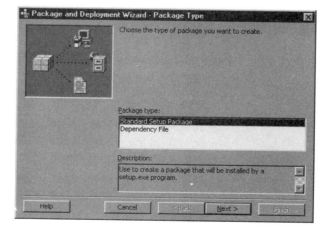

4. Choose to create a Standard Setup Package. This type of package installs an application using a `setup.exe` program. Clicking the Next button takes you to the Package Folder page of the wizard.

5. In the Package Folder page, choose where the package is to be assembled. The folder where the package is assembled defaults to the same folder as your project file. To avoid clutter, you might want to create a new folder under your project file folder to contain the package. After setting the folder name, click the Next button.

6. You are now on the Included Files page, shown in the following graphic. This page shows you a list of all the files that the wizard found that need to be included in your installation routine. The page also has an Add button that enables you to select additional files from an open dialog box. This is where you add any data files, initialization files, or other files you think are needed.

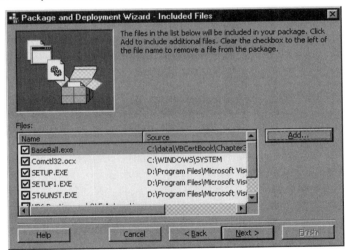

7. After adding any required files, click the Next button to proceed to the Cab Options page. Here you select whether to package all your files in a single `.cab` file or multiple `.cab` files. Multiple files are required if you are using a floppy disk-based distribution. After making your

selection, click the Next button. (The Cab Options page is shown below.)

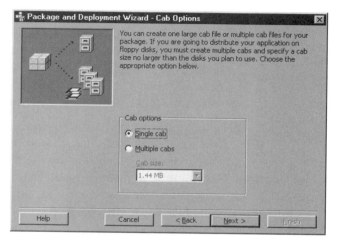

8. On the next page (the Installation Title page), you enter the title of the application. This title is displayed by the setup program as your application is installed. After specifying the title, click the Next button.

9. The Start Menu Items page of the wizard (shown below) enables you to select the Start menu items and groups that will be created by the setup program. By default, a new group and a single item are created for your application. You can accept the defaults or modify them using the buttons on this page. Click Next when you are happy with the Start menu configuration.

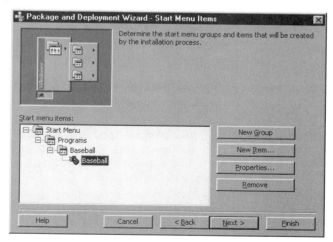

10. Next, the Install Locations page of the wizard enables you to specify the location of certain files in your setup routine. The location is where the file will be installed on the user's machine. For most installations, you will probably accept the default location and click the Next button.

11. The Shared Files page enables you to specify whether a file can be shared by more than one program. You typically share files if they are an Automation server or an ActiveX control that you created. After specifying any shared files, click the Next button.

12. You have now arrived at the Finished page, the last page of the wizard. This page enables you to specify a name for the setup script. The name enables you to retrieve and reuse the setup script for recreating the installation routine at a later date. After specifying the name, click the Finish button. The wizard then goes to work creating the .cab files for your package. When it is finished, you are returned to the original screen of the Package and Deployment Wizard shown in Figure 18.1.

13. After the package is completed, you need to handle the deployment of your distribution package. To start the deployment process, click the Deploy button on the main screen of the wizard. This brings up the first Deployment screen, which enables you to choose the package to deploy. The package choice defaults to the latest package associated with the project you selected. After confirming the package selection, click the Next button.

14. The Deployment Method screen, shown in the graphic below, lets you choose whether to deploy to floppy disks (if you created multiple .cab files), to a folder (used for CD-ROM or network distribution) or to the Web. For CD-ROM distribution, choose the folder option. You can then copy the files from the chosen folder to the CD-ROM at a later time. If you are deploying via floppy disks, choose the floppy

disks option. After you have made your selection, click the Next button.

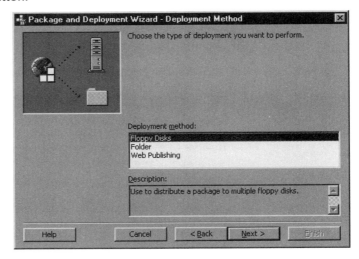

15. The Folder screen enables you to specify the folder where the package will be deployed. After choosing the folder, click the Next button. If you are creating a floppy disk-based installation, you instead choose the location of the disk drive.

16. After choosing the disk drive or folder where the installation files will be copied, click the Next button. This takes you to the final screen where you can name the script and finish the deployment. Clicking the Finish button on the last screen starts the process of copying the files to the target folder or to the target disk.

Depending on the type of application you are packaging, you may encounter other screens in the Package and Deployment Wizard. For example, if you are working with a database application, you need to select the database drivers to include in the setup. Driver selection is handled through a screen such as the one shown in Figure 18.2.

FIGURE 18.2

Database driver
selection screen

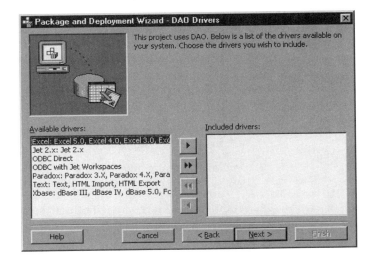

Creating a Network-Based Installation Program

Microsoft ✓ *Exam* *Objective*

Plan and implement network-based deployment for a desktop application.

Similar to a disk-based installation program is a network-based installation program. With network-based installation, the files are copied to a central location that is accessible to everyone who needs to install the software. By placing the installation files on the network, each user can install the program directly from the network drive without having to worry about swapping out floppy disks.

For managed systems, network installation allows the Management Information Systems (MIS) group to remotely install the application on all the required client machines. This, then, requires no effort on the part of the user to install the program. Exercise 18.2 shows how to create a network installation of a program. Because the packaging portion of the installation effort is the same as for disk-based installation, the exercise starts with the deployment screens of the Package and Deployment Wizard.

EXERCISE 18.2

Deploying Applications across a Network

1. After creating an installation package, as described in steps 1 through 12 of Exercise 18.1, you need to select the project and click the Deploy button of the Package and Deployment Wizard.

2. On the first deployment screen, select the package that you wish to deploy over the network; then click the Next button.

3. On the Deployment Method screen, select the Folder method. Then, click the Next button.

4. On the Folder screen of the wizard, click the Network button. This brings up the Browse for Folder dialog box shown below. From this dialog, select the folder on the network server where you wish to have the setup files copied. After you select a folder and return to the Folder page of the wizard, click the Next button.

5. On the final page of the wizard, you can specify a name for the deployment script and click the Finish button to handle copying the files.

Creating a Web-Based Installation Program

Microsoft
✓ *Exam*
Objective

Plan and implement Web-based deployment for a desktop application.

The final method of installation that you can create with the Package and Deployment Wizard is a Web-based installation. Using Web-based installation enables you to distribute your applications over the Internet. This saves you the trouble of mailing disks to remote users and saves users the trouble of handling disks during the installation process. Another advantage of using Web-based installation is that you are sure that users are getting the latest version of your program. Also, any updates to the application are instantly available.

The process of creating a Web-based installation program is not very different from creating a disk-based or network-based installation program. Exercise 18.3 shows you how to create a Web-based installation program.

EXERCISE 18.3

Creating a Web-Based Installation Program

1. Create a package for your application just as you would for a disk-based or network-based installation. This process is described in detail in steps 1 through 12 of Exercise 18.1. With a Web-based application, you might want to create multiple .cab files. Creating multiple files enables users to download smaller files, lessening the chance that the file transfer will be interrupted in the middle of a file.

2. Click the Deploy button on the main page of the wizard.

3. Choose the package that you wish to deploy for the application.

4. Select Web Publishing as the deployment method.

5. Select the files from the package that you want to deploy. The file list (shown below) includes the SETUP.exe file, a Setup.1st file, and the

.cab files for the package. You can choose to include any or all of the files to be deployed. After choosing the files, click the Next button.

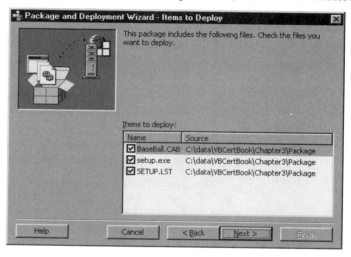

6. The Additional Items to Deploy screen enables you to specify additional items that need to be deployed along with your package files. These items might include graphics files or Web pages that are related to the application.

7. After selecting all the files to be deployed, you need to specify the URL where the files will be placed. You also need to choose the Web Publishing Protocol. You can choose either HTTP Posting or FTP transfer.

8. After you specify the location and protocol, you can click the Finish button to publish the files. Typically, when you start to publish the files, you need to specify your user ID and password for the server to which you are sending files. The wizard then logs onto the Internet and attempts to post the files to the location you specified.

After the files have been successfully transferred to the Internet, you need to create a Web page that makes it easy for users to download all the files associated with the installation routine.

Summary

As you can see, even after you complete the design, coding, and testing of the program, you must attend to several other tasks. It is not difficult to create an effective setup program, and it is an important part of the overall programming process. This chapter showed you how to create setup programs for various types of installations using the Package and Deployment Wizard. The information in this chapter covered the following exam objectives:

- Use the Package and Deployment Wizard to create a setup program that installs a desktop application, registers the COM components, and allows for uninstall.

- Deploy application updates for desktop applications.

- Plan and implement floppy disk-based deployment or compact disc-based deployment for a desktop application.

- Plan and implement network-based deployment for a desktop application.

- Plan and implement Web-based deployment for a desktop application.

Review Questions

1. How would you create disks for installing your program from floppy disks?

   A. Copy the necessary files to multiple floppies using Windows Explorer.

   B. Use the Package and Deployment Wizard to create a single `.cab` file and the setup program; then copy the files to floppies.

   C. Use the Package and Deployment Wizard to create multiple `.cab` files that will fit on floppies; then deploy the files to floppies.

   D. Zip all the files into a `.zip` file that spans multiple floppies.

2. Why would you need to modify the Setup.1st file?

   A. To customize the installation of an application

   B. To specify which program to install

   C. To add forms to the setup program

   D. None of the above

3. What Internet information do you need to specify to facilitate a Web-based installation? Check all that apply.

   A. The name of the Web page the users will access to download the files

   B. The URL of the server you will be publishing the files to

   C. The transfer protocol to use for publishing the files

   D. The IP address of your Web site

4. What tasks does the Package and Deployment Wizard perform for you? Check all that apply.

   A. Compresses your files into a .cab file

   B. Determines the files that need to be included in the installation routine

   C. Error checks your program

   D. Creates a Setup.exe program to install your application and register components

5. Which types of files are not automatically added to your installation package by the Package and Deployment Wizard? Check all that apply.

   A. The program executable file

   B. Database files

   C. Private .ini files

   D. Required .dll files and custom controls

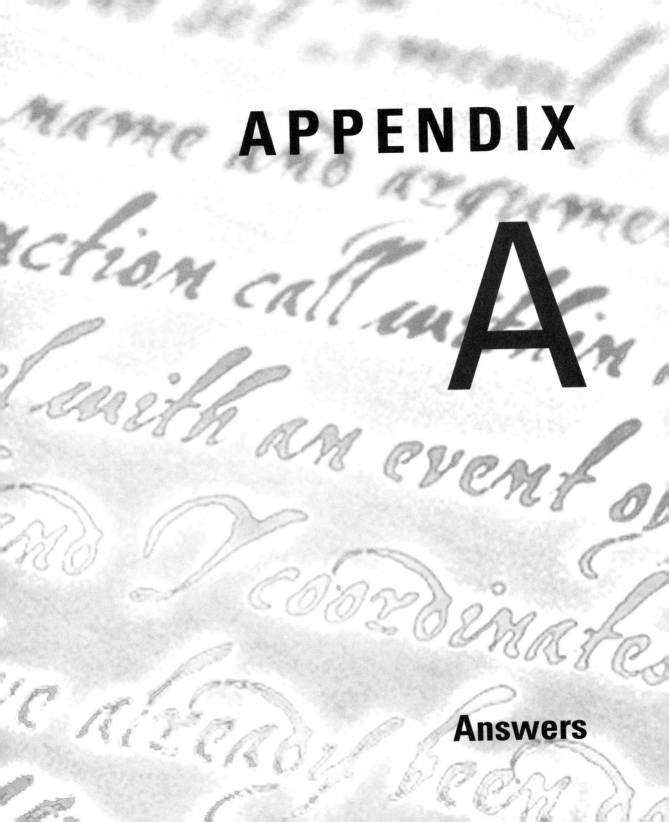

APPENDIX A

Answers

Chapter 1 Answers

1. What is the sequence in which the following events are triggered when a form is loaded?

    A. Initialize, Resize, Paint, and Load

    B. Load, Initialize, Resize, and Paint

    C. Initialize, Load, Paint, and Resize

    D. Initialize, Load, Resize, and Paint

    Answer: D

2. What is the sequence of events when a form is unloaded?

    A. Unload, QueryUnload, and Terminate

    B. QueryUnload, Unload, and Terminate

    C. Unload only

    D. QueryUnload and Unload

    Answer: D

3. How can you keep the user from exiting a form by using the Close item on the Control menu or by clicking the Close button?

    A. Place code in the Unload event.

    B. Place code in the QueryUnload event.

    C. This can only be done using a Windows API call.

    D. This cannot be done in Visual Basic.

    Answer: B

4. How do you create a read-only property in a form?

    A. Create only a Property Let procedure.

    B. Create only a Property Get procedure.

    C. Create both a Property Get and Property Let procedure.

    D. Declare a Public variable in the Declarations section of the form.

    Answer: B

5. Given the following code segment, how many instances of the form are created and displayed?

```
Dim frmVar1 As frmPerson, frmVar2 As frmPerson
Set frmVar1 = New frmPerson
Set frmVar2 = frmVar1
Load frmVar1
frmVar2.Show
```

A. None

B. Three

C. One

D. Two

Answer: C

6. Given the following code, what happens when the frmPerson.Show method is called?

```
Dim frmVar1 As frmPerson, frmVar2 As frmPerson
Set frmVar1 = New frmPerson
Set frmVar2 = frmVar1
Load frmVar1
frmPerson.Show
```

A. The current instance of the form is displayed.

B. A second instance of the form is created and displayed.

C. An error occurs.

D. Nothing.

Answer: B

7. Which event(s) enable you to determine which key was pressed by the user? Check all that apply.

A. Click

B. KeyPress

C. KeyDown

D. KeyUp

Answer: B, C, D

8. Which event(s) allow you to determine if a control or Shift key was pressed by the user? Check all that apply.

   A. Click

   B. KeyPress

   C. KeyDown

   D. KeyUp

   Answer: C, D

9. When is the Terminate event of a form triggered?

   A. When the user moves to another form or program

   B. When the form is unloaded

   C. Never

   D. When all references to the form are deleted

   Answer: D

10. Which event is triggered when the user moves to another form?

    A. Unload

    B. Deactivate

    C. Terminate

    D. Load

    Answer: B

Chapter 2 Answers

1. Which control lets you display information in a hierarchical structure?

   A. TreeView

   B. ListView

   C. ListBox

   D. StatusBar

   Answer: A

2. Which style of StatusBar panel can be modified by your program?
   Check all that apply.

   A. sbrText

   B. sbrCaps

   C. sbrNum

   D. sbrIns

   Answer: A

3. How do you update the status of a sbrCaps style panel?

   A. It is handled for you automatically by the control.

   B. You need to place code in the KeyPress event of the form.

   C. You must place code in the KeyPress event of the StatusBar.

   D. You use a Windows API call to find out when the key is pressed.

   Answer: A

4. Name the two techniques for identifying a Panel object in the Panels
   collection.

   A. Refer to it by the Index property.

   B. Refer to it by the Text property.

   C. Refer to it by the Style property.

   D. Refer to it by the Key property.

   Answer: A, D

5. What property of the ProgressBar determines how much of the bar is filled?

   A. Min

   B. Max

   C. Value

   D. All of the above

   Answer: D

6. What is the purpose of the ImageList control?

  A. To display bitmaps for the user to view

  B. To provide a repository for images used by other controls

  C. To allow easy editing of icons

  D. Both A and B

Answer: B

7. What are valid methods of adding a picture to the ImageList control? Check all that apply.

  A. Select a picture using a dialog box in the property pages.

  B. Set the Picture property of the ImageList control to the name of a PictureBox control.

  C. Set the Picture property of the ListImage object to the Picture property of another control.

  D. Set the Picture property of the ListImage object using the Load-Picture command.

Answer: A, C, D

8. What does a button of a button group on a toolbar do?

  A. Shows you the current status of an option

  B. Enables you to select one option from several

  C. Simply starts a function of the application

  D. Provides a space in the toolbar

Answer: B

9. All of the following statements are true about toolbars except:

  A. You can have only one toolbar on a form.

  B. Toolbars can be positioned anywhere on the form.

C. Toolbars can be customized by the user.

D. Toolbar buttons can display both text and images.

Answer: A

10. What do you have to do to allow the user to customize the toolbar?

A. Write code to add buttons or remove buttons based on the user selection.

B. Set the AllowCustomize property to True and the control takes care of the rest.

C. You cannot do this with Visual Basic toolbars.

D. You don't have to do anything. Toolbar custom action is automatic with any toolbar you create.

Answer: B

11. How many root nodes can a TreeView control have?

A. One

B. Up to five

C. Maximum of two

D. No limit

Answer: D

12. What must you specify to make a new node the child of another node? Check all that apply.

A. The Key value of the node to which it is related

B. The text of the related node

C. The Relationship must be specified as tvwChild

D. The image to be associated with the new node

Answer: A, C

13. What property determines whether lines are drawn between parent and child nodes? Check all that apply.

A. Appearance

B. Style

C. Indentation

D. LineStyle

Answer: B, D

14. What advantages does the ListView control have over the standard ListBox? Check all that apply.

A. ListView can display multiple columns of data.

B. ListBox is limited in the number of items that are allowed.

C. Only the ListView can be sorted.

D. ListView enables you to sort on different fields and to specify the sort order.

E. ListView can display headers over columns of information.

Answer: A, D, E

15. Which of the following views displays the Text property of the List-Item objects? Check all that apply.

A. Icon view

B. Small icon view

C. List view

D. Report view

Answer: A, B, C, D

16. Which views display the detailed information of a ListItem that is contained in the SubItem array? Check all that apply.

A. Icon view

B. Small icon view

C. List view

D. Report view

Answer: D

17. Which property of the ListView control determines which field a sort is based on?

   A. Sorted

   B. SortOrder

   C. SortField

   D. SortKey

Answer: D

Chapter 3 Answers

1. What properties are required to be specified for a menu item? Check all that apply.

   A. Checked

   B. Index

   C. Name

   D. Caption

   Answer: C, D

2. How can you enable the user to access a menu item from the keyboard? Check all that apply.

   A. Define an access key by designating a letter in the Caption property.

   B. Define a shortcut key by setting the Shortcut property in the Menu Editor.

   C. The user can press F10 and use the cursor keys.

   D. Define a shortcut key by setting the Shortcut property in code.

   Answer: A, B, C

3. All of the following statements about access keys are true except:

A. You can have items on different menus with the same access key.

B. The user must hold the Alt key while pressing the access key to open a top-level menu.

C. All top-level menus must have a unique access key.

D. Access keys are indicated to the user by an underlined letter in the caption.

Answer: C

4. Which of the following statements about pop-up menus are true? Check all that apply.

A. A pop-up menu can be used as a main menu.

B. A pop-up menu can be created from a sub-level menu.

C. A pop-up menu can have multiple levels.

D. A pop-up menu can be activated by any event the developer chooses.

Answer: A, B, C, D

5. Which Form event would you use to activate a pop-up menu when the user clicks the right mouse button? Check all that apply.

A. MouseDown

B. Click

C. MouseUp

D. MouseMove

Answer: A, C

6. What is the proper syntax for activating the pop-up menu fmtFormat?

A. Popup = fmtFormat

B. Set PopupMenu = fmtFormat

C. Me.PopupMenu fmtFormat

D. Me.PopupMenu = fmtFormat

Answer: C

7. Which menu item properties can you change at run time?

   A. WindowList, Caption, Index, Checked

   B. Name, Caption, Index

   C. Caption, Checked, Enabled, Visible

   D. Caption, Checked, Visible, Shortcut

Answer: C

8. What does the WindowList property do?

   A. Maintains a list of all forms in your program

   B. Enables you to add menu items to any menu at run time

   C. Keeps a list of MDI child windows

   D. Works with any application

Answer: C

9. What is the proper syntax for adding an item to a menu array?

   A. filMRUFile.AddItem 1

   B. filMRUFile.Load 1

   C. Load filMRUFile(1)

   D. Load New filMRUFile

Answer: C

10. Which command is used to remove an item from a menu array?

   A. Delete

   B. RemoveItem

   C. Drop

   D. Unload

Answer: D

11. When removing items from the menu array, which of the following best describes restrictions in doing this?

   A. You can remove all elements of the array.

   B. You must keep at least one element of the array.

   C. You cannot remove any elements that were created at design time.

   D. You cannot remove any elements of the array.

Answer: C

Chapter 4 Answers

1. How do you create the first element of a control array?

   A. Set the Index property of a control while in the design mode.

   B. Use the Load statement to load a control with an index value of zero.

   C. Use the CreateObject statement to create an instance of the control.

   D. Change the Index property of a single control at run time.

Answer: A

2. Which of the following restrictions apply to adding a control to a control array at run time? Check all that apply.

   A. The form must be visible when the control is added.

   B. The control array must already exist.

   C. The Index value must be the next sequential number after the upper bound of the array.

   D. The Index of the new control must be unique.

Answer: B, D

3. Which of the following are properties of a control array?

   A. Count, Type, and Name

   B. Count, Item, LBound, and UBound

   C. Count, Name, and Index

   D. Index, LBound, and UBound

Answer: B

4. Which of the following statements can be used to change the value of a property in an element of a control array?

   A. txtMember.Top = 120

   B. txtMember(0).Top = 120

   C. txtMember.0.Top = 120

   D. txtMember0.Top = 120

   Answer: B

5. What are the restrictions on removing controls from a control array? Check all that apply.

   A. The control must have been created in design mode.

   B. The control must have been added at run time.

   C. The control element must exist.

   D. All data must have been unloaded from the control.

   Answer: B, C

6. Which of the following statements removes a control from an array?

   A. Delete txtMember(5)

   B. Remove txtMember(5)

   C. Unload txtMember(5)

   D. Load txtMember(5) vbRemove

   Answer: C

Chapter 5 Answers

1. What are the three types of Property procedures that can be created for a class?

   A. Add, Retrieve, Remove

   B. Item, Add, Remove

   C. Let, Set, Get

   D. Let, Get, Object

   Answer: C

2. Which Property procedure is used to retrieve the value of a property?

A. Retrieve

B. Get

C. Item

D. Value

Answer: B

3. How do you create a method for a class?

A. Use a Method procedure declaration.

B. Use a Property Set procedure.

C. Create a Public procedure in the class module.

D. Create a Private procedure in the class module.

Answer: C

4. What command triggers an event created in a class?

A. RaiseEvent

B. SetEvent

C. Trigger

D. FireEvent

Answer: A

5. How do you create a Public class in a standard executable?

A. Set the Public property to True.

B. Set the Instancing property to SingleUse.

C. No special requirements.

D. You cannot create a Public class in a standard executable.

Answer: D

6. What does the Friend declaration do?

  A. Makes a class available for use by any program

  B. Makes the methods of the class usable by other parts of the program in which the class is defined

  C. Limits your program to creating a single object from the class

  D. Keeps you from having to specify the object name to reference the methods of the class

Answer: B

7. What does the Instancing property do?

  A. Sets the number of objects that can be created from the class

  B. Determines whether the class inherited properties from another class

  C. Specifies how the class in an ActiveX server can be used by other programs

  D. Specifies how the class in a standard program can be used by other programs

Answer: C

8. How do you use a class in your program?

  A. Simply call the methods and properties like any other procedure.

  B. Create an object based on the class using the Set statement or New keyword.

  C. Use the Call statement to access the class directly.

  D. Drag a copy of the class from the Project window to the form where you will need it.

Answer: B

9. Which of the following statements can be used to create an object based on a class? Check all that apply.

A. Set oUser = New cUser

B. oUser = cUser

C. Dim oUser As New cUser

D. CreateObject("cUser")

Answer: A, C

Chapter 6 Answers

1. What three methods does the Collection object support?

A. Load, Unload, Count

B. Add, Remove, Item

C. Add, Delete, Index

D. Add, Remove, Sort

Answer: B

2. What method is common to all collections?

A. Add

B. Delete

C. Remove

D. Item

Answer: D

3. What is the only property supported by a collection?

A. Name

B. Index

C. Count

D. Type

Answer: C

4. What does the Forms collection contain?

  A. A list of all forms in a project

  B. A list of all currently loaded forms

  C. A list of all visible forms

  D. All the child forms of an MDI application

Answer: B

5. How are forms added to the Forms collection?

  A. By adding a form to a project

  B. By using the Add method of the Forms collection

  C. By using the Load statement

  D. By activating a form

Answer: C

6. What does the Controls collection contain?

  A. A list of all controls on a form

  B. A list of all the controls used by your program

  C. A list of visible controls

  D. The names of all control arrays on the form

Answer: A

7. What are key differences between a control array and the Controls collection? Check all that apply.

  A. A control array contains controls of a single type; the Controls collection contains controls of many types.

  B. The elements of a control array all have the same name; the elements of the Controls collection can have different names.

  C. The elements of a control array do not share any events; the elements of the Controls collection do.

  D. A control array is simply another name for the Controls collection.

Answer: A, B

8. How do you determine the type of a control?

   A. Use the IsType function.

   B. Use the TypeOf clause.

   C. Check the Type property of the control.

   D. Use the prefix of the control name.

Answer: B

9. Why is it important to determine the type of a control?

   A. To process only controls that support a given property.

   B. Some control types are not included in the Controls collection.

   C. For programmer information only.

   D. To skip controls that are part of an array.

Answer: A

10. What are the two methods of referencing an element of a collection?

   A. Using the name value or the Index value

   B. Using the Index value and the Key value

   C. Using the name and type

   D. Using name and Key

Answer: B

11. Which of the following code segments can be used to process all the controls on a form? Check all that apply.

   A.

```
For I = 0 To Controls.Count - 1
    Debug.Print Controls(I).Name
Next
```

B.

```
For All Controls
    Debug.Print Control.Name
Next Control
```

C.

```
Dim chgControl as Control For Each chgControl In Controls
    Debug.Print chgControl.Name
Next chgControl
```

D.

```
For I = 0 To Controls.UBound
    Debug.Print Controls.Item(I).Name
Next I
```

Answer: A, C

Chapter 7 Answers

1. In setting up the ADODC, which property do you use to specify the database that the control will link to?

A. ConnectionString

B. RecordSource

C. LockType

D. CursorType

Answer: A

2. What is a valid setting for the RecordSource property? Check all that apply.

A. The name of a Table in the database

B. The name of a Query in the database

C. A valid SQL Select statement

D. The name of another ADODC

Answer: A, B, C

3. Which CursorType setting would you use if you wanted to create a read-only cursor?

   A. Dynamic

   B. Keyset

   C. Static

   D. Read-only

   Answer: C

4. In setting up a text box as a bound control, which property specifies the field of the recordset to be displayed?

   A. Name

   B. DataSource

   C. DataField

   D. Text

   Answer: C

5. Which list controls let you create the selection list from a table in a database? Check all that apply.

   A. Standard ListBox

   B. DataList

   C. Standard Combo Box

   D. DataCombo

   Answer: B, D

6. Which property of the DataList specifies the display field for the list?

   A. RowSource

   B. ListField

   C. DataSource

   D. DataField

   Answer: B

7. Which property of the DataList control specifies where the list information comes from?

A. RowSource

B. ListField

C. DataSource

D. DataField

Answer: A

8. How do you handle adding and deleting records in a database program using the ADODC?

A. Set the appropriate properties of the ADODC (AllowAddNew, AllowDelete).

B. Write program code to invoke recordset methods (AddNew, Delete).

C. Either A or B can be used.

D. Neither A nor B is correct.

Answer: B

9. Which items must be specified as part of the criteria for the Find method?

A. Field name, comparison operator, comparison value

B. Field name, database name, comparison value

C. ADODC, bound control name, comparison value

D. Field name, comparison operator, bound control name

Answer: A

10. What must you do with literal dates in a search criteria for the Find method?

A. Enclose the date in single quotes.

B. Enclose the date in double quotes.

C. Enclose the date in # symbols.

D. No special treatment is required.

Answer: C

Chapter 8 Answers

1. Which object handles the link to a specific database?

   A. Connection

   B. Command

   C. Database

   D. Recordset

Answer: A

2. Which object provides the link to specific data?

   A. Connection

   B. Command

   C. Database

   D. Recordset

Answer: D

3. Which object is responsible for handling transaction processing?

   A. Connection

   B. Command

   C. Database

   D. Recordset

Answer: A

4. Which of the following is a valid data source for the Open method of the Recordset object? Check all that apply.

   A. The name of a table

   B. The name of a stored query

   C. An SQL statement

   D. The name of a data control

Answer: A, B, C

5. What is the proper method of referring to a field in a recordset in order to retrieve the value of the field? Check all that apply.

A. RSProd!ProductName

B. RSProd(ProductName)

C. RSProd("ProductName")

D. RSProd.Fields(3)

Answer: A, C, D

6. Which statement is valid for setting the ProductName field to a new value?

A. Set ProductName = "Syrup"

B. RSProducts!ProductName = "Syrup"

C. SetFieldValue "ProductName", "Syrup"

D. RSProducts.Fields(3).Set "Syrup"

Answer: B

7. To modify the value of a field, what is the proper sequence of commands?

A. Assign the value of the field and then invoke the Edit and Update methods.

B. Invoke the Edit method and then assign the value of the fields. The Update method is not needed.

C. Invoke the Edit method, assign the values of the fields, and then invoke the Update method.

D. Invoke the Edit method, assign the values of the fields, and then invoke the Commit method.

Answer: C

8. What is the proper method to use to add a record to the recordset?

A. Edit

B. NewRecord

C. Add

D. AddNew

Answer: D

Chapter 9 Answers

1. Which object provides a link to a database or data source?

   A. Connection

   B. Command

   C. Recordset

   D. Data Environment

   Answer: A

2. Which object provides a link to a particular set of records in a database?

   A. Connection

   B. Command

   C. Recordset

   D. Data Environment

   Answer: B

3. What are valid sources of data for a Command object? Check all that apply.

   A. A database table

   B. A Data control

   C. A stored procedure

   D. An SQL statement

   Answer: A, C, D

4. Which properties must be set to bind a control to a Data Environment?

   A. DataSource and DataField

   B. DataField and DataFormat

   C. DataMember and DataField

   D. DataSource, DataMember, and DataField

   Answer: D

5. What does a child Command object do?

  A. Provides clarification of the parent command.

  B. Handles the master records of a master/detail recordset.

  C. Handles the detail records of a master/detail recordset.

  D. There are no child command objects.

Answer: C

6. Which method of the DataReport enables the user to preview the report information?

  A. PrintReport

  B. PrintForm

  C. Preview

  D. Show

Answer: D

Chapter 10 Answers

1. Which of the following is not true of In-Process servers?

  A. An ActiveX DLL is an In-Process server.

  B. They are faster than Out-of-Process servers.

  C. They can run as a stand-alone application.

  D. They run in the same process space as the client.

Answer: C

2. Which of the following is an advantage of an Out-of-Process server? Check all that apply.

  A. It can run as a stand-alone application.

  B. An Out-of-Process server has more multithreading options than an In-Process server.

  C. It can handle more objects in a single project than an In-Process server.

  D. It is faster than an In-Process server.

Answer: A, B

3. Which of the following settings of the Instancing property apply only to Out-of-Process servers? Check all that apply.

A. Private

B. Public Not Creatable

C. MultiUse

D. SingleUse

Answer: D

4. What is the advantage of multithreading?

A. It enables a single object to execute on more than one processor.

B. It significantly speeds up any server operations.

C. Multiple objects can run in separate threads and avoid blocking each other.

D. There is no advantage to multithreading.

Answer: C

5. Which of the following multithreading models uses the most resources?

A. Apartment model

B. Single Threaded

C. Thread Pool

D. Thread per Object

Answer: D

6. Which setting of the Instancing property creates all client objects from the same instance of the server object?

A. Private

B. Public Not Creatable

C. MultiUse

D. SingleUse

Answer: C

7. How do you create a property for a server object?

    A. Declare a variable as Public.

    B. Use Property procedures.

    C. Create a Friend variable.

    D. Use a Sub procedure.

Answer: B

8. What statement is used to trigger an event?

    A. LoadEvent

    B. Trigger

    C. RaiseEvent

    D. Event.Raise

Answer: C

9. How do you display a server form from a client application?

    A. Use the Show method and specify the form name.

    B. Call a method of the server object that creates and displays an instance of the form.

    C. Use a server event to show the form.

    D. You cannot create forms in a server project.

Answer: B

10. What is the advantage of asynchronous processing?

    A. There is no advantage.

    B. The server can accomplish other tasks while the requested task is running.

    C. The client can accomplish other tasks while the requested task is running.

    D. It enables the client to display a server form.

Answer: C

11. What keyword must be used in a declaration statement to enable an object to respond to events?

    A. Notify

    B. New

    C. WithEvents

    D. UseEvents

Answer: C

Chapter 11 Answers

1. Which statement or function do you use to create an object variable?

    A. Dim oWord As Word.Application

    B. Set oWord = Word.Application

    C. Set oWord = CreateObject("Word.Application")

    D. Dim oWord As String

    Answer: A

2. How do you set up early binding in an application?

    A. Declare a variable as Object.

    B. Declare a variable as Variant.

    C. Use the CreateObject Function.

    D. Declare a variable as a specific object type.

    Answer: D

3. How do you declare an object variable for late binding?

    A. Declare a variable as Object.

    B. Declare a variable as Variant.

    C. Use the CreateObject Function.

    D. Declare a variable as a specific object type.

    Answer: A

4. Which of the following statements creates an instance of an object? Check all that apply.

A. Dim oWord As Object

B. Dim oWord As New Word.Document

C. Set oWord = New Word.Document

D. Set oWord = CreateObject("Word.Document")

Answer: C, D

5. What are advantages of early binding? Check all that apply.

A. Objects are created faster.

B. You can use an early bound variable with any object.

C. Information about properties and methods is available while you program.

D. There are no advantages.

Answer: A, C

6. What are advantages of late binding? Check all that apply.

A. Objects are created faster.

B. You can use a late bound variable with any object.

C. Information about properties and methods is available while you program.

D. There are no advantages.

Answer: B

7. Which of the following statements show the proper use of the New keyword? Check all that apply.

A. Dim oWord As New Object

B. Dim oSheet As New Excel.Sheet

C. Set New oSheet = CreateObject("Excel.Sheet")

D. Set oWord = New Word.Document

Answer: B, D

Chapter 12 Answers

1. Which of the following statements is true about creating ActiveX controls?

   A. You must create the control completely from scratch.

   B. You can use only a single standard control in the creation of an ActiveX control.

   C. You cannot add properties to a standard control to enhance its capabilities.

   D. You can use multiple standard controls as well as drawing methods to create the interface of your control.

   Answer: D

2. What statement is used to trigger an event in your ActiveX control?

   A. LoadEvent

   B. RaiseEvent

   C. FireEvent

   D. Trigger

   Answer: B

3. Which property statement is required for a read-only property?

   A. Property Get

   B. Property Let

   C. Property Set

   D. Property Read

   Answer: A

4. How do you create a method of a control?

   A. Use a Method declaration statement.

   B. Create a Sub or Function procedure and declare it as Public.

   C. Create a Sub or Function procedure and declare it as Private.

   D. Creation of the method is automatic because all procedures in a control are public.

   Answer: B

5. What does the Control Interface Wizard do for you? Check all that apply.

   A. Designs the visual interface of your control

   B. Helps you create properties, methods, and events for your control

   C. Lets you assign properties of the control to properties of the constituent controls

   D. Handles the code for storing property changes

   Answer: B, C, D

6. What is the purpose of property pages?

   A. To make it easier for you to create properties of your control

   B. To provide a developer with easy access to the properties of your control

   C. To automatically test the property settings of your control

   D. To link the properties of your control to the properties of its constituent controls

   Answer: B

7. Which of the following programs can use ActiveX controls that you create? Check all that apply.

   A. Visual Basic

   B. Microsoft Office

   C. Microsoft Visual FoxPro

   D. Internet Explorer 3 or higher

   Answer: A, B, C, D

8. Which event is used to store developer settings for your control?

A. WriteSettings

B. StoreProperties

C. WriteProperties

D. Save

Answer: C

9. What is a PropertyBag?

A. Another name for property pages

B. An object used to store developer settings for a control

C. A made-up term

D. A list of properties that can be included in a UserControl

Answer: B

10. What method is used to retrieve developer settings for your control?

A. The Read method of the UserControl object

B. The Retrieve method of the PropertyBag object

C. The ReadProperty method of the PropertyBag object

D. The ReadProperty method of the UserControl object

Answer: C

Chapter 13 Answers

1. What is the primary object used in creating ActiveX documents?

A. UserControl

B. Form

C. UserDocument

D. Class Module

Answer: C

2. How many documents are allowed in a single project?

    A. Maximum of 5.

    B. There is no set limit.

    C. Maximum of 10.

Answer: B

3. Which of the following is not allowed in an ActiveX document?

    A. Custom controls

    B. User-created controls

    C. OLE container control

    D. Database controls

Answer: C

4. How do you store information from an ActiveX document so it is available when the document is reloaded?

    A. Write the information to a file.

    B. Use the methods of the PropertyBag object.

    C. It cannot be done.

    D. Specify the initial settings in the Hyperlink object.

Answer: B

5. What does the Document Migration Wizard do for you?

    A. Helps you move documents to another folder

    B. Helps you create an ActiveX document from an existing program

    C. Creates a file that lets you distribute your document over the Internet

    D. Lets you move from one document to another

Answer: B

6. Which of the following can run an ActiveX document? Check all that apply.

   A. Internet Explorer

   B. Visual Basic development environment

   C. Windows Explorer

   D. Office Binder

Answer: A, B, D

7. Which file do you load to run an ActiveX document?

   A. .dob

   B. .vbd

   C. .cab

   D. .vbp

Answer: B

8. How do you display one document from another?

   A. Use the Show method of the document.

   B. Use the NavigateTo method of the Hyperlink object.

   C. Use the Display method of the document.

   D. Use the Navigate method of the UserDocument object.

Answer: B

9. How do you pass information from one document to another?

   A. Set the value of a property in the target document.

   B. Use a global variable to contain the data.

   C. Use the PropertyBag.

   D. You cannot pass data between documents.

Answer: B

Chapter 14 Answers

1. Which of the following statements is used to turn off error handling in a procedure?

   A. On Error GoTo line

   B. On Error Resume Next

   C. On Error GoTo 0

   D. Error Off

   Answer: C

2. Which of the following statements tells Visual Basic to retry the statement that caused the error?

   A. Resume Next

   B. Resume

   C. Retry

   D. Resume line

   Answer: B

3. Which statement is used with deferred error handling?

   A. On Error GoTo line

   B. On Error Resume Next

   C. On Error GoTo 0

   D. On Error Defer

   Answer: B

4. Which of the following are drawbacks of deferred error handling? Check all that apply.

   A. It runs slower than immediate error processing.

   B. Errors may occur between the original error and your error handler.

   C. Your error code is spread throughout your procedure instead of being located in a single place.

   D. If multiple errors occur, your program will crash.

   Answer: B, C

5. What does the Clear method of the Err object do?

   A. Transfers error handling to the next higher procedure.

   B. Generates a run-time error.

   C. There is no Clear method.

   D. Resets the properties of the Err object.

Answer: D

6. Which of the following is a required argument of the Raise method?

   A. Description

   B. Number

   C. Source

   D. Helpfile

Answer: B

7. What is the purpose of the Raise method?

   A. To transfer error handling to the next higher procedure

   B. To generate a run-time error

   C. To trap errors that occur in your program

   D. To reset the properties of the Err object

Answer: B

8. What happens if you use a Resume statement outside of an error-handling routine?

   A. Your program retries the statement that generated the error.

   B. Nothing happens.

   C. An error occurs because the Resume statement cannot be used outside an error handler.

   D. Your error handler enters an infinite loop.

Answer: C

9. What are some ways that you can centralize error handling? Check all that apply.

   A. Write a class to encapsulate functions and include the error handling in the class.

   B. Place an On Error GoTo procedure statement as the first line of your program and write an error procedure.

   C. Have the error-handling code in each procedure call a function that identifies the error and indicates the appropriate action.

   D. Place your function in a Public procedure that includes error-handling capabilities.

Answer: A, C

Chapter 15 Answers

1. Which of the following tools helps you avoid errors in your programs? Check all that apply.

   A. Auto Syntax Check

   B. Require Variable Declaration

   C. Call stack

   D. Immediate window

Answer: A, B

2. Which of these tools displays the value of a variable? Check all that apply.

   A. Immediate window

   B. Watch window

   C. Call Stack window

   D. Locals window

Answer: A, B, D

3. Which of these tools shows you the properties of a form and its controls?

   A. Watch window

   B. Immediate window

   C. Auto Data Tips

   D. Locals window

   Answer: D

4. Which of these tools enables you to change the value of a variable? Check all that apply.

   A. Watch window

   B. Immediate window

   C. Auto Data Tips

   D. Locals window

   Answer: A, B, D

5. How can you cause a program to pause execution? Check all that apply.

   A. Set a breakpoint in code.

   B. Set a watch to break when the value changes.

   C. Insert the Stop command in your program.

   D. Right-click the mouse on the program while it is running.

   Answer: A, B, C

6. How are the scope of a variable and the scope of a watch related?

   A. The scope of the variable determines the scope of the watch.

   B. The scope of the watch determines the scope of the variable.

   C. The scope of the watch and scope of the variable are set independently and are, therefore, unrelated.

   Answer: C

7. Which command do you use to pause execution after a procedure when you are stepping through a program?

   A. Step Into

   B. Step Out

   C. Run to Cursor

   D. Step Over

Answer: D

8. What Visual Basic element must you use to debug an ActiveX DLL?

   A. Call stack

   B. Immediate window

   C. Project group

   D. Compiler

Answer: C

9. When is the program code of a User Control running and able to be tested? Check all that apply.

   A. When the control is being built

   B. When the control is being added to another project and the properties are being set

   C. When a project containing the control is running

   D. During compilation of the control

Answer: B, C

Chapter 16 Answers

1. Which compilation option typically produces the smaller executable file?

   A. Compile to native code.

   B. Compile to P-code.

   C. Both options produce the same size file.

Answer: B

2. Which compilation option typically produces the faster executable?

   A. Compile to native code.

   B. Compile to P-code.

   C. Both options produce equally fast programs.

   Answer: A

3. Which compiler options would be a benefit for a program to be run on a Pentium Pro machine? Check all that apply.

   A. Favor Pentium Pro™

   B. Create Symbolic Debug Information

   C. Assume No Aliasing

   D. Remove Safe Pentium™ FDIV Checks

   Answer: A, D

4. How can you set the value of conditional compilation arguments? Check all that apply.

   A. Use the #Const directive.

   B. Use the Const statement.

   C. Use an assignment statement in your program.

   D. Use the Project Properties dialog box.

   Answer: A, D

5. What are reasons for using conditional compilation? Check all that apply.

   A. To maintain multiple versions of a code

   B. To incorporate debug information

   C. To compile a single module for testing

   D. To create demonstration programs

   Answer: A, B, D

6. What compiler options can lead to unexpected results from your program? Check all that apply.

    A. Remove Integer Overflow Checks

    B. Remove Floating Point Error Checks

    C. Create Symbolic Debug Info

    D. Favor Pentium Pro™

    Answer: A, B

7. How can you access version information about your program that is input in the Make dialog box?

    A. It is unavailable while your program is running.

    B. Through the properties of the App object.

    C. Through the properties of the Program object.

    D. Read the header information in your code files.

Answer: B

Chapter 17 Answers

1. HelpFile is a property of which object? Check all that apply.

    A. Form

    B. Common Dialog

    C. Project

    D. App

    Answer: B, D

2. How do you make a specific topic appear when the user presses F1 on a control?

    A. Pass the control name to the Common Dialog.

    B. Set the value of the HelpContextID property of the control.

    C. Set the value of the Index property of the control.

    D. Set the ToolTipText property of the control.

    Answer: B

3. What happens if there is no specific topic for a control when the user presses F1?

   A. The Topic not Found error is displayed in the help file.

   B. Help is not accessed.

   C. The HelpContextID of the control's container is used.

   D. Windows 95/NT help is shown.

   Answer: C

4. What happens if the topic assigned to a control is not in the help file?

   A. The Topic not Found error is displayed in the help file.

   B. Help is not accessed.

   C. The HelpContextID of the control's container is used.

   D. Windows 95/NT help is shown.

   Answer: A

5. Which two properties of a Common Dialog must be set before trying to display help?

   A. HelpFile

   B. HelpContext

   C. HelpCommand

   D. HelpKey

   Answer: A, C

6. Which method of the Common Dialog is used to display help information?

   A. Help

   B. OpenHelp

   C. ShowHelp

   D. Assist

   Answer: C

7. Which files are created by the Help Workshop? Check all that apply.

   A. Help Topic files

   B. Help file (`.hlp` extension)

   C. Help Project file

   D. Help Contents file

Answer: B, C, D

8. Which groups of controls can be linked to a specific help topic?

   A. Any control that is visible on the screen

   B. Only controls with a HelpContextID property

   C. All controls

   D. Only menu items

Answer: B

Chapter 18 Answers

1. How would you create disks for installing your program from floppy disks?

   A. Copy the necessary files to multiple floppies using Windows Explorer.

   B. Use the Package and Deployment Wizard to create a single `.cab` file and the setup program; then copy the files to floppies.

   C. Use the Package and Deployment Wizard to create multiple `.cab` files that will fit on floppies; then deploy the files to floppies.

   D. Zip all the files into a `.zip` file that spans multiple floppies.

Answer: C

2. Why would you need to modify the `Setup.lst` file?

   A. To customize the installation of an application

   B. To specify which program to install

   C. To add forms to the setup program

   D. None of the above

Answer: A

3. What Internet information do you need to specify to facilitate a Web-based installation? Check all that apply.

A. The name of the Web page the users will access to download the files

B. The URL of the server you will be publishing the files to

C. The transfer protocol to use for publishing the files

D. The IP address of your Web site

Answer: B, C

4. What tasks does the Package and Deployment Wizard perform for you? Check all that apply.

A. Compresses your files into a .cab file

B. Determines the files that need to be included in the installation routine

C. Error checks your program

D. Creates a Setup.exe program to install your application and register components

Answer: A, B, D

5. Which types of files are not automatically added to your installation package by the Package and Deployment Wizard? Check all that apply.

A. The program executable file

B. Database files

C. Private .ini files

D. Required .dll files and custom controls

Answer: B, C

APPENDIX

B

Glossary of Terms

Access key A key combination (such as Alt+F) that enables the user to open a main menu, or a single key that enables the user to select a menu item.

ActiveX documents A specialized Visual Basic application that can run within a Web browser.

ActiveX server Any program that exposes objects to other programs for use while running as a stand alone application.

Alias Another name by which a procedure is identified for use in an application.

Asynchronous operation Program execution in which multiple instructions can be run simultaneously.

Bookmark property An identifier for a specific record in a recordset.

Breakpoint A debugging tool that pauses the execution of the program at a specific point.

Callback procedure A procedure in an application that can be called by a function in a DLL routine.

Child form A form that is contained within a parent form.

Class A structure that provides a definition of an object. A class defines the data (properties), tasks to perform (methods), and notifications (events) of an object.

Class modules The code structures that implement classes in Visual Basic.

Collection A grouping of similar objects, such as forms, recordsets, controls, and so on.

Common Dialog control A control that enables the programmer to easily create Open, Save, Help, Print, Color, and Font dialogs for a program.

Conditional compilation Visual Basic compiles only parts of a program as they are needed.

Control array A group of controls of the same type that have the same name. Members of the array are identified by the Index property. Arrays are used for easier processing of multiple controls.

Controls collection   A special collection that provides a reference to every control on a given form.

Dynamic-link library (DLL)   A file that contains object definitions for use by client programs. A DLL works as an in-process ActiveX server.

Early binding   Declaring a specific object type is known as early binding of the object.

Encapsulation   The data about an object and the code used to manipulate the data are contained within the object itself. The data is stored as the properties of the object and the code as the methods of the object. Encapsulation enables the object data and code to stand alone, independent of outside routines.

Explicit declaration   A means of defining the data type of a variable by specifying the type in the declaration statement.

Forms collection   A special collection that provides a reference to every loaded form in an application.

Friend declaration   Enables the programmer to make a property or method available to other modules in the current project (the one in which the class is defined), without making the routine truly public.

Global variable   Another name for Public variable.

Hyperlink   A string that identifies a link to another document or Web page.

Implicit declaration   A means of defining the data type of a variable by placing a particular symbol at the end of the variable name.

In-Process server   An ActiveX server that is contained in a .dll file and runs in the same process (memory) space as the client application.

Inheritance   Enables one object to be created based on the properties and methods of another object. With inheritance, it is not necessary to code the properties and methods that are derived from the parent object. The programmer has to code only new or modified properties and methods.

Invalid value error   An error that occurs when the programmer tries to assign a value to a variable that the variable is not capable of handling.

Jump   A link between two topics in a help file.

Late binding   Declaring a generic object variable is known as late binding of the object.

Local variable   A variable that can be used only in the procedure in which it is defined.

Logic error   An error that does not cause a program to crash, but does cause a program to yield incorrect results.

Method   A procedure that provides an object with the ability to perform a task.

Modal form   A form that must be exited before other forms of an application may be accessed.

Module level variable   A variable declared at the beginning of a form or code module that is available to all procedures in the module, but not outside the module.

Multithreading   Processing multiple parts of an application in separate threads (typically on multiple processors).

Native code   Machine-level instructions that make up an application.

Object browser   A Visual Basic tool that lets the programmer see the properties, methods, and events of an object.

Open database connectivity (ODBC)   A specification that provides a consistent means to communicate with many types of databases.

Out-of-Process server   An ActiveX server that is contained in an .exe file and runs in a separate process (memory) space from the client application.

P-code   An interpreted code that is between the "English-like" commands that programmers enter and the machine code that computers use.

Parent form   A form that provides a container for other child forms of the application.

Polymorphism   Relates to the use of the same method name in various objects; for example, a Print method for the printer, a form, or a picture box. Although the name of the method is the same, the code for the method in each object can be different. However, because the code for the method is encapsulated in the object, each object knows how to perform the correct task when the method is called.

Pop-up A small window that contains additional information about a topic. The window "pops up" in response to a mouse click on a particular style of text.

Procedure A self-contained segment of code that performs a specific task.

Programming interface The structure through which programs communicate with one another.

PropertyBag A storage device for maintaining information for an ActiveX document or ActiveX control.

Public variable A variable that can be accessed from anywhere in the program.

Query A SQL statement that is used to retrieve or modify data.

Recordset An object that contains the information used by an application.

Registry A database in Windows 95 and Windows NT that contains information about the settings of the computer.

Remote data Data located in a database server such as Oracle or SQL Server.

Run-time error An error that occurs while a program is running.

Shortcut key A key combination that directly invokes a menu option.

Status bar A bar at the bottom of a form that provides the user with additional information about the application.

Synchronous operation Program execution in which one instruction must be completed before the next instruction can be started.

Syntax error An error in the "wording" of a line of program code.

Thread pooling A method of multithreading in which a specific number of threads are allocated for processing. Objects use these threads in a round-robin fashion.

ToolTip A small window that provides additional information about a control. The ToolTip pops up when the user rests the mouse cursor on the control for a few seconds.

Trapping an error   Handling an error within an application so the user does not see the original error information, and so the program does not crash.

Watch   A debugging tool that tracks the value of a variable or expression.

Index

Note to the Reader: Throughout this index **boldfaced** page numbers indicate primary discussions of a topic. *Italicized* page numbers indicate illustrations.

SKILLS MEASURED BY EXAM 70-176	PAGE

Deriving the Physical Design

Assess the potential impact of the logical design on performance, maintainability, extensibility, and availability.	12
Design Visual Basic components to access data from a database.	357
Design the properties, methods, and events of components.	147, 150

Establishing the Development Environment

Establish the environment for source code version control.	4
Install and configure Visual Basic for developing desktop applications.	3

Creating User Services

Implement navigational design.	6, 8, 10, 25, 89, 99, 103, 109
• Dynamically modify the appearance of a menu.	103
• Add a pop-up menu to an application.	99
• Create an application that adds and deletes menus at run time.	109
• Add controls to forms.	6
• Set properties for controls.	8
• Assign code to a control to respond to an event.	10, 25
Create data input forms and dialog boxes.	42, 52, 56, 64, 72, 129, 185, 189
• Display and manipulate data by using custom controls. Controls include TreeView, ListView, ImageList, Toolbar, and StatusBar.	42, 52, 56, 64, 72
• Create an application that adds and deletes controls at run time.	129
• Use the Controls collection to manipulate controls at run time.	189
• Use the Forms collection to manipulate forms at run time.	185
Write code that validates user input.	121, 122, 124, 126
• Create an application that verifies data entered at the field level and the form level by a user.	122, 124
• Create an application that enables or disables controls based on input in fields.	126
Write code that processes data entered on a form.	19
• Given a scenario, add code to the appropriate form event. Events include Initialize, Terminate, Load, Unload, QueryUnload, Activate, and Deactivate.	19
Add an ActiveX control to the toolbox.	46
Create a Web page by using the DHTML Page Designer to dynamically change attributes of elements, change content, change styles, and position elements.	391
Use data binding to display and manipulate data from a data source.	239
Instantiate and invoke a COM component.	321, 323
• Create a Visual Basic client application that uses a COM component.	321, 323
• Create a Visual Basic application that handles events from a COM component.	321
Create callback procedures to enable asynchronous processing between COM components and Visual Basic client applications.	303
Implement online user assistance in a desktop application.	304, 486, 497
• Set appropriate properties to enable user assistance. Help properties include **HelpFile**, **HelpContextID**, and **WhatsThisHelp**.	486
• Create HTML Help for an application.	497
• Implement messages from a server component to a user interface.	304
Implement error handling for the user interface in desktop applications.	408, 415
• Identify and trap run-time errors.	408
• Handle inline errors.	415

Exam objectives are subject to change at any time without prior notice and at Microsoft's sole discretion. Please visit Microsoft's Training & Certification Web site (www.microsoft.com/train_cert) for the most current listing of exam objectives.